# THE MYSTERY

# OF

# WEALTH

## Political Economy—
## Its Development
## and Impact on World Events

by

JOHN HUTTON

Member of the Directing Staff, Henley
The Administrative Staff College, Oxfordshire, England

# STANLEY THORNES (PUBLISHERS) LTD

First published in 1979 by:
Stanley Thornes (Publishers) Ltd
EDUCA House
32 Malmesbury Road
Kingsditch
CHELTENHAM GL51 9PL
England


ISBN  0  85950  470  0  Library Edition


ISBN  0  85950  475  1  Sewn Paperback Edition

Text set in 11/13 pt VIP Sabon, printed by photolithography and bound in
Great Britain at The Pitman Press, Bath

# Preface

I was initially stimulated to write this extended essay after being asked to lecture on economic concepts, systems and growth to Senior Managers coming to Henley from a wide variety of countries. It soon became apparent that if I was going to talk meaningfully about complex and contentious political, economic and social issues with such diversely experienced students it was necessary to approach the underlying ideas in a holistic way. There was little point in talking to people from Eastern Europe or developing countries, increasingly influenced by Marxist philosophies, be they of the Russian or Chinese varieties, unless considerable attention was given to the economic doctrines of Karl Marx. Conversely, it was also essential to give fair coverage to the ideas of the *laissez-faire* school, from Adam Smith through to the various debates about the schisms from classical and neo-classical orthodoxy by John Maynard Keynes and his successors. I have conceived of the economic thinker in three different roles: that of a scientist of man; a prophet of revolutionary change; and a social cum systems engineer of the future possibilities open to mankind. I then consider the way the main lines of contemporary thought, debate and action derive from underlying philosophical and historical debates about scarcity, wealth and welfare which in large part have been developed during the past two centuries. It is remarkable the degree to which economic doctrines, initially developed against the late 18th and 19th century British experience, of the transformation from a small population agrarian and commercial country into a large population urban and possibly 'post industrial' nation, have come to have such a wide impact throughout the world. For good or ill the British cum Western European and North American experience, as viewed by minds as diverse as Adam Smith, David Ricardo, John Stuart Mill, Karl Marx, John Maynard Keynes and many others, continue to dominate the world's thoughts about the creation and distribution of wealth and welfare in a scarce world. This book is primarily a study of the history and impact of such thoughts on every day life. I have therefore included at the beginning of the book brief accounts of the Principle Historic Personae, their lives and influence and at the end of a Chronology of Events running between 1750 and 1977. There is also included a list of the Nobel Prize winners in Economic Science awarded between 1969 and 1977. The purpose is to enable the reader to see, in easily comprehensible form, the main developments of the past two hundred or so years of the industrial age, against the lives and preoccupations of the political and economic thinkers of the same period. Finally, some tentative remarks are included about a possible 'convergency' between the various doctrines and systems reviewed, and we look to the future 'shocks' prospects for the world economy in this, the last quarter of the twentieth century.

*The Administrative Staff College,*                          John Hutton
*Greenlands,*                                               December 1977
*Henley-on-Thames,*
*Oxfordshire.*

# Acknowledgments

The preparation of this book extended over several years; from Spring to Christmas of 1976, being mainly concerned with final reading and preparing the first draft. Throughout this period my ideas were most helpfully commented on, at various points and stages, by many of my colleagues. I am particularly indebted to Sir James Lindsay, Director of International Programmes, for his encouragement and enthusiasm at this first stage, and for the opportunity of trying out some of the ideas in lectures and discussions with Senior Managers attending the Henley International Operations programme. The second, revised, draft was written between January and May 1977, typing being undertaken by Rosemary Daniels and Dorothy Wharton at different periods of time. At this stage I received many additional helpful comments from a number of people, notably Sir Noel Hall; my father Mr. H. F. Hutton, and Mr. Michael Shanks. I have also received helpful stimulation and support from a number of others including from within the college; Professor Thomas Kempner, Mr. Harry Slater, Mr. Phillip Montagnon, Professor Bernard Taylor; also Professor Tibor Mende, C.E.I., Geneva, Professor Naoto Sasaki, Sophia University, Tokyo, Mr. Tad. Rybczynski of Lazard Brothers and Professor R. D. Robinson from the Massachusetts Institute of Technology. I am also greatly indebted for the ongoing assistance in finding sources and checking facts which have been undertaken by Miss Gail Thomas and Miss Anne Halliwell in the College Library. I also owe much to my wife Rosemary Laura Hutton for her assistance with various facets of the book.

This is largely a work of perception and synthesis, as opposed to extensive scholarship from original texts, and as such I have relied on many sources, both books and journals, most of which are either referred to in the text and/or are listed in the short reading list. Of particular assistance, in the formative stages, was Sir Eric Roll's *A History of Economic Thought* and the information about economists and their lives contained in Seldon's and Pennance's *Dictionary of Economics*. I have also relied extensively on the services of *Chambers Encyclopaedia*, and the Tavistock *A Dictionary of the Social Sciences* for much of the background information contained in the work. There are many thousands of facts, references and names which I have checked as carefully as possible. However, in its everyday and doctrinal aspects scarcity, wealth and welfare is a large, diverse and rapidly changing field of study, and errors and omissions may well exist. I should, therefore, be grateful for the indulgence of readers for any especially flagrant omissions which may come to mind. It will be appreciated that this is a literary work and that statistics have only been used in support of specific lines of argument, and not as a substantive element in the preparation of the work as a whole. It may appear to readers that I have relied unduly upon Anglo-Saxon sources for philosophical ideas and examples of their application to problems. To some extent this is true and reflects the intellectual myopia induced by a British education. Yet it remains my view that the political and economic concepts influencing the world today are largely derived from the British, the Western European and North American experience of scientifically based 'industrial' transformation and change. It would be of interest to speculate upon what sources will be used by an author writing a similar book a hundred years hence.

The Author and Publishers gratefully acknowledge permission to reproduce copyright material from the following sources.

Page 16, Fig. 1.   World Population, 1950–1972; source *UN Demographic Yearbook*, 1973. Reproduced by permission.

Pages 331–4, an excerpt from *The Future of the World Economy* by Prof. Wassily Leontief. Copyright United Nations (1977). Reproduced by permission.

Page 18, Fig. 2.   World Rich and Poor, 1974.
Pages 400–1, 405.   Appendix V. Tables III and XI.
Source *The Economist Diary*. Reproduced by permission of *The Economist*, London.

Pages 75–6. *War in European History* by Michael Howard. Copyright Oxford University Press (1976), by permission of Oxford University Press.

Page 80.   *World Bank Report*, 1975. Reproduced by permission of the World Bank, Washington, D.C.

Pages 122–3.   Extracts from *Ramsay MacDonald* by David Marquand published (1977) by Jonathan Cape, London.

Page 144, Fig. 15.   Growth Rates in 16 Major Industrial Countries in Annual Compound Increase Terms, 1870–1976.

Page 150, Fig. 16. Some Recent Changes in the Share of World Exports in Major Areas, 1955–76.

Page 202, Fig. 27. Contribution to Economic Growth.
The above are reproduced by permission of T. M. Rybezynski, Lazard's Bros. & Co. Ltd. London.

Pages 149/151. Excerpt from The Policy Challenge from OECD *Economic Outlook* No. 20, December 1976.
Page 200, Fig. 26 Civilian Employment by Main Sectors of Economic Activity, 1974.
Page 207, Fig. 28. Gross Fixed Capital Formation by Products, 1973.
Page 216, Fig. 29. Use of Gross Domestic Product at Market Prices, 1974.
Page 221, Figs. 30–1. Taxes and Actual Social Contributions 1974; Social Security Expenditure as Percentage of Gross Domestic Product at Market Prices.
Page 290, Fig. 37. Gross Flow of Capital and Technical Assistance from International Agencies to the Third World.
Pages 399–404, Appendix V. OECD Statistical Tables.
All the above are published by OECD, Paris and are reproduced by permission.

Pages 158–161, Fig. 17. List of the World's Top 50 Companies, reprinted from the *World Business Directory*, 1974 by special permission; copyright 1974 Time Inc.

Pages 166–7, Fig. 19. Perlmutter's Model – Types of Head Office Orientation towards Subsidiaries in an International Enterprise, reproduced by permission of Dr. H. V. Perlmutter, University of Pennsylvania.

Page 178, Fig. 21. W. W. Rostow's Five Stages of Economic Growth (1959), copyright Cambridge University Press.

Page 181, Fig. 22. Growth Cycles according Jay W. Forrester. Reproduced by permission of Prof. J. W. Forrester, Massachusetts Institute of Technology, Cambridge, Massachusetts.
Page 183, Fig. 23 Maslow's Hierarchy of Human Needs from *Motivation and Personality* by A. H. Maslow, published in 1970 by Harper and Row, New York.

Page 227, Fig. 32. Monopolised and Oligopolised Products in the U.K., 1970; published in *Hansard* 6th April, 1970, reproduced by permission.

# Contents

# Lists of Maps, Diagrams and Tables

# Global Perspectives, Dilemmas and Opportunities

"Let observation with extensive view,
Survey mankind, from China to Peru;
Remark each anxious toil, each eager strife,
And watch the busy scenes of crowded life."

Samuel Johnson (1709–1784)
*Vanity of Human Wishes*

"An age that melts with unperceiv'd decay,
And glides in modest innocence away."

*Ibid*

"Human history becomes more and more a race between education and catastrophe."

H. G. Wells (1866–1946)
*The Outline of History*

"One World or None."

*Book title of a report on the full meaning of the atomic bomb, published by the Foundation of American Scientists in 1946.*

"Man is a singular creature. He has a set of gifts which make him unique among the animals: so that, unlike them, he is not a figure in the landscape – he is a shaper of the landscape. In body and in mind he is the explorer of nature, the ubiquitous animal, who did not find but has made his home in every continent."

Jacob Bronowski (1908–1974)
*The Ascent of Man*

The mystery of wealth and material affluence in a world of scarcity has attracted and baffled many of the best minds of succeeding generations, involving as it does a bewildering mixture of philosophical puzzles, historical accidents and practical concerns. Since the onset of the modern industrial age, in the late 18th and early 19th century, the study of economic phenomena, its development and change, has taken on many of the characteristics of a secular 'religious' fervour, and has frequently occasioned doctrinal debates of unusual and prolonged ferocity. In everyday speech politics is thought of as being concerned with the philosophical and practical aspirations of society. As such it focuses on questions of power and, in economic distribution terms, 'who gets what'. Conversely economics, in its purest sense, is thought of as being concerned with the resources and the means by which both individuals and society achieve material goals. In Professor Lionel Robbins classic 1935 essay on *The Nature and Significance of Economic Science* it was defined as a relationship 'between ends and scarce means which have alternative uses'. In this Robbins was questioning Professor Edwin Cannan's earlier definition of economics as a study of 'material welfare'. In practice political ends, and economic means, become hopelessly entangled, and in recent times political economy has become widely regarded as a useful generic term to describe a complex and changing relationship between the creation of wealth out of scarcity and its use in various ways.

*     *     *     *     *

Since the Polish astronomer Nicolaus Copernicus' (1473–1543), and Galileo Galilie's time (1564–1642), man's perception of his world has encompassed the idea of its being a near sphere revolving around the sun. Today he can actually see it in this way on television, or in the cinema, as coloured moving pictures taken from outer space. It is sobering to recognise that, for good or evil, whatever material life has to offer, is contained in this glittering sphere. Even more salutory is to recognise that some two-thirds of the planet Earth is covered by oceans, while of the remaining third much of the surface consists of inhospitable regions; from northern and southern polar belts, to snow-covered uplands; to extensive areas of yellow, arid deserts extending across North Africa to Central Eurasia and South Western North America, to South America's and Africa's green swamps and jungles. Those parts of the world which human beings intensively occupy are limited in spacial extent, and confined in altitude, between sea level and at best 10,000 to 12,000 feet above this.

Turning to the contemporary state of mankind, as Professor Tibor Mende in the concluding remarks to his wide-ranging book *From Aid to Recolonisation* points out:

"The merely quantitative aspects of the population problem have received abundant publicity. Following centuries of near stagnation, from about 1650 onwards world population doubled in two centuries, reaching 1 billion by about 1850. It had doubled again by 1930, after eighty years. The next doubling, from 2 to 4 billion, will have been accomplished in only forty-five years. And beyond 1975, the rise from 4 to 8 billion will probably require less than thirty-five years. Children now in primary school may very well reach retirement age in a world with over 12 billion people. Indeed, in the totally improbable case of present growth rates continuing unchecked by 2200, the grandchildren of our grandchildren may be condemned to live in a world where 500 billion people will give the surface of all the continents a population density equal to that of the biggest cities today. What is practically certain is the doubling of the world's population by the end of the century. And behind that figure are related problems which cluster around three main themes: food, environment, and equality."

Of the present population of mankind of some four billion souls, over half, approximately two billion, are concentrated in Asia; including an estimated 900m in China; over 800m in the Indian sub-continent, with a further 138m in Indonesia and 113m in Japan. Europe, including European Russia, has a further population of some 600m; Africa nearly 400m (including over 61m in Nigeria and 26m in Egypt); North America 338m; South America 212m and the Soviet Union, as a whole 252m. The industrial and scientific based leadership centres of the world are largely confined to dense clusters of activity, extending from California to the Middle West and North Eastern seaboard of the U.S.A., in North Western Europe and European Russia as far east as the Ural Mountains and in the few Asian centres, notably Japan. Only a small fraction of the world's people are directly involved in industrial processes. The rest live in a derivative state dependent to a large, and perhaps, increasing extent on the technological leadership and wealth-generating possibilities of concentrated, but vulnerable, economic, social and industrial systems.

Looking in the mid 1970s at the world economy, a rapidly changing, and highly confusing situation is apparent. After a 'golden age' of more than two decades of unprecedented growth the O.E.C.D. member countries (the industrialised nations of Western Europe, North America, Australasia and Japan) have slowed to virtual stagnation with

FIG. 1.  WORLD POPULATION, 1950–1972

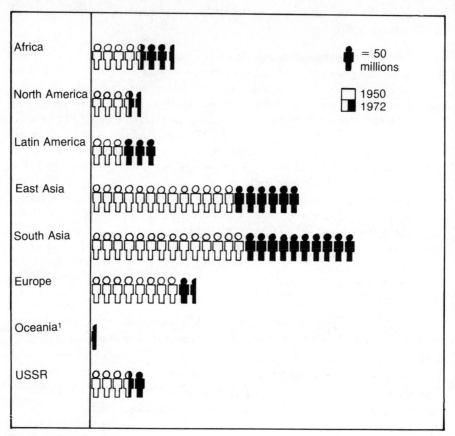

[1] 1972 figure only: 1950 = 13 millions.
*Source:* UN Demographic Yearbook 1973.

Demography underlies the political economy of scarcity, wealth and welfare. As Fig. 1 shows, in 1950 the world's population was estimated to total nearly 2.5 billion, which by 1972 was thought to have risen to some 3.8 billion. During this period the population of Africa nearly doubled, by rising from some 250 to 375 million; Latin (South and Central) America from 150 to 300 million; East Asia from 650 to 950 million and South Asia from 700 to 1200 million. However within the industrially developed countries population increases were far less dramatic; North America rose from 175 to 225 million; Europe from 400 to 475 million; and U.S.S.R. from 175 to 250 million.

serious implications for both immediate employment and welfare, and longer term growth prospects. Whereas throughout the 1960s the industrial countries' growth rates averaged better than 5 per cent per year, by the mid 1970s these had fallen to a static or slowly growing state. For the first time since the great depression of the 1930s world economic activity, as reflected in the growth of output and trade in the industrialised countries, levelled off to what amounted to a stationary state. Conversely, the quadrupling in oil prices, which followed on from the OPEC price adjustments of 1973 onwards, has radically improved the standing of a number of the Middle Eastern states. Today, in per capita income terms, amongst the richest countries in the world are two oil producing sheikdoms. Both Kuwait and the United Arab Emirates have an estimated 10,000 U.S. dollars per annum per capita income in gross national product. Of the other major oil producers the long term position of Saudi Arabia, with its huge power resources, is particularly favourable. The changing balance of power in favour of the oil producers has affected the international balance in many other ways. the United States, with over 6 per cent of the world's known petroleum resources, compares unfavourably with the Soviet Union, which is thought to have over 12 per cent, of known world resources. Thus in the 1970s, the balance of world power, in energy and political terms, has shifted away from the great social democracies of North America and Western Europe, towards those other 'new rentier' areas of the world, which still have an abundant supply of critical oil supplies.

Turning to the less developed countries of Africa, Asia and Latin America, only the oil producing countries have proved able to continue their economic growth during the mid 1970s recession. For most less developed countries, bereft of both cheap energy and higher technology, the result was a sharp check to expectations for future development. All such countries have been substantially and unexpectedly restricted by the slow-down in the industrial countries' growth rates, and by the sharp relative rises in the price of imported petroleum-based fuels. Most less developed countries, particularly those in Asia and Africa with average per capita incomes below some 200 dollars per year, have had little or no improvement in living standards since the early 1970s. There is an awareness of the problems highlighted by the North–South dialogue, and of the need for the advanced industrialised countries to assist in raising the living standards of the great masses of mankind living in the less developing world. Yet, how far this will prove to be practically possible remains to be seen. In such circumstances of change in *real politic* and trading

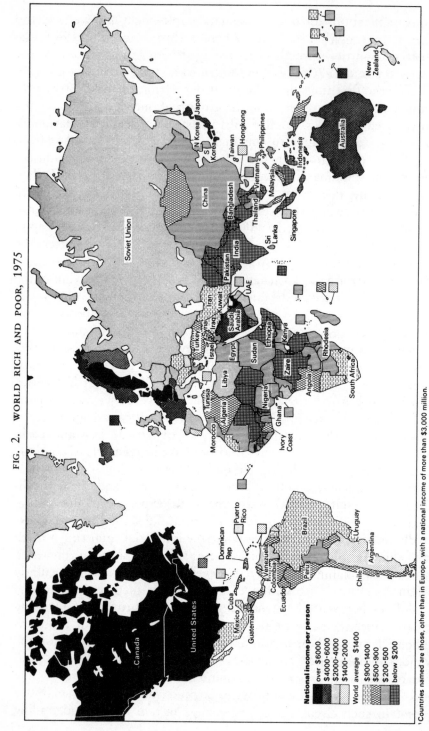

FIG. 2.   WORLD RICH AND POOR, 1975

Source: The Economist Diary 1978
Reproduced by kind permission of *The Economist* – London

Countries named are those, other than in Europe, with a national income of more than $3,000 million.

**National income per person**

- over $6000
- $4000-6000
- $2000-4000
- $1400-2000
- World average $1400
- $900-1400
- $500-900
- $200-500
- below $200

relationships and, with the great uncertainty to economic prospects as a whole, it is difficult and unwise to ignore the rapidly changing world beyond our own shores. Since the end of the Second World War all the Western free market economies have been influenced by the working of such agencies as the International Monetary Fund and the General Agreement on Tariffs and Trade, which did so much to facilitate the unprecedented post-war 'golden age' of growth for the international economy. Most immediate, from a current British viewpoint, is a new relationship with European partners, following on from the final acceptance of membership of the European Economic Community in 1975. Ironically, this membership coincided with the deepening onset of the repercussions of the OPEC managed price rises, from the previous year. Related to these developments has been the national and international problems of dealing with periodical monetary crises, affecting first one country and then another, and extending rapidly throughout the international system. Especially disturbing has been the re-emergence of unemployment as a critical problem in the leading Western industrial economies. Another oft-associated issue has become the role and responsibilities of great multinational enterprises, for investment, output and employment creation throughout the world. Again of special and particular significance was the Soviet Union's critical dependence on the United States, during the mid 1970s, for at least part of its essential supplies of food grains. This led to world-wide repercussions in price levels of foodstuffs. There has also been growing awareness within the Soviet led Council for Mutual Economic Assistance – C.M.E.A.; more usually known in the Western World as the COMECON group as a whole, of the need for new trade opportunities, both by export of primary and consumer durable products abroad, and to satisfy desires for a wider range of products, and freedom of choice at home. Throughout the Western world there is strengthening concern as to the impact of the 'Japanese economic miracle', which from an extreme distance, is now able to offer intense competition for a wide range of local manufacturers of consumer products, from transistor radios, to motor cycles and cars and such like.

Meeting in London on 7th and 8th May 1977, the Heads of States of seven of the world's richest industrialised countries (U.S.A., the United Kingdom, France, West Germany, Japan, Italy and Canada) defined seven pledges for their immediate future policies. These priorities neatly summarised current world economic dilemmas, as perceived by the leaders of the major industrialised nations in this, the final years of the 20th century.

They were:

1.  To create more jobs and at the same time reduce inflation.
2.  To meet national economic growth targets.
3.  To improve world financing facilities, by making more resources available to the International Monetary Fund.
4.  To expand trade and thereby increase job opportunities, while rejecting protectionism.
5.  To conserve energy and reduce dependence on oil.
6.  To set up an urgent study of nuclear problems.
7.  To help the world's poorer countries, with an increased flow of oil for their vital needs.

*    *    *    *    *

The irony surrounding these intense and widening preoccupations with the state of the world as a whole is that, viewed in a historical global context, the existence of man as a thinking animal remains tenuous. In the advanced urban and industrial nations of East and West the fear of nuclear holocaust has, since the Helsinki and related conferences of the early 1970s, been averted by détente. Yet, as the North–South dialogue continually emphasises in many of the less developed countries, the individual life span is still not much more than 30 years. Only during the present century has Western science based urban cum industrial society successfully increased the average life expectancy to near 70 years, approaching the Bible's sevenfold span. Life, for much of mankind, continues to be what that pessimistic English political philosopher, Thomas Hobbes, long ago described as 'solitary, poor, nasty, brutish, and short'. To escape the ferocity and limitations of brute nature, man moved into society, into what the French philosopher of freedom, Jean-Jaques Rousseau, later described as a 'social contract'. Though the 'savage' may have a nobility lost to civilised man, of necessity he has sought the chains of society, in order to escape from the pressing inadequacies of nature in the raw.

Such speculations naturally lead us back to the underlying nature of human society, and to those conventions relating to the phenomena and mystery of wealth. Where it comes from, and who it goes to, remains the preoccupation of philosophers and practical men alike. Is there an ideal system or mechanism by which individual man, and society as a whole, can escape from the finiteness of the material world, be rewarded for his contribution to productive processes, yet recognise the claims of equity and welfare? In agricultural societies, from Old Testament times onwards, one learns of fat years being followed by lean years, of abundance being all too frequently followed by famine, plague, pestilence and death. In William the Conqueror's England the Domesday Book of 1086 sought to catalogue national wealth, while later, King John's Magna Carta of 1215 listed associated political, economic and social problems in one document. In the modern urban and industrial economies, cushioned by the 'value adding' powers of the scientifically based system, much of economic policy, in these post 'Keynesian revolution' times, have been concerned with seeking to regulate business fluctuations so as to maintain full employment, and at the same time facilitate a smooth upward pattern of economic growth. Are such fluctuations part of a natural cyclical process, by which periods of expansion and growth leading to over indulgence and sloth, are followed by necessary periods of retribution and absolution? Certainly, until the impact of the thought of the Cambridge economist John Maynard Keynes was felt in Western democratic society, this was a widely held belief by many of classical thought and persuasion. As the experience of recent years shows, the Keynesian system has yet to prove itself as an ongoing world-wide answer to such problems.

Wealth, therefore, its definition and creation, its distribution, ongoing production and retention remains central to our understanding of human life and habitation, in both its historical and contemporary aspects. Yet many of the key elements of the wealth creating process remain profound mysteries. Affluence, its existence or absence, continues to attract concern focused on man's relationship to himself as a consumer, to his fellow as a rival or partner, and to the state of nature as an origin of abundance and scarcity. The practical applications of these concerns remain at the heart of economic debate, doctrine and analysis. Such concerns underline the global dilemmas and opportunities facing mankind now, and into the foreseeable future. Overshadowing all the forecast rise of the world's population from some 4 billion today, to 8 billion three decades or so hence, presents the most fundamental political economy issue confronting the future of mankind in this last quarter of the 20th century.

# Principal Historic Personae, Their Ideas and Influence

"Lives of great men all remind us
We can make our lives sublime,
And, departing, leave behind us
Footprints on the sands of time."

Longfellow (1807–1882)
*A Psalm of Life*


"Life is the art of drawing sufficient conclusions from insufficient premises."

Samuel Butler (1835–1902)
*Notebooks, Life*


"Let us now praise famous men –
Men of little showing –
For their work continueth,
And their work continueth,
Broad and deep continueth,
Greater than their knowing."

Rudyard Kipling (1865–1936)
*A School Song*, Stalky & Co


"The ideas of economists and political philosophers are more powerful than are commonly understood, indeed the world is ruled by very little else. Practical men, who believe themselves to be quite exempt from any intellectual influences, are usually the slave to some defunct economist."

John Maynard Keynes (1883–1946)
*The General Theory of Employment, Interest and Money*

Saint Thomas Aquinas (1225–1274)

Sir Thomas Gresham (1519–1579)

Thomas Mun (1571–1641)

Sir William Petty (1623–1687)

John Locke (1632–1704)

Francois Quesnay (1694–1774)

David Hume (1711–1776)

Sir James Steuart (1712–1780)

Adam Smith (1723–1790)

Anne-Robert-Jacques Turgot (1727–1781)

Jeremy Bentham (1748–1832)

Thomas Robert Malthus (1766–1834)

Jean Baptiste Say (1767–1832)

Robert Owen (1771–1858)

David Ricardo (1772–1823)

Thomas Tooke (1774–1858)

Robert Torrens (1780–1864)

Johann Heinrich von Thünen (1783–1850)

Friedrich List (1789–1846)

Nassau William Senior (1790–1864)

Antoine Augustin Cournot (1801–1877)

John Stuart Mill (1806–1873)

William Thomas Thornton (1813–1880)

Karl Marx (1818–1883)

Herbert Spencer (1820–1903)

Walter Bagehot (1826–1877)

Marie-Esprit Léon Walras (1834–1910)

William Stanley Jevons (1835–1882)

Carl Menger (1840–1921)

Alfred Marshall (1842–1924)

Francis Ysioro Edgeworth (1845–1926)

John Bates Clark (1847–1938)

Vilfredo Pareto (1848–1923)

Eugen von Bohm-Bawerk (1851–1914)

Knut Wicksell (1851–1926)

Friedrich von Wieser (1851–1926)

Thorstein Veblen (1857–1929)

John A. Hobson (1858–1940)

Frank W. Taussig (1859–1940)

Edwin Cannan (1861–1935)

Gustav Cassel (1866–1945)

Irving Fisher (1867–1947)

Vladimir Ilyich Lenin (1870–1924)

Wesley Clair Mitchell (1874–1948)

Arthur Cecil Pigou (1877–1959)

William Henry Beveridge (Lord Beveridge) (1879–1963)

Sir Ralph George Hawtrey (1879–1975)

John Maynard Keynes (Lord Keynes) (1883–1946)

Joseph Alois Schumpeter (1883–1950)

John Maurice Clark (1884–1963)

Sir Dennis Holme Robertson (1890–1963)

Ernst Friedrich Schumacher (1911–1977)

Harry S. Johnson (1924–1977)

## SAINT THOMAS AQUINAS (1225–1274) Canonised 1323

An Italian friar of the Dominican Order, who after studying theology in Paris, became one of the leading scholars and teachers of his day. His opinions came to carry great weight in the medieval Church, and his points on doctrine were generally regarded as decisive, and influence Catholic thinking to the present day. In economic thinking the late medieval Church was torn by conflict: whereas secular practice went in the direction of increasing the lending of money at interest and justifying it by reliance on Roman law, the Church at the Lateran Council of 1179 declared the first of a number of stringent prohibitions of usury.

Saint Thomas caused the Church's doctrine towards usury and a 'just price' to be founded as much on Aristotelian argument as on Scriptures. The former regarded money as a barren means of exchange; usury which made money 'yield fruit' was unnatural. Saint Thomas took up this view and combined it with traditional Roman law which distinguished whether goods were consumed or not. He concluded that to demand interest, in addition to return of a loan, was to seek an unjustifiable gain. In fact as the commercial age developed, the practise of taking interest grew, and from the 14th century onwards the temporal authorities became much more concerned with fixing maximum rates for a 'just price' than in preventing usury as such. Nevertheless the concept of a just price for money and for other goods has persisted to the present day, and is frequently at variance with the terms of *laissez-faire* supply and demand, or 'what the market will bear'. In Britain his ideas live on in the present day Government Price Commission, and in much else besides.

Elsewhere price and wage tribunals and controls have also become part of the armoury of contemporary democratic governments in seeking to regulate market forces in the 'public interest'. The spirit of good Saint Thomas might therefore be seen as an early expression of the 'bring down prices at a stroke' school of political economy.

## SIR THOMAS GRESHAM (1519–1579)

A Tudor statesman and financial adviser to the Cecils and to Queen Elizabeth I, who led an enquiry into the debasement of coinage. Depreciation of the value of the nation's currency against the prices of other commodities, a phenomenon which we today call inflation, has a long lineage. His conclusion, which became known as 'Gresham's Law', was 'that bad money drives out good'. By this he meant that when debased and good currency circulate together, people tend to hoard the good and try to pass on the debased in repayment of debts. In time the least acceptable coins become the commercial exchange value of the whole currency, while the more acceptable ones are withheld by the public and are kept for other uses, notably as a store of value. The failure of money to provide in one and the same form both a means of exchange and an effective store of value, has bedeviled attempts by contemporary democratic western governments, in their use of Keynesian demand management measures, to seek a sustained and stable growth rate.

Gresham was successful enough in his own dealings, as a Freeman of the Mercers' Company, to be able to propose and finance the building of the Royal Exchange, and also to found Gresham College. Seven professors were appointed to lecture in astronomy, geometry, physics, law, divinity, rhetoric and music. Between 1597 and 1768 the College was housed in Gresham House. Thereafter the lectures were delivered at the Royal Exchange until 1841, when a new Gresham College was built. The College is today associated with the City University, London.

## THOMAS MUN (1571–1641)

The son of a London mercer who traded in Italy and the Middle East and also became a director of the East India Company. He wrote *A Discourse of Trade from England unto the East Indies* in 1621, and *England's Treasure by Forraign Trade* in 1630, which was published posthumously by his son in 1664. His writings contained a synthesis of many of the most developed 'mercantilist theories' of his time, including the importance of foreign trade creating a surplus in bullion for a national economy; and the need to have a stock of capital to finance exports, so as to yield a surplus later on. He was aware of the importance of invisible exports, emphasising the desirability of overseas trade being carried on British ships, which was used in support of the Navigation Acts, which between the rivalry with Holland in the 17th and the eventual triumph of *laissez-faire* trade philosophies in the 19th century, underpinned England's colonial system.

Mun's main contribution to theory lies in his explanation of the 'balance of trade', and his expression of early mercantile capitalist concepts. His work was later quoted by Adam Smith in his *An Enquiry into the Nature and Causes of The Wealth of Nations* published in

1776. Mercantilism, as a guide to the practical conduct of national and international affairs, was strongly attacked by Smith and his followers of the classical school, notably David Ricardo, who developed the theory of comparative advantages as applied to international trade. Nevertheless protectionist trade policies persist – through the 'autarchical' measures followed by most leading industrial states in the depression years of the 1930s – to those of the Soviet inspired COMECON group of centrally planned economies today.

## SIR WILLIAM PETTY (1623–1687)

An early English statistician and economist, who linked the subjects together. A friend of the Admiralty Secretary and diarist, Samuel Pepys (1633–1703), and a founder member of the Royal Society, which became the leading association of scientists in Great Britain.

Petty's best-known work was *Political Arithmetik*, probably written in 1672, but not published until 1691, as it contained opinions thought likely to offend France. He was a Commissioner of Land Distribution under Cromwell in Ireland and published the *Political Anatomy of Ireland* in 1672. He also published *The Treatise of Taxes and Contributions* 1662, and *Quantulamcunque, a Tract Concerning Money* in 1682, in which he discussed the theory of value, fiscal policy and foreign exchange. His importance in the history of economic theory was that he broke away from earlier traditions and provided a beginning for classical economics and a 'statistical basis' for economic knowledge which continues to stand it in good stead.

Petty described his approach as 'Instead of using only comparative superlative words, I express myself in terms of number, weight or measure; use only arguments of sense, and consider only such causes as have visible foundations in nature'. He drew particular attention to the tendency for national employment to shift, with increased economic development, in the direction of services, and this became known as 'Petty's Law'. In the modern urban and industrial economies the move from agrarian into factory and thence into service employment for much of the workforce, has become a universal phenomenon, associated with development and growth and 'high living standards'. Daniel Bell in a book entitled *The Coming of the Post Industrial Society*, published in 1974, has outlined a further phase of possible economic, social and political developments in the modern 'service based' high mass consumption societies.

## JOHN LOCKE (1632–1704)

The son of a Somersetshire country lawyer, who was educated at Westminster and Christ Church, Oxford, Locke was originally intended for the Church, but early in his career he became a lecturer in Greek and rhetoric at Oxford. Later he became a physician to a powerful patron, in the first Earl of Shaftesbury. He also became a Fellow of the Royal Society, and for a while, Secretary to the Council of Trade and Foreign Plantations. However acute political conflicts, following the restoration of Charles II and the disaster of the Monmouth Rebellion of 1685, led him to live abroad in France and in the Low Countries until the Ascension of William of Orange in 1688.

Locke is best known for his *Two Treatises of Civil Government*, in which he attacked the divine right of kings and the need for an absolute ruler, as postulated by Thomas Hobbes (1588–1679) in his *Leviathan*. Hobbes had suggested that in order that man escape from brute nature, he needed to live within the security of an all-seeing centrally controlled state. However for Locke, man is subject to the laws of reason, which teaches all that no one ought to harm another in his life, health, liberty or possessions. People constitute in themselves a power superior to government. This was an idea which later came to have great weight in the Convention assembled in Philadelphia in 1787 to frame the Constitution of the United States. Again Locke's idea of the sanctity of 'private property' had an important impact on the way the early classical economists thought about the ideal functioning of the *laissez-faire* system, which was to so dominate economic development during the late 18th and throughout much of the 19th century.

## FRANCOIS QUESNAY (1694–1774)

French philosopher and physician to Louis XV (1710–1774) and his influential mistress Madame de Pompadour (1721–1764). A leading member of an important group of 18th century French intellectuals known collectively as physiocrats; to their contemporaries as *les economistes*. These included Mirabeau (1749–1791), Mercier de la Riviere (1720–1793), La Trosne (1728–1780), Du-pont de Nemours (1739–1817) and several others. Their bible was Denis Diderot's (1713–1784) huge 28 volume *Encyclopedia* or *Dictionaire Raisonne des Sciences, des Arts et des Metiers*. Jean Jacques Rousseau's (1712–1778) ideas of the need for civilised man to accept the chains of a *Contrat Social* also had much influence on their thought.

Quesnay was best known for his *Tableau economique* 1756, an early input-output table of the economy as a whole. It is thought that Quesnay was influenced in his ideas by the earlier writings of a little known Irish economic writer, Richard Cantillon (1680–1734), who as a banker lived in Paris and London and was eventually murdered. His view that only agriculture yielded a surplus over costs of production influenced later French thought about the origins of wealth. The physiocrats were united by a belief in common natural law and the idea that, in marked contrast to mercantilist trade surplus and bullion ideas, wealth derived only from the soil. Industry was unproductive because it merely combined things already produced, while commerce simply moved them around. Agricultural activity alone yielded a *produit net*, a free gift of nature, worth more than the costs of production. They proposed that agriculture should be fostered, and that domestic and foreign trade should be free of restrictions. They criticised prevailing mercantilist policies through an advocary of *laissez-passez*, the removal of all obstacles to domestic trade. Physiocratic ideas of the critical importance of the agricultural system as a basis of wealth continue to have an important meaning in much of the world. The European Economic Community's common agricultural policy bears a strong physiocratic flavour, in its support of the agricultural system against the claims of other interests.

## DAVID HUME (1711–1776)

The son of a small landowner who attended Edinburgh University and later worked for brief periods in a Bristol trading house, in France, as a tutor to the Marquis of Annandale. In 1752 he became a member of the Faculty of Advocates in Edinburgh. As a young man Hume was greatly influenced by the writings of the French aristocrat and philosopher Charles Louis Montesquieu (1689–1755) about the natural laws governing human life. Montesquieu's writings, from his *Lettres Persanes* to his *Causes de la grandeur des Romains et de leve decadence* had a profound effect – especially on the development of democratic ideas in Western Europe and North America. Hume's own works *Treatise on Human Nature* (1739–1740) and *Political Discourses* (1752) established his reputation as a leading 'natural law' philosopher; and as a critic of 'mercantilistic ideas' of trade regulations he had an important formative influence on Adam Smith.

## SIR JAMES STEUART (1712–1780)

A Scottish lawyer, who having supported the Young Pretender, went into eighteen years of exile following the defeat of the Stuart cause by the Hanoverians at Culloden Moor in 1745. During his exile he took up a study of political economy, and in 1767 published a book on *Principles of Political Economy* which was subsequently overshadowed by Adam Smith's *Wealth of Nations*, published nine years later. Steuart was important for his early study of finance and for turning attention to the problems of 'population increase', which Malthus was to develop further in his *Essay on the Principle of Population* published in 1798.

## ADAM SMITH (1723–1790)

A Scottish philosopher, man of letters and economist, who after an unprofitable time at Balliol College, Oxford, later held academic posts in Edinburgh and Glasgow. He is generally regarded, with Karl Marx and John Maynard Keynes, as being one of the three great economists of all time. (Skinner and Wilson's recently published *Essays on Adam Smith* provides the most recent and comprehensive assessment of his life and work.) While in England, Smith was a member of Dr. Samuel Johnson's (1709–1784) famous literary circle, which included most of the leading figures in London literary and artistic society of the day. In 1759, after returning to Scotland, he published a series of lectures on *The Theory of Moral Sentiments*, the sixth of which was the propensity of man to 'truck, trade and exchange'. This book led him to being offered the post of tutor to the young Duke of Buccleuch, which between 1764 and 1766 involved a Grand Tour of Europe. During this time, Smith met the French physiocrats, including the statesman cum economist Turgot. He also conversed with the great philosopher and satirist Voltaire (1694–1778), whose writings in *Candide* and other works were later to have such an impact on the ideas which led to the outbreak of the French Revolution in 1789. While in Toulouse, Smith delivered part of a lecture which became the beginning of his great work on *An Enquiry into the Nature and Causes of the Wealth of Nations*. He returned to Britain in 1766, settled in Kirkcaldy and finally published his book in 1776.

In contrast to the mercantilists and physiocrats, Smith argued that increasing wealth arose primarily out of the division of labour, inherent within the new industrial system, and went on to describe 'social harmony' as being dependent on man's balance of conflicting motives, in a search to satisfy individual self interest which would benefit society, but also limited by the self interest of others. He was impressed by the idea of the 'invisible hand' underlying economic activity and, in marked contrast to the mercantilists, of the desirability of government having a minimum role in the running of an economy. Smith thereby established the classical *laissez-faire* model and systematised most economic thought for several generations, around an idealised concept of free markets. He provided an intellectual justification for a newly emerging commercial and industrial class, which was increasingly anxious to rid Britain, and later Western Europe, of mercantilistically inspired governmental regulations and controls. Prophetically published in the same year as the American Declaration of Independence, *The Wealth of Nations* suggested that the American colonies would inevitably become one of the foremost nations of the world, and indeed that the capital of the British Empire would one day have to move across the Atlantic – from London to Philadelphia. *The Wealth of Nations* became the guide for economic activity, which served the capitalistic expansion of Britain and her Empire and much of Western Europe and the United States for the following century. Smith was truly said 'to have persuaded his own generation, and governed the next'.

## ANNE-ROBERT-JACQUES TURGOT (1727–1781).

A French statesman and economist who originally studied theology, but later became a lawyer and finally Secretary of State for the Navy in 1774 and thereafter Controller of General Finance. However his attempted financial and taxation reforms provoked much opposition, and he was dismissed in 1776 to be replaced by Jacques Necker (1732–1804), another intellectually formidable, if ultimately unsuccessful, reformer of the *ancien regime*. Turgot was much impressed by physiocratic notions of wealth deriving primarily from the soil, and of Quesnay's theory of a *produit net*. He wrote a book *Reflections sur la Formation, et la Distribution des Richesses* published in 1766, in which he suggested the idea of the division of labour, the productivity of labour and the effects of competition on markets. He also discussed the 'Law of variable proportion' which describes the relationship between inputs of productive resources (or factors) and the resulting output of goods. In particular he drew attention to the optimistic implications for economic growth of increasing returns. These are, however, eventually followed by decreasing returns – when a variable factor, say labour or investment in drainage improvements – are combined with a finite factor, such as land.

Turgot was in regular correspondence with Adam Smith and thereby had considerable influence on the early development of the classical *laissez-faire* model with its hopes for the 'division of labour' and 'competitive markets' leading to increasing returns. However the possibility of eventual decreasing returns, arising out of the finiteness of nature, had much influence on the pessimistic views for future growth later propagated by Malthus and also to a degree by Ricardo.

In his public life, Turgot, as Finance Minister during the first two years of Louis XVI's reign, attempted to restore economic stability to the *ancien regime* with the formula: 'No increase in taxation, no loans, no bankruptcy'. 'Salvation must be attained by increased production, wise economics and sound administrative reforms.' These and later reformist policies might have succeeded, but for the foolish extravagance of the Court party led by Queen Marie-Antoinette (1755–1793) and for expenditure caused by intervention in the American War of Independence against Britain. Some two decades later Revolutionary France, under Napoleon Bonaparte, was in sufficiently straitened circumstances to sell the whole of her remaining North American Empire, from the Mississippi to the Rocky Mountains, and from the Gulf of Mexico to Canada to the newly expanding U.S.A., under the terms of the 1803 'Louisiana Purchase' for the paltry sum of $15 m. 'Plus ça change, plus c'est la même chose'.

## JEREMY BENTHAM (1748–1832)

An English philosopher, lawyer, social reformer and classical economist educated at Westminster and Oxford. His *Defence of Usury* published in 1787, was his first essay on economics, and a logical application of Adam Smith's principles. His later works included *The Principles of Morals and Legislation* published 1789, and *Manual of Political Economy* in 1825. In thought he followed the *laissez-faire* principle, envisaging a structure of institutions which would create a free society and in which 'the greatest happiness of the greatest number' is the foundation of all morals and legislation. His utilitarian 'calculus of pleasure and pain' – in an economic sense, pleasure coming from consumption up to the point of satiation, and pain coming from forgoing, but being necessary to allow saving and investment – had much influence on the thinking of classical economists of succeeding generations.

Bentham's utilitarian disciples, including James Mill (1773–1836), founded University College London, as a non-Sectarian University, the forerunner of the University of London and other civic universities in Britain. This was at a time when non-members of the Church of England were excluded by the religious Test Acts from graduating at Oxford or Cambridge. After death Bentham's brain was dissected and his body subsequently embalmed, and kept at University College, where it may be viewed to this day, dressed in his thinking clothes and broad-brimmed hat. As his own auto-icon he unwittingly, therefore, provided an early forerunner of a utilitarian use of a corpse, which Lenin and other Soviet leaders were later to emulate in a tomb outside the Kremlin in a rather more grandiose and public style.

After his death, one story which circulated in intellectual and literary London was that Bentham's dissected head had yielded nothing more remarkable than a kind of oil, which was almost unfreezeable. Indeed the only 'utility' which could be thought for it was for oiling chronometers, which were going to polar latitudes. However Thomas Peacock (1785–1866), is reputed (in the Oxford Book of Literary Anecdotes) to have told James Mill that the less he said about it the better:

> ". . . . just because if the fact once becomes known, just as we see now in the newspapers that a fine bear is to be killed for his grease, we shall be having advertisements to the effect that a fine philosopher is to be killed for his oil."

## THOMAS ROBERT MALTHUS (1766–1834)

An English country gentleman and clergyman, who came to fame on the basis of his essay on *The Principle of Population as it Affects the Future Improvement of Society* published in 1798. In this work he was developing ideas about population problems perceived earlier by the Scottish Economist Sir James Steuart in the 1760s. Malthus, whose ideas fell on more receptive ears, stated that whereas 'population when unchecked increased in a geometrical ratio, subsistence only increases at an arithmetic ratio'.

Subsequently he became Professor of Political Economy at Hailey-bury College, a newly established school for young men intended for the East India Company, where he remained until his death in 1834. He thereby joined the ranks of a number of leading economic thinkers, from Thomas Mun in the 17th century, to James Mill and later his brilliant son, John Stuart Mill, and William Thomas Thornton in the mid 19th century who worked for the company. Malthus' other main economic works included *An Enquiry into the Nature and Progress of Rent* of 1815; *The Poor Law* 1817; *Principles of Political Economy* 1820; and *Definitions of Political Economy* 1827. Malthus also became a founder member of the Political Economy Society, a Fellow of the Royal Society, and gave evidence to many parliamentary committees.

Malthus was stimulated to write his original essay by the optimistic passages about population, contained in Adam Smith's *Wealth of Nations*, and also by the pessimistic implications for growth of the 'law of variable proportions', leading at first to increasing, and then to decreasing, returns, as first discussed by the French statesman cum economist Turgot. These forebodings prompted Malthus to write his essay in which he argued that, while the means of subsistence tended to grow in an arithmetic progression 1,2,3,4 etc., population grew in a geometric progression 2,4,8,16, etc., every 15 years or so. The main effect of his ideas on economic doctrine was to wipe away some of the optimism for growth and progress generated by Smith and others, and to bring back into focus the underlying 'finiteness of nature', land and food production capacity, etc., acting as a restraint on the development of the economy as a whole. Again in contrast to Ricardo, Malthus was impressed by the problems of gluts and periods of under-consumption, views which later had an effect on Karl Marx and his followers, and were also referred to by John Maynard Keynes in his *General Theory* published in 1936.

Malthus also influenced Ricardo to think in terms of a 'subsistence wage' being essential, to allow capitalists sufficient returns to finance the future through the wage fund and investments in new machinery and stock. His pessimistic views had an influence on the way the post-1834 Poor Law Reforms were harshly applied in Britain. In economic thought, through his pessimistic interpretation of the implications of 'diminishing returns' for growth, Malthus influenced Ricardo and caused economists to become known – in Thomas Carlyle's (1795–1881) telling phrase – 'Respectable Professors of the Dismal Science'.

Malthusian ideas of runaway population and scarce resources look set for a strong revival; especially in the U.S.A. where ever expanding new frontiers kept such gloomy thoughts at bay for many generations. 'The world models' developed at the Massachusetts Institute of Technology (M.I.T.) represent an ambitious attempt to bring together forecasts of population growth, resource depletion, food supply, capital investment and pollution into one general model of the future. Two recent books, *World Dynamics* (1971) by Jay W. Forrester and the *Limits to Growth* (1972) by Dennis L. Meadows, have promoted these views. A further book, *Thinking about the future – A Critique of the Limits to Growth* (1973) by the Science Policy Research Unit at Sussex University, suggests that the Malthusian style 'assumptions made at M.I.T. may be unduly pessimistic'. The President's Energy Advisor Mr. James Schlesinger – in his gallant, if apparently forlorn current attempt to wean the American public off 'gas-guzzling' – is also prone to invoke the wisdom of Parson Malthus.

## JEAN BAPTISTE SAY (1767–1832)

A French economist who became interested in the new political economy after reading Smith's *Wealth of Nations*. Following the Napoleonic wars he was sent by the new Royalist French Government to study economic conditions in Britain, and he later published a book on *Angleterre et les Anglais*. The Chair of Industrial Economy was founded for him at the Conservatoire des Arts et Metiers in 1819, and in 1831 he was appointed Professor of Political Economy at the College de France.

Say's conception of an economic equilibrium that supply created equivalent demand became known as 'Say's Law of Markets', and had much influence on subsequent 19th and 20th century classical and neo-classical thought. However at much the same time, the Swiss economist and historian Jean Sismondi (1773–1842), in his *Nouveaux Principes d'Economic Politique'* published in 1819, was questioning the view that competition was establishing an equilibrium between production and consumption, and suggested that over-production and crises were an inevitable part of the economic system. Say's ideas of an automatic equilibrium tending to full employment were at a much later time also powerfully criticised by John Maynard Keynes. Indeed a refutation of Say's law became central to Keynesian ideas of the need for government intervention on the demand side of the economy, so as to raise aggregate demand and combat persistent under-employment of labour and other resources in the economy as a whole.

## ROBERT OWEN (1771–1858)

An early Welsh cotton master and socialist pioneer, who in 1815 wrote about the revolutionary impact of industrial development on people in his *Observations on the Effect of the Manufacturing System.* He is best remembered for the principles which he originally pioneered in a textile factory, established in Manchester in 1819. These included sick and retirement pay, no child labour, and a generally paternalistic view of workers' needs. Owen later further developed these ideas in a new business at Lanark, in Scotland. He subsequently moved to the United States to establish a model industrial community based on Owenite ideas, at New Harmony in Indiana, but following the failure of this returned to Britain. Owen is principally noted in the history of political and economic thinking for his early espousal of the ideas of industrial 'welfare' and 'co-operation'; of Socialism and of adult education. He was also a founder member of the British trade union movement by his involvement with the abortive National Consolidated Trade Union, following the repeal of the Combination Acts in the 1830s. The example of Owen and his ideas inspired socially minded economic thinkers, of all shades of opinion, for many generations to come.

In France the utopian social reconstruction theories of Francois Fourier (1772–1837) had a similar influence. As with Owen, many Fourierist colonies were started after his death, in both France and the United States. All eventually failed. Nevertheless the criticism by Owen and Fourier in their different ways of early 19th century social conditions, stimulated socialist reformers for many years to come.


## DAVID RICARDO (1772–1823)

A wealthy stockbroker and brilliant intellect who was successful enough to retire at the age of 42, to become influential in public life, and be elected to Parliament in 1819. During the last decade of his life Ricardo became greatly interested in the new science of political economy and wrote a number of important works, including *The High Price of Bullion* in 1810, followed by an essay *On the Influence of a Low Price of Corn on the Profits of Stock* in 1815 and by *Proposals for an Economical and Secure Currency* in 1816. At this time Ricardo was involved in a public controversy with another leading economic writer Charles Bosanquet (1769–1850) about taxation and prices etc. However, Ricardo's most important work became *The Principles of Political Economy and Taxation* which first appeared in 1817, with the third edition, to which reference is usually made, being published in 1821.

For Ricardo the most important problem of economics was 'to

determine the laws which regulated distribution' of economic produce. His idea of value was 'a quantity of labour theory'. He dismissed 'scarce' non-reproducible commodities and concentrated analyses on the mass of goods which may be increased by human industry. He sought to demonstrate that the exchange values of commodities would be proportional to the quantities of labour embodied in them, including the stored up labour in the form of machinery, etc. He gave particular emphasis to the need of the capitalist to have sufficient profits to maintain and finance future machinery and stocks, and also to afford the 'wage fund' which was the payment to workers in advance of the products of their efforts being sold. The idea of the wage fund persisted in classical economic doctrine, up to its detailed criticism by William Thomas Thornton in his work *On Labour* published in 1869.

For Ricardo the explanation of the 'distributive shares' of the three factors of production – land, labour and capital – was implicit in his theory of value, once the scarcity rent of finite land had been eliminated. His theories of distribution and taxation had much influence on later classical economists – they suggested that, as population expanded, the increase in demand for food would raise rents and the price of food – hence wages would rise and profits would fall, which in turn augured badly for financing future growth, for the introduction of new machinery and stock and for financing the wage fund. Thus, the harmonious 'community of interests' suggested by Adam Smith in his *Wealth of Nations* no longer seemed possible.

Ricardo also wrote extensively about the *Theory of Comparative Advantages* as applied to international trade, and advocated the repeal of the Corn Laws which restricted the flow of cheap foodstuffs into Britain from their introduction in 1815 until their repeal by Sir Robert Peel's (1788–1850) Government in 1846 following the disaster of the Irish potato famine, (the Great Hunger), in the years 1844–1847. Ricardo's theories – notably the labour theory of value – also had a powerful critical influence on Karl Marx, in the later development of his alternative views about the working of the economic and social system as a whole.

## THOMAS TOOKE (1774–1858)

An English merchant cum classical economist, who in 1819 wrote the *Merchant's Petition* against protective tariffs. He later published a six volume *History of Prices and of the State of Circulation During the*

*Years 1793—1826.* A leading proponent of the 'banking school' who argued, against Robert Torrens' 'currency school', that the volume of currency was not determined solely by the quality of gold and paper notes in circulation, but included bank deposits and bills of exchange. Tooke supported freedom for the individual banks in their note issue – in light of the needs of trade. He considered that price fluctuations were caused by changes in general conditions of supply and demand for commodities rather than by changes in the supply of money alone – a debate which in various forms continues to the present day.

## ROBERT TORRENS (1780–1864)

An important English classical economist, friend of both Malthus and Ricardo, who, like the latter, was for a brief period a Member of Parliament. Early in his career he was an officer in the Marines and saw active service in the Napoleonic Wars. He later became a novelist and developed an interest in political economy. His *Essay on the External Corn Trade* in 1815, established his reputation, and he later wrote widely on money and banking. In his *Letter to Lord Melbourne* published in 1837, he suggested that the Bank of England, which originally had been established as a joint stock company in 1694 to deal with the Government debt created by Charles II, should be divided into two departments. One would be the issue department, to hold the bullion reserve and deal with the note issue, and the banking department to conduct general business.

Torrens became a leading exponent of the 'currency principle' which led to the Bank Charter Act of 1844 and the way the relationships between the Bank of England and the Joint Stock banking system subsequently developed: with the Bank as a 'lender of last resort' by variations in 'bank rate' and by its use of 'open market operations'. In general, members of the 'currency school' felt that the primary duty of the Bank of England was to maintain a sufficient reserve of bullion to safeguard the stability of public credit. They considered that the total amount of metallic currency varied with inflows and outflows from abroad. If the nation's credit base was to remain stable a mixed currency should work in the same way – with the volume of paper notes being kept in strict proportion to the amount of gold in the system. In opposition, the 'banking school', led by Thomas Tooke, maintained that individual banks should be free to decide how many notes to issue – subject to convertability to gold on demand.

## JOHANN HEINRICH VON THÜNEN (1783–1850)

A German agricultural economist who was a son of a landowner in Aldenburg. He had estates in Mecklenburg and ran a model farm there. Von Thünen was mainly concerned with the principles determining the best system of cultivation, especially in terms of the distance from the market. He was a founder of modern theories of 'industrial location' and his analysis also caused him to build up a theory of rents, similar to that of Ricardo's. However, because of his denial of the 'subsistence theory of wages' and his thinking about various ideas leading to 'marginal analysis', von Thünen played an important role in assisting in the development of later economic theories as developed in England by Stanley Jevons and in Vienna by Carl Menger, and others of the Austrian school, in Vienna and elsewhere.

## FRIEDRICH LIST (1789–1846)

An influential German civil servant and economist. After spending some years in America engaged in a variety of activities, including mining and railway development, he wrote a book on the importance of tariffs, etc., for encouraging growth in developing countries. List's *Outlines of American Political Economy* published in 1827, revealed his ideas at that stage. On returning to Germany he developed these views further, giving them an historical foundation which fitted well into the intellectual environment of his country at that time. These ideas were included in the book *Das Nationale System der Politischen Oekonomie* (1841) in which he emphasised the importance of the nation state, and developed the theory of 'national economic development' in an industrial age. As such, List's ideas coincided with the creation of the Zollverein in 1833 when Prussia agreed with four other leading German states to withdraw tariffs against one another's goods and maintain a uniform external tariff. Behind this wall Germany emerged under Prussian leadership as a modern industrial state, capable of challenging first France, and later Great Britain for leadership in the Western European world.

## NASSAU WILLIAM SENIOR (1790–1864)

An influential early classical economist, educated at Eton and Oxford, who from 1825 onwards was a Professor of Political Economy at Oxford. Senior was influential on many Royal Commissions, in which he generally represented the classical viewpoint. His opinions on one Royal Commission that long hours were necessary because all profit derived from the last hour worked, later received vituperative attack from Karl Marx. In his *An Outline of the Science of Political Economy* he stated his views on the scope and method as being purely a 'deductive science'. Senior, together with Professor John Elliot Cairnes (1823–1875), of Trinity College, Dublin, and others, also conducted a long controversy with John Stuart Mill over 'the scope and method of economics'. Similar debates developed with even greater fervour during the second half of the 19th century in Austria and Germany. In general the 'Austrian school', led by Carl Menger, took a 'deductive scientific' viewpoint, whereas the historians, under the leadership of Gustav Schmoller, emphasised an 'inductive' approach to knowledge. These issues continue to divide practitioners of political economy to the present day. In particular the American 'institutional' or 'evolutionary' school is very much within the traditions of the historical inductive approach. In contrast, others within the more mathematical aspects of economics, in both its 'micro' and 'macro' economy aspects, would be seeking to develop the claims of theory with scientific rigour and 'predictive' powers.

## ANTOINE AUGUSTIN COURNOT (1801–1877)

A French professor of mathematics at the University of Lyons who also had a wide knowledge of economics. His main publications include *Recherchés sur les Principes Mathématiques des Richesses* (1863), *Revue Sommaire des Doctrines Economiques* (1877). He established the idea of 'supply and demand functions' which were used to show how price was formed under conditions of pure monopoly, duopoly and perfect competition. He is considered to be a founder of modern mathematical economics, which today play such an important role in our perception and understanding of the economic system as a whole.

## JOHN STUART MILL (1806–1873)

The English political philosopher and economist, who received a remarkable education from his father, James Mill, who had been a close friend of Ricardo and Bentham, and was one of the leading intellectuals and classical economists of his time. The elder Mill had published *Elements of Political Economy* in 1821, but was better known for his extensive *History of British India* published in 1817–1818, which led him to holding senior appointments with the East India Company in London.

Following in his father's footsteps, the younger Mill served with the East India Company until 1858, when, following the Mutiny, it lost its Charter. From 1865 to 1868, like Ricardo before him, he became a Member of Parliament, but after the death of his wife, he retired and spent his last years at Avignon, in Southern France. His system of logic first appeared in 1843 and immediately established his leading position in the intellectual community. His *Principles of Political Economy* published in 1848, were largely based on Ricardo, though he did include a substantial chapter on the need for a 'stationary state' which could be mitigated by a 'liberal society'. Throughout much of his writing Mill was engaged in controversy with others of classical persuasion, notably Nassau Senior and John Elliot Cairnes, about the scope and methods of political economy. In general Mill's main contribution to economic thought was that he sought to mitigate the harsher elements of the classical Malthusian/Ricardian model by liberal opinion and gradual social reform. As such it also stands in marked contrast to the social revolutionary ideas being developed by Karl Marx, and his supporters at the same period. The debate between those who look for a liberal solution, and those whose hopes lie in revolutionary change, persist throughout the world to the present day.

Edmund Clerihew Bentley (1875–1956) later wrote these witty lines about the dilemmas of the great man thus:

> John Stuart Mill,
> By a mighty effort of will
> Overcame his natural bonhomie
> And wrote *Principles of Political Economy*.

## WILLIAM THOMAS THORNTON (1813–1880)

Another of the group of talented 19th century economists, James and his son John Stuart Mill, and Thomas Robert Malthus who were employed by the East India Company. From 1858 Thornton was First Secretary of Public Works in the India Office. A close friend of the younger Mill, Thornton became a powerful critic of many aspects of classical Ricardian doctrines. His first publications were *Over Population* in 1846, and *Plea for Peasant Proprietors* in 1848, reflecting an interest in economic development problems. However he is best remembered for his detailed criticisms of the idea of the 'wages fund' which were included in his work *On Labour* published in 1869. In turn he influenced John Stuart Mill and other classical cum neo-classical economists about the working of the system as a whole.

## KARL MARX (1818–1883)

The second of the 'big three' economic thinkers, Marx, together with Adam Smith in the 18th century and John Maynard Keynes in the 20th century decisively influenced the way people think about economic, political and social doctrines to the present day. (David McLellan's recently published book, *Karl Marx – his life and thought*, gives a full account of Marx's varied and often tumultuous life.)

He was born of Jewish parents, who later converted to Christianity, in Trier in the Rhineland, shortly after it had reverted to Prussian rule. During an uneven career at the Universities of Bonn and Berlin, Marx came under the influence of the works of the Prussian philosopher Georg Wilhelm Hegel (1770–1831) and the French social-ist philosopher Claude-Henri Saint-Simon (1760–1825). Subsequently, following various literary cum revolutionary activities, including editorship of the *Rheinische Zietung*, he fled to Paris where he edited the *Deutsch-Franzosische Jahrbucher*, and then moved to Belgium and England. His interest in political economy developed from his friend-ship with Friedrich Engels (1820–1895) the son of a wealthy German family of Manchester textile manufacturers. Engels himself had made an extensive study of the misery of industrial society, as it had developed in early 19th century Lancashire. *The Communist Manifesto* written jointly by Marx and Engels in 1848, owed much to the example of the English Chartist list of grievances which had been promulgated in England during the 1830s. Marx and Engels saw human society as being locked into an 'historically determined' series of stages – primitive communism, slavery, feudalism and capitalism following each other through revolutionary change. Within the capitalist stage an inevitable rupture between the bourgeoisie owners of the means of production and the property-less industrial proletariat would occur. They con-sidered that in the conflict between these two social classes the capitalist system inevitably contained the seeds of its own destruction.

Marx in his later writings was much influenced by Ricardo's labour theory of value, which emphasised the contribution of labour in the creation of wealth. However he suggested an additional 'surplus value' which was that part of total value, which accrued to the capitalist rather than to the worker. He ascribed to the capitalist classes an insatiable

thirst for 'surplus value', and built up a theory of 'capitalist accumulation' which suggested that the working of the capitalistic system
inevitably caused the control of productive resources to fall into fewer
and fewer hands, and create an increasingly impoverished proletariat,
incapable of sustaining demand for industrial products – ideas which in
their different ways both Malthus, and later John Maynard Keynes,
also perceived. Again, like the Swiss economist, Sismondi, at an earlier
time, Marx predicted increasingly disastrous commercial and 'trade
crisis' extending throughout the capitalist world.

Many of Marx's later published theories, as expressed in the three
editions of *Das Kapital* published between 1867 and posthumously in
1894, reinforced the views of a growing band of socialists, who like
himself, developed their thought from the basis of Ricardo's labour
theory of value. During the second half of the 19th century the rapid
worldwide development of the capitalist system and, in particular, the
growth and wider distribution of income as a whole, seemed to refute
many of Marx's grimmer forebodings of economic collapse, this being
followed by revolutionary and social turmoil – eventually leading to 'a
dictatorship of the proletariat'. For the Marxists', the extension of
imperialism and empire, especially deriving from the 'scramble for
Africa' following the Berlin Conference of 1885, signalled a further
phase of capitalistic world exploitation and a way out of collapsing
markets and profits at home. The influence of many of Marx's
underlying ideas contained in Lenin's programme following the 1917
Russian Revolution, and in revolutionary movements elsewhere, has
caused Marx and his views to have a powerful influence on world
history. Today the practical application of Marxist ideas are split
between many factions within the increasingly diverse Marxist influenced societies, from post Stalin (1879–1953) Russia to post Mao
Tse-Tung (1896–1976) China, and their various client states. Tito's
Yugoslavia early on showed the possibility of breaking political and
economic subservience to the Soviet industrial system – and no doubt,
many more such schisms are to come.

## HERBERT SPENCER (1820–1903)

An assistant editor of *The Economist*, who in 1850 published a book
on *Social Statics* in which he sought to demonstrate that *laissez-faire*
liberalism would establish a social equilibrium, if allowed to operate
freely. In this, like many other mid- and late-Victorian intellectuals of
all shades of the political spectrum, he was influenced by 'Malthusian'

ideas of finite nature, and of 'Darwinian' ideas of an evolutionary social progress, coming out of a 'struggle for survival'. It will be recalled that Charles Darwin (1809–1882) lived at the same period as both Marx and many classical cum neo-classical economic thinkers. He had a profound, if varied impact, on their views of life and its meaning. Spencer, in the book *Man versus the State* published in 1884, made a powerful attack on all forms of state intervention in market and social processes, which had a great success amongst those of like mind in Britain and America. He thereby powerfully influenced middle class opinion of his own time and later about the class structure, and the apparent social and biological justification which was said to underlie the working of the *laissez-faire* market system as a whole. Indeed he stimulated a debate which has continued fiercely throughout the western democratic world to the present day.

## WALTER BAGEHOT (1826–1877)

An English economist, lawyer and banker, who after education at University College London, was called to the bar and entered his father's banking and shipping business in Bristol. Later, between 1860 and 1877, he became an influential editor of *The Economist*, and his book *Lombard Street* published in 1873, is a detailed study of finance and banking, as conducted at that time. His other important works include the still widely admired *The English Constitution*; *Physics and Politics*; *Universal Money*; and *Postulates of English Political Economy*. A man of flexible and liberal persuasion Bagehot early on recognised the limitations of Ricardian style classical economics. He considered political economy as a science not of rigorous laws, but rather of social tendencies. His idea of 'psychological cycle' of optimism and pessimism was an early attempt to explain trade cycle fluctuations against business confidence. Many of Bagehot's original writings are currently being edited by *The Economist* into a new series of works.

## MARIE-ÉSPRIT LÉON WALRAS (1834–1910)

A French economist originally trained as a mining engineer who became a Professor of Political Economy in Lausanne in 1870. In his writings he divided analysis into pure, social and applied. In his first book *Eléments d'Economie Politique Pure* 1874–1877 he developed a 'marginal utility' theory a few years later than Jevons in England and Menger in Austria – but independently of them. Walras was an enthusiastic social reformer. However, his most outstanding contribution to economic thought was in his analysis of the conditions of 'general equilibrium'.

## WILLIAM STANLEY JEVONS (1835–1882)

An important mid-nineteenth century British economist, who after early university education in London and a period in Australia as Assayer in the Royal Mint in Sydney, returned to become a Professor of Political Economy at Manchester, and later at University College London. Jevons was interested in most aspects of economics, but especially that which linked statistical investigations to theory. In this sense he was in the tradition established by Sir William Petty two hundred years before. His *Theory of Political Economy* (1871), brought together various earlier utility analyses into a comprehensive theory of value, exchange and distribution. He sought to provide a mathematical exposition of the laws of the market and the theory of value. It was in this work that he formulated a development of concept of 'marginal utility' which paralleled ideas originally thought of by a number of Western European thinkers, including Johann von Thünen, in connection with agriculture and markets, and Heinrich Gössen (1810–1858). It was also being undertaken contemporaneously by Carl Menger of the Austrian school, and Léon Walras at the University of Lausanne.

Jevons made several other highly original contributions to mid 19th century neo-classical marginal utility economics. At one stage he sought, by elaborate historical and statistical research, to explain the incidence of 'trade cycles' in just over 10-year frequencies, as being related to the incidence of similar cycles of sunspots – which in turn influenced grain harvests in the U.S.A., Russia, and other countries, and thus affected food prices, industrial wages and costs, and so on. Likewise in 1864, he published an important book on *The Coal Question* which, on the basis of marginal analysis was, by cutting into less and less productive seams, facing rapidly diminishing returns, as foretold by classical economists from Malthus onwards.

In fact new technology and new pits, plus alternative fuels, saved the day, at least up to the present time. However Jevons' ideas about sunspots, harvests and prices look due for a revival, in light of current preoccupations with world climatic conditions and grain supplies.

Later a student of Jevons, Philip Henry Wickstead (1844–1927), a philosopher, medieval scholar, theologian and economist, who had been educated at University College London, made a most comprehensive non-mathematical statement of the marginal theories of economics, in *The Scope and Method of Political Economy in the Light of the Marginal Principle* (1914).

## CARL MENGER (1840–1921)

An influential Professor of Economics at the University of Vienna from 1873 to 1903 – except for the period 1876 to 1878, when he became private tutor in political economy and statistics to Prince Rudolf of Austria 1858–1889. The said Prince, a man whose interests also ran to anticlerical thought, literature, liberal politics and Hungarian actresses, was later to die in a suicide pact with his mistress, Maria Vetsera, in a shooting box at Mayerling in 1889. In 1900 Menger became a life member of the Austrian Upper House, which indicates the close links maintained between the academic and governing establishments of the Vienna of his time. Published in 1871, his work *Grundsatze der Volkswirtschaftslehre*, marked an independent discovery, from Jevons in England, of the concept of 'marginal utility' and is considered to be one of the best non-mathematical statements of the principle. Under Menger's leadership the 'Austrian school' became engaged in a long controversy with Gustav Schmoller, who was a leading proponent of the 'inductive' or historical approach, as opposed to the 'deductive' approach to economic doctrine. In many ways these debates related to those between Nassau Senior, the younger Mill, Cairnes and others in Britain, about the scope and methods of economic science.

## ALFRED MARSHALL (1842–1924)

Godfather of the Anglo-Saxon neo-classical tradition. Educated at Merchant Taylors' School and at St. John's College, Cambridge, he became a Lecturer and later a Professor of Political Economy at Cambridge in 1885 – a position he held until his retirement in 1908. Early in his academic career he visited the U.S.A. to study the tariff system, which was facilitating the rapid industrialisation of America at that time.

His main contribution is contained in the book *Principles of Economics* published 1890, and also in *Industry and Trade* in 1919. In the former he successfully brought together two streams of thought; the older, classical view and the newer, 'marginal utility' view, as expressed by Jevons and others. He created a precise theory of 'value' and 'distribution'.

Marshall considered that the main work of the economist was to study the behaviour of man within the framework of institutions in which they live. This required that facts be collected, arranged and interpreted carefully and the dangers of presenting interpretations as theories of universal validity be avoided. Like Marx he also believed that institutions affected a man's behaviour and was largely determined by them, and thereafter looked for a common denominator in order to make economics a 'scientific subject'. He considered that economics was confined to those aspects of human behaviour which could be measured in terms of money, and were reflected in the price mechanism, and his principles thus set out to examine the general relationship between supply, demand and value. For Marshall, economic behaviour was based upon a delicate 'Benthamite' balance between the search for satisfaction, and the avoidance of sacrifice.

This approach enabled him to treat utility and costs as joint determinates of value, like the blades of a scissor 'neither cutting solely by its own action'. He also divided economic analysis into a number of different time periods, basing much of his theory on 'static conditions'. Though Marshall intended his work to be mainly used by the layman and the business man, he had a wide impact on the development of neo-classical inspired economics throughout the English-speaking world. Marshallian concepts, such as the 'elasticity of demand' and 'substitution', are still to be found in the works of contemporary market economists.

However many historical and institutional thinkers felt that the 'marginal utility' school had led economic thought into a blind alley. Thus Professor Henry Sidgwick (1838–1900), who was a contemporary of Marshall's at Cambridge, showed a strong interest in his *Principles of Political Economy* – published in 1883, in the social issues presented by classical economic doctrines.

Marshall is reputed to have done most of his creative thinking while on family walking holidays in the Swiss Alps, or in his summer house in his Cambridge garden. At his death in 1924, in the best Cambridge tradition, he left his family an excellent well stocked wine cellar, which remained largely untouched until after the passing of his widow in the 1940s. By this time most of the wine had deteriorated badly – thus disproving the adage, 'that an old wine tastes much nicer'. Economic doctrines are prone to suffer a similar fate, if left unused too long.

# FRANCIS YSIDRO EDGEWORTH (1845–1926)

An Anglo–Irish economist who after education at Trinity College, Dublin and at Oxford came to economics, via mathematics and ethics. He became a professor of political economy in London and at Oxford. Early on he developed the concept of the 'indifference curve'. In other works he presented ideas on the *Theory of Monopoly* published in 1897, and the *Theory of Distribution* published in 1904. He used statistics and economics in regard to economic theory, and thereby established a path that many others have subsequently trod. Most of his work consisted of articles and journals which were collected and published as *Papers relating to Political Economy* in 1925.

# JOHN BATES CLARK (1847–1938)

An important American economist educated at Brown University and Amherst College, who later attended the university at Heidelberg, and finally became a Professor at Columbia University. He was best known for his work on *Distribution of Wealth* (1899), in which he extended the marginal principle into an analysis of production and distribution, and also introduced the concept of 'marginal product'. He was especially influential in extending neo-classical theories, in the context of the United States which, during his lifetime, experienced enormous economic expansion and growth.

# VILFREDO PARETO (1848–1923)

An Italian mathematical economist who became involved in contemporary political problems. His mathematical interests led him to succeed Léon Walras to the important chair of economics in the University of Lausanne. His main contribution to economic theory was included in his *Manual of Political Economy* published in 1906. His argument that utility was not measurable led him to develop the concept of the 'indifference curve'. This led to an important shift in neo-classical economic theory from the 'cardinal' to the 'ordinal' aspects of utility. It was henceforth unnecessary to assume utility was measurable. A more satisfactory theory of consumer behaviour could therefore be developed, on the assumption that the utility from different combinations of goods could be ranked in order of preference by consumers.

## EUGEN VON BÖHM-BAWERK (1851–1914)

An Austrian statesman and Minister of Finance who, in 1904, became a Professor of Economics in Vienna. His main interest in economics was in the theory of capital. In his *Positive Theory of Capital* published in 1889, he applied the idea of marginal utility more closely to the theory of interest, using productivity and wage fund theories. His concept of 'time preference' had considerable influence on the development of neo-classical thought. In general his career suggests the close ties which existed between government and academic circles in the Vienna of his day. For all that, such links do not seem to have done much towards assisting the ramshackle Austro–Hungarian Empire of Emperor Franz Joseph (1830–1916) to move itself into the modern age.

## KNUT WICKSELL (1851–1926)

An influential Swedish Professor of Economics at the University of Lund, who studied in Austria, Germany and England. His main contribution to economics consisted of a 'theory of interest' and the general level of prices, which anticipated many modern ideas of money and interest. He also assisted to establish economics as a strong subject in the Scandinavian academic system, where it has remained influential to the present day.

## FRIEDRICH VON WIESER (1851–1926)

An Austrian economist and sociologist, who after some years in government service, became a Professor at the University of Prague, and later followed Carl Menger in the important Chair of Economics at the University of Vienna. As a leading exponent of the 'Austrian school' Wieser developed Menger's approach to value theory, including the term 'marginal utility', and gave his name to a law of costs – that the cost of a commodity was the 'alternatives forgone' in producing it.

## THORSTEIN VEBLEN (1857–1929)

An eccentric American economist and sociologist of Norwegian descent, who began to train for the Lutheran Church but later went to Yale and Cornell, and became a Professor of the newly opened University of Chicago in 1892. Irregular in his domestic arrangements, Veblen, on more than one occasion, fell victim to conventional prejudices in favour of matrimony. The president of at least one 'Ivy League' University is reputed to have offered Veblen a post if he would give an undertaking not to seduce the wives and daughters of faculty members. Veblen apparently responded that there was no danger of this as he had already viewed the ladies in question. He didn't get the post in question either.

Veblen's main works on *Theory of the Leisure Class* (1899) and *Theory of Business Enterprise* (1904), with their highly emotive descriptions and analysis, of what he described as 'conspicuous consumption' and of the tendency for the capitalist system to have unnecessarily high rates of obsolescence and depreciation, had a powerful impact. Veblen also gave weight to the influence of a new class of technocratic engineers who would understand the working of industry, and increasingly adopt a controlling role in the working of society.

These ideas affected the thinking of many, and led Veblen to become known as the founding father of 'institutional economics' in the United States, a group of socially and institutionally minded economists, some of whom later became influential in the Roosevelt 'New Deal' administration of the 1930s. They encouraged, not without considerable opposition, the introduction of Keynesian 'demand management' ideas into the running of the contemporary American economy. In recent years the American Institutional school had adopted a further title as the 'Evolutionary school', claiming for economics an integrating partnership role with the other social sciences. As such they are opposed to the idea of the development of economics as a precise predictive science in its own right. In general they are in favour of 'planning' for both the demand and supply sides of the economy, while retaining those human values and rights which are integral to the Anglo-Saxon concept of political and social freedom.

## JOHN A HOBSON (1858–1940)

Educated at Oxford, he became a schoolmaster and later a University extension lecturer, specialising in social studies and economics. He became known through his *Physiology of Industry* (published in conjunction with G. E. Mummery in 1889) and later published some thirty-five other works including *Imperialism* (1902), which powerfully influenced Lenin, in his own later work on the same theme, published in 1916. Other books by Hobson included *The Industrial System* published in 1909, *Work and Wealth* in 1914, *The Economics of*

*Unemployment* in 1922. Early on Hobson suggested a theory of 'under-consumption', based on the idea that expectations on capital and consumption goods become unbalanced because of excess saving by a wealthy minority. In this he was developing ideas orginally hinted at by Malthus, and also held by Sismondi and Marx. Hobson's views were unpopular with the leading neo-classical economists of the time, committed as they were to Say's *Law of Markets* that supply created its own demand. His ideas on the more exploitive aspects of imperialism, which were later taken up and developed by Lenin, were also unlikely to have ingratiated him with many establishment figures of his time. The most productive middle years of Hobson's life coincided with the highest point in imperialist sentiment and policies – as reflected in the empire policies espoused by such powerful men as Joseph Chamberlain (1836–1914), Cecil Rhodes (1853–1902) and others of like persuasion. His somewhat unfashionable views about both capitalism and empire may explain why he was never offered a permanent academic post. However, his ideas about under-consumption received belated recognition from Keynes in his *General Theory* published in 1936.

## FRANK W. TAUSSIG (1859–1940)

Educated at the Universities of Washington, Harvard and Berlin, he became an influential Professor of Economics at Harvard between 1892 and 1935. Between 1917 and 1919 he was Chairman of the U.S. Tariff Commission, and in 1919 he went to the Versailles Peace Conference to help draft post-war commercial policies. In his earlier work he brought together theoretical and practical questions – *Wages and Capital* published in 1896, and *Principles of Economics* in 1911. His *Aspects of the Tariff Questions* published in 1915, and *International Trade* published in 1927, included his main contribution to 'international economics'.

## EDWIN CANNAN (1861–1935)

A British economist educated at Balliol College, Oxford, who as Professor of Economics from 1897 onwards, played a leading role in developing the London School of Economics and Political Science. His major work, *A History of Production and Distribution* published in 1893 established his reputation. Cannan was mainly concerned with the history of economic ideas, and his edited edition of *The Wealth of Nations* published in 1904, was a standard work of reference. He was widely regarded as a critic of the classical tradition and his definition of economics as a study of 'material welfare' was later criticised in the 1930s by Professor Lionel Robbins, who redefined economics as the study of one aspect – that involving 'scarcity and choice' – of all human behaviour.

## GUSTAV CASSEL (1866–1945)

Another significant Swedish Professor of Economics at the University of Stockholm, who during his early career was much influenced by Alfred Marshall at Cambridge. He made important contributions to the theory of interest and to analysis of the 'trade cycle'. He was also widely known for his *Theory of Social Economy* published in 1918, and for his writings about monetary policies during and following the First World War.

## IRVING FISHER (1867–1947)

An American mathematical economist who was educated at Yale and later spent two years studying in Berlin and Paris. He became a Professor of Political Economy at Yale in 1898. Author of many books including the *Nature of Capital and Income* (1906); *The Rate of Interest* (1907); *Purchasing Power of Money* (1911), and *The Theory of Interest* (1930). Fisher was in the quantitative tradition originally established by Sir William Petty in the 17th century. All his works are mathematical and made Fisher a pioneer of the development of mathematical economics and econometrics, which were to take such an increasing role in contemporary economic doctrines and analysis. He was particularly associated with development of the 'Quantity Theory of Money' – that is $MV = PT$ where M is the quantity of money (including bank deposits) and V is the circulation of money – that is the average number of times which a unit of money is spent during a defined period for a quantity of goods and services T – whose average price is P. Fisher made a working model of the price system, using a large water tank and floats. (This idea was later developed by A. W. Philips at the London School of Economics into an elaborate model which simulated the flow of national income.)

Fisher's 'quantity theory of money' underlies much of modern discussion about monetary economics, and John Maynard Keynes recognised Fisher's work as having an important influence on his own theoretical developments. It thereby underlies contemporary Keynesian and 'monetarist' debates about the uncertain relationship between aggregate money supply and inflation rates for the economy as a whole.

In recent times there has been, and continues to be, a great debate between monetary economists – notably led by Professor Milton Friedman of the University of Chicago – and Keynesian (and even those dubbed neo-Keynesian) economists, about the relationship between the quantities of money circulating (the money supply however defined) and rates of inflation. This debate is in turn related to arguments about the relative merits of fiscal, as opposed to monetary, policies in the day to day running of the economy, which are discussed in greater detail later in the book. It has also made Western democratic politicians peculiarly vulnerable to the validity, or otherwise, of computer based forecasts and outcomes. This factor, together with ongoing instant news coverage and recall inherent in modern news media techniques, makes the contemporary politicians lot 'not a happy one'.

## VLADIMIR ILYICH LENIN (1870–1924)

Better known as a revolutionary than as an economist, but influential nevertheless. Lenin was the son of a local inspector of education, whose elder brother was executed in 1887 for attempting to assassinate Tzar Alexander III. Lenin was expelled from Kazan University but later read widely of Marx and other revolutionary authors. In 1897, after spending a year in gaol for revolutionary activities, he was sent to Eastern Siberia where he and his wife translated into Russian, Sidney (1859–1947) and Beatrice (1858–1943) Webb's *History of Trade Unionism*, and Lenin completed his book on *The Development of Capitalism in Russia*. In this he concluded, following the abolition of serfdom in 1862, that capitalism would soon become the dominant element even in agriculture. The peasants would become both less homogeneous and would also be moving into industrial employment. He felt that properly handled they could provide the beginnings of a revolutionary industrial proletariat.

Lenin left Russia in 1900 and spent many years in exile in Britain, France, Austria, Hungary and Switzerland, where he emerged as a revolutionary leader of international repute. In 1916, influenced by Hobson's ideas about imperialism, he published his own work *Imperialism, the Highest Stage of Capitalism*. Returning to Russia in 1917 to take charge of revolutionary activities, he was wounded in an assassination attempt a year later. However, he survived to facilitate the Bolshevik seizure of power and to guide Russia through post-revolutionary turmoil. He strongly influenced early plans for social and industrial development, including the *New Economic Policy* of 1921. In this Lenin pragmatically utilised private enterprise and the existing peasant-based agriculture to recreate a shattered economy. It was only after his death, in Stalin's first Five Year Plan of 1929, that collectivised agriculture became an important part of the Soviet economy.

Lenin was very much a political economist, in the style which would have appealed to Karl Marx, and possibly Adam Smith. He was skilled in statistical analysis and in debate about economic policy. Like Marx, Lenin concentrated attention on class analysis, and in seeking determinants for growth and change. He was impressed by the tendency for modern industrial capitalism to be distinguished by that department of social wealth which consists of the means of production, and for 'constant capital' to grow faster than 'variable capital'. He later became involved with problems of imperialistic expansion by the industrial and commercial centres of the world over the less developed areas of tropical Africa, Asia and Siberia etc. He considered this expansion to be necessary in order to avoid a decline in profits, which would take place if capitalists continued to invest in their own country. Capital had to be exported to backward areas where profits were high, wages were low and raw materials cheap. Lenin thus stimulated debate about colonial development and 'exploitation', which continues strongly to the present day. His work on *The State and Revolution* written in 1917, suggested a somewhat idealistic hope that the powers of 'scientific management' and 'bookkeeping' would be able to solve all the problems of running a centrally planned modern industrial society.

After his death Joseph Stalin (1879–1953) carried on with many of Lenin's ideas for industrialising Russia, but from the 1929 Five Year Plan onwards in a far more ruthless way. Another collaborator Leon Trotsky (1879–1940) was expelled from the Communist Party in 1927, exiled in 1929, founded the fourth Communist International in 1937 and, alas, ended up with an ice axe in his skull in Mexico in 1940. His political followers – the Trotskyists – maintain their policy of continuing the 'world revolution'.

## WESLEY CLAIR MITCHELL (1874–1948)

An influential Professor of Economics at Columbia University, who originally studied under Thorstein Veblen at Chicago, and was influenced by his 'institutional' ideas. He studied at Halle and Vienna, was a member of many governmental bodies and a founder member of the American National Bureau of Economic Research. Mitchell's own research, though influenced by institutional ideas, was statistically based and mainly involved study of 'business cycles' and other cyclical activities in the functioning of the American economy. His books included *Business Cycles* (1913), *Business Cycles: the Problem and its Setting* (1927), and *Measuring Business Cycles* in 1946. He is of importance because he perceived the need to relate the changing historical and institutional basis of modern industrial society, to the possibilities of mathematically based measurement and prediction techniques.

## ARTHUR CECIL PIGOU (1877–1959)

Pigou, who was educated at Harrow and King's College, Cambridge, succeeded the grand old man Alfred Marshall to the Chair of Political Economy at Cambridge in 1908. His main purpose was to extend and clarify the theoretical apparatus of his great predecessor. However he is best known for his pioneering book on the *Economics of Welfare* (1920). In this Pigou examined policies, in relation to their effects on the distribution and size of the national output, and on the divergence and the effects of economic activity on those who conducted it (i.e. marginal private net product) and on society as a whole (marginal social net product). This distinction has subsequently been widely applied in national economic planning. Pigou was a contemporary of John Maynard Keynes and later came into considerable controversy with him over most aspects of the working of the neo-classical model, and in particular on the appropriate government policies in response to what the then Prime Minister, Mr Ramsay MacDonald (1866–1937) called the 'economic blizzard' and 'unemployment crises', of the late 1920s and early 1930s. At the same time the former Liberal wartime Prime Minister, Mr. David Lloyd George (1863–1945) was calling with support from Keynes, for the Treasury to run a deficit to help mop up persistent unemployment, and get the economy moving back to full employment.

## WILLIAM HENRY (LORD) BEVERIDGE (1879–1963)

A British economist and public servant who later became Lord Beveridge. As a young civil servant he was involved in the establishment of Employment Exchanges under Winston Churchill in 1909, and later filled many different roles, including Director of the London School of Economics, between 1932 and 1937. He was elected a Liberal Member of Parliament from 1944–45, and was Master of University College, Oxford, between 1937–1945. His main publications were *Unem-*

*ployment – A Problem of Industry* published in 1909; *Full Employment in a Free Society* in 1944, and *Voluntary Action* 1948.

Beveridge is particularly associated with the drafting of the wartime Coalition Government's post-war plans for developing the 'Welfare State', and as such was regarded as an extremely influential figure in the development and application of both Keynesian and welfare ideas, to modern urban industrial society. Indeed he saw his famous 1942 report as the practical embodiment of what Churchill and Roosevelts' 1941 Atlantic Charter had said the soldiers were fighting for. While the soldiers, sailors and airmen were killing the enemy, Beveridge went on to prepare his plans for killing the terrifying giants of 'want, ignorance, squalor, idleness and disease'. At the time a national conference of Free Churchmen identified his report with 'practical Christianity', all they said was missing from it was the sixth giant, 'Sin'. For her part that formidable reformer Beatrice Webb reportedly found it 'a queer result of this strange and horrible war' that Beveridge of all people – should have suddenly risen into the limelight as an accepted designer of 'new world order'.

## SIR RALPH GEORGE HAWTREY (1879–1975)

An English civil servant and economist, who after a highly distinguished career in the Treasury from 1904 to 1945, then became a Professor at the Royal Institute of International Affairs until 1952. He was probably a greater scholar than Keynes, though not as influential. He wrote extensively on monetary theory and practice, and their relationships to employment policies. He was especially significant by his early involvement with Keynesian ideas in the war and post-war running of the British economy. In particular he emphasised the influence of the 'rate of interest' on the changing volume of stocks of goods in various phases of the 'trade cycle'. Towards the end of his active working life Hawtrey's principal publications were *The Balance of Payments and Standard of Living* 1950, and *Cross Purposes in Wage Policies* 1955. Nevertheless he remained an influential voice in economic and political affairs well into the 1960s.

## JOHN MAYNARD (LORD) KEYNES (1883–1946)

The most influential economist of his day, who was later created Baron Keynes in 1942, in recognition for his many academic and public services. (The classic *The Life of John Maynard Keynes* was written by Sir Roy Harrod in 1951.) Keynes is generally regarded as one of the three 'greats', together with Adam Smith and Karl Marx. The philosopher Bertrand Russell (1872–1970) regarded Keynes as the cleverest man he had ever met, though he is supposed to have told the young Keynes that he himself had not taken up economics, as he found it too easy. The son of John Neville Keynes, who was a lecturer and Registrar of Cambridge University, John Maynard Keynes was educated at Eton and King's College and was early interested in mathematics and philosophy. After a brief period in the India Office where he researched the monetary problems of the rupee, he returned to Cambridge to become a lecturer in economics in Alfred Marshall's department, and was later elected a Fellow of King's.

During the First World War, while still a comparatively young man, Keynes played an important role as an adviser in the Treasury on Allied Loans. Later, at the 1919 Paris Peace Conference, he was chief representative of the Treasury. His recommendations on the need for moderation in German Reparations were rejected, and he resigned, recording his views in the *Economic Consequences of the Peace* published 1919. This book gave a prophetic insight into what became the economic causes of the Second World War, and made him the centre of controversy about the economic, political and social reconstruction of Europe. During the depression years Keynes both taught at Cambridge and held a number of City directorships. He was particularly associated with, and interested in, the work of Sir Dennis Holme Robertson, another leading Cambridge economist, whose main interests were in monetary theory and 'trade cycle analysis'. In 1930 Keynes published a two-volume *Treatise on Money* and in 1936 published his doctrinally revolutionary *General Theory of Employment, Interest and Money*. In his *Treatise on Money* Keynes had argued the importance of the relationship between 'savings and investment' as the cause of the trade cycle. However in the *General Theory* he sought to explain the factors affecting the level of employment and this became the basis of subsequent Keynesian-based 'demand management' ideas.

The 'General Theory' changed the way many economists and democratic statesmen thought about the management of the hitherto *laissez-faire* economic system. In particular Keynes rejected Say's Law of Markets, that supply would create its own demand, leading in the long run to a naturally restored level of full employment. Instead he advocated, and justified on an intellectual basis, significant government intervention in free market processes to facilitate the maintenance of full employment. Keynesian ideas of demand management policies have subsequently become an integral part of most economic and financial planning undertaken in the Western democratic countries since 1945.

During the Second World War Keynes again returned to the Treasury, and towards the end of the war played a leading part in setting up the Bretton Woods Conference in 1944, from which emerged the International Monetary Fund and the International Bank, immediately after the war. As such these have had a major impact on post-war international trade and development. Many of Keynes' ideas were also included in post-war policies about domestic employment and welfare policies. The British Coalition Government's White Paper on *Employment Policy* (1944), marked the acceptance, at the governmental level, of the implications of the Keynesian revolution. His emphasis on national totals or aggregates also stimulated the development of 'macro-economics' – the study of the behaviour of large groups – which other economists, in both Britain and America, have made the basis for statistically based social accounting and national economic planning.

More recently Keynesian thinking has tended to be interpreted as a 'special', rather than a 'general', policy for encouraging full employment. Increased attention has been directed to structural questions, particularly as reflected in the need for the economy to be managed on the supply, as well as on the financial, demand side. Questions of the availability of markets, of adequate capital investments, of appropriate machinery, of skilled labour, raw materials and critical energy have increasingly preoccupied government and business planners. Again on the financial demand side, debate has shifted on to issues associated with money as a store of value, and of a tendency for Keynesian-type policies to be associated with high inflation rates. In turn, this has stimulated a so called 'monetarist counter revolution' dating particularly from Professor Milton Friedman's first *Wincott Memorial Lecture* in 1970. In this lecture Friedman suggested that the way government spending was financed mattered greatly in determining its economic impact – in short that 'money mattered' a lot. By the eighth *Wincott Memorial Lecture* in 1977 Professor Alan Walters was suggesting that no model 'whether monetary or Keynesian' could foretell accurately the performance of the economy in the next two years.

## JOSEPH ALOIS SCHUMPETER (1883–1950)

An Austrian economist educated in Vienna, who after the First World War, was for a time Finance Minister of the Austrian Republic, but later became a Professor at Bonn, and in 1932 moved to Harvard. A powerful general intelligence enabled Schumpeter's writing to cover all branches of economics, most notably in *Capitalism, Socialism and Democracy* published in 1942. In his early book on *Theory of Economic Development* published in 1912, and in *Business Cycles* in 1939, he analysed the capitalist system and suggested that 'innovations made by entrepreneurs' are the strategic critical factor in economic development, and occupy a central position in the process of the trade cycle. Schumpeter also foresaw a decline in power of the family firm, and the transference of political power away from traditional ruling class toward managers of great enterprises. In this he was echoing similar ideas developed by Thorstein Veblen and a number of other institutionally minded economists. In many ways Schumpeter was also part of the German 'historical school' of economic thinking, which to some extent related to Marxist ideas, of the development and modification of economic and social systems over time, although his conclusions were markedly different. His broad historical and institutional approach had a wide influence on the teaching of economics in the U.S.A., and on the work of many other authors on political economic and social topics. In recent years 'the poverty of historicism' has been challenged by Professor Karl Popper, who has argued strongly that there can be no prediction of the course of human history by scientific or other rational methods.

## JOHN MAURICE CLARK (1884–1963)

The son of John Bates Clark who taught at Columbia University from 1915 and succeeded to his father's chair in 1926 – he wrote an important book on the *Economics of Overhead Costs* (1923), which led to the development of 'dynamic analysis', in place of Marshall's static assumptions. Influential, like his father before him for the dissemination of both neo-classical and later Keynesian theory in the context of the United States economy and institutions.

Clark also developed and introduced the concept of the 'acceleration principle' i.e. the relationship between the rate of growth and the demand for consumer goods and the rate in the demand for producers' goods which subsequently had an important influence on the development of the Keynesian theory. In 1936 he published *Essays in Preface to Social Economics*.

## SIR DENNIS HOLME ROBERTSON (1890–1963)

An author and public speaker of great style, wit and distinction who was a leading member of the group of economists and men of public affairs based mainly in Cambridge and London who, during the depression years of the 1930s debated with John Maynard Keynes about the deficiencies of neo-classical economics, and led to the change in doctrines which later became known as the 'Keynesian Revolution'. However, he by no means fully accepted all of Keynes's strictures on the deficiencies of traditional economic thinking, which so dominated policy making at that time.

Robertson was chiefly known for his interests in monetary theory and practice and in trade cycle analysis which in turn influenced the development of Keynes's own ideas on these issues. He frequently prefaced his lectures and essays with apt quotations from Lewis Carroll's *Alice in Wonderland*. A prolific author he is particularly remembered for his *Essays on Monetary Theory* published in 1930, and *Britain in the World Economy* published in 1954.

He was successively Reader in Economics at Cambridge between 1930–38; the Sir Ernest Cassell Professor at the London School of Economics between 1938–44, an adviser to the Treasury throughout the Second World War and finally, Professor of Political Economy at Cambridge from 1944 onwards. Following his retirement in 1957 he became a member of the Council of Prices, Productivity and Incomes and played a major part in writing its early reports. In this role he was beginning to take 'Keynesian' ideas for the better management of the economy beyond the boundaries originally envisaged in the 1930s.

## ERNST FRIEDRICH SCHUMACHER (1911–1977)

Born in Germany Schumacher first came to England in 1930, as a Rhodes Scholar to study economics at New College, Oxford. He later briefly taught economics at Columbia University in the U.S.A. Always pragmatical by nature he then moved into a combination of journalism, farming and business activities and only returned to academic life at Oxford during the second World War. Later he became an Economic Adviser to the British Control Commission in Germany, and from 1950 to 1970 had a similar role with the National Coal Board in London. In this capacity he was one of the first, during the later 1950s onwards, to draw attention to the impending 'energy crises' implicit in growing dependency on scarce, finite and politically uncertain supplies of oil from the Middle East. He also became the originator of the concept of 'intermediate technology' for developing countries, a founder chairman of the Intermediate Technology Development Group in London, and a Director of the Scott-Bader Institute.

Schumacher and his ideas came to a wider public awareness through the publication in the early 1970s of his challenging book *Small is Beautiful* – a study of economics as if people mattered. In the preface to this work he drew attention to his main theme by a quotation from the work of the great economic historian Professor R. H. Tawney in his book *Religion and the Rise of Capitalism*.

> The most obvious facts are most easily forgotten. Both the existing economic order and too many of the projects advanced for reconstructing it break down through their neglect of the truism that, since even quite common men have souls, no increase in material wealth will compensate them for arrangements which insult their self-respect and impair their freedom. A reasonable estimate of economic organisation must allow for the fact that unless industry is to be paralysed by recurrent revolts on the part of outraged human nature, it must satisfy criteria which are not purely economic.

## HARRY S. JOHNSON (1924–1977)

One of the great 'internationalists' of the post-Second World War generation of economists. A Canadian by birth Johnson first graduated from the University of Toronto in 1943, and later served with the Canadian forces in Europe. In 1954 he joined the Cambridge Economics Faculty in England, where he soon demonstrated an incompatibility with many of the mores and attitudes of what he increasingly regarded as an isolated and chauvinistic institution. In particular he found it claustrophobic in its enshrinement of the ideas of John Maynard Keynes – and hostile to the North American style of empirical economics which he sought to foster. He later moved to Manchester and thence to hold joint professional appointments at the London School of Economics and at the University of Chicago. In fact the Chicago of Milton Friedman and others of like mind with its espousal of monetarist economics, and concern with political freedom and the beneficial working of the free market mechanism, became his intellectual home. During his last period in Britain as a Professor of Economics at the London School of Economics between 1966 and 1974, Britain's decline into 'second class' industrial status, and the widespread interventionist government which increasingly applied, confirmed all his worst fears and prejudices about the conduct of economic affairs. His many books and some 400 articles cover most aspects of contemporary economic thinking. At the time of his death in Geneva he was developing and refining a new monetary theory of the balance of payments.

Chapter 1

# THREE PERSPECTIVES OF THE ECONOMIST: SCIENTIST, PROPHET OR ENGINEER

*"Laissez-faire"*.

Adam Smith (1723–1790)

"It follows, from the relation between alienated labour and private property, that the emancipation of society from private property, from servitude, takes the political form of the *emancipation of the working class*, not in the sense that only the latter's emancipation is involved, but because this emancipation includes the emancipation of humanity as a whole. For all human servitude is involved in the relation of the worker to production, and all the types of servitude are only modifications or consequences of this relation."

Karl Marx (1818–1883)
cited from *Selected Writings in Sociology and Social Philosophy*

". . . I believe myself to be writing a book on economic theory which will largely revolutionize – not, I suppose, at once but in the course of the next ten years – the way the world thinks about economic problems."

Letter from John Maynard Keynes (1883–1946) to George Bernard Shaw, 1 January 1935

The contemporary world of men on the moon, television pictures from outer space, instant international communication via satellite; nuclear fission, OPEC and the energy crisis; of Concorde, computers and multi-nationals; of Polaris submarines and détente yet widespread tensions; of the north/south dialogue between the haves and have-nots on a global scale; of big government and economic growth targets but unemployment and calls for protectionism; of the automobile and suburban affluence; of hamburgers from the deep-freeze; may all seem far removed from the circumstances of past generations. Yet, our ideas about the many complex dilemmas arising from the scarcity of natural resources, and desires for consumption and equity have deep philosophical and historic roots. We now variously see the economist as a sort of scientist of man; as a prophet of inevitable revolutionary change; or as an engineer cum systems technocrat of the future possibilities open to mankind.

\*     \*     \*     \*     \*

The first view with which we are still highly familiar in the modern Western democratic world, is associated with an attempt to develop economics as a natural law, a hoped for Newtonian system of the science of man. This school of thinking derived from the philosophers of the 18th century age of enlightenment. In Britain it developed from the works of a number of talented men of letters. They included the works of the English philosopher John Locke, who emphasised the importance of private property as an essential adjunct to political freedom. This, at a later time, formed a basis for the principle of 'no taxation without representation' and for the refutation of the principle of a divine right of kings. Another important thinker was David Hume, the Scottish philosopher, who was in turn influenced by the writings of Charles Louis Montesquieu, the French aristocrat and philosopher, about the natural laws governing human life. The changing intellectual climate stimulated in Britain by Hume in the middle of the 18th century powerfully influenced a young Scottish philosopher, Adam Smith, who in 1759, published a book *The Theory of Moral Sentiments* in which he listed six pre-dispositions of man of which the sixth was a natural tendency 'to truck, to trade and to exchange'. He later developed his thinking about 'economic man' into further work which was published as a book under the general title of *An Inquiry into the Nature and Causes of the Wealth of Nations* published in 1776. In *The Wealth of Nations* Smith presented, for the first time, a coherent view of what has become known as a *laissez-faire* model of economic activity; emphasising the importance of free markets and of the need to break down artificial and harmful constraints to trade. His ideas about the efficacy of generating economic growth through the pursuit of self-interest, and from the inherent economies of scale beginning to flow from the division of labour in the new factory system, just beginning in his native Scotland and England, was to become the secular 'religion' of the emerging industrial age. The many subsequent schisms which have occurred between economists of all faiths and complexions often take on a fervour normally limited to those associated with strongly doctrinal faith.

In the year 1776 three other important works were published which, coming together, had an impact on thinking about the way the new capitalist system evolved, in both its philosophical and practical applications. In Philadelphia the Declaration of Independence was proclaimed. In its drafting the young lawyers, guided by Benjamin Franklin (1706–1790) were influenced by John Locke's ideas of both the sovereignty of people over monarchs and of the inalienable right of individuals to pursue life, liberty, happiness and the possession of private property. The Americans having shaken off their mercantile colonial shackles, were increasingly to regard *laissez-faire* doctrines, at least domestically, as the basis for national economic development. The development of the United States came to involve a fundamental dichotomy, tariff protection against cheaper overseas imports going hand in hand with the enthusiastic espousal of a *laissez-faire* economy at home. Two important books published in the same year – Edward Gibbons' (1737–1794) *Decline and Fall of the Roman Empire*, tracing the decline of a system based on slavery, and Jeremy Bentham's early writings on *Fragments of Government*, had an important impact on the way that classical economic doctrine was influenced and developed by other authors; notably David Ricardo, Thomas Malthus, James Mill and his precocious and intellectually formidable son, John Stuart Mill. Later still, a neo-classical school, running in England from Stanley Jevons to Alfred Marshall, led to the development of 'marginal analysis' and mathematical approaches, still used as a basis of our perception of the working of *laissez-faire* markets and industry to the present day. The 'marginal utility' school of analysis also had a major contribution from the 'Austrian school' and several leading American economists. Professor Milton Friedman, the 1976 Nobel Prize Winner, of the University of Chicago, is today the most outspoken of contemporary economists, in advocacy of the classical *laissez-faire* tradition in the conduct of economic affairs. Professors Ludwig von Mises, the 1974

Nobel Prize Winner, Friedrich A. Hayek, and Lord Lionel Robbins, have also been important spokesman for classical doctrines and their application to present day problems.

*    *    *    *    *

A second highly significant line of thinking and language about economic concepts and systems derives from very different origins. It stems from German sources, primarily philosophical and historical in background, but often goes forward to express social criticisms and, in some cases revolutionary fervour and prophesies. This type of economic thinking makes no pretence at being 'value free' in the way that the exponents of the English classical deductive school from Ricardo onwards considered they were developing the new science of political economy. Rather, Karl Marx, in association with his friend Friedrich Engels, both of whom had been variously impressed and influenced by Hegelian and Saint-Simon social philosophies, put forward a historically deterministic model of society, in which man is inevitably locked into a bitter two opposing class conflict, between a small group of rulers; from slave owners; to feudal landlords or 19th century capitalist masters and a large mass of toilers; be they slaves, landless peasants or a propertyless industrial proletariat. In their 1848 *Communist Manifesto*, which was inspired by the English Chartists' lists of reforms of 1839, Marx and Engels suggested four stages which society has passed through, which may be likened to a *Paradise Lost* scenario; from tribal communism, to a state of slavery as represented by the ancient kingdoms of Babylon, Egypt, Greece and Rome; to feudalism as it had developed in Western Europe under the domination of medieval Church and Kingdom; and finally to monopolistic commercial and industrial capitalism, as it seemed to be developing in England in the middle of the 19th century. The common denominator running through the three Marxist stages of slavery, feudalism and capitalism, was the domination of the many by the few, who control the means of production available in the society. Marx later went on to develop two further stages to which he considered that society must inevitably evolve; the first being socialism and the common ownership of property and means of production which would follow the revolutionary overthrow of the capitalist system, and in which each would be rewarded according to his labour need. This would eventually be followed by full communism in an industrial urban society, when the production of wealth would be so abundant that each would be rewarded according to his need. At this stage, according to Marx, the

State would wither away and an earthly paradise would presumably be attained, within the context of urban and industrial life.

It requires little insight to recognise the impact of Marxist doctrines on much of our present day world. The paradox is that the revolution which Marx saw inevitably occurring in the rapidly developing industrial states of Britain and Western Europe did not happen in the way anticipated. Rather, from Russia of 1917 onwards most of the Marxist inspired revolutions have occurred in basically peasant agrarian societies, and his ideas have been used as part of the intellectual apparatus to justify the use of a surplus, derived initially at least from the produce of agriculture, to finance a process of rapid industrial and urban development. The Marxist model was developed by Lenin and later intensified by Stalin as the basis of a philosophical and practical programme to industrialise Russia, following the over-throw of the Tsarist regime in 1917, and the taking of power, following prolonged civil war between the Whites and the Reds, by a Communist regime. The industrial urban and military society of the Soviet Union of today, with its powerful apparatus of central planning, owes much to the basic ideas which Lenin, Stalin and their disciples built onto Marx's original ideas. The Soviet Stalinist pattern of forced, centrally planned massive industrialisation based initially on the surplus of agriculture and only later on the surplus from industry, has also been applied in other East European COMECON member states. However in recent years the harshness of application seems to have been ameliorated by more liberal social and political attitudes in many countries.

Another line of Marxist development has been in China where the 1949 Revolution under the leadership of Mao Tse-Tung has been followed by an intense phase of agrarian self-help, based on the use of certain Marxist ideas as justification for the euthanasia of an absentee landowning and colonialist rentier class, and its replacement by a self-help peasant economic system, with the gradual development of an urban industrial system as well. How much the Chinese model owes to Marx and Mao and how much it owes to other more traditional cultural values in China remains a matter for keen debate. It must always be recognised that whatever the ideological complexion may be, China must feed nearly one quarter of the world's total population, from perhaps 7 per cent of the world total arable land.

The Chinese model of what seems to be a more gradual approach, giving particular emphasis to the intensification of peasant agricultural production, the elimination of the landowning class, and the ejection of external commercial influences, has a powerful appeal in many recently independent ex-colonial agriculturally based countries.

\*   \*   \*   \*   \*

A third category of economic thinking might be broadly described as the economist as a social engineer or guardian, in Keynes' phrase of 'the future possibilities of mankind'. In the Western democratic world we associate the concept of the economist as a guiding interventionist force with the work of John Maynard Keynes particularly as expressed in his *The General Theory of Employment, Interest and Money* published in 1936. From this complex but great work comes the idea of financially based demand management to make the capitalist system work more smoothly, and to ride over short-term cyclical fluctuations in trade and business. Throughout the history of economic thought, from Malthus to Marx and many others, 'under-consumption' fears had been expressed. However, the important classical school of economic thinking which developed from the ideas of Adam Smith and David Ricardo assumed, on the basis of Say's Law, that supply created equivalent demand and that given time an overall 'full employment' equilibrium would apply. Jean Baptiste Say was sent by the French Government to England in 1814 to study economic conditions, and he was later a Professor of Political Economy at the College de France. His 'law of markets', based on his conclusions at that time, had much influence on the development of classical and neo-classical thought, as it applied to the overall functioning of the capitalist system. However, the prolonged and persistent unemployment and restricted income growth during the late 1920s and early 1930s throughout the industrial world led to criticism of the idea of an equilibrium with full employment being inevitably achieved by the *laissez-faire* functioning of the market. Eventually this criticism led to the development of new bases for Western democratic economics, focused on the Keynesian model of demand management by government intervention in fiscal and monetary policies.

Since the end of the Second World War, all the Western economies have become powerfully influenced by these ideas. Related to these concepts has been a widespread development in mathematically based information-gathering and assessment techniques. Within the domestic management of the major Western industrial countries, there has been extensive use of Keynesian demand management methods. Internationally, the unprecedented post-war expansion of international trade owes much to the Bretton Woods Conference in 1944, and the subsequent creation of the International Monetary Fund in 1946 and the General Agreement on Tariffs and Trade in 1947. Both institutions influenced the post-war development of freer and greatly expanded trading and financial arrangements, especially between the advanced Organisation for Economic Co-operation and Development member industrial states. A further, related, development was the extension of the *laissez-faire* ideals in the creation of larger trading areas, of which the European Economic Community is the outstanding example. Indeed, much of the imperative behind the creation of the European Coal and Steel Community in 1951, and the Treaty of Rome which established the European Economic Community in 1957 and the European Atomic Energy Community in 1958, was to prevent a reintroduction of highly nationalistic *autarchical* trading and industrial policies, such as had been followed by the major industrial countries during the depression years of the 1930s.

It would, of course, be misleading to suggest that the application of Keynesian ideas is the only example of the economist as a type of engineer of future possibilities, etc. In recent years Nobel Prizes in Economic Science have been awarded for mathematically based theoretical and applied work of this sort, of which details are listed at the end of the book. For instance in the United States the pioneering work of Professor Simon Kuznets and his colleagues, in respect of statistical calculation of national income and product and its components, provided the quantitative basis to the Keynesian revolution in economic thought. Again examples of the economist as a systems technocrat are also with us in the centrally planned economic systems of the Soviet led Marxist inspired Council for Mutual Economic Assistance group of nations. A leading Soviet economist Leonid Kantorovich was jointly awarded with Tjallings Koopman of the U.S.A., the 1975 Nobel Prize for work on The Theory and Practice of Resource Allocation. The use of the concept of national input and output tables associated with the American Professor Wassily Leontief, and cost benefit analysis techniques of the Dutch Professor Jan Tinbergen, also have had a powerful impact on the way the world, both West and East, is run, and in this sense at least 'convergency' might be said to apply. Leontief's work has been widely used as a basis for applying Keynesian concepts to the running of advanced economies and as a means of thinking about world economic prospects as a whole. Tinbergen's ideas of primary and secondary benefits, originally developed to support investment in the inter-war years Zuider Zee reclamation schemes, have been used as a basis for analysing and justifying major capital investment projects

throughout the world. Other innovations have applied to the managerial economic techniques associated within the cost and market forecasting activities of major national and multinational enterprises. Indeed
one of the consequences of Western democratic governmental policies
to demand manage their economies has been to create an elaborate
forecasting industry; to predict the effect of such policies on business
activity in general – and the fortunes of individual firms and industries
in particular, often on an international basis. Recently forecasting and
related 'Delphi' techniques have also been used to establish long into
the future, scenarios of resource and technical needs, affecting future
economic and social developments and needs. The ideas of Mr. Herman
Kahn and the Hudson Institute of *The Year 2000* and of Mr. A. Tofler's
*Future Shock* have been built into long-term perspectives of future
needs.

Thus in attempts to manage technically the modern highly complex
urban industrial and service based society, *laissez-faire* inspired
economics has moved substantially away from its origins as a
philosophical model of the way a 'free will' and 'choice' society should
ideally operate, to a much more structured system of thinking and
planning to direct society towards the achievement of broadly agreed
economic, social and political goals. In most Western democratic
countries these goals have come to include a Keynsian managed high
even rate of growth, somehow matched with a moderate rate of
inflation, low unemployment and reasonable balance of payments
stability, etc. Yet the idea of economics being as much a science of ends
as of means is in conflict with many of the earlier tenets of classical cum
neo-classical economic thinking, which considered that, as far as
possible, economics should be 'value free'. The role of the economist as
a demand manager at the macro-national and international economic
level and as an adviser cum manager at the enterprise level is beset with
implicit 'value' judgements as to the desirability of particular pan-
national, national or corporate goals. Yet in theory at least it remains
primarily the task of the statesman, politician or company director to
define such goals, and for the economist to suggest the least costly way
of achieving them, within the constraints which inevitably apply in a
finite, and far from perfect world.

Chapter 2

# THE GREAT DEBATES: SCARCITY, WEALTH AND WELFARE

"When Adam delved and Eve span,
Who was then a gentleman?"

*At the time of the Wat Tyler uprisings*
*by unions of labourers resisting*
*Parliamentary laws fixing wages, and*
*unions of villein farmers resisting*
*the customs of the manor 1381.*

Attributed to John Ball

L'etat, c'est moi,
The State, it is me.

Louis XIV (1638–1715)
The Sun King

"Commerce which has enriched the citizens of England
has helped to make them free, and that liberty in turn
has expanded commerce. This is the foundation of the
greatness of the state."

Voltaire (1694–1778)
*Lettres Philosophiques (Letter X)*

"For what were all these country patriots born?
To hunt, and vote, and raise the Price of Corn?

Year after year they voted cent per cent,
Blood, sweat and tear wrung millions – why?
for rent!"

Lord Byron (1788–1824)
*The Age of Bronze*

"It is an Age of Machinery in every outward and inward
sense of that word."                        *Signs of the Times*

"Captains of Industry."                        *Past and Present*

"Man is a tool-using animal ... Without tools he is
nothing, with tools he is all."

> Thomas Carlyle (1795–1881)
> *Sartor Resartus*

"Knowledge advances by steps, and not by leaps."

> Thomas Macaulay (1800–1859)
> *Essays and Biographies. History*

"Annual income, twenty pounds, annual expenditure
nineteen nineteen six, result happiness.
Annual income twenty pounds, annual expenditure
twenty pounds ought and six, result misery."

> Charles Dickens (1812–1870)
> Mr. Micawber in *David Copperfield*

"The Workers have nothing to lose in this (revolution)
but their chains. They have a world to gain.
Workers of the World, Unite!

> Karl Marx (1818–1883), and
> Friedrich Engels (1826–1895).
> *The Communist Manifesto*

"All progress is based upon a universal innate desire on
the part of every organism to live beyond its income."

> Samuel Butler (1835–1902)
> *Notebooks, Life*

"You shall not press down upon the brow of labour this
crown of thorns, you shall not crucify mankind upon the
stake, even the peppered stake of monetarism."

> William Jennings Bryan (1880–1925)

## The Early Beginnings and Scholasticism

As has been suggested in the foregoing, political cum economic and social debates have underlaid most accounts of the life of man in society, from the biblical account of the garden of Eden, onwards. Many economists, including Adam Smith and Karl Marx, have commenced their enquiries with some idealised departure point in mind. For some this required that the original life of man, in the 'primitive state' have a Hobbesian quality of hardship and deprivation – for others the life of Rousseau's 'noble savage' had an idyllic aspect – which, alas, had been necessarily lost, or alienated, by the move into the chains of 'civilised' living. In fact, during the latter years of the 'age of reason' the explorations and discoveries by European seamen and traders suggested both alternatives as very real possibilities. Captain James Cook (1728–1779) during his great voyages of discovery certainly found what at least superficially may have seemed a sunlit paradise in Tahiti, and a history of barbarism and cannibalism elsewhere. Poor Cook himself succumbed to the latter, in a brawl on a beach in Hawaii in 1779. Sir Eric Roll, in his definitive *History of Economic Thought*, traces the beginnings of attempts to formalise thinking about economic issues through from the Bible, to the political philosophers of the essentially slave based states of Greece and Rome, and then on into the Dark Ages, and early medieval Europe. Scholasticism is the phrase most commonly used to describe the underlying ideas of the medieval schoolmen who wrote, generally from the security, peace and calm of monasteries, from the 9th to the early 15th century. One of the most important of these was the 13th century Saint Thomas Aquinas, though there were many others as well. Most of their writings are from the years before the onset of widespread trading and commercial ideas, and the emergence of the mercantalistic military sovereign state, out of the husks and debris of the Reformation, and the release of energies associated with the Renaissance.

The medieval doctrines most closely associated with such temporal economic and social issues was the rightness or otherwise of usury – the charging a rate of interest for the use of money generally confined at the time to non-Christian, Jewish moneylenders and merchants. The movement to England of such a group from Lombardy led to the establishment of a specialised financial system, distinct from both the other trades and from the Church and the Royal Court, and in time this became Lombard Street, the centre of the financial life in Britain to the present day. Gradually the restrictive and inflexible concept of Saint

Thomas' 'just price' had to be adapted to meet the rapidly changing trading and commercial needs of a new age. In a sense the decline of the hold of scholasticism doctrines marked the acceptance of the Church to the workings of supply and demand markets, and opened the door to great economic and social developments in the future. The essential element in these new temporal developments was the production and distribution of material wealth, distinct from any spiritual justification of its rightness or otherwise. In short, the gaining and use of wealth was power itself, too serious a thing to be left in the hands of the Pope in Rome, or his Cardinals and Bishops. The age of mercantilism and the all-seeing nation state was about to dawn.

In practice, for long periods of time financial matters remained largely in the hands of Jewish communities, often living in ghettos. These resourceful and skilled people, with a wide network of contacts throughout the known world, and free from the dogmas of the medieval Church and canon law, were able to handle money and, notwithstanding the strong attitude of the medieval Church and the sophisticated arguments as put forward by Aquinas and others, the practice of taking interest grew with economic expansion and development. Indeed, as Roll emphasises:

> "Law authority became increasingly concerned with the regulation rather than with the prohibition of interest; and decrees fixing maximum rates became more frequent in the fourteenth century. When we reach the age of discoveries of the fifteenth and sixteenth centuries the channels for profitable investment grow to such an extent that the doctrines of the earlier canonists become hopelessly out of keeping with economic practice. Important modifications appear in the theory of usury, as they had done in the theory of the 'just price'."

Roll further suggests that with the development of commerce and the opportunity for monetary transactions in the later Middle Ages, two tendencies arose. On the one hand secular practice went in the direction of increasing the lending of money at interest and justifying it by a reliance on Roman Law; on the other hand:

> "The Church, alarmed by the new development, made its original prohibition more emphatic and universal. At the great Lateran Council of 1179 the first of a series of stringent prohibitions of usury was decreed. And the growth of the religious orders, most of which put a complete asceticism in the forefront of their principles, was another symptom of the same movement."

It was from these contentious beginnings that later mercantilistic ideas of national economic development and trade began to develop. In turn these ideas were subsequently attacked and modified by a variety of new thinkers, from the 18th century French physiocrats to 19th century *laissez-faire* economists, and political scientists. In Chapter 1 we briefly considered the economist as scientist of man; a prophet of revolutionary change, or engineer of a desired future. We can now look in greater detail, at the historical and philosophical origins of each of the main schools of thought, and consider how they relate to each other, and continue to have a significant impact on the practical conduct of business and political life in the contemporary world scene.

## Mercantilism and the Classical Model 1776–1870

In advocating the *laissez-faire* system Adam Smith and his followers were not speculating in a vacuum, but writing about the needs of the world they saw to be changing rapidly around them. Smith was arguing against what had become known as the mercantilistic doctrines of state regulation as they affected economic activity both at home and abroad. In political theory the writings of Thomas Hobbes in his *Leviathan*, with the justification for an all seeing powerful monarchy was at one with ideas for the central regulation of trade affairs by government. In practice, mercantilism was a system of economic regulation doctrines which to a greater or lesser degree were followed by all the major nation states, in 16th to 18th century Europe. These ideas had developed out of the break up of the feudal world of Church and State jointly maintaining an agrarian system; to the extension of the new nation states into wide areas of imperial trading adventures, often with rapidly acquired colonial empires linked to a mother country, by bonds of both sentiment and self interest. The very success of Great Britain in her successful scramble for commercial wealth and advantages abroad were later to underpin the move into a more industrialised society at home. Despite the rapid growth in their overseas trade, the expansionist minded rulers of the European states thought of the wealth of the world as being finite, and that any increase of trade by one nation could only, in the long run, be at the expense of the trade of its rivals. Thus a nation's wealth was best held in the form of bullion, which among other things enabled the 'Leviathan' state to maintain or purchase the military capacity necessary for its defence. Mercantilism also supported the view that labour skills and traditional basic industries needed to be protected and closely regulated, a view which fitted well with the self interests of

FIG. 3. MERCANTILISM: A NATIONALISTIC 'SELF SUFFICIENT' SYSTEM OF 16TH TO 18TH CENTURY WESTERN EUROPE

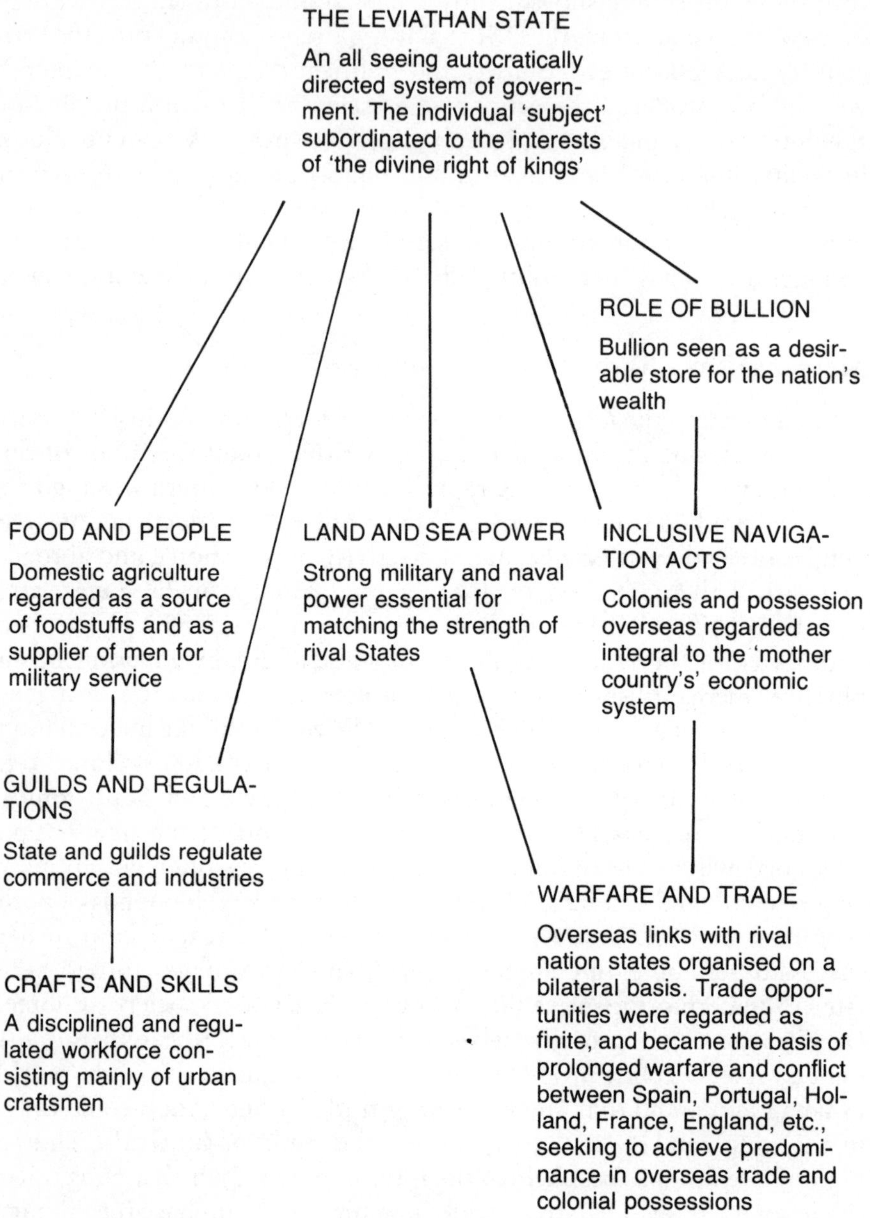

**THE LEVIATHAN STATE**

An all seeing autocratically directed system of govern- ment. The individual 'subject' subordinated to the interests of 'the divine right of kings'

**ROLE OF BULLION**

Bullion seen as a desir- able store for the nation's wealth

**FOOD AND PEOPLE**

Domestic agriculture regarded as a source of foodstuffs and as a supplier of men for military service

**LAND AND SEA POWER**

Strong military and naval power essential for matching the strength of rival States

**INCLUSIVE NAVIGA- TION ACTS**

Colonies and possession overseas regarded as integral to the 'mother country's' economic system

**GUILDS AND REGULA- TIONS**

State and guilds regulate commerce and industries

**CRAFTS AND SKILLS**

A disciplined and regu- lated workforce con- sisting mainly of urban craftsmen

**WARFARE AND TRADE**

Overseas links with rival nation states organised on a bilateral basis. Trade oppor- tunities were regarded as finite, and became the basis of prolonged warfare and conflict between Spain, Portugal, Hol- land, France, England, etc., seeking to achieve predomi- nance in overseas trade and colonial possessions the still vigorous medieval trade guilds. The best way to run a national economy was to have a continuously favourable trade balance with the rest of the world as a whole, and with individual trading partners in particular. Pushed to its logical extreme such a policy inevitably led to a 'beggar one's neighbour' stance.

Such mercantilistic doctrines relating to the overseas trading of a centrally regulated all-seeing state, plainly had a powerful influence on the conduct of economic, political and social life throughout Western Europe. Perhaps the leading academic study of such doctrines as a whole was undertaken by Professor Eli Heckscher (1879–1952) and published as *Mercantilism* in 1931. However it remains a great debate among economic historians whether the political or the economic aspects of the collapse of feudalism were the most decisive factors in formulating the system. Early on the seafaring nations of the Peninsula, Spain and Portugal, acquired large colonial empires, with huge resources of gold and silver. Later France, England and the Low Countries joined in the race for 'God, gold and glory' abroad. In England in 1630 the merchant Thomas Mun prepared a defence of the East India Company under the title of *'England's Treasure by Forraign Trade'*, in which he justified the export of bullion for a short period, providing that it brought back more bullion in the longer run. In his justification Mun was, in fact, drawing attention to what he called stock or the need for capital to finance a particular volume of overseas trade, but pointing out that the expenditure of capital at one moment in time in the form of the export of gold coin could be justified if it brought back more gold coin in the longer run. In France, Mercantilism is especially associated with Jean-Baptiste Colbert (1619–1683) who from 1665 was Louis XIV's, The Sun King's, (1638–1715) Controller-General of Finance – and encouraged trade at home and abroad.

Professor Michael Howard, in his recent book on *War in European History*, describes the important relationship between mercantilistic trade doctrines and warfare thus:

> "The whole mercantilist argument had indeed an elegance and coherence in theory which was not, unlike so many elegant economic arguments, disproved in practice. Trade did engender wealth; wealth, if the government could get at it, could be translated into fleets and armies; fleets and armies, if properly equipped and commanded, did increase state power. As the English writer Charles Davenant observed at the end of the seventeenth century: 'Nowadays the whole art of war is reduced to money: and nowadays, that prince who can best find money to feed, cloath and pay his army, not he that has the most valiant troops, is surest

76                                                    THE MYSTERY OF WEALTH

of success and conquest'. And during the quarter-century of wars
between 1689 and 1713 when the British, the Dutch, and their continental allies engaged in almost continuous struggle against the France of
Louis XIV – a struggle both for wealth and for power – it was the greater
capacity of the maritime powers to mobilise their resources, particularly
their financial resources, that eventually carried the day. To the Bank of
England and the Treasury, the whole mechanism which came into being
for the raising of loans and the establishment of credit, must go at least as
much responsibility for ultimate British success in that war – as indeed in
all subsequent wars – as is due to the generalship of Marlborough and to
the professional competence of armed forces by land and sea. There was
little point in winning – let alone risking – a major battle if there were not
to be any resources left over for a campaign the following year."

Mercantilistic notions are by no means dead in our present age.
During the great depression of the 1920s and 1930s many countries
reverted to policies of national self-interest and protectionism, which
closely equated to such doctrines. These policies were generally
described in economic literature as being 'autarchical'. Again, many
contemporary ideas about the importance of favourable national trade
balances stem from the mercantilistic notions of the importance of these
to the successful conduct of a national or pan-national economic
system. Critics of such potentially *laissez-faire* trading systems as the
European Economic Community would deplore any tendency for it to
become at the same time an inward looking protective trade system
against the rest of the world. This would be regarded as detrimental to
wealth creation possibilities of worldwide free trade. As will be
examined in greater detail later, since the end of the Second World War
free trade policies have also been encouraged by the existence of the
1947 General Agreement on Tariffs and Trade. Conversely however,
the Soviet and primarily Eastern European COMECON trade bloc
have tended to follow protectionist mercantilistic-type trade policies.
Moreover as the impact of Eastern European, Japanese and Asian
competition has been felt in many critical markets – from footwear to
textiles, steel and motor vehicles protectionist attitudes and policies
have re-emerged strongly throughout – in Western Europe and in the
U.S.A. and indeed anywhere where local industries are apparently
threatened by destructive competition from cheaper imports.

*     *     *     *     *

Apart from opposing such restrictive and reactionary mercantilistic
policies in both their international and domestic aspects, another

FIG. 4. PHYSIOCRATIC IDEAS OF NATIONAL WEALTH DERIVING FROM THE LAND AND FROM THE 'PRODUCT NET' OF TENANT FARMERS IN 18TH CENTURY FRANCE

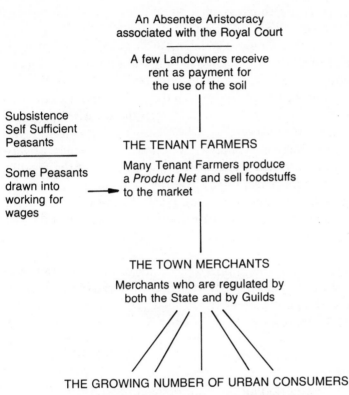

An Absentee Aristocracy
associated with the Royal Court

A few Landowners receive
rent as payment for
the use of the soil

Subsistence
Self Sufficient
Peasants

THE TENANT FARMERS

Some Peasants
drawn into
working for
wages

Many Tenant Farmers produce
a *Product Net* and sell foodstuffs
to the market

THE TOWN MERCHANTS

Merchants who are regulated by
both the State and by Guilds

THE GROWING NUMBER OF URBAN CONSUMERS

Many consumers who are supplied through
a commercial system of regulated prices,
terms and conditions of service and so on

For the physiocratic thinkers economic wealth derived ultimately from the bounty of the soil and the toil of peasant and larger tenant farmers who produced a surplus for sale to the market. However the 'parasitical' hand of merchants, bolstered by medieval guild and state regulation of prices and terms of service, hindered the efficient flow of goods to the rapidly increasing numbers of urban consumers. The physiocrats therefore advocated a policy of 'laissez-passez' which was later extended by the classical economists, taking their lead from Robert Turgot and Adam Smith, to a doctrine of 'laissez-faire' for the economy as a whole.

important school of economic thought also influenced Smith in his advocacy of *laissez-faire* attitudes. In 18th century France a prominent group of physiocratic thinkers and hopeful reformers of the *ancien regime*, associated with the Court of Louis XV (1710–1774) and particularly with the King's physician, François Quesnay, suggested that the wealth of the nation derived mainly from the land. In fact many of the physiocrats' basic ideas about land and wealth are thought to have derived from the earlier writings of the Irish economist and banker Richard Cantillon. They divided society into three classes – landlords, merchants and tenant farmers – of whom only the latter were regarded as being the productive group. They supported policies of *laissez-passez*, by which they meant encouraging a free flow of the produce of the soil to the market place, unhindered by mercantilistic trade monopolies or regulation by government agencies. The physiocrats designed a 'Tableau Economique', a sort of primitive input/output table which sought to demonstrate that all wealth ultimately derives from the basis of the soil.

Physiocratic ideas of the importance of land as an essential basis of national wealth are by no means extinct. During the early years of the United States, Thomas Jefferson (1743–1826) the highly intelligent third president, advocated the idea of a democracy based on small farmers, each with land up to 50 acres in extent. Jefferson also became an early and enthusiastic supporter of extending the new States' western frontiers, at the expense of Spain, France and the Indians alike. Likewise, at a later period in a very different context, the Prussians, and later Adolf Hitler, claimed the need for a greater Germany to have Lebensraum in the east, for settling its expanding population. Particularly associated with these ideas were the writings of a German General cum University Professor Karl Haushofer (1869–1946) who wrote extensively about geo-politics. In some of his work he had been much influenced by the ideas of the 'Eurasian heartland' suggested by the British geographer Sir Halford Mackinder (1861–1947). At the present time the European Economic Community agricultural system, as expressed through the Common Agricultural Policy, might to some seem to be based on a physiocratic notion, concerning the importance of the soil and the produce from agriculture, as a fundamental basis of wealth for society. Policies advocated by the World Bank also increasingly support the continued development of the agricultural basis of developing countries, as opposed to encouraging a headlong rush of resources into seeking to create a high mass consumption urban and industrial society based on the Western European and American

FIG. 5. TABLEAU ECONOMIQUE

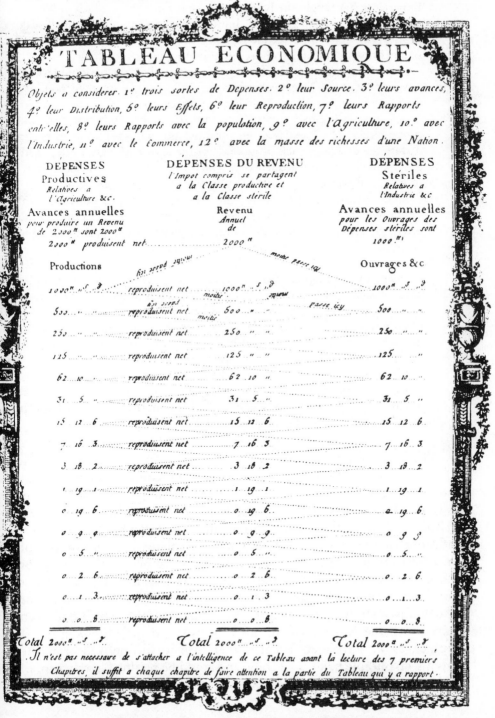

Reproduction of the Tableau Economique from the *Elemens de la Philosophie rurale* by the Marquis de Mirabeau

(Reprinted from Oncken's *Geschichte der National konomie* by the courtesy of the publishers, Messrs. C. L. Hirschfeld.)

pattern. To quote from the Bank's 1975 report:

"Experience has taught the Bank that, in many instances, a lack of finance alone is not the only factor limiting production among small-scale producers. Frequently, technological, procedural, and manpower constraints thwart the effective use of additional investment.

Overriding these factors, however, is the need, at the national level of government, for a strong commitment to 'rural development policies'. Such commitment is required if the impact of programs designed to attack the problems of rural poverty are to be both effective and broad-based. The Bank is in no position, nor would it want to be, to dictate the design of such programs, for the choice of ways to deal with the problem, and the sequence in which they are used, will necessarily reflect local conditions as well as narrower technical considerations.

In some instances, present policies must change if programs for rural development are to be effective. The Bank's analysis indicates that all too often, government policies discriminate against agricultural production in favour of manufacturing or processing industries; in addition, policies designed to keep food prices low for the large urban market have frequently been adopted to the disadvantage of the small farmer. In other cases, national fiscal policies – through high levels of indirect commodity taxation and low effective rate of income or property taxes, the poor often pay a considerably larger share of their income than the rich, for instance – must be made consistent with the commitment to rural development.

Elsewhere, land policies, involving land reform or settlement schemes, to name but two, must be designed to aid the rural poor. Technologies of relevance to and within the means of the smallholder must be made available and promoted."

                    *     *     *     *     *

Whether he intended it or not Adam Smith played a decisive role in the development of economic thought and subsequent doctrines about how the 'ideal' *laissez-faire* market system should apply and operate. His original lectures at the University of Glasgow, where he held the Chair of Moral Philosophy, led to his first major work on *The Theory of Moral Sentiments* in 1759 and later, stimulated by a grand tour of mercantilistically influenced Europe, as a tutor to the Duke of Buccleuch, he returned to Scotland and began work on his great enquiry into the nature and causes of the *Wealth of Nations*. This was essentially a study of the creation of national wealth which had been very much the concern of the mercantilists and the physiocrats; the former, as we have seen, believed that such wealth derived primarily from a favourable balance of trade and could be retained in the form of bullion, while the latter believed that it derived primarily from the

FIG. 6.   ADAM SMITH'S CLASSICAL 'LAISSEZ-FAIRE' FREE MARKET SYSTEM, LATE 18TH AND EARLY 19TH CENTURY BRITAIN

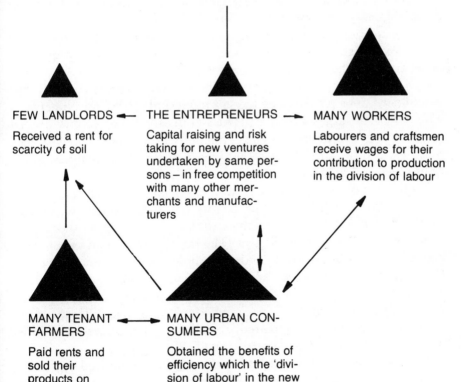

CONSTITUTIONAL GOVERNMENT

The desired role of government limited to law and order, diplomacy and warfare, money and the maintenance of property rights

FEW LANDLORDS ◄— THE ENTREPRENEURS —► MANY WORKERS

Received a rent for scarcity of soil

Capital raising and risk taking for new ventures undertaken by same persons – in free competition with many other merchants and manufacturers

Labourers and craftsmen receive wages for their contribution to production in the division of labour

MANY TENANT FARMERS ◄—► MANY URBAN CONSUMERS

Paid rents and sold their products on open market

Obtained the benefits of efficiency which the 'division of labour' in the new and expanding factory system allowed efficient use of land – and in freeing the flow of trade between farmers and consumers.

In contrast, Smith, in analysing the origins of national wealth, emphasised the importance of effectively utilising a nation's stock of labour skills. He began with a celebrated description of the 'division of labour', which increases wealth because it increases the 'dexterity of the labour force, saves time and permits the use of mechanical devices'. The limits to the theoretical division of labour were set by the size of the market and the stock of capital at hand. From this basis he then went forward to consider the question of economic growth and put forward a view, counter to that held by the mercantilists, that freedom for the individual within an economic society could lead to the greatest possible increase in wealth. The arguments Smith used were based on those originally put forward in his *Theory of Moral Sentiments* about the basic motivations of man, particularly his propensity to 'truck, trade and to exchange'. He described a system of 'social harmony' as being dependent on the delicate balance of man's conflicting motives: the search for satisfying individual self-interest could benefit society but would need to be restricted by the self-interest of others. Manufacturers would seek the largest possible profit, but in order to do so they needed to produce goods desired by the community as a whole. Likewise they must learn to produce them in the right quantities and qualities, at the right place and at the right time.

Smith went on to suggest the delicate mechanism of 'an invisible hand at work' in the market for the factors of production; land, labour, capital and risk-taking, providing a harmony so long as the factors sought the largest possible returns. The right goods would therefore be produced at the right prices and the whole society could achieve the largest possible wealth, so long as free competition was allowed to work. However, if, as in the mercantilistic model, competition was restricted by governmental or guild regulations the efficacy of the invisible hand would be impaired, and the wealth creating possibilities open to society would remain frustrated.

The enormous success that the *Wealth of Nations* enjoyed was due to Smith's ordering of economic thinking around the central concept of free markets, and the philosophical and practical justification this provided for the newly emerging capitalist class, who were interested in ridding Britain, and later other Western European countries, of mer-cantilistic type controls affecting the development of wider trade at home and abroad.

As with the physiocrats Smith further categorised society into productive and non-productive groups. For Smith, the capitalist and working classes formed the bulk of the former, and the ruling aristocracy, legal and military establishments formed the bulk of the latter. Such a view was obviously popular with those 'on the make' in the new factory system. It also led to a strong belief that good government was less government, and that expenditures on defence, welfare and education were at best suspect, and at worst positively harmful, to the creativity and efficiency of society as a whole. It was said that Smith 'persuaded his own generation and governed the next'. However his broadly optimistic view of future growth was to receive checks, notably by the writings of the Reverend Thomas Malthus, who was concerned about the problems of population increase running ahead of the resources available to sustain them, and David Ricardo who later analysed, in more rigorous fashion, the working of the *laissez-faire* market and industrial system.

*     *     *     *     *

Thomas Malthus, a country curate and the son of a well-educated landowner, first came to fame with the publication of his famous essay on *The Principle of Population as it Affects the Future Improvement of Society* published in 1798. This first edition, with its broad generalisations and religious undertones, attracted both attention and adverse criticism, and he later spent some years travelling on the Continent gathering data to support his thesis, which was included in a second edition published in 1803.

Arising out of his original essay on population, Malthus acquired a wide reputation and became a close friend of David Ricardo with whom he had a long correspondence. Like his great contemporary, Lord Byron (1788–1824) following on the publications of the first two cantos of his poem *Childe Harold's Pilgrimage*, Malthus, following the publication of his first essay on population, 'woke up and found himself famous'. Ironically this essay might never have been written if his father had not been an over-enthusiastic admirer of the optimistic French philosopher, the Marquis de Condorcet (1743–1794) whose ideas were translated and propagated in England by William Godwin (1756–1836). Young Malthus was also disturbed by the chapters on population in Smith's *Wealth of Nations* and by the 'law of diminishing returns' as stated by another French philosopher, Robert-Jacques Turgot. Turgot was far more than merely a philosopher. In a varied and active life he was an attempted reformer of the *ancien regime*, Navy Minister and early economist, who wrote a significant book *Reflexions sur la*

FIG. 7.   THOMAS ROBERT MALTHUS : THE LATE 18TH CENTURY POPULATION INCREASE
TO SUBSISTENCE DILEMMA

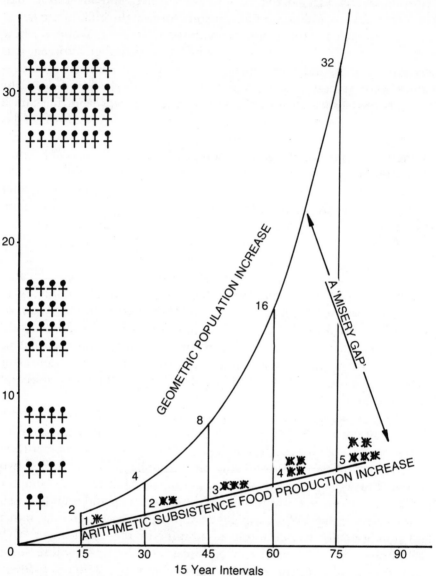

Population when unchecked increases in a geometric ratio, subsistence only increases at
an arithmetic ratio.

*Formation et Distribution des Richesses* in 1766, and was also in regular correspondence with Adam Smith. Malthus' misgivings about the wisdom of these gentlemen prompted him to write his essay which argued that while the means of subsistence tended to grow in an arithmetic progression, population grew in a geometric progression. Indeed on his original basis he thought that the British population might begin to double every 15 years or so. In fact the real rate of increase proved to be far below this. Later he modified his theory into a more general view that increases in population would need to be restricted by moral restraint, failing which would lead only to a society characterised by vice and misery. The problems associated with population increasing more rapidly than available resources was later to diminish as a crucial problem in the advanced Western European industrial countries. Falling death rates were to be matched by falling birth rates, while the expanding economic system proved capable of producing sufficient to support the gradually increasing population, and generally increasing standards of affluence. Moreover as the 19th century moved on, massive emigration to America and elsewhere ameliorated population pressures on domestic resources. Yet in many of the less developed countries, especially in Asia and Latin America, the Malthusian dilemma of falling death rates and rising birth rates, unaccompanied by sufficient rises in overall production or possibility of massive emigration elsewhere, continues to pose grave problems of starvation, degradation and misery.

In his own day the main effect of Malthus' essay was to wipe away the optimistic hopes about the future before mankind which had been generated by the French philosophers and in Britain by Smith, Godwin and others. To Malthus as Britain's population increased, marginal less fertile land would need to be brought into cultivation, and the increase in food production would not keep pace with demand. Thus famine could be avoided only if the population engaged in moral restraints; by marrying later and having fewer children. His ideas later had much influence on the old Tudor derived Poor Law system, which in 1834 was amended, to take a somewhat harsher view of the needs of the poor for more than a subsistence income. In economic philosophy, Malthus' interpretation of the law of diminishing returns, as applied to the relationship between labourers and land, had a considerable influence on David Ricardo, and through his writings caused the economics, in Thomas Carlyle's phrase, to become known as the 'dismal science'. As will be seen later, his writings also powerfully influenced Karl Marx in his perception of the working of the British political economy; of a landless peasantry forced off the land to join a 'reserve army' of the unemployed industrial proletariat, readily disciplined to subsistence living, and dependant on feast and famine and on the ups and downs of the trade cycle.

\*     \*     \*     \*     \*

David Ricardo was an English economist of formidable intellect, who in the last decade of his life became the leading exponent of the classical school of political economy, building on the *laissez-faire* model originally suggested by the writings of Smith. For much of his life Ricardo was a successful man of business, a stockbroker who by the age of 42 was able to retire and devote himself to the study of political economy and to public affairs. He was elected to Parliament in 1819, and his early interests lay in monetary problems arising out of the Napoleonic Wars and led to an important essay *The High Price of Bullion* (1810). This was followed in 1815 by an essay on the *Low Price of Corn and the Profits of Stock*, and in 1816 by the *Proposals for an Economical and Secure Currency*. His most important work *Principles of Economy and Taxation*, appeared in 1817, and the 1821 edition is one to which reference is usually made. This work embodied Ricardo's main ideas on the theory of value and distribution, words which dominated much of English classical economic thinking from that time onwards.

In contrast to his friend and disputant Malthus, he considered that to determine the laws which regulate the distribution of economic produce is the principal problem in political economy. Ricardo's idea of value was a quantity of labour theory. In opposition to Malthus he discounted the importance of rents, the return to finite and irreproducable commodities, especially land, and concentrated his analysis to the mass of goods which may 'be increased by human industry'. He therefore sought to demonstrate that the exchange values of commodities will be proportional to the quantities of labour embodied in them, including stored up labour in the forms of machines, etc. The simplicity of this original proposition was later extended, requiring the use of proportions of capital and labour of varying qualities, but Ricardo retained it as a fundamental element in his theory. For Ricardo the explanation of the distributive shares of the three factors of production: land for which the price is rent, labour for which the price is its wage, and capital for which the price is interest, is implicit in his theory of value. In essence these are still ideas which have a powerful impact on our perception of the working of the economic system to the present day.

For Ricardo the price of land as rent was regarded as a surplus over the costs of production, and to the extent to which it was determined by

FIG. 8.   INDUSTRIAL AND SOCIAL DEVELOPMENTS AFFECTING THE POLITICAL
ECONOMY OF BRITAIN AND IRELAND BETWEEN 1815 AND 1851

1815   Peace in Europe followed by an economic slump and great social
       distress
       Corn Laws introduced strengthening home agriculture by preventing
       cheap grain imports
1816   Spar Field riots
1817   Suspension of Habeas Corpus
       Thomas Robert Malthus published *The Poor Law*
       David Ricardo published *The Principles of Political Economy and
       Taxation*
1819   The 'Peterloo massacre' in Manchester
       Gag Acts increase powers of magistrates
1820   Cato street conspiracy
       Merchants begin movement for Free Trade
1821   Population census 15.4 million
1822   New Corn Laws provide improved Colonial preferences
1825   20 per cent reduction in tariffs and Navigation Laws amended
1825   Stockton to Darlington railway inaugurated
1827   Macadam made Inspector General of Roads
1829   Robert Stephenson demonstrates 'The Rocket' and introduces The
       Railway Age
1831   Truck Act prevented payment of wages in kind
1832   The Great Parliamentary Reform Bill – greatly extends franchise
1833   Abolition of slavery in the British Empire
1834   The Tolpuddle Martyrs
       Poor Law Amendment Act
1837   Queen Victoria's reign began (1837–1901)
1838   Transatlantic steamship by Isambard Brunel
1840   Railway system begins to expand rapidly at the expense of the canals
       and roads
1841   Population census 20.2 million
1842   Second Chartists petition to parliament
       Mines Act restricted employment of women and children underground
1843   Poor Law. Outdoor labour test reform
1844   Rochdale Pioneers established commercial aspects of the co-operative
       movement
       Bank Charter Act introduced stronger central banking system
1845   Irish potato famine. Mass starvation leading to one million deaths out
       of total population of 8 million
1846   Sir Robert Peel's repeal of the Corn Laws allowing import of cheap
       food grains
1848   John Stuart Mill published his *Principles of Political Economy*
       Marx and Engels published their *Communist Manifesto*
       Revolutionary turmoil throughout Europe
       Discovery of gold in California
1851   The Great Exhibition demonstrates British industrial leadership and
       the high point for 'laissez faire' as an economic doctrine

differing fertility in the extent of the land. The price that would warrant production on the poorest worst situated land, would yield a surplus over production costs on more favourable plots, which would be appropriated in rent by landowners. Thus for Ricardo, rent could be ignored as an element in the cost of production. Indeed as he emphasised, corn is not high in price because a rent is paid but 'a rent is paid because corn is high'. He went on to use this proposition to argue for the repeal of the Corn Laws, which between 1815 and 1846 played a key role in the operation of the English and Irish political economy, preventing the import of cheap grain from overseas and thereby sustaining the returns to agriculture and to the rentier landowner and the agricultural classes, at a higher level than would otherwise have been the case.

Ricardo accepted Malthus' view of an 'elastic supply' of labour which would receive a natural real wage. Indeed he thought of labour as being paid out of a national 'wage fund' which, divided by the number of workers on offer, was equivalent to the real wage. In turn the real wage in the England of his time was, in his view, sufficient for subsistence and modest comfort by the average labourer. For Ricardo profit was a residual over wage cost and indeed he considered there would be no rise in the value of labour, without a fall in profits. He thought of capital in terms of a 'gross revenue' which would be sufficient to enable society to stay where it was. Over and above the gross revenue was the possibility of a 'net revenue' which was a true surplus. This revenue would enable the capitalist to invest in new machines, or alternatively to increase the wage fund to pay for workers. The net revenue used to increase the wage fund was an advance made by the capitalist classes to workers in anticipation of the work they would undertake. In the Ricardian model the role of the entrepreneur was clear, he should pursue 'self interest' and obtain the net revenue which would enable the purchase of new machinery and the maintenance of the wage fund.

In the working of his system Ricardo took a somewhat pessimistic view of the opportunities for increasing productivity from factory activities, and indeed generally assumed 'constant returns to scale'. Equivalent inputs of capital and labour would soon lead to a constant rate of return from such inputs. At the time he was writing the possibilities of large economies of scale in huge manufacturing enterprises was still some way off. Even in textiles, factory sizes were still relatively small, by later standards. This assumption inevitably led to a pessimistic view of possibilities of growth. Indeed his assumptions

FIG. 9.   DAVID RICARDO: BRITAIN'S ECONOMIC DILEMMA 1815 ONWARDS
HOW TO MOVE TO AN INDUSTRIALLY BASED WORLD FREE TRADING SYSTEM

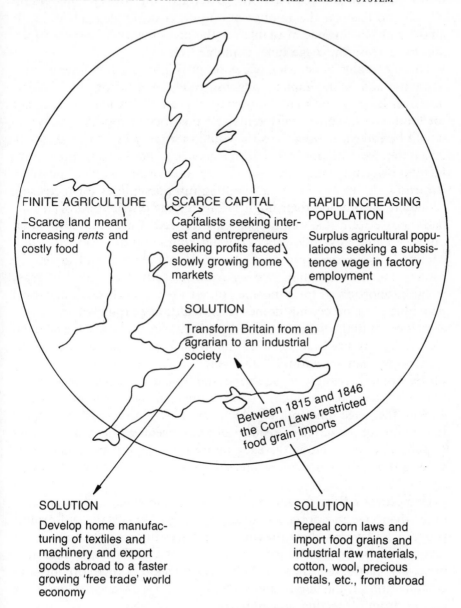

FINITE AGRICULTURE

–Scarce land meant increasing *rents* and costly food

SCARCE CAPITAL

Capitalists seeking interest and entrepreneurs seeking profits faced slowly growing home markets

RAPID INCREASING POPULATION

Surplus agricultural populations seeking a subsistence wage in factory employment

SOLUTION

Transform Britain from an agrarian to an industrial society

Between 1815 and 1846 the Corn Laws restricted food grain imports

SOLUTION

Develop home manufacturing of textiles and machinery and export goods abroad to a faster growing 'free trade' world economy

SOLUTION

Repeal corn laws and import food grains and industrial raw materials, cotton, wool, precious metals, etc., from abroad about growth, given the onset of constant returns, in relatively small factories, assumed a stationary or slowly growing society; only gradually able to increase the amount of output, critically dependent on the amount of net revenue available for the investment of new machines, and to increase the wage fund available.

This generally pessimistic view of possibilities of industrial productivity had wide implications for other aspects of the classical doctrine. It suggested that as population grew the increasing demands for food would tend to raise rents and the price of food, hence wages would be forced up while profits would inevitably be squeezed to fall. Thus the 'community of interest' between the various productive factors originally suggested by Smith no longer seemed possible. Ricardo's gloomy views about the long run possibilities for increasing economic wealth and their implications for the distribution of income had a powerful influence on other classical economists and also, later, on Marx and his followers. Looking to the future Ricardo, with Malthus, could see only an increase of population and given the assumption of 'diminishing returns' from agriculture, a relative increase in the proportion of total income going to rents. Both saw only small possibilities of increasing domestic agricultural output, which would therefore lag in the long run behind population growth and the demand for food. This situation made it important that labour should not be paid more than its natural 'subsistence' wage. If this was exceeded, profit would inevitably be squeezed and would allow less net revenue than was necessary to allow for investment in new machinery or to expand the wage fund, out of which capitalists would wish to employ labour for future activity. Again profit also seemed destined to fall; as population grew, and as the existing obsolete capital stock competed with new investment coming onto the static or only slowly growing market.

Domestically Ricardo and his followers could think of few policies, other than law and order measures, which would sustain and protect property and would allow the capitalist classes sufficient income for net investment, to finance future new investment and the wage fund and, hopefully, facilitate growth. Labour policies should, therefore, prevent combinations, trade unions and such like, and discourage the labouring classes from expecting much beyond a 'subsistence wage' and of encouraging as much effort and thrift as possible. Soon after this time the Tolpuddle Martyrs (1834) and other labour 'trouble makers', including Luddites, who broke up machinery, were prosecuted, and shipped off as convicts to the convict settlements of New South Wales,

Tasmania, or worse. In line with Adam Smith's doctrine, Ricardo obviously regarded government as having a minimal role confining itself to law, order and defence, with minimal taxation being levied on rents, which was a form of income no one could escape from, and on luxury goods. Like Edward Gibbon, in his great history of *The Decline and Fall of the Roman Empire*, Ricardo believed that 'all taxes must, at last, fall upon agriculture'.

For Ricardo the main hope lay in expanding the economy, not by domestic manipulations of returns to the different factors, but rather by opening Britain up to the import of cheaper foods from abroad, and conversely by encouraging manufacturers to seek new expanding markets abroad. In this way the economy would be able to escape from the narrow confines of its limited markets at home, and by free trade and *laissez-faire* would be able to benefit from the advantages of 'comparative costs' and the 'international division of labour' abroad. He therefore advocated the repeal of the Corn Laws, which from the end of the Napoleonic wars, restricted the import of cheap food grains into Britain and Ireland. However the eventual triumph of the 'Manchester school' and the Anti-Corn Law League did not occur until 1846, following the disasters of the Irish potato famine. In the middle 1840s it is estimated that over one million people perished, or one eighth of Ireland's total population at that time.

*     *     *     *     *

It should be recognised that the subsequent rapid development of the industrial system, which had been presaged by Adam Smith's writings, and was later interpreted and guided by the precepts of Malthus, Ricardo and others of the classical school, was, as much as anything else, based on an unprecedented flow of original scientific ideas and inventions, and their application to industrial processes. These developments made possible the increasingly rapid transformation of Britain from a small population agricultural society to a much larger population, industrial and urban society. The increases in population were particularly marked, rising from an estimated seven million in 1776 to over 15.4 million in the year of the Census, 1821. At this time most of the population were still engaged in agricultural employment, though textiles, mining, iron making, etc., was expanding rapidly. By the Census of 1901 the United Kingdom's population was to exceed 38 million, and the population was very largely engaged in urban based industrial and domestic employment.

Inventions which we associate particularly with the development of the early factory system were initially involved with the changes in the traditional textile industry. These include Kay's early invention of the Flying Shuttle in 1733, and Hargreave's Spinning Jenny in 1764. This was soon followed by Watt and Bolton's steam engine in 1769, which was put to work in the new industrial factories, and also the introduction of Compton's Spinning Mule in 1779. In the industrialisation of the textile industry, both cotton and wool, set the pace of change. About the same time transport possibilities were revolutionised by the opening of the Bridgewater Canal by Brindley in 1772, and this led to half a century of feverish canal developments, which was only to be halted with the introduction of the railway system in the 1840s. Other important scientific developments, which would have a profound effect on both social and industrial life, included Dr. Jenner's development of vaccination against smallpox in 1796. In the first half of the 19th century, concomitant as it were with the rise and fall of Napoleon's Europe and the relative peace and stability which followed the Congress of Vienna in 1815, were inventions within which the basis of British manufacturing continued to develop and multiply. In 1815 Humphry. introduced his Miner's Safety Lamp, and in 1827 Macadam was made first Inspector General of Roads, and a wider application of his improved system of road building followed. Two years later, in 1829, Stephenson's Rocket had its first run, and instituted the onset of the railway age, and in 1831 Faraday invented the dynamo. Towards the end of that decade, in 1838, Brunel had put into service the first Atlantic steamship, which was soon to be followed by an iron steamship service in 1844. Finally in 1847, Dr. Lister had demonstrated the use of chloroform in operations. While the foregoing represent only a limited list of major scientific and industrial applications, nevertheless they underpinned the developments which were transforming the nature of British social, political and industrial life at the time. They provided the backdrop against which the ideas of the classical school of political economy developed, bridging as it were the move from a small agrarian society to a large-scale industrial society based, increasingly after 1846 and the repeal of the Corn Laws, on the import of cheap foodstuffs from abroad and the wide export on a free trade basis of manufactured goods, textiles, railway equipment, ships and Welsh steam coals, to all parts of the world. In turn they established a pattern of industrial and social transformation and change which, ever since, the other advanced industrial nations have sought to emulate and surpass.

*     *     *     *     *

Following on from Malthus and Ricardo, many Victorian intellectuals, both alarmed and impressed by the transformation of industry
and society going on around them, took up an interest in a study of
political economy. One such, who had a considerable influence in his
time, was Herbert Spencer, who in 1843 became Assistant Editor of
The Economist, which was developing into an influential weekly
newspaper on public affairs. The Economist also became the home in
1860 of Walter Bagehot, who wrote a powerful work on *The Evolution and Nature of the English Constitution*, which is still highly
regarded to the present day. Bagehot, in another work, *Physics and
Politics*, included a passage which summed up the mid-Victorian
ambivalence towards progress and welfare when he wrote, 'The most
melancholy of human reflections perhaps is that, on the whole, it is a
question whether the benevolence of mankind does most good or
harm'.

In general Bagehot was a cleverly advanced thinker well able
to view many of the more rigorous aspects of Ricardian inspired
economics with a sceptical mind. However in 1850 his fellow journalist
cum philosopher Spencer, had published a book on *Social Statics*, which
attempted to show that *laissez-faire* liberalism would establish a 'social
equilibrium', if allowed to operate in an unchecked way. This belief he
formulated as the law of equal freedom, by which he meant every man
should have freedom to do as he wills, providing that he influences not
the equal freedom of any other man. Later Spencer's most widely read
book was to be *Man versus the State* published in 1884, which had a
great critical success by those of like mind, in both Britain and America.
In this work, he included a powerful attack on all forms of state
intervention which he considered was taking place in the England of his
day. Indeed he saw on all sides the disappearance of individual freedom,
as the direct consequences of state intervention. For Spencer freedom
provided the conditions for progress by the elimination of the unfit,
whilst state intervention preserved the unfit and led to what he regarded
as an undesirable state of 'economic and social' stagnation. His defence
of individual *laissez-faire* type freedom gained him much popularity
amongst the increasingly successful and entrenched urban middle
classes. As time went by his views drew strong censure from the more
collectively and socially minded members of the intelligensia. While it
cannot be said that Spencer had an important influence on any original
development in economic doctrines, nevertheless, in company with a
number of other intellectuals, he powerfully influenced the perception
that many of the middle classes had of the social and political balance of

their time, and in the underlying working of the system as a whole —
lines of debate which persist to the present time.

Spencer certainly provided ample fuel for his many enemies of all
shades of left wing and socially reformist opinion. Given the many
changes which influenced Victorian life it was hardly surprising that for
many years the debate about the attitude of the classical economists
towards the role of government and of social welfare generally, divided
the intellectual community. Later, liberal social historians and political
activists such as Sydney and Beatrice Webb, the Hammonds, Professor
G. D. H. Cole and many others, came to depict the classical economists
as apologists for the developing system of industrial capitalism, and for
the widespread pauperism, large profits and exploitation, which was
considered to be an integral part of it. Other commentators went
further to discredit them, as simply ciphers for the new industrialists
and opponents of social reform, and claimed they had supported a
system of *laissez-faire*, in which the state stood aside, and allowed the
successful few to dominate the many. In particular, this view was
vigorously espoused by Marx and his many subsequent disciples, and is
considered in somewhat greater detail later. However many contemporary economists such as Lord Robbins, Ludwig von Mises,
Friedrich von Hayek, and Milton Friedman, would hold the view that
attitudes of the classical economists in opposing government action in
principle, and in favour of complete freedom of economic activity, must
be seen against the context of their times. To this way of thinking the
early classical schools were essentially reformers, seeking to expose the
defects of reactionary mercantilistic traditions and habits of thought,
which had lingered on from previous centuries. It is natural therefore
that they should emphasise the liberating aspects of *laissez-faire*
theories, and of the advantages, both pecuniary and spiritual, of
breaking man away from the dead hand of government. In fact all the
classical economists, in one way or another, were prone to suggest ways
in which their principles should be moderated in light of some
particular welfare goal. Indeed close reading of the works of many of
the classical writers often suggest that what they were contemplating
was not so much *laissez-faire* as an active policy of non-interference by
government in economic activity. Thus they hoped for an active state of
Benthamite inspired laws and institutions which would enable the
market economy to work to the 'social advantage'.

These types of liberalising debates necessarily took a number of
forms. Adam Smith, for instance, had early recognised the need to
maintain certain public works and institutions, which can never be for

the interest of an individual or a small number of individuals to maintain, because the profit would never repay the expense to any individual or small number of individuals, though it may frequently do more than to repay it to a 'great society'. He also recognised the need for public expenditure on 'defence before opulence', and the case for Britain to maintain the Navigation Acts, so as to keep her naval supremacy secure. Other classical economists, including Mill, envisaged direct state intervention favouring the assistance for 'infant industries', help for backward peoples and limited dividends from public companies. However in general, all these interferences were intended to encourage a system of freedom, so as to provide security to enable increased opportunities and knowledge, or to reduce excessive power, so that the market economy would work for the general good, and be open and receptive to future innovations. As the industrial age developed, and the many social abuses of highly urbanised industrial life became more manifest, many classical economists also perceived the need for more sophisticated social policies. Both Smith and Malthus suggested the need for subsidising schools, while even Nassau Senior, in a famous report on handloom weavers, said that 'both the ground landlord and the speculating builders ought to be compelled by law to take measures which would prevent the towns they create being centres of disease'. Other classically minded thinkers opposed the payment of wages in goods, and supported the implementation of the Truck Act, which prevented this. They also supported the Factory Acts, 1833 and 1844, restrictions on the employment of children; and on the employment of women and children underground in the 1842 Mines Act, etc.

In general the early classical thinkers made very broad assumptions about man and his environment. Man was to be seen seeking his own interest, which meant not so much self interest but the interest of any human being, and especially his family and descendants he chose to benefit by his efforts, through the ongoing possession and retention of accumulated wealth and property. As Locke had emphasised and the American colonists had endorsed, the possession of property facilitated political freedom as well. While the industrial society was obviously getting richer, the world was still poor, and incentive had to be given to those who were able to contribute more than the average to the common weal. Hence the classical economists spent much time concerning themselves with arguments which were geared to suggesting self interest leading to overall social advantage. They thought that only a market economy could reconcile these objectives with personal freedom which, underlying all else, was their fundamental concern. In this they were powerfully influenced by ideas stemming from Locke and Bentham of the nature of a free society as a whole.

*    *    *    *    *

By the middle of the 19th century the most influential classical economist was John Stuart Mill, who had received an extraordinary education from his father, James Mill, a friend of Ricardo and Bentham and in his own right one of the leading intellectuals of the early 19th century. By inclination a philosopher, Mill considered that in economics he was nothing more than pure Ricardian, though his main work on the *Principals of Political Economy* (1848), contained original thought. It was a comprehensive survey of economic doctrine as it was understood at his time and became the standard mid 19th Century work on the subject. Throughout much of his life Mill conducted an extensive debate with other classical economists about the scope and methods of political economy. Professor Nassau Senior in particular sought to establish its claims to being a 'deductive science'. On the other hand William Thomas Thornton, an influential colleague of Mills', in the East India Company, was critical of classical methods. In practice Mill tolerated most of Malthus' and Ricardo's dismal forebodings about the workings of the economic system, and in particular until quite late in his life he accepted the wage fund theory, which so dominated classical doctrine from Ricardo onwards. However he hoped to mitigate the worst excesses of the classical system by the benefits of liberal government and society. Mill included in this book a famous account of the 'stationary state', which suggested that the increase of wealth and affluence must sometime come to an end, and society enter upon stationary condition. In the words of Sir Eric Roll, in his *A History of Economic Thought*, Mill suggested that:

> "Improvements in technique, the law of diminishing returns, the accumulation of capital, and the working of competition combine to produce declining profits, rising rents, and, if population is restrained from rising unduly, an improvement in the condition of the working classes. But although advances in technique and the export of capital might ensure a continuance of progress even in highly developed countries, the arrival of the stationary state cannot ultimately be postponed."

In hindsight Mill appears to have looked somewhat complacently upon this state of blissful equilibrium in which the competitive struggle would disappear and in which wealth would be more evenly divided, as a result both of individual prudence and of legislation. As with Malthus and Ricardo before him, his vision served again as an argument for the need of restricting population growth. More generally however, he looked for a compromise in the field of economic doctrine which would be in line with the liberal hopes he expressed in respect of the possibilities of Benthamite social and public planning, leading to 'the greatest happiness for the greatest numbers'. In such a world a rational choice of pleasure and pain by the individual in his economic activities should ensure an adequate balance being struck, between the delights of consumption on the one hand, and the need for abstinence via saving and investment on the other. While Mill's economics lacked some of the rigour of other systems, he was free from doctrinaire views, and brought into public debate generally a practical concern with human welfare, combined with a spirit of toleration, which were eventually to stand it in good stead. It is not too fanciful to suggest that much of current conflict between economic and political doctrines in the world at large may still be seen as polarising between the liberal compromise suggested by Mill, and the revolutionary historical determinism propounded by Marx and Engels in the Communist manifesto, originally promulgated in that year of Revolutions, 1848.


## Karl Marx and the role of Capital in Economic Analysis 1848–1883

The historical deterministic nature of Marxist thinking has already been emphasised; in fact Karl Marx, the man, during the course of active life, extending from a childhood in Germany to the last 33 years of his life in London, tried many choices. By training, a lawyer and philosopher, by vocation, a journalist and revolutionary and an important figure in the history of sociology, economics and political thought, Marx liked to regard himself as a 'Darwin of the Social Sciences'. It will be recalled that Charles Darwin (1809–1882) lived contemporaneously with Marx and published his highly controversial *Origin of the Species by Means of Natural Selection* in 1859, and *Descent of Man* in 1871. Both Marx and Darwin, in their different ways, had been influenced by Malthus' essay on population, containing as it did the idea of a struggle for survival and natural selection. However Marx's subsequent reputation as a scientist, at least in the West, has suffered from the extreme variety of his activities and from the conflicts which, from the outset, have beset Marxism as a political ideology.

FIG. 10.   KARL MARX, MID-19TH CENTURY ONWARDS

### (1)   THE HISTORICAL DETERMINISTIC CONFLICT SYSTEM

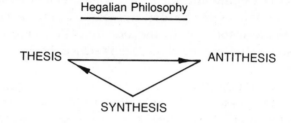

The materialist dialetic moving through time and conflict situations

### (2)   HISTORICAL SOCIAL EVOLUTION THROUGH REVOLUTIONARY CONFLICT SCENARIO

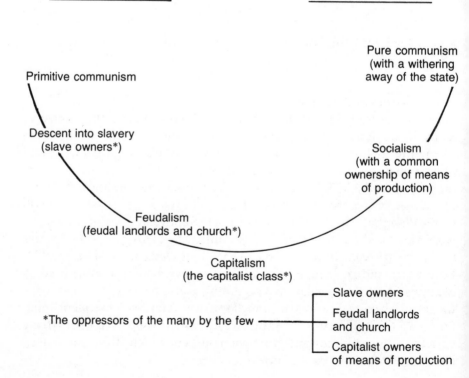

As David McLellan, in his recent book on *Karl Marx — his life and thought*, points out:

> "It may seem paradoxical that Karl Marx, whom so many working-class movements of our time claim as their Master and infallible guide to revolution, should have come from a comfortable middle-class home. Yet to a remarkable extent he does himself epitomise his own doctrine that men are conditioned by their socio-economic circumstances. The German city (Trier) in which he grew up gave him a sense of long historical tradition and at the same time close contact with the grim realities of the underdevelopment then characteristic of Germany. Thoroughly Jewish in their origins, Protestant by necessity yet living in a Catholic region, his family could never regard their social integration as complete. The sense of alienation was heightened in Marx's personal case by his subsequent inability to obtain a teaching post in a university system that had no room for dissident intellectuals."

Again from the same source we have this quotation from a letter written by Heinrich Marx to his young son, Karl Marx, while the latter was at the University — which gives a remarkable foretaste of problems to come.

> "I feel myself suddenly invaded by doubt and ask myself if your heart is equal to your intelligence and spiritual qualities, if it is open to the tender feelings which here on earth are so great a source of consolation for a sensitive soul; I wonder whether the peculiar demon, to which your heart is manifestly a prey, is the Spirit of God or that of Faust. I ask myself — and this is not the least of the doubts that assail my heart — if you will ever know a simple happiness and family joys, and render happy those who surround you."

Finally we have left to us this vivid picture by Annenkov of what the young Marx was like during an early visit to London on a spring evening in 1846:

> "Marx was a type of man formed all of energy, force of will and unshakeable conviction, a type highly remarkable in outward appearance as well. In spite of his thick, black mane of hair, his hairy hands, and his coat buttoned up all awry, he had the appearance of a man who has the right and the power to demand respect, although his looks and his manners might appear peculiar sometimes. His movements were angular, but bold and confident, his manners were contrary to all social practice. But they were proud, with a touch of disdain, and his sharp voice, which rang like metal, sounded remarkably in accordance with the radical judgements on men and things which he let fall. He spoke only in the imperative, brooking no contradiction, and this was intensified by the tone, which to me was almost painfully jarring, in which he spoke. This

tone expressed the firm conviction of his mission to reign over men's minds and dictate their laws. Before my eyes stood the personification of a democratic dictator such as might appear before one in moments of fantasy."

Marx's interest in political economy came through his friendship with Friedrich Engels (1820–1895), the son of a wealthy family of German and Manchester based textile merchants. Engels studied both the lives of the English working classes and the theories of the English classical economists, and his critique influenced Marx. In 1845 Engels had published a highly critical book of life in Manchester and the industrial North under the title *Conditions of the Working Class in England*. Engels was a prolific author in his own right; especially on military affairs which interested him both intellectually, and as a means of furthering the Proletarian Revolution. He was proud of his early experience as a Prussian one-year volunteer and for his active role in the Badan insurrection of 1848. He was known as 'the General' by his friends. *The Communist Manifesto*, which was strongly influenced by the English Chartists' List of Grievances of the same period, was written jointly by Marx and Engels, and published in 1848. After moving to England in 1850, Marx began a systematic study of English industrial conditions, as seen through the eyes of Engels in Manchester, from the powerful writing of Charles Dickens (1812–1870); Elizabeth Gaskell (1810–1865); Caroline Norton (1808–1877) and others, about the lives of the industrial poor, and in the literature found in the British Museum library. He soon developed a vituperative debate with the works of the English classical school; notably that of parson Malthus, stockbroker Ricardo, and reactionary Professor Nassau Senior, which has continued to the present day. In particular Marx, and others of like interest, had been powerfully impressed by the attempts of the Welshman, Robert Owen, the early industrialist cum philanthropist, who had attempted to improve the life of working people by running model industrial communities, initially in New Lanark, in Scotland, from 1800, and later in New Harmony, in Indiana, in 1825. He had later returned to England to become a recognised leader of working class improvements, and was instrumental in the founding of the abortive National Consolidated Trade Union, in 1833. Owen was the founding father of British Socialism, the Cooperative Movement, adult education and much else besides. Stimulated by such examples, in 1859 Marx published his *Critique of Political Economy*, which contained the essence of his economic ideas, later developed at length in *Kapital* – the first volume of which appeared in 1867, second and third edited by

Engels in 1885 and 1894, and a tripartite volume was published in 1904–1910.

Some flavour of Marx's general views on the British political, economic and social scene is given by this early extract of his writings, originally published in 1844:

> "It will be agreed that England is a POLITICAL country. It will be agreed, further, that England is the COUNTRY OF PAUPERISM; indeed, the term itself is of English origin. A study of England is, therefore, the surest way of becoming acquainted with the RELATIONS between PAUPER-ISM and POLITICS. In England the distress of the workers is not PARTIAL, but UNIVERSAL, not limited to the manufacturing districts, but spread over the countryside. The movements here are not just appearing; they have recurred at intervals for almost a century.
>
> How, then, does the ENGLISH bourgeoisie and the government and press which are associated with it regard PAUPERISM? In so far as the English bourgeoisie blames politics for the existence of pauperism, the WHIG accuses the TORY, while TORY accuses the WHIG, of being responsible for it. According to the Whig, the chief cause of pauperism is the monopoly exercised by the great landowners and the laws prohibiting the import of corn. According to the Tory, the whole evil springs from liberalism, from competition, and from the too greatly extended factory system. Neither of the parties regards politics in general as a cause, but each one only the policy of the other party; neither party even dreams of a reform of society.
>
> The most convincing expression of English opinion on pauperism – we are still referring to the opinion of the English bourgeoisie and government – is English POLITICAL ECONOMY, that is to say, the scientific reflection of English economic circumstances."

As a basis for his economic analysis Marx accepted Ricardo's 'labour theory of value', in that he agreed that the value of commodity is determined by the quantity of labour embodied in its production. However Marx then went on to observe that only part of the total value of production went to the labour force as wages, and this led to his theory of 'surplus value', in which a significant part of total value accrues to the capitalist rather than the worker. Marx ascribed to the newly emergent capitalist class an insatiable desire for surplus value, and developed an elaborate theory of capitalist accumulation, which suggested that the ownership of the means of production would inevitably fall into fewer and fewer hands. Supporting the new factory system was a rapidly increasing propertyless proletariat, a reserve army of unemployed paupers. Many had been forced off the land by the agricultural enclosure movements, and at less than full employment, toiled for a Malthusian subsistence wage. Marx did, however, recognise that during periods of prosperity associated with up-swings in the 'trade cycle', workers might obtain more than a subsistence wage. Marx's prophesy of an inevitable revolution leading to the overthrow of capitalism and its replacement with socialism, was based on the belief that with the onset of increasingly serious trade fluctuations and commercial crises, the numerous members of the 'expropriated working classes' would overthrow the capitalists and their lackeys, who owned or controlled the means of production. Following this revolution a dictatorship for the proletariat would be established which would introduce a socialist economic system and society.

In place of Ricardo's gross and net revenues, the latter of which supported both investment in new machinery and the wage fund, three categories of capital are included in Marx's economic model. 'Constant capital', defined as the value of plant and raw materials used up in production; 'variable capital', the value of labour power expended during a particular period of time; and third, and most important, 'surplus value' going to the capitalists as profit, rent or interest, and re-invested for further accumulation. Marx defined the ratio of surplus capital over variable capital as the 'rate of exploitation'. This could be increased by requiring the working classes to toil longer working hours for the same wage, by allowing wages to fall below subsistence in the short run, or by improving the productivity of labour with machinery. Given the assumption of a subsistence wage, unbridled competition in the labour market would inevitably lead to a large surplus derived from the employment of the pauper workforce, accruing to the capitalist classes.

Marx differed from Ricardo in a particularly important way, in that he increasingly recognised the possibilities of technical change facilitating industrial productivity and returns to increasing scale. Marx saw clearly the possibility, inherent in large scale industry of substantially increasing returns and a reduction in the real costs of production. He was, of course, writing several decades after Ricardo, by which time the scale and operations of industry had grown vastly. New technologies and economies of scale were apparent for all to see, and Britain was increasingly moving into the leadership of a rapidly expanding world capitalist economy. The Great Exhibition of 1851 marked a high point in Britain's emergence as the leading industrial nation, importing foodstuffs and raw materials and exporting manufactured textiles and railway equipment, machinery, ships and Welsh steam coals to world markets. The successful, if initially derided, holding of the first great international exhibition, under the leadership of Prince Albert (1819–1861), Queen Victoria's (1819–1901) talented consort was a remarkable achievement in its own right. Over 100,000 exhibits were displayed in Joseph Paxton's (1803–1866) Crystal Palace erected in Hyde Park. This was modelled on the Duke of Devonshire's Green-houses at Chatsworth and was the world's first large prefabricated iron and glass structure. It was later moved to Sydenham in Kent and served as an exhibition building until destroyed by fire in 1936. Yet from the 1880s onwards the competitive power of the north eastern regions of the United States, and later a unified industrialising Germany, France and the Low Countries were to present a growing threat to British industrial supremacy. However London in the second half of the 19th century was also rapidly becoming a financial centre, for both public and private investment on a world-wide basis. Within this expanding and rapidly changing scene Marx saw only the prospect of ceaseless competitive struggle between capitalists, constantly seeking new investment outlets sufficient to keep ahead of their competitors. All were trapped in a 'devil take the hindmost' ruthlessly competitive market. He emphasised the accumulative tendencies of the capitalist classes with their concentration on seeking power, faced however with a long run fall in the rate of profit, due to an eventual drying up of rewarding investment possibilities. Associated with this picture of remorseless decline was a steady tendency for the 'immiseration' of the working class, at best surviving on subsistence, or at worst on less than subsistence, wages. Part of the immiseration process arose from des-truction of traditional crafts by new technology, in pursuit of labour saving schemes. Ultimately, like Malthus before him and Keynes long after him, Marx perceived the problems of 'under-consumption' and of a tendency for a failure of aggregate demand. For Marx this occurred both due to the inability of capitalists to re-invest rapidly enough in capital goods, and also because of the disproportionate distribution of income within the population as a whole eventually failing to create adequate consumer demand to sustain the markets for new productive capacity.

Marx speculated at length about the outcome of the trade cycle. Indeed in England, from the end of the Napoleonic era, waves of desperation had broken out over the country, in 1811–1813, in 1815–1817, in 1826, in 1829–1835, in 1838–1842, in 1843–1844 and in 1846–1848. The instability of political and social life deriving from economic recession was a central feature of British life. Marx foresaw a continuing series of increasingly serious slumps, due to a lack of true profitability, which in turn led to speculative activities by capitalists to avoid the falling profits deriving from surplusses of goods. Such rises inevitably led to a rush for liquidity in the form of money, the collapse of the credit system, of workers being laid off and wages cut, and of small capitalists being bankrupt. For Marx all this derived from under-consumption, because of the narrow basis upon which aggregate demand within the society as a whole was based. He also perceived the difficulties of large organisations in accurately forecasting future demands, and the problems this created for planning the appropriate investments for future expansion and growth. As all the world knows, Lenin later took many of Marx's ideas and developed them as the basis for revolutionary Communism, on an international scale. Whether Marx himself would have recognised all the present varieties of Marxism remains a great unanswerable question!

*     *     *     *     *

In retrospect, looking beyond the plight of mid 19th century industrial Britain, one of the most remarkable aspects of Marx the man, was his ability to take a wide ranging prophetic view of the way the world as a whole was shifting. The following passages, also quoted by McLellan, were written in 1849, following the discovery of gold in California. For Marx the flow of population westward, and the rapid expansion of the American railway system, meant that New York and San Francisco were taking the place in world trade then held by Liverpool and London. He continued thus:

> "The fulcrum of world commerce, in the Middle Ages Italy, more recently England, is now the Southern half of the North American continent . . . Thanks to the gold of California and to the tireless energy of the Yankees both coasts of the Pacific will soon be as thickly populated, as industrialized and as open to trade as the coast from Boston to New Orleans is now. The Pacific Ocean will then play the same role the Atlantic Ocean is playing now and the role that the Mediterranean played in the days of classical antiquity and in the Middle Ages – the role of the great water highway of world commerce – and the Atlantic Ocean will sink to the level of a great lake such as the Mediterranean is today."

As McLellan emphasises, in Marx's view:

> "The only hope for Europe of avoiding industrial, commercial and political dependence on the United States was 'a revolution which would transform the mode of production and intercourse in accordance with the needs of production arising from the nature of modern productive forces,

thus making possible the development of new forces of production which would maintain the superiority of European industry and counteract the disadvantages of geographical situation'. Marx finished the article with a remark on the recent beginning of Chinese socialism and the social upheaval brought about by contact with the West, an upheaval that 'must have the most important results for civilization'."

Again a second article on current affairs, written in April 1849, dealt more specifically with the possibilities of revolution in Europe:

"Marx thought he saw an approaching crisis in Britain due to over-investment, particularly in the key wool industry. The interaction of this crisis with the imminent upheavals on the continent would give to the latter a 'pronounced socialist character'. In Britain the crisis would drive from power both Whigs and Tories to be replaced by the industrial bourgeoisie, who would have to open Parliament to representatives of the proletariat, thus 'dragging England into the European revolution'."

While the Revolution as Marx foresaw it did not occur in either England or in other advanced industrial countries, nevertheless it still provides a chilling and, at times, plausible, alternative to some of the easy optimism of the early classical school inspired more by Adam Smith, than the later forebodings and pessimism of Malthus and Ricardo. Again from John Stuart Mill had come the idea of a 'stationary state', which, hopefully guided by liberal principals, could equate with Bentham's prescription of policies conducive to the 'greatest happiness for the greatest number'. Perhaps the most important English follower of Marx, in the development of economic thought, was John A. Hobson, a university extension lecturer who published a number of important works, including *The Physiology of Industry* with A. E. Mummery in 1889. In his earlier work Hobson suggested a theory of under-consumption based on a 'Marxian view' that expenditure on capital and consumption goods becomes unbalanced, because of excess savings by a small wealthy property owning class. Hobson also expressed critical views about colonial developments and capitalism in his work on *Imperialism* published in 1902. Significantly Vladimir Ilyich Lenin also drew extensively on these ideas in his own work on *Imperialism, The Highest Stage of Capitalism*, published in 1916 while he was still in exile in Zurich, waiting for the revolutions which he felt must come. Lenin's work was an analysis of economics in relation to international politics and provided a theoretical background for revolutionary policy in time of war. In particular Hobson and Lenin were both impressed by the way the capitalist system had extended into the new European colonial empires, which had developed in the second half of the 19th century. Both looked to a decline in profits, which they felt would take place if capitalists continued to invest only in their own countries. Thus the need for the major industrial powers to establish colonies and to invest where profits were high, wages were low and raw material cheap. Lenin's *Imperialism* was published just shortly before the Russian Revolution, and his move back to his homeland to take charge of the Revolution and, following triumph in the civil war, to impose his views on Russia's subsequent political, economic and industrial development. The practical application which these views took, in both the period up to Lenin's death in 1924, and in the subsequent Stalinist regime are considered in greater detail later in the book.

Many of Hobson's views about under-consumption problems and especially about the exploitive aspects of imperialism were unacceptable to the leading neo-classical economists of his time. However he eventually received belated recognition for this contribution to economic thinking about under-consumption and its effect on aggregate demand from Keynes in *The General Theory of Employment, Interest and Money*, published in 1936.

## The Development of Neo-Classical Doctrines 1870–1930

Neo-classical economic ideas developed against the background of the unprecedented and rapid, if uneven, expansion of the free enterprise property owning capitalist system, during the second half of the 19th century. As we have seen, the classical economists, Ricardo and, more importantly, Mill, had foreseen the possibility of a 'stationary state' which at best might be mitigated by liberal social measures; while Marx and Engels looked forward to a collapse of the capitalist system in its entirety and its replacement by a socialist system of common ownership of property, a dictatorship of the proletariat and an eventual 'withering away of the state'. In reality, technology and gradually improved education and knowledge, continued to bring in increasing benefits to industrial productivity, incomes increased and became somewhat more evenly distributed, and abroad new markets and sources of raw materials and foodstuffs supply expanded for British and other European countries.

Indeed the new European colonial empires and much of North and South America developed rapidly, as sources of raw materials and as markets for manufacturers, and as safe repositories of surplus wealth for investment, and as new homes for surplus population. Whereas both the classical and the Marxian economists had foreseen the possibility of static wages and a declining rate of profit, real wages were able to rise significantly above the Malthusian subsistence rate, and profits generally grew as well. Most importantly the returns to land did not appear to require an inevitably increasing share of national income. In Britain, the Repeal of the Corn Laws in 1846, and the import of cheaper foodstuffs from abroad, eventually destroyed from the 1870s onwards the power of domestic grain producing agriculture for nearly 100 years, while encouraging the expansion of food production abroad, in the U.S.A. and in the new white Dominions, Canada, Australia, New Zealand and South Africa, and also Argentina. While between the 1850s and 1870s British agriculture enjoyed considerable prosperity from that time onwards, the grain growing regions – especially in the eastern counties, experienced great social distress leading to collapse of incomes and emigration of population. Yet Mill's ideas of the need for the 'stationary state' receded and the interest of economists in the processes of economic development and its eventual resolution by benign liberal stability, or Marxist social revolution, diminished. The surplus of total national output over the output adequate to keep the population at subsistence level, and to keep the capital stock intact and expanding, grew rapidly. This enabled the dropping of the 'subsistence wage' theory, breaking the simple classical and Marxist connection between the uneven distribution of incomes, and its critical importance to sustain adequate savings and investment in the economic system as a whole.

*    *    *    *    *

Important theoretical developments followed on these real improvements in economic and social circumstances. In turn the old Political Economy evolved into formal economics increasingly concerned with what became known as 'marginal analysis'. This became the basis of much modern micro economic theory, based as it is on the analysis of the utility of successive units of a commodity or service, while the costs of successive units are the cost of factors of production. Marginal analysis first emerged in a clear form in 1871, with the publication by Professor W. S. Jevons of his *Theory of Political Economy* in that year. However as Jevons acknowledged in his preface, to some extent he was building on the foundations laid by a German economist, Herman Heinrich Gossen, who had postulated three laws in a book published in

1854. The works of two other economists: Carl Mengers' *Principles of Economics*, and Léon Walras' *Elements d'Economie Politique Pure* in 1874, also contributed similar ideas, and these were subsequently taken up and developed by many other economists both of the 'Austrian school' and elsewhere.

The marginal utility analysis of Jevons and Menger explained for the first time the allocation of expenditure by the consumer and formulated a maximisation solution. By the end of the 19th century the concept of the margin was being widely applied to the theory of distribution, and the allocation problems of the producer. In essence, since successive units of a commodity have different degrees of significance, significance attached to the effects of a loss, for addition of the marginal last unit. This applies to consumer goods, to factors of production, land, labour, capital, etc., and to services rendered by them. Marginal analysis deals with the logic of choice, and is applied where limited resources need to be allocated amongst a variety of ends, and where the object is to maximise satisfaction. The consumer allocates income in order to derive the most satisfaction from the whole of it. The producer allocates expenditure on various factors of production out of limited resources in order to maximise monetary returns, earnings or profit. The allocation problem of the consumer is, in fact, based on the law of 'diminishing marginal utility'. Equilibrium in distributing a given income is reached when total utility or satisfaction is maximised. This requires that the marginal utility of a unit of expenditure to be the same for all goods. Similarly, the solution to the allocation problem of the producer is based on the law of 'variable proportions'. Equilibrium in the distribution of given outlays is reached when factors are combined to the proportions which maximise physical output or minimise the cost of producing it. That is, when marginal physical product per unit of outlay is the same for each factor. Full productive equilibrium, however, requires an output that will maximise profits. Thus a further condition of equilibrium must be added. The use of all factors will be expended to the point when the additional marginal cost per unit of output is equal to the additional marginal revenue per unit obtained for its sale.

*     *     *     *     *

In Britain during the last quarter of the 19th century and the early years of the present century, the development of what became known as the neo-classical school of economics was especially associated with Professor Alfred Marshall, who for many years taught at Cambridge. An influential contemporary of Marshall's at Cambridge was the

FIG. 11.   MARSHALLIAN CONCEPTS OF DEMAND AND SUPPLY ELASTICITY

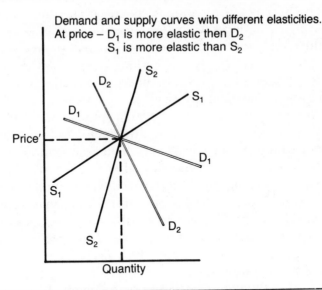

Demand and supply curves with different elasticities.
At price – $D_1$ is more elastic then $D_2$
$S_1$ is more elastic than $S_2$

1. Price elasticity of demand is defined as the responsiveness of demand to changes in price.

2. It is found by the formula:

$$\frac{Percentage\ change\ in\ quantity\ demanded}{Percentage\ change\ in\ price}$$

3. There are three demand curves with constant elasticity: the infinitely elastic curve, the unitarily elastic curve, and the curve with zero elasticity.

4. All other demand curves have elasticities which change along the curve. For such curves elasticity refers to a particular point on the curve, i.e. to a particular price.

5. Total revenue to the producer (i.e. total expenditure by the consumer) varies with price. Since fluctuations in price depend on the elasticity of demand, total revenue varies with elasticity.

6. Elasticity of demand chiefly depends on the availability of close substitutes.

7. Elasticity of supply is defined as the responsiveness of supply to changes in price. Its formula is similar to that given in note (2) above.

8. Prices fluctuate widely if supply or demand are inelastic.

9. Prices are stable if supply or demand are elastic.

10. Primary producers suffer more from fluctuating prices than secondary producers.

11. Besides price elasticity of demand and supply, income elasticity of demand, and population elasticity of demand are also of interest.

Professor of Moral Philosophy, Henry Sidgwick, who was also persuasive in drawing attention to the social questions underlying classical doctrines, with ideas which have persisted in our conception of the oft confused relationship between wealth creation and human welfare to the present day. Marshall's earliest work was on the *Economics of Industry* published in 1879, but perhaps his most significant contribution to economic thought was contained in his *Principles of Economics* published in 1890. In this important work Marshall brought together two streams of thinking. Those of the earlier classical school with those of Jevons and the marginal utility school. He fitted them into a precise theory of 'value' and distribution: costs of production explaining supply and utility explaining demand. Somewhat at variance with the mathematical determinism being suggested by Jevons, he considered that the principal task of the economist was to study the behaviour of men in the framework of the institutions in which they live. This meant that facts must be collected, arranged and interpreted, and the temptation must be avoided of presenting interpretations of theorems without universal validity. Again like Marx and his followers, Marshall perceived that institutions change and men's behaviour is influenced by them. In his attempt to make economics a scientific subject, he sought to find a common denominator to measure the activities of men, and his analysis was confined to aspects of human behaviour which could be measured in terms of money and were reflected in the price mechanism.

He set out to examine the general relationship between supply, demand and value. Influenced by 'Benthamite' pleasure–pain ideas, he regarded man's economic behaviour as a delicate balance between the search for satisfaction and the avoidance of sacrifice. This approach enabled Marshall to treat 'utility' and cost as joint determinants of value, likening them to blades of a pair of scissors, neither cutting solely by its own action, and then going on to apply this general idea to the whole field of economic activity. The individual consumer obtained income by balancing the disutility of effort with the utility derived from spending the income derived from it. Likewise the pattern of his expenditure was determined by the utility to be obtained from a commodity at the expense of the utility foregone in not buying others. The same theme underlay the activity of the whole economic community in its production and distribution of wealth.

As time went by Marshall became increasingly aware of the difficulty of analysing such economic activities under rapidly changing circumstances, and he therefore based his theories on a foundation of 'static conditions'. He analysed the influences between market value which was determined in the short run when supply was fixed, and normal value which was determined in the short run when supply could be increased with unchanged equipment and stocks of labour. In a third stage, the long period, he took into account the situation when the amount of a plant can be changed. Finally, he emphasised that all value must be considered in non-static periods, when all economic data such as taste, technology, population and the like are likely to be changed.

He primarily intended his work for the use of the layman and the businessman. However he soon came to have a wide influence amongst his fellow economists and a major impact on the teaching of the subject throughout the Western world. In America the neo-classical model was taken up and developed by Professor John Bates Clark, best known for his book on the *Distribution of Wealth* published in 1899, in which he introduced ideas of marginal products, and by his son John Maurice Clark who succeeded to his father's chair at Columbia University in 1926. The latter's book *Economics of Overhead Costs* published in 1923, was significant in development of 'dynamic analysis' as a move on from static states of Marshall. He also developed the idea of the 'accelerator principle' – the relationship between the rate of growth in the demand for consumer goods and the rate of growth in demand for capital goods – which later played an important part in Keynesian thought. In 1936 he published essays in *Preface to Social Economics.*

Meanwhile at Cambridge, in England, the influence of both Sidgwick and Marshall influenced many of the succeeding generation of British and Western European economists, including Arthur Pigou, the creator of 'welfare economics' who, in 1908, followed Marshall to the Chair of Political Economy at Cambridge, and the Swede, Gustav Cassel who became Professor at the University of Stockholm in 1904, and wrote widely about trade cycles and monetary policies. Marshall also fostered the early advancement of the young John Maynard Keynes, who later went on to become an astringent critic of the relevance of the neo-classical model, to the political and social needs of the inter-war depression years. Nevertheless Marshallian methods of reasoning and concepts, such as 'elasticity of demand' and 'substitution', are still to be found in the works of present day economists concerned with working of the *laissez-faire* market economy.

Concerning ideas about the mystery of wealth, it is clear that economics had come a long way from the 'dismal science' views, which had so characterised classical thinking during the first half of the 19th century. As we have seen, for Malthus, Ricardo and their followers, wealth creation possibilities were limited by the scarcity of fertile land and other finite resources, of which productivity improvements could mitigate only temporarily and slightly the tendency towards diminishing returns, or at best constant returns to scale. By the time the later neo-classical economists were fully developing their ideas, technical and industrial progress, and widespread improvements in education, had produced a marked tendency towards what appeared to be historically continually increasing returns to new investments in industry. Real wages in the United Kingdom in 1900 were estimated to be approaching double the level which had applied in 1850. Many of our ideas of late Victorian and Edwardian optimism about economic growth, and gradually beneficial Fabian Society inspired social change, stem from this time. Important thinkers associated with this influential group of intellectual gadflys cum social and political reformers included the Irish dramatist and wit, George Bernard Shaw (1856–1950), who early on wrote amusingly about Economics, Herbert George Wells (1866–1946), novelist and perceptive prophet of the future, and perhaps most significant of all, Sydney and Beatrice Webb, who together had a profound influence on the intellectual development of the Labour Party, and the founding of the influential journal the New Statesman and the London School of Economics and Political Science. Later important members included the Oxford historian and economist G. D. H. Cole (1899–1959), Kingsley Martin (1897–1969), editor of the New Statesman between 1931 and 1960, and many other socialist intellectuals, hopeful for non-violent change.

While Marshall and his contemporaries recognised that some forms of production would show a tendency to diminishing returns, the main belief was that many of the main forms of production, given the right inputs of education, technical know-how and investment would show a tendency to increasing returns to scale. The widespread introduction of mass production techniques following on the pioneering work of Henry Ford (1863–1947) in America, and William Morris, later Lord Nuffield (1877–1963) and others in England, in the early motor industry, seemed to confirm the trend. Marshall came to believe in a gradual autonomous growth of technical knowledge and of wants in society, which would build up as the new physical possibilities of resources and income, available for the employment and the satisfaction of the workforce, grew. He also believed that as the economic system developed man was tending to become more unselfish, and therefore more predisposed to work and more inclined to save for the future. Yet he remained aware of the continuing classical dilemma of population growth and the pressure that this represented in terms of the need for land resources to support it both for foodstuffs and mineral exploitation and in England for space to house the still growing population in towns and suburbs. The idea of new garden suburban towns far beyond the confines of the early and mid-Victorian industrial cities was being promoted by Ebenezer Howard (1880–1928) in his book *Garden Cities of Tomorrow* published in 1902, and other social reformers. Indeed Marshall suggested that rental income might once again exceed the aggregate of income derived from all other forms of material property.

Regarding international trade, Marshall was well aware of longer-run problems, which continue to have great meaning to our present age. Throughout much of the second half of the 19th century, notwithstanding the long depression which had borne especially harshly on rural people of the mid 1870s to 1890s, world trade and commerce had expanded rapidly, on the basis of *laissez-faire* and on Britain's industrial, financial and trading leadership in many parts of the world. However America, Germany, France and other industrial nations were also developing rapidly, and only gradually and intermittently shedding protectionist attitudes and policies. Towards the end of the century an upsurgence of imperialistic sentiments meant that all the major industrial powers were looking for colonies to acquire, where it was hoped that raw materials would be abundant, labour was cheap, markets unlimited and profitability high. However Marshall saw that those primary agricultural and mineral producing countries, which had surplus raw materials to sell, could eventually obtain 'an upper hand' in international bargains, and that the old industrial countries might eventually have to face a cyclical deterioration in their terms of trade; that is the ratio of export to import prices. He also foresaw the growing competition of manufactured exports from the less developed world, where lower labour costs would more than compensate for 'technical inferiority'. The example of the development of India's cotton textile industry which for long had been restricted in the interests of Lancashire and of Japan's growing competitive industrial strength, were very much in mind. In general however, the neo-classical school simply extended and refined Ricardo's doctrine of comparative costs. They stressed the advantages of international trade to a country, and its effects on raising real national incomes. They looked to the opening of new markets and the foreign trade which allows a nation to reap the benefits of further international specialisation in a division of labour.

The resulted increase in income would also create a larger volume of saving, and raise the worldwide possibilities of further capital investment and wealth creating processes. They were, however, conscious of problems associated with the supply of raw materials and the spread of technology abroad.

Marshall also foresaw the continued development of trade between the major industrial countries, (such as has expanded enormously in the post-Second World War years), but took the view that labour and capital would inevitably tend to be more mobile within its own country than to other countries, where linguistic and cultural obstacles needed to be overcome. From early on he had been particularly interested in the 'infant industry' argument as it had been applied in the United States, and was to be increasingly applied in other developing industrial nations as well, including the British dominions of Canada, Australia, New Zealand and South Africa. He considered that tariffs to protect local industries might be justified where the income developed by a few high cost progressive industries could eventually be spread by introducing new external cum internal economics of scale, over a greater part of the industrial system of the whole country. Nevertheless he believed that free trade, like honesty, generally remained the best policy.

In sum, the Anglo–Saxon neo-classical tradition, as developed by Marshall and others before the outbreak of the First World War, reflected an optimistic liberal view of future development and wealth making possibilities. The Edwardian 'Indian summer' of the upswing in mood from the 1900s onwards nourished a strong euphoria amongst the possessing classes; of the possibilities of economic improvement without anyone having to actually give up what they already had. In this it was a world away from the dismal prescriptions of Malthus and Ricardo, the struggle for survival of Spencer, the hopefully liberal 'stationary state' of Mill, or the revolutionary historical determinism cum revolutionary turmoil of Marx. It assumed continued political and social evolution and beneficial change, and importantly the absence of wars between the great civilised industrial powers. It also assumed that in industrial populations there would persist a will to work and develop, combined with habits of thrift and a steady build-up of adequate education and labour skills. It believed that labour, certainly within countries, tended to be mobile to the best opportunities, and there would be a rapid flow of knowledge to new situations. It emphasised 'qualitative improvements in population', in the gradual widening and deepening of the capital stock, in the finding of new raw materials and improvements in the techniques of manufacture. The neo-classical doctrine probably failed to recognise adequately the influence of destabilising influences including labour unrest at home and imperialistic rivalry abroad and to depend overly on economic rationality of judgement. It believed in the ability of the price mechanism within the context of a modern industrial society, to strike the right balance between present savings and future investment needs. It certainly looked upon the rate of interest as a key determinant between the present savings and future investment in wealth generating activities. It assumed that in the long term, harmonious development was possible, with an underlying assumption, in line with Say's 'law of markets', that an economy naturally tended to full employment and maximum income, within the constraints of existing slowly developing stocks of technology, basic raw materials and knowledge, etc. It was the apparent failure of this assumption, the failure of supply to create automatically its own demand, which, in the 1930s led to the major schism in Western neo-classical economic thinking, and the development of the Keynesian model which advocated a more interventionist role for financial demand management in the economy as a whole. Thus in the development of economic doctrine, the effect of Keynes was to shift the balance of interest away from supply questions which had so pre-occupied most classical and neo-classical thinkers, towards the maintenance of demand questions which had first been mooted by the 'under-consumption' fears of Malthus and Sismondi, and later, in their different ways, by Marx and Hobson.

All these many and complex developments eventually brought into sharp focus the possible contribution of the mathematical/statistical aspects of economics as well. Indeed while much of the original work in these areas by the Italian mathematical economist Vilfredo Pareto and others had been concerned with supply questions – as the impact of the 'Keynesian message' became felt the mathematical basis of dynamic macro equilibrium became more critical, to both theoretical thinking and public policy debate. In Britain much of this work was early associated with Sir Roy Harrod, and the data developed by the National Institute of Economic and Social Research. In turn this has become part and parcel of the way the present 'Keynesian economy' is managed, regarded and judged by the world at large.

The relationship between longstanding ideas of money and the Keynesian revolution is therefore the next step in our examination of the development of economic debates and doctrine through time.

## Money and the Keynesian Revolution 1930 onwards

As any economic and social system begins to move away from a simple state of pure barter, some form of money, in its purest form as a neutral means of exchange and hopefully as a store of value, becomes essential. Whether man enjoys this dependence on money is a question of some controversy. For Marx money represented 'the alienated essence of man's work and being; this alien essence dominates him; and he adores it'. Whatever the theory, in practice money must be in some finite and scarce form, not easily reproducible, but sufficiently compact to provide security of store and easy mobility of movement. Indeed, in his desires for money man has normally looked for a commodity which, on the one hand may be safely kept away from the grasp of others, but paradoxically can easily be transferable to others, when a transaction is undertaken. The need for security and liquidity of wealth, in one item, is paramount. Many different goods have been tried to fulfill these somewhat contradictory wealth holding and wealth transferring needs. The author has seen an extensive use of sea shells in the upland areas of Papua New Guinea, and of the rare sea shells in the various islands of Melanesia. One reads of the use of other scarce natural commodities in some areas; salt was traditionally a form of money in those areas where it was not easily obtainable, but was nevertheless essential for human life. In early Colonial America, in Virginia and in the Carolinas, tobacco was used as a form of money. In ancient China one learns of the use of printed paper money, which was then later re-invented, by the Bank of Amsterdam in the 16th century, as a form of money and credit which became widely negotiable throughout the Low Countries and the trading centres of Europe.

In general, however, man has preferred portable wealth in the form of coins, generally made of such durable precious metals as gold, silver, copper and nickel. Ranking as one of the oldest professions in the history of mankind is that of the debaser of the coinage, either of clipping coins of some of their weight, or sometimes by sweating them. From this phenomenon. came Sir Thomas Gresham's, dictum as a financial adviser to Queen Elizabeth I that 'bad money drives out good'. By this he meant that when a debased and a good currency circulate together people tend to hoard the good, and try to pass on the bad in repayment of debts. The rush in recent times of international speculators in and out of gold and various international currencies reflects an updated version of shrewd Sir Thomas's law.

In early 18th century France a peripatetic Scottish financier, one John

Law (1671–1729) had founded the Banque Génerale in 1716 which became a Royal Bank two years later – issuing paper currency. Having acquired a monopoly of trade with Louisianna in 1717 he established a vast stock company, which merged with the Bank in 1720. Excessive uncontrolled speculation led to frenzied buying and selling and ruin for many – together with Law's rapid departure for other less threatening scenes. Meantime back home in Scotland, much of the liquid wealth of the Highland Chiefs was kept in the form of gold and silver buttons, which were both conveniently on hand as a store of value, and at the same time were readily cut-offable and usable as a means of exchange. Certainly, buttons were infinitely more portable and useful as a liquid form of wealth than the Chief's other form of wealth, which depended primarily on his standing as a leader of the Clan, and its communal ownership of large herds of cattle and sheep.

Dr. Samuel Johnson (1709–1784), during his famous travels with James Boswell (1740–1793) in the Western Isles and the Hebrides between August and November 1773, commented on many aspects of life, from 'uneasiness of discipline, to resentment of exaction, rents and emigration' – following the disasters of the '45 uprising and the subsequent Hanovarian inspired land clearances. These led to the mass exodus of Highland people abroad, notably to the North Americas, and led Johnson to remark adversely on the governmental policies which had 'made a desert and called it peace'. Boswell commented on some of the other economic and social changes thus:

> "In the Islands, as in most other places, the inhabitants are of different rank, and one does not encroach here upon another. Where there is no commerce nor manufacture, he that is born poor can scarcely become rich; and if none are able to buy estates, he that is born to land cannot annihilate his family by selling it. This was once the state of these countries. Perhaps there is no example, till within a century and half, of any family whose estate was alienated otherwise than by violence or forfeiture. Since money has been brought amongst them, they have found, like others, the art of spending more than they receive; and I saw with grief the chief of a very ancient clan, whose Island was condemned by law to be sold for the satisfaction of his creditors."

Again the lack of coin on many of the Islands to pay rents, and the implications of the existence of money for social usage, and customs is also commented upon:

> "The payment of rent in kind has been so long disused in England, that it is totally forgotten. It was practised very lately in the Hebrides, and

probably still continues, not only in St. Kilda, where money is not yet known, but in others of the smaller and remoter Islands. It was perhaps to be desired, that no change in this particular should have been made. When the Laird could only eat the produce of his lands, he was under the necessity of residing upon them; and when the tenant could not convert his stock into more portable riches, he could never be tempted away from his farm, from the only place where he could be wealthy. Money confounds subordination, by overpowering the distinctions of rank and birth, and weakens authority by supplying power of resistance, or expedients for escape. The feudal system is formed for a nation employed in agriculture, and has never long kept its hold where gold and silver have become common."

In the expanding world of commercial, and later, industrial capitalism, the wide extension of the use of bank notes in Lowland Scotland and in England became a critical step towards a more flexible monetary based economy. From its original foundation in 1694 the Bank of England was a highly innovative institution in developing the use of paper money and credit creation, as a national asset backed for many years, except during periods of crises and war, by a fixed relationship and convertibility with gold. Throughout the 19th century the Bank of England's role, both domestically and internationally, was greatly extended and defined. It came to include the means by which the amount of credit made available through the associated Joint Stock banks were controlled by the use of the bank rate and by open market operations. Again the note issue of the English and Scottish banks after the passing of the Bank Charter Act, 1844, became the main source of legal tender available in Britain. In fact between 1820 and 1860 there was an ongoing public debate by members of the 'currency school' led by Robert Torrens, a friend of both Malthus and Ricardo, against the views of the 'banking school'. The latter held, against the terms of the 1844 Act, that the total number of notes in circulation would best be regulated by competition between the banks – and would vary according to the needs of trade. Nevertheless the example of the functioning of the Bank of England in relation to the Joint Stock banks, was later used as the model for the development of central banking in most other countries in the Western world. In America the creation of the Federal Reserve System in 1914 marked the eventual adoption of a strong central banking system, originally unsuccessfully advocated by the First Secretary of the Treasury, Alexander Hamilton (1757–1804), to the needs of that rapidly expanding *laissez-faire* economy.

*     *     *     *     *

In classical economic doctrine, money was assumed to have four functions: a means of exchange; a measure of value; a standard for deferred payments and a store of value. However in the day to day use of money its function as a 'means of exchange' and as a 'store of value' (at least in the short term), has most meaning. The neo-classical quantity theory of money, as further developed by Professor Irving Fisher at Yale in the early years of the 20th century, asserted that the general price level depended on the amount of money in circulation and it was usually formulated in terms of a quantity equation: $MV = PT$ where M is the quantity of money (including bank deposits) and V is the velocity of circulation of money: that is, the average number of times which a unit of money is spent during a defined period for a quantity of goods and services, T whose average price is P. The equation stated that the total quantity of money spent in a period MV is equal to the volume of transactions multiplied by the price of each transaction. It is therefore essentially a truism and did not show a causal connection between the variables in the equation. Nevertheless it did provide a rudimentary outline of the problems involved in money in that it was obviously true that the supply of money has some influence on price level and may be well significant a cause of monetary inflation.

For the neo-classical economists the price of money, as reflected in the rate of interest, maintained an equilibrium between a total community's savings and its investment activities. Money was essentially passive, reflecting simply the willingness of holders of money to retain it against a particular rate of interest. However if the rate of interest rose they would be prepared to forgo liquidity for the satisfaction of a particular rate of return. Throughout much of the second half of the 19th century and well into the 20th century the yield on consols, i.e. undated British Government Stocks, was $2\frac{1}{2}$ per cent – an adequate return in a non inflationary age. In the total working of the economy the traditional view of the passive, facilitating role of money saw Say's law of markets linking micro ideas of firm and industry equilibrium, to what Keynes later saw as *macro* needs for maintaining overall aggregate demand. What was good for the individual, in striking a balance between present consumption and forgoing by saving for investment and future reward, was also held, via the medium of passive money and the rate of interest, to be good for the firm, the industry and for the economy as a whole. Internationally it was also assumed, before 1914 and between 1925 and 1931, through the medium of the gold standard and later through the possibility of exchange rate adjustments, that a balance of payments on international account, would be maintained.

Say's law of markets – of supply creating an equivalent demand – had, as we have seen, been held and reiterated by the leading economic thinkers from Ricardo onwards. Indeed as Keynes aptly put it 'Ricardo had conquered England just as surely as the Holy Roman Inquisition conquered Spain'. However the prolonged depression, or slump in economic activity, which developed after the First World War, caused profound questioning about the overall functioning of the economic and industrial system. In the United Kingdom there was a persistence of high levels of unemployment, which between 1921 and 1940 did not fall below 10 per cent, and in many areas, struck by the decline of the old staple industries, cotton textiles, ship-building, heavy machinery and coal mining etc., persisted at 20 to 40 per cent levels. The neo-classical solution to these high levels of employment was to suggest that wage rates had been artificially inflated during the First World War and that once these had been adjusted down to their real wage level, the economy would move back into an 'equilibrium state', matching the real resources readily available on the supply side, with the aggregate market needs on the demand side.

The British 'illness' was further confused, by no means for the last time, by the fact that during this period the £ Sterling was maintained, after restoring the gold standard in 1925, at a relatively high rate of exchange against the dollar (£1 to $4.87), which kept imports cheaper than they might otherwise have been and exports more expensive. The acceptance of this rate by the then Chancellor of the Exchequer, Mr. Winston Churchill (1874–1965), occasioned Keynes to write a famous essay on *The Economic Consequences of Mr. Churchill*. Indeed an underlying reason for the National Strike in 1926 and the way in which it was handled by the Government, led by the Conservative Prime Minister Mr. Stanley Baldwin (1867–1947), was the classically derived belief that the answer to the economy's problems could be achieved by reducing the average wages of mine workers by some 10 per cent – this would therefore enable British coal to become competitive once again in overseas markets. It is an indication of the change in circumstances that at that time coal exports were still regarded as being essential to Britain's overseas trade. In 1924 some 260m tons of coal had been produced, of which some 75m tons had gone for export. However many influential people felt that if the £ Sterling exchange rate was adjusted in a downwards direction this would have created unprecedented problems on the External account, especially for the Bank of England in relation to overseas holders of sterling. Since the creation of the national debt in the 17th century the British Government has never 'defaulted', unlike virtually every other major banking system, at one time or another.

Throughout the 1920s the gradual loss of faith in the working of the competitive *laissez-faire* equilibrium model became particularly reflected in the writings of John Maynard Keynes. Keynes, a Cambridge economist and contemporary and friend of Bertrand Russell, the philosopher, of Rupert Brooke (1887–1915) the poet, and others of the Bloomsbury group of literati, had early come to the attention of the public at large with his devastating inside critique of the Versailles Peace Treaty – *The Economic Consequences of the Peace* (1919). In this the activities of the Big Four and especially David Lloyd George (1863–1945), the British Prime Minister, received astringent criticism. Keynes' increasingly critical views of the course of political and economic events were expressed in newspaper articles and in his two volume *Treatise on Money* published in 1930, and later in his *General Theory* published in 1936 he suggested that the old ideas of equilibrium needed to be abandoned. Keynes suggested the need to reject Say's law of markets and for positive intervention by government to encourage aggregate demand to restore an equilibrium, with unused underemployed supply possibilities. At this time the widespread existence of unemployed workers, machines and immense surplus stocks of coal above ground and other raw materials, were apparent for all to see. In the circumstances of this time he suggested that the Government, rather than run a financial surplus or seek to balance its Budget, should in fact be prepared to run a deficit, a proposal against all the canons of sound finance, as supported by traditional neo-classical economic doctrines. Indeed in 1929 the British Treasury had published a refutation of policies then advocated by the former Liberal wartime Prime Minister and statesman, Mr. Lloyd George, that the Treasury should be prepared to run a financial deficit to create sufficient demand to mop up persistent unemployment. In their view any demand created in this way, by expenditure on new public works, roads, buildings, etc., would simply be at the expense of real resources which should be going into the private sector. Their answer to the unemployment problems of the economy were to let wages and other costs eventually move down to their natural level so that Say's law could, in the longer run, once again begin to work. Unfortunately, as Keynes provocatively pointed out, 'in the long run we are all dead'.

A recently published life of the first Labour Prime Minister, Mr. Ramsay MacDonald (1866–1937), by Mr. David Marquand, gives a remarkable insight into how the 'economic blizzard' cum unemployment crisis affected the political, social and intellectual life of Britain in the late 1920s and early 1930s. They also go some way to illustrate the dilemmas facing Keynes and others, in the application of neo-classical doctrines to changing circumstances.

As Marquand emphasises:

> "The Trade revival which accompanied Labour's return to office lasted for nearly six months. Then the tide turned. The Wall Street crash stopped the flow of American lending which had sustained the fragile prosperity of Europe. By the early months of 1930, the worst trade depression of the century was unmistakably under way. In January 1930, 1,533,000 people were out of work, and by June 1931, two years after Mac-Donald's triumphant appearance before the crowds at King's Cross station, it had reached 2,735,000.
>
> These figures spelt suffering and degradation for the unemployed and their families and gnawing fear for millions of others who thought that they might become unemployed. For the Labour Party, which had consistently proclaimed that unemployment was the inevitable consequence of the social order which it alone was committed to transform, and which now found itself presiding over the worst increase in unemployment in living memory, they spelt failure, bitterness and a sense of guilt, all the more corroding for being unadmitted. For MacDonald, they spelt a kind of baffled anguish verging on despair."

At that time it has been suggested that when MacDonald called on George V, with whom he had a close relationship, he found his sailor monarch less than sympathetic: 'You got us into this bloody gale, now get us out of it!' – or words to that effect.

Later, following on from the Treasury's rejection of Lloyd George's ideas in the previous year:

> "Early in 1930 Sir Oswald Mosley, the young Chancellor of the Duchy of Lancaster, sent MacDonald a copy of a long memorandum on the economic situation, on which he had been at work for well over a month, and which has gone down in history as the 'Mosley Memorandum'. It made three main assertions – that the machinery of government should be drastically overhauled, that unemployment could be radically reduced by a public-works programme on the lines advocated by Keynes and the Liberal Party, and that long-term economic reconstruction required 'a mobilisation of national resources on a larger scale than has yet been contemplated'.
>
> The existing administrative structure, Mosley argued, was hopelessly inadequate. What was needed was a new department, under the direct control of the Prime Minister, consisting of an executive committee of ministers and a secretariat of civil servants, assisted by a permanent staff

of economists and an advisory council of outside experts. The immediate problem of unemployment could be solved by making road-building a national responsibility, by raising a loan of £200 million and spending it on roads and other public works over the next three years, by raising the school leaving age and by introducing earlier retirement pensions."

MacDonald greatly valued the young Mosley's support and made a conciliatory offer to him on the following lines:

"... I have had a talk with the Minister of Transport and he is as firm as ever upon (1) the utter impossibility of a purely national responsibility for the building of roads of a certain class, and also upon (2) the comparatively small effect that could be had by the application of this policy as regards the numbers on the unemployed register ... This is surely a case where *pros* and *cons* can be hammered out on the committees and in the departments concerned ...

MacDonald hoped that the explosion could somehow be contained; Mosley wanted action, not investigation – and still less compromise. He wished to save his country and believed, not wholly without cause, that he had found the way to its salvation. If the cabinet wished to adopt his plan, well and good; if not, he would rather fight than talk. The Treasury and the Ministry of Transport were equally intransigent on the other side – the Ministry of Transport, because it believed that the road proposals were unworkable, the Treasury, because it believed that a vast development loan spelt national bankruptcy.'

Again in the words of Marquand's account:

'On February 3rd, the Cabinet had a rambling and inconclusive discussion about the memorandum, and eventually referred it to a committee headed by Snowden, Chancellor of the Exchequer. After interminable delays, the committee reported back to the Cabinet on May 1, and the stage was set for one of the most remarkable struggles in recent British history.'

As was to be expected, the Snowden committee condemned the memorandum root and branch, Mosley's administrative proposals, the committee claimed 'cut at the root of the individual responsibilities of Ministers'. They could be reconciled with the principles of parliamentary government only if the proposed new department were confined to an advisory role. Though the Snowden committee did not say so in so many words, the implication was clear. State action to reduce unemployment was inherently suspect, and the Government's existing policies were already pressing against the margin of safety. To go further would be to plunge the country into ruin."

Having made his peace with Lloyd George and other Liberals an important new theoretical element that Keynes brought into this debate was to elevate the role of money from its previously passive position. His investigations supported the significance of money as a link between the past and present and the future, and he introduced the idea that individuals held money with at least three motivations in mind; for transactions, for precautionary and for speculative motives. He suggested that the demand for money reflected the liquidity preference of individuals to hold money for one of these three purposes. The supply of money was a reflection of the quantity of money which the Bank of England allowed in circulation. The price of money for investment in the total economy was the going rate of interest which at that time, given the very depressed general circumstances, was around $2\frac{1}{2}$ per cent per annum. The demand for money for investment purposes by businessmen and others was a reflection of the marginal efficiency of capital, which was influenced by their state of confidence as to expectations of the future and of the profit to be derived from investing in new machines and stocks, etc. It was also influenced by the supply price of the new machines and raw material stocks which could be purchased with money borrowed. The link between private savings and real investment in machinery was much less direct than neo-classical doctrine suggested. If business expectations of future reward were very poor, a very low rate of interest would not necessarily induce new investment. In Keynes' phrase, 'one could take the horse to water but not make it drink'.

Turning to the consumption side of the economy again, Keynes saw this as being influenced by two elements. The supply side, for money to spend, was influenced by the total size of income within the national economy, while the demand side of consumption was a reflection of 'individuals' propensity to consume'. If income was low for society and individuals, the propensity to consume beyond a certain point would also tend to be low, as they would lack confidence to run down savings and consume at the expense of their desire to hold money for precautionary motives. The 'propensity to consume' was a critical point in Keynes' new system. The individual consumer depends on both objective data about the society in which he lives and his subjective attitudes towards consumption. The objective data meant there was an important influence of income on the level of prices, Keynes felt that with the exception of changes of money income, no change in economic condition would significantly affect the propensity to consume. In a sense, Keynes' preoccupation with the need for confidence to encourage the propensity to consume by individuals, and indeed the willingness to invest by businessmen, went back to 'under-consumption theories' which both Malthus and Marx, in their different ways, saw as an Achilles heel to the *laissez-faire* market system.

Two other important concepts also underlay what later became known as the Keynesian model. First there was a multiplier, an inherent part of Keynesian theory, though it had been developed earlier by Mr. R. F. Kahn, later Lord Kahn. The essence of the multiplier is that it compared the relative size of a given initial increase in investment and the total inherent ultimate increase in income for the community as a whole. Thus the multiplier effect of any investment could have an overall increase on the income possibilities of the society. The size of the multiplier depended on the 'marginal propensity to consume', and if this was high then the multiplier was high. A second underlying consideration was the working of the accelerator which, while included in the Keynesian model, was originally the work of the American Professor J. M. Clark. Whereas the multiplier showed the effect of alteration of changes of investment on income and consumption, the accelerator shows the effect of changes of consumption on investment. Overall, the multiplier depends on consumer tastes and habits, whereas the accelerator depends on a technical principle, in the narrow sense in that it depends on the durability of machines etc.

More generally, Keynes' reputation, ranking with Adam Smith and Karl Marx, as one of the three great economists, lay in the clear break he sought to make with neo-classical theory by seeking to demonstrate both to members of his profession, to the Government and to the general public at large that the *laissez-faire* economic and industrial system could persist in an equilibrium with a large volume of under-employed resources for virtually indefinite periods of time. Before Keynes, most traditionally educated economists had, following on from Ricardo, tended to concentrate their attention on the distribution of the national product, rather than its size. Generally because of the underlying assumption of a close link between money savings and real investments, under-employment of labour, falling wage levels and falling prices for new machines, equipment and of raw materials would create forces tending to restore activity onto an upward growth path. The orthodox neo-classical thinkers had tended to explain unemployment as being due to institutional rigidities within the wage and price system, and their policy recommendations, whether they applied to labour, or for that matter to other forms of industrial collusive price fixing, were largely concerned with the removal of rigidities.

FIG. 12  KEYNESIAN MODEL FOR DEMAND MANAGEMENT OF AN ECONOMY OVER TIME

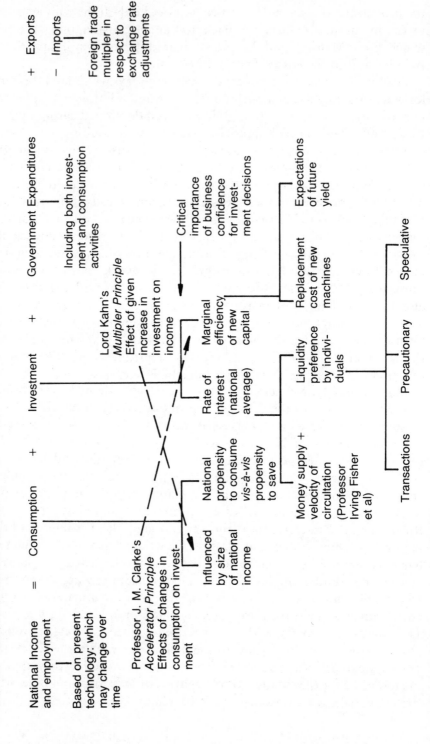

## A. Some underlying assumptions

(i) In contrast to neo-classical theory money ceases to be regarded as a 'passive link' between savings and investment.

(ii) The need for government intervention, to maintain full employment and income is recognised. (This represented a rejection of the classical Say's law of markets – that 'supply creates an equivalent demand'.)

(iii) Of reasonable supply elasticity of real resources of labour, raw materials, energy, capital goods etc. up to the point of *full employment and income*. Beyond this point 'more money chases less goods' and *inflation* applies. (Money loses its value relative to goods.)

(iv) The need for governments to manage external trade balances over time: imports and exports (both visible and invisible) need to be broadly equal, with capital transfers and loans making up the difference (e.g. U.K. resort to I.M.F. loan 1976).

(v) The fundamental assumption of trying to retain substantial elements of the flexibility assumed in the *laissez-faire* model – especially on supply side of economy (e.g. the work of N.E.D.O. committees).

## B. Some policy options, for promoting full employment, with a steady rate of growth, and reasonable balance of payments stability over time, etc.

(i) Monetary: adjust interest rates or money supply with direct controls over new lending and capital issues etc.

(ii) Fiscal: Government may budget for a deficit during recession, or a surplus during inflationary boom. It may also adjust taxation levels, both direct and indirect – and conversely put public expenditures up or down as is considered to be appropriate.

(iii) Direct controls: over wages and prices – through 'social contract' type policies, with rationing as a last resort. It may also be encouraged to apply trade controls, etc., tariffs and quotas (however it needs to conform with G.A.T.T. and E.E.C. regulations).

(iv) Exchange rate adjustments vis-a-vis other major currencies. The effectiveness of such policies depends on the working of the trade multiplier.

(v) The accelerator principle relates to the effects of changes in consumption on investment.

(vi) The multiplier principle relates to the effect of a given increase in investment on income.

(vii) The accelerator principle, the multiplier principle and the foreign trade multiplier, all influence the way the model works over time.

In his *Treatise on Money* in 1930, Keynes had begun to argue the importance of the relationship between savings and investment as an underlying cause of the trade cycle. In his general theory he 'moved on to explain the factors underlying the level of employment, at least in the shorter term'. The communities' expenditure on consumption and on investment goods determined the level of economic activity, but as incomes rose savings also tended to increase. On the other hand, a relative fall in expenditure caused the economy to spiral down into a depression. His ideas about interest, which differ from the orthodox doctrines, were widely assumed to show that the system was liable to stay in this position, unless expenditure was increased in some way. The policy recommendations which followed on from Keynes' analysis suggested that the Government, as Lloyd George and others had proposed, should be responsible for running a budget deficit to finance new public works and thus to generate expenditure that would remove unemployment, and to seek to maintain aggregate demand at a level that would create full employment. The theory also suggests that the reverse process would be capable of checking and removing inflationary conditions. This has in fact been the basis of much of the Keynesian style attempts to fine-tune the British economy since the war. In practical, economic, social and political terms, Lord Beveridge's war-time Coalition Government's White Paper on employment policy 1944, marked the acceptance of the Keynesian revolution as a basis of national policy, as reflected in the need to maintain employment levels. In America New Deal economics, and later post-war employment legislation, stemmed from a small group of economists, principally at Harvard, who gradually introduced the Keynesian message to the Roosevelt, and later Truman, administrations, in Washington. Similar ideas linked to a widespread introduction of mathematical based forecasting techniques have also been applied throughout the remainder of the Western democratic mixed economy world since the end of the Second World War.

It is important to recognise that during the interwar period, when Keynes was writing so prolifically about Britain's domestic problems, that the economy was afflicted by persistent under-use of virtually all real resources. It was therefore reasonable to assume the supply of labour, capital, management and raw materials etc. were relatively elastic, given the high degree of under-employment that obviously existed. Thus a small increase in price would bring onto the market any amount of the real resources of capital, raw materials, fuel and labour, etc., necessary to the functioning of the economic and industrial system.

Moreover Britain was still one of the most powerful industrial and trading countries in the world, with the terms of trade, during the 1930s, moving somewhat in its favour. It was able to obtain more raw materials and foodstuff imports for given exports of manufactures than had previously been the case. In fact the world depression had a generally more disastrous impact on primary producing countries than the advanced industrial countries. It is also worth emphasising that in the 1930s most of Britain's basic energy needs came from domestic coal resources, and that the coal miners had for many years been under-employed, and large unused stocks of coal lay above ground. Through-out the 1930s Britain's trade balance, taking visibles and invisibles together, was reasonably strong, and it was always possible to raise an international loan at very low rates of interest if this had been necessary. In the generally under-employed circumstances of the time the suggestion that Government intervention policy might go some way to re-creating and stimulating aggregate demand and bring onto the market readily available resources, was a reasonable policy; once Say's law had been abandoned and the assumption of the validity of always seeking to balance the budget had been dropped, as a basis of sound economic thinking. Moreover up to the point of full employment of real resources, this could be achieved without any serious threat to money as a store of value. Inflation and losses of monetary value in the terms of the 1970s had less meaning to economists and public policy makers in the 1930s. While the awful example of the great German inflation of the Weimar Republic of the early 1920s was well known, for most Anglo-Saxon economists unemployment and deflation were the 'dragons' on hand which had to be slayed.

*     *     *     *     *

Since the end of the Second World War much of the Western world has been influenced by Keynesian aggregate demand management policies. Indeed it is impossible to think about the functioning of contemporary Western democratic governments, without Keynesian concepts and policies coming to mind. For instance in the late 1950s the Radcliffe Committee (on the working of the monetary system) reported to the effect that bank rate controls should be supplemented by increased use of physical and other controls. Needless to say some thought the committee had underestimated the power of monetary policy – while others thought that it had not gone far enough in advocating physical controls, in place of interest rates and controls over the money supply. More recently, certainly from the mid-60s onwards, economists have become re-aware of underlying constraints affecting the economy which make aggregate demand management in the Keynesian way appear to be less and less effective. In particular once full employment, however defined, has been achieved, inflation and the loss of money as a store of value has become a fact of life in most Western mixed economies, in a way inconceivable to pre-war theorists, conditioned by years of stagnation and falling price levels. However of particular significance since 1973 has been the large increase in the price of crude oil, coming into the Western countries from Middle Eastern sources. Critical supply constraints have also increasingly appeared in respect of labour with higher and improved skills, and the need for modern high technology industries to constantly re-tool and upgrade investment programmes. There has also been a suggestion of a serious deterioration in capital investment output ratios in many key industries, which is a further constraint to be overcome. There is certainly a need for a constantly increasing level of research and development activity, to support the ongoing progress of industrial economies increasingly competitive with each other in both domestic and third country markets. As both Marx and Marshall foresaw, industrial, and also consumer goods, competition on a world scale places an acute strain on what Schumpeter called the 'recreative powers', of advanced technically based systems. All of these types of supply constraints Keynes was able to take as solvable, at least in the short term, in a world characterised by mass under-employment of all real resources.

In retrospect, perhaps one of the most remarkable features of 'Keynesian revolution' was the way in which it shifted, at least for a time, the balance of economic debates away from supply, to demand considerations. As indicated by Fig. 13 for much of the period from the publication of Smith's *Wealth of Nations* in 1776 to the Great Depression of the 1930s, much of economic theory had tended to concentrate on questions of cost. For Smith the way ahead had been seen in promoting a division of labour in new manufacturing systems, which would enable a rapidly increasing population to escape the limitations of life and the 'diminishing returns' inherent in agriculture. The Malthusian dilemma of population outrunning subsistence never fully applied in the Western world. However, for Ricardo and later for Marx the impact of steam power and new technologies signalled the possibility of rapid development in the industrial system, though for the latter, historical determinism and the need for violent change into a

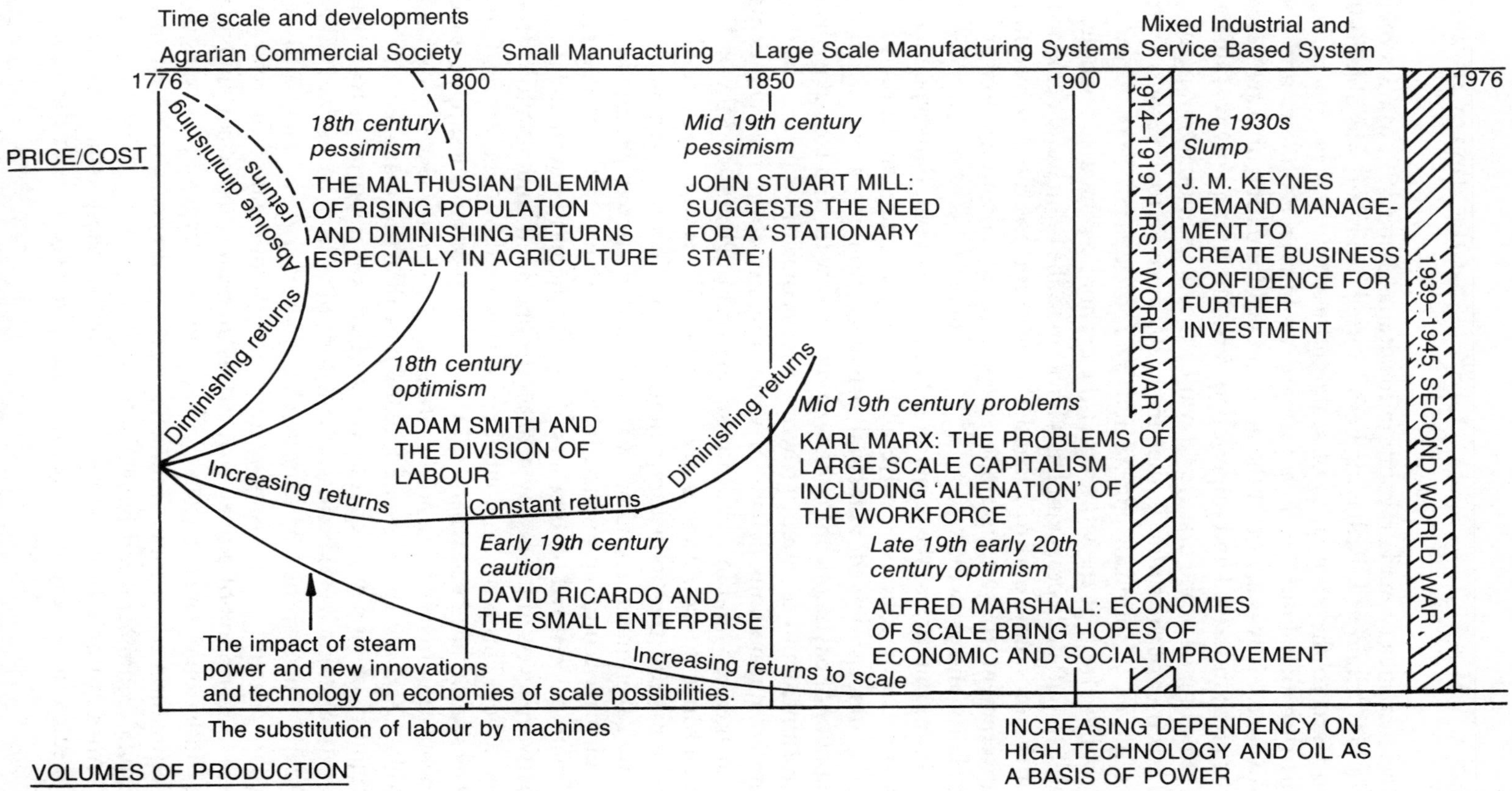

FIG 13. THREE COST CURVES UNDERLYING THE GREAT DEBATES 1776–1976

socialist society made revolution inevitable. Later still, Marx's revolution in Britain at least having been averted, Marshall was able to look forward to the economies of scale and extension of the international division of labour, leading forward to further economic and social advance. He was aware of the need for a continuation of peace between the great industrial and Imperial powers. This tranquility was shattered by the impact of the first world war on the international trading system. The onset of the slump in the late 1920s forced a total reconsideration of the easy optimism engendered by neo-classical ideas. Keynes, by looking afresh at the working of the economic system as a whole, was able to put intellectual emphasis back on to the money and demand side of the economy, and to suggest the need for positive intervention by government to sustain employment and to encourage longer term stability and growth.

In recent years the apparent failure of Keynesian type demand management policies to solve all the problems inherent in the running of a modern mixed industrial urban economy – from inflation to balance of payments difficulties, to runaway wage and lack of industrial investment and economic growth – has become the subject of lively and indeed acrimonious debate, at various points of the financial demand management and interventionist spectrum. Professor Milton Friedman's first *Wincott Memorial Lecture* of 1970 is widely regarded as the beginning of the 'monetary counter' revolution – suggesting that the way government spending was financed mattered greatly in determining its economic impact. In particular much of the contemporary debate has centred on two sets of issues, one has been the relationship between levels of unemployment on the one hand, and inflation rates on the other. This has commonly been represented by 'The Philips Curve'. The second has been whether, by the control of money supply, governments can directly influence inflation rates and inter alia employment as well. Certainly the view of Friedman is that the management of the quantity of money in circulation is of critical importance to inflation levels, and much else besides. At the time of writing (Autumn 1977) Dr. Arthur Burns in his capacity as chairman of the U.S. Federal Reserve Board is actively exposing a strong opinion of the need for restraint in 'the recent burst of money growth', as an attack on the continued level of 'inflationary expectations'. In his view, these type of expectations are detrimental to business confidence and a willingness to invest in new capital equipment and plant, etc.

An admirable brief summary of many of these issues, as they are reflected in the United Kingdom and to some extent in the U.S.A., in both a practical and doctrinal sense, is given by Mr. G. D. N. Worswick, in his Lloyds Bank Review articles, January 1977, *The End of Demand Management*. As Worswick points out in his summary of demand management, in post-war Britain:

> "The rationalisation of unemployment in a capitalist economy was hardly new. The Marxian theory of capitalist crisis had been available for a long time. The Keynesian theory, however, had two great advantages. First, it could be conveniently presented in terms of the newly emergent system of national income accounting, which lent itself to quantitative analysis. Secondly, it offered a programme of practical action within the capitalist economy, by contrast with the Marxian analysis which seemed to offer no alternative to the destruction of the existing system and the construction of a totally new one."

Mr. Worswick concludes that:

> "My conclusion is that, if the limited role of demand management in securing full employment is recognised, and it is buttressed by other instruments of policy, above all incomes policy, one can envisage the return to low unemployment and low inflation. But it is quite wrong to believe that there exists some ideal demand management technique, whether discretionary or the application of some simple budgetary or monetary rule, which alone would do the job."

Finally the point about the General Theory was not that it provided a final solution – but that it gave a new start.

Chapter 3

# TRADE, DEVELOPMENT AND GROWTH

---

"A war and traffic are incompatible. Let this be received as a rule that if you will profit, seek it at sea, and in quiet trade; for without controversy it is an error to affect garrisons and land-wars in India."

> Sir Thomas Roe
> Ambassador for James I (1566–1625)
> To the Court of the Mogul Emperor

"To found a great empire for the sole purpose of raising up a people of customers, may at first sight appear a project fit only for a nation of shopkeepers. It is, however, a project altogether unfit for a nation of shopkeepers; but extremely fit for a nation that is governed by shopkeepers."

> Adam Smith (1723–1790)
> *Wealth of Nations*

"My celestial Kingdom has no need for the trinkets of foreign Barbarians."

> *Translation of a reply from the Manchu to the request from envoys of George III (1738–1820) for trade concessions in China.*

"The Continent will not suffer England to be the workshop of the world."

> Benjamin Disraeli (1804–1881)
> Speech, House of Commons, 15 March 1838

"Protection is not a principle, but an expedient."

> Ibid 17 March 1845

"Wake up, England."

> *Title of a reprint in 1911 of a speech made by the*
> *King when Prince of Wales in the Guildhall on 5 Dec*
> *1901 on his return from a tour of the Empire.*

"I venture to allude to the impression which seemed generally to prevail among their brethren across the seas, that the old country must wake up if she intends to maintain her old position of pre-eminence in her colonial trade against foreign competitors."

> George V of Great Britain (1865–1936)
> Speech

"Quinquireme of Nineveh from distant Ophir
Rowing home to haven in sunny Palestine,
With a cargo of ivory,
And apes and peacocks,
Sandalwood, cedarwood, and sweet white wine.

Dirty British coaster with a salt-caked smoke stack,
Butting through the Channel in the mad March days,
With a cargo of Tyne coal,
Road-rail, pig-lead,
Firewood, iron-ware, and cheap tin trays."

> John Masefield (1878–1967)
> *Cargoes*

## Protectionism or *laissez-faire*

The relationship between the domestic economy and overseas trade has already been referred to, in various contexts. In the middle ages the Northern German Hanseatic League organised the trading activities of most seaports on the Baltic and North Sea Coasts. At the same time mercantilistic trade philosophies increasingly assumed that the amount of world trade available was finite and that the nation state could best pursue its interests by seeking to acquire, at the expense of its competitors, as much of the going trade as possible. Wealth accruing from trade could be held in the form of bullion, a store of value which could be readily used, at a later date, to purchase what ever the nation wished to have, notably, throughout most of 16th to 18th centuries, munitions and ships of war and the employment of large mercenary armies. Among mercenary soldiers the poverty struck, but willing-to-travel Scots, Irish and Swiss were most highly regarded. Later in the scramble for Eastern empires, all the great European trading companies relied on locally recruited mercenary troops. In economic doctrine we especially associate such mercantilistic policies with the 'age of discovery' and of the European nation states pursuing their expansionist rivalries through piracy and plunder and the creation of monopolistic trading companies such as the Hudson Bay Company and East India Company. These great enterprises pre-dated the emergence of more *laissez-faire* free trade philosophies in the 19th century; initially in Britain under the influence of Smith and Ricardo, and finally, more spasmodically in other parts of Western Europe, and the U.S.A. as well.

Throughout much of the 19th century two governmental philosophies cum trade policies increasingly supported Western Europe and American expansion, and have therefore influenced our thinking about economic development to the present day. One, we have seen, was the Adam Smith and Ricardian inspired ideas of free trade involving the abolition of tariff barriers to exports or imports. This was the reversal of the protectionism associated with mercantilism, which had dated back to the Middle Ages. Associated with this move to *laissez-faire* was the adoption by Great Britain, and later by other countries, of the gold standard, and the increasing valuation of major currencies, and in particular the £ Sterling in terms of a given weight of gold. This persisted as a fully convertible reserve currency until Britain finally moved off the gold standard in response to the domestic and international circumstances of the great depression, in 1931. Between 1914 and 1925 Britain was off the gold standard as an emergency wartime cum post-war measure. The domestic implications of Britain's return, and eventual abandonment, of the gold standard, have already been discussed in the previous sections on Keynes and his influence.

\*     \*     \*     \*     \*

Free trade was first fully adopted by England with the Repeal of the Corn Laws in 1846, and the final triumph of the Manchester Free Trade School, over the agricultural protectionist landowning interests. Again the scrapping of the historic Navigation Acts in 1849 marked the end of some 200 years of protective measures in the colonial shipping trade. Britain as a nation, based on the rapidly increasing productivity of new textile, metal manufacturing and shipbuilding industries in, Manchester and in the Midlands; on the Tyne and Tees and Clydebank in Scotland, increasingly enjoyed the beginnings of extremely lucrative markets abroad, combined at the same time with little or no competition at home from foreign competitors. Gradually other Western European countries also came to believe that free trade was the magical means by which Britain had been able to put herself far ahead in industrial and commercial development, and in turn sought to follow her lead, lowering their own tariff barriers during the 1850s and 1860s. In particular the move to free trade within different parts of Western Europe was associated with the Zollverien, a tariff or customs union of independent sovereign states, establishing a common fiscal policy, between themselves and against the rest of the world. This had been created in 1833 when Prussia agreed, with four other leading German states, to abandon tariffs against each other's goods, and maintain a uniform external tariff. By the middle 1830s, with the exception of the three Hanseatic cities and the three major states, Austria, Hanover and Oldenburg, Germany was for most purposes an increasingly unified economic union. Uniform currency, weights and measures followed, which eventually completed the union, and after the success of Prussia against the Hapsburgs and Austria in 1866, and against the France of Napoleon III in 1870, became the basis of a creation of a greater Germany under the leadership of the House of Hohenzollern, which lasted until the overthrow of the regime in 1918. Again the former British colonies in Canada, following the Durham Report of 1849, and Australia, following Federation in 1901, abandoned trade barriers and established common currencies, etc., with each other. However the former colonies were later to erect tariffs as a means of promoting industrial development. Finally the Imperial Preference systems, which applied between Britain and the Commonwealth from 1931 onwards, and also the European Economic Community, from the late 1950s onwards, also shows some of the characteristics of a Zollverein.

It would be wrong to suggest, however, that free trade in the mid-19th century had a triumphant or easy progress amongst the developing industrial nations. There were often periods of marked revision from free trading policies, particularly as Continental manufacturers became increasingly aware, that during periods of trade depression they were unable to meet the competition of inexpensive foreign products in their own markets. At about this time the Prussian economist and Civil Servant, Friedrich List (1789–1846), the inventor of 'national economics', was warning Europe against the 'crafty and spiteful' commercial policy of England who wish to deny others the use of state power which had, in his view, established her commercial leadership. The onset of widespread and repeatedly serious business and trade fluctuations, affecting the economies of many countries, was a phenomenon in which Marx was to show great interest.

FIG. 14   THE EVOLUTION OF THE INTERNATIONAL ECONOMY, IN BROAD TERMS 1776–1976

| Broad Periods and Main Themes | Nature of International Monetary System | Degree of Freedom for International Trade | Degree of Freedom for International Capital Movement | Pace of Technological Change | Efficiency of Resources Allocation | Labour Markets | Government Policies | Investment Incentives |
|---|---|---|---|---|---|---|---|---|
| 1776–1815 The Gradual abandonment of mercantilism. | An era still dominated by mercantile conflicts and the Napoleonic Wars | Greatly hindered by wars and by mercantilistic traditions. | Very restricted and limited to mercantile trade links. | Beginnings of 'Agricultural and Industrial Revolutions' heralds technical change possibilities. | Restricted by nature of era. Communications and trasport difficulties. | Tended to restrictive and dominated by combinations and dominance of underlying agrarian system. | Dominated by war and revolutionary threats. Growing awareness of population growth for economic development. | The move from a mercantile agrarian to industrial society. Total uncertainty inhibits investment in new technologies. |
| 1815–1870 The Gradual Triumph of laissez-faire. | Congress of Vienna assures peace in Europe. Gold standard (£) gradually became basis of value | Corn Laws in Britain restricted trade between 1815 and 1846. Mercantile and agrarian protectionism persisted elsewhere. | Beginnings of international investment flows. | Industrial development stemming from Britain's Industrial Revolution gathers momentum. | Beginnings of greater efficiency in international division of labour. | Laissez-faire philosophies used against combinations and unions. | Increasing adoption of laissez-faire attidues towards labour in many countries. | Growing confidence stemming from extension of peace in Western Europe and elsewhere. |
| 1870–1913 A mixture of laissez-faire and national development protectionism policies | Gold (£) standard. Rigid exchange rate – wage flexibility. (Deflation biased). | Very free. Rise of tariffs in the second half. | Almost completely free. | Mainly process innovation. Slow growth in lead countries. | International allocation helped by free trade and factor movement. | Weak unions – wages flexible downwards. | No concern with unemployment. | Basic longterm stability fosters investment. Longterm instability hinders it. |

| | | | | | | | | |
|---|---|---|---|---|---|---|---|---|
| **1914–1920** | *The First World War brings controls and emergency measures* | | | | | | | |
| **1920–1938** The era of autarchy and stagnation. Low growth in output and restricted trade. | Gold exchange standard collapsed 1931. Fluctuating rates – large debt. | Tariffs and quantitative restrictions. | Severe controls. | Low rate of capital growth – process innovation re-inforced by product innovation. | International allocation marred by restriction on trade and capital movement. | Governments try to enforce downward flexibility resulting in social conflict. | Concerned with price and exchange rate stability – acceptance of unemployment. | Longterm and shortterm instability hinders investment. |
| **1939–1950** | *The Second World War brings controls and emergency measures* | | | | | | | |
| **1950–1970** The return to free trade. The era of G.A.T.T. and high growth in output and trade. | Gold ($) standard and fixed but not rigid rates. Ample credit (8). | Liberalisation of trade and move towards customs unions. | Gradual freeing of labour and capital movements. | Dynamic – reinforced by backlogs. Product and process innovation. R. & D. increasing. | Efficiency helped by liberalisation of trade and capital movement. | Stronger unions – no downward flexibility – social climate relaxed. | Priority given to high employment. | Favourable longterm and shortterm prospects and financial stability and low real interest rate. High investment. |
| **1970–1976** The fears of a strong return to protectionism accompanying slower growth. 'The energy crises' years 1973 onwards. | Floating rates since 1971/73. | Free trade maintained – spread of restrictions outside G.A.T.T. since 1975. | Free capital movement but restriction on labour. | Pace checked and some deterioration in output to capital ratios. | Efficiency inhibited by low capacity utilisation. | Strong unions – strong upward bias in wage expectation. | More emphasis on price stability than unemployment. | Shortterm and longterm instability hinder investment. |

*Source:* compiled jointly by T. M. Rybczynski and J. Hutton, 1977.

Classical economists thought of trade fluctuations as deriving mainly from natural causes, such as seasonal factors and disasters which affected food supplies and prices. However Marx was more impressed with the idea that capitalism itself, its organisation, structure and behaviour, was prone to instabilities. He believed that capitalism on a worldwide basis was inevitably subject to fluctuations, which would eventually lead to its destruction through social revolution, and an evolution into a Socialist, and later a Communist, world. In fact during the 1870s, faced by deteriorating trade, several Continental nations reverted to protectionist policies. This was particularly initiated by manufacturing interests in the less or barely industrialised nations at the time, notably Russia, Spain and Italy, and was later followed up by protective measures being re-adopted by an increasingly united Greater Germany and also by France.

In a number of Western European countries the agricultural interests joined industrialists in lobbying for government protection against foreign competition. Farmers were prepared to support *laissez-faire* trade policies as long as they were seen to produce a surplus for export, and enable them to buy foreign farm machinery and other consumer goods cheaper. However when, from the 1870s onwards, Russia and the United States began selling increasing quantities of grain to Western European markets, the domestic agricultural system was threatened and a Continental crisis, affecting both agriculture and industry, persisted. It was clear that the claims of the farmers for protection against cheaper foodstuffs from elsewhere frequently found a sympathetic hearing from governments. During the second half of the 19th century physiocratic notions of the need for nations to be as self-sufficient in food production frequently re-asserted themselves. Governments felt that diminished home food production would necessarily render them both subject to domestic political pressures and more vulnerable in time of war. Moreover the desire to raise revenue via import tariffs for more public works, for social reforms and for the support of the growing industries, also affected policy.

Thus many countries gradually re-introduced some form of tariff protection for domestic, industrial and agricultural interests during the second half of the 19th century. Only in Great Britain, Belgium and Holland, where industrialisation and widespread commercial trading was most established, was there a strong resistance towards the swing back to trade protectionism; and indeed in these countries the industrial and commercial urban interests tended to outweigh agrarian concerns. Nevertheless in Great Britain the plight of the rural poor in Ireland,

Scotland, Wales and even in the Eastern counties, remained a persistent cause for social and political concern. The main classical economics solution was the massive emigration of the unemployed or displaced rural poor to the New World, Australasia, Southern Africa and elsewhere.

\* \* \* \* \*

Some of the complexities of the relationship between money and the domestic working of an economy in the neo-classical and the contemporary Keynesian demand management economy have already been referred to. Concerning money and its relationship to international trade, it is of great importance that in 1816 Britain had adopted the standard relationship which defined the £ Sterling as an equivalent of 113 grains of gold. At the time this moving on to a 'gold standard' was in marked contrast to the situation applying in the other Western European countries, which had entered the industrial age maintaining extremely confused, and out-of-date systems of finance. However gradually, with increased industrialisation, came monetary reform and then, as the industrial nations became increasingly wealthy, saw the discovery and exploitation of great new deposits of gold in California, Australia, New Zealand, Alaska, South Africa, and elsewhere. During the second half of the 19th century and certainly from the 1870s onwards, most of the major industrial nations were able to accumulate gold reserves, and to define their currency in that metal which made possible the orderly settlement of international accounts. This meant that a trader holding a standard currency – pounds, francs, marks or dollars – could turn it into gold, or into another currency on demand. At the same time the universal move into a more uniform form of monetary system led to a wide recognition of a new phenomenon, which became known as the world economic cycle. As Marx had perceived, with the rise of modern capitalism came trade fluctuations and crises, which could no longer be simply attributable to catastrophes of nature or, as Jevons suggested, to sun spots and their effects on harvests, and in turn on food prices and industrial costs and production. In fact, as industrial and trading activities became more widely extended, financial crises were no longer confined to single countries or areas, as the previous agricultural crises had generally been, but were felt throughout the whole commercial world. One of the first of such crises mainly attributable to the nature of capitalism per se developed from the collapse in 1875 of an insurance company in New York. Several American banks closed, railways went into bankruptcy and some thousands of smaller firms eventually collapsed. These catastrophes in turn affected the prices of raw materials and agricultural products, and within a few months the effect of the 'New York' crisis was noted in the industrial areas of Northern Britain and Scotland, Germany and France, and eventually in Russia and Latin America. So integrated had the world capitalist economy become that a financial crisis and collapse in one place starting from apparently minor beginnings, could soon send reverberations around the world. However the more optimistic neo-classical economists, taking the lead from Marshall, felt that the long-term path was upwards, and that, notwithstanding intermittent financial, commercial and industrial crises, the long-term trend to growth, given the necessary disciplines of thrift and application to task, should follow a steadily upward path.

*     *     *     *     *

During the 20th century controversy between *laissez-faire* and protectionist policies and doctrines have continued unabated and in many guises. Modern trade protectionist ideas, originally considered by such influential economists as Professor F. W. Taussig at Harvard, still have a powerful influence in many parts of the world today. As we have seen in the 1920s and '30s virtually all the industrial nations, faced with the disastrous effects of the world slump on their traditional industries and trading relationships, reverted to protectionist policies, pursuing tightly controlled autarchical trade policies, including barter, and sought to balance trade on a bilateral country to country basis. The creation of the Imperial Preference system in 1931 signified a reversion by Britain and her Empire to a mutually inclusive protectionist trading system, as a means of economic survival and recovery, in an increasingly autarchial world trade situation. Since the end of the Second World War highly protectionist trade policies have been pursued in the centrally planned economies of the Soviet inspired COMECON group of countries, extending throughout the Soviet sphere of influence, from Eastern Europe to Mongolia and Cuba. In theory, at least, each socialist member state was initially expected to develop socialism in its own country, the surplus derived from domestic agriculture being used initially to finance the industrialisation of the economy as a whole. In many cases this 'do it yourself' system soon proved to be grossly inefficient and a considerable volume of mutually advantageous barter trade developed between the members of the Marxist inspired group. Nevertheless in these trading relationships with each other, much is still arranged on a virtually barter basis, using non-convertible currencies as units of account. Again, until recent years and the expansion of trade between Eastern and Western Europe, much of the Eastern Marxist economic system has remained an internal trading community drawing raw materials, coal and oil, etc., from the Soviet Union, and exporting, on a barter basis, manufactured and consumer goods in exchange.

In contrast to the protectionist self-help barter philosophy of the Soviet led group, since the end of the Second World War much of the Western world has sought to move back towards a more *laissez-faire* world trading system. Following the Keynesian inspired Bretton Woods Conference of 1944 the creation of the International Monetary Fund in 1945, and of the General Agreement on Tariffs and Trade, negotiated in Geneva in 1947, were intended to encourage an expanding free trading world, reaping the advantages of the international 'division of labour' and 'specialisation'. It is important to emphasise that the advantages of such trade were originally deemed to be most obvious between countries with tropical and temperate climes, or with complementary, as opposed to competitive, production of goods. Ricardo, for instance, originally drew particular attention to the advantageous trade between Britain and Portugal in exchanging cloth for wine. Likewise, as we have seen, much of the development of Britain's trade during the 19th century was based on exchanging raw materials and foodstuffs grown in tropical and expanding temperate colonies – Canada, Australia, New Zealand and Southern Africa – in exchange for exports of machinery and manufactures which Britain could produce more cheaply than they could. However as the populations of these nations expanded, a considerable degree of local industrialisation and protection of 'infant industries' became well nigh inevitable.

The classical Ricardian principle of comparative cost or advantage is that, under given technological conditions, the increased product obtainable by 'specialisation' and 'exchange', rather than from a policy of 'self-sufficiency' and economic isolation, will be maximised when each country or region specialises in the production of these goods and services in which its 'comparative advantage' is largest (that is, its comparative cost of production is least). The principle of comparative advantage will pay only if the ratio between production costs differs in the two countries concerned. This qualification is necessary as trade itself may cause cost ratios to change, making trade less, or more, worthwhile. Clearly in contemporary circumstances many industrial and consumer goods produced in different countries are differentiated by branding and design differences, and trade may be deemed to be worthwhile even though cost ratios are the same. These types of goods,

FIG. 15 GROWTH RATES IN 16 MAJOR INDUSTRIAL COUNTRIES, IN ANNUAL COMPOUND INCREASE TERMS 1870–1976

| | Output | Exports | Exports to Output Ratios | Tangible Reproducible Non-Residential Capital Stock | Capital Stock to Output Ratios | Output per Head of Population |
|---|---|---|---|---|---|---|
| 1870–1913 | 2.5 | 3.7 | 1.48 | 2.8 | 1.12 | 1.5 |
| 1913–1950 | 1.9 | 1.1 | 0.58 | 1.6 | 0.84 | 1.1 |
| 1950–1970 | 4.9 | 8.6 | 1.76 | 5.6 | 1.14 | 3.8 |
| 1970–1976 | 3.0 | 6.0 | 2.0 | 6.3 | 2.1 | 2.4 |

Note: The figures above indicate the compound annual rates of growth per annum in 16 major industrial countries – as calculated by Mr. T. M. Rybczynski of Lazard's Bank.

FIG. 15 (*continued*)

As can be seen during the 43 year period 1870 to 1913, the annual compound rate of expansion of output in these countries of 2.5 per cent, was considerably exceeded by the growth in their total export of 3.7 per cent compound per annum. This was during a period characterised, by a growing volume of manufactured exports being exchanged for primary foodstuffs and industrial raw material, on a complimentary basis. Throughout this period output per head of population in the industrial counties are on average thought to have increased by some 1.5 per cent per annum.

The period 1913 to 1950, which included the devastating effects of two world wars, and the prolonged slump of the 1930s, saw an overall collapse of the rate of export increases to some 1.1 per cent per annum, against the average increase in output of 1.9 per cent. During the same period average output per head was thought to have increased by 1.1 per cent. This was successively an era of retrenchment, autarchy and eventual rearmament for many economies.

The period 1950 to 1970 became, under the influence of a rapidly growing, increasingly freer trading world, a golden age for international trade. During this period the volume of exports rose at some 8.6 per annum, compared to total output increases of 4.9 per cent. During the same period, output per head of the industrial nations' population rose by 3.8 per cent. The expansion of international trade was especially associated with the increasing flow of manufactured goods between the leading industrial countries, and at the same time with some relative falling off of trade between former colonial primary producing countries and their mother countries. Britain's eventual full membership of the E.E.C. in 1975, represented a late recognition of the changing facts of international trade. In the 1960s the growth of oil traffic, especially from the Middle East to Western Europe and the U.S.A., also became a key element in world trading activities.

Finally between 1970 and 1976, output on average grew at only 3.0 per annum – and generally fell below that figure after the energy crises of 1973–74. Export volumes also fell, but remained twice those of output. Likewise output per head of population also fell to average 2.4, well below that of the period for most of the postwar era, but considerably above the levels of growth which had usually applied in the previous century.

from machine tools to cars and household consumer goods, sell as much on service and adequate delivery, etc., and also on the subjective utility satisfactions of customers, as on price alone. The classical explanation of gains from trade lies in differences of comparative advantage, translated into differences in comparative costs, and differences in money prices once the monetary exchange rates between the nations is known. However a more fundamental question is what causes the differences in such comparative costs. One is that countries naturally differ in their endowments of natural and acquired resources such as climate, productive land and minerals, human skills, existing capital stock, technical know-how, etc., and they will tend to have a comparative advantage in the production of goods which require those of which they have a relatively plentiful supply. They will then tend to export these goods in exchange for goods whose production requires resources which are relatively scarce and therefore expensive to them.

*     *     *     *     *

In Britain modern theories of trade flows are especially associated with the work of the 1977 Nobel Prize winner Professor J. E. Meade who in 1951 published the first volume of his work *The Theory of International Economic Policy*. He shared the prize with Professor Bertil Ohlin of Sweden who published *Inter-regional and International Trade* as far back as 1933. Despite the apparent theoretical advantages of free trade on a comparative cost basis, in many situations, governments continue to find good reasons for discouraging the free flow of trade and for promoting or supporting industries of their own. One traditional form of justification is the argument originally used by J. S. Mill for 'infant industries', a term used to justify protective measures to advance expanding industries in Western countries against foreign competition during their growth to maturity. The argument in favour of what may be argued to be temporary protection for infant industries, is that in encouraging a pattern of specialisation different from that which would freely emerge under free trade, a country will eventually derive benefits which will more than compensate for the economic wealth sacrificed in the short term. As is well known throughout much of the 19th and early 20th century American infant industries developed behind tariffs against British and Western European manufactured imports. Again the original Australian Commonwealth tariffs introduced in 1906 looked to a cost disability of up to 30 per cent over world prices, as being justified if it allowed infant manufacturing industries to develop. Nevertheless, in theory such a tariff provides no justification for a permanent subsidy to individual industries unless additional external economies of community benefits are expected to grow. The difficulty is of assessing such economies accurately, and the probability that such measures, originally described as temporary or emergency or developmental, will become part of the permanent fiscal structure, making the argument of doubtful longer term value as a guide to sound policy. Nevertheless, the infant industry argument will remain a powerful one in countries seeking to develop industrial capacity for the first time.

It is of interest that the similar argument is often applied in the present time for the support of 'mature industries' which a country is unable to let go into permanent decline, given the employment and investment involved in particular basic industries. People in Britain have been familiar for many years with the arguments advanced to justify the protection of mature or declining industries, from cotton textiles, ship-building, coal mining, and a host of others. The short term social and political costs of allowing a long established, if internationally inefficient, 'lame duck' industry to decline, is often too much for governments to contemplate. In some cases they may consider that the traditional industry is being destroyed by 'dumping', that is by import of manufactured goods from other countries which are not reflecting the true costs of manufacture and marketing in their export prices. Such criticism has in recent years been levelled widely against imports of cars and other consumer durable household goods from Japan and other Far Eastern and Eastern European sources. The response of government in these circumstances is often to introduce a system of quantitative restrictions for a period of time, which it is hoped will give the industry a breathing space to re-invest and re-tool itself up to a point of providing effective competition with the cheaper imports.

\*     \*     \*     \*     \*

It is important to recognise that for most of the post-Second World War years the 'golden era' of growth in world trade was substantially supported by the strength of the U.S. dollar with, its linkage to gold at $35 per fine oz. Between 1950 and 1970 world exports expanded at some 8.6 per cent compound per annum compared to an output increase of 4.9 – both unprecedented fast rates of growth. Fortress America had emerged from the war with her industrial and agricultural capacity greatly enhanced and was faced with the possibility of a never-ending trade surplus with the rest of the world – which conversely at the time seemed to be faced with a perpetual dollar shortage.

The Marshall Plan, for the reconstruction of Western Europe from 1947 onwards; the outpouring of resources associated with the Korean War boom; the gradual industrial rebuilding of Western Europe and Japan, were very much based on the investments, the 'know-how' and the markets of a freer trading, highly successful American economy. However, from the early 1960s several awkward dilemmas began to emerge. One was the tendency for dollars to stay in Europe, as opposed to being repatriated back to the U.S.A. Another was that the growing costs of the Vietnam War combined with no cut backs in the U.S. domestic economy, began to adversely affect trade balances and financial confidence. The completion of the 'Kennedy Round' of tariff reductions in 1967 coincided with the beginnings of serious doubts about the American economic leadership and external trade position. In 1971 the U.S. Treasury effectively demonetised gold, and since that time the international trading system has had to learn to live with 'floating exchange' rates, highly susceptible to the fundamentals of trade balances, inflation rates, productivity ratings, political risks, etc., comparing one country to another. The energy crises from 1974 onwards – and the quadrupling of oil prices – was as much as anything else based on a recognition of oil as a vital asset, useful both as a highly liquid fuel, and as an alternative 'store of value' for the international economy as a whole. North America, Western Europe and Japan's critical dependency on oil imports for much of their energy needs has further emphasised the dependency of the world's economic system on this volatile base. Ironically, at the time of writing the three nations with the strongest currencies, the Japanese yen, the West German deutsche mark and the Swiss franc, have no oil reserves of their own. However, they seem to be able to sustain highly 'productive' and for the time being, viable economies.

In recent times a further complication, in the case of the United Kingdom, has been full membership since 1975 of the European Economic Community which is committed to a rapid extension of free trading on a Community wide basis. The member states are pledged to a complete abolition of tariffs for manufactured goods traded between themselves and the extension of free trading over the whole market: plainly this can have traumatic effects on the short term survival prospects of many companies. The immediate effect of Britain's membership of the E.E.C. was a very rapid deterioration in the visible trade balance between Britain and her European partners, going from a surplus on visible trade of some £44 million in 1970 to a deficit of £2,372 million in 1975. The British response, at least in the short term, has not been by seeking to retain tariffs, but rather by allowing Sterling devalution against other European currencies to give the home industry at least temporary respite against the competitive force of more cost efficient rivals in other parts of the Community. Moreover the artificially maintained rate for the green £ has been used to protect British domestic food prices from the full impact of European Community prices. Put simplistically, German industrial workers subsidise French and other Continental farmers to supply British consumers! Needless to say, in a trade dependent economy reliant on both the import of raw materials and foodstuffs, and export of manufactures, such devaluations are soon useless, unless accompanied by measures to rapidly improve manufacturing methods and to raise 'productivity' and 'value adding' capacity. Again in the longer run sufficient basic scientific and technical research needs to be undertaken, both to provide a new knowledge base, and a platform for the creation of new industrial activities. A long standing criticism of Britain's performance in this respect has focused less on the national ability to generate new knowledge, (witness the jet engine, radar, artificial fibres, etc. etc.), but more on the failure to translate these into positive advantages in terms of production and new products, widely sellable on world markets. This in turn has been seen by some as relating to British education's traditional preference for pure as opposed to applied subjects – which it is suggested makes us good at original concepts, but bad at industrial applications to produce sufficient sellable goods against international competition.

*   *   *   *   *

Finally the following extract from the O.E.C.D. *Economic Outlook* No. 20, December 1976, gives a clear indication of the close connections between domestic and international trade issues which are seen to apply in the contemporary Western industrial world. Under the heading – The Policy Challenge – the report states that:

"On the basis of the forecasts presented above, economic policy will be faced with three major problems over the coming twelve months:

(a) The rate of inflation, although decelerating, is likely to remain high in most countries.

(b) The growth of activity may be insufficient to reduce unemployment. And the investment that most countries require, if they are to make good the deficiencies of past years and cope with the problems of the years ahead, may be very slow to materialise.

FIG. 16   SOME RECENT CHANGES IN THE SHARE OF WORLD EXPORTS IN MAJOR AREAS, 1955–1976

| Exports From / To | Average of 1955/59 compared to 1970 | | | | 1970 to 1976 | | | |
|---|---|---|---|---|---|---|---|---|
| | Industrial Countries | Developing Countries (including O.P.E.C.) | Centrally Planned Economies | World Total 1970 | Industrial Countries | Developing Countries (including O.P.E.C.) | Centrally Planned Economies | World Total 1976 |
| | % | | | | % | | | |
| Industrial Countries | +9 | −10 | +1 | 69.2 | −7.7 | +1.2 | +1 | 63.0 |
| Developing Countries (including O.P.E.C.) | +3 | −5 | +2 | 17.8 | +5.4 | −0.3 | +0.1 | 25.4 |
| Centrally Planned Economies | +5 | +7 | −11 | 10.5 | +0.3 | −0.1 | −1.1 | 9.6 |
| World | +7 | −7 | 0 | 100 | −2.3 | +3.0 | −0.2 | 100 |

*Note:* These tables indicate the great strength of exports by industrial countries during the past two decades. The growth of relative trade in the 1970s by the developing countries (including O.P.E.C.) is almost entirely the result of the growth and strength of oil exports, on which both Western Europe and the U.S.A. have become increasingly dependent.

(c) The divergence in economic performance between individual countries will probably remain considerable.

The challenge to policy lies in the need to reduce the spread between
the performances of the more and the less successful countries, without
endangering the record of the former.

Action to reduce the gap requires, in the first place, fully adequate
stabilisation policies by the governments of the less successful countries.
This will entail severe domestic demand restraint, supplemented where
possible by arrangements which limit the growth of incomes, until cost
increases are reduced and net exports lead to recovery. Such action may
be politically difficult, and the temptation to resort to soft options in the
form of generalised or sectoral protection may grow. The need to resist
this, and to adhere to the principles that underlay the adoption of the
O.E.C.D. Trade Pledge in 1974, can hardly be over-emphasised in a
world where *all* are grappling with unemployment problems and protectionist lobbies are strong. Special trade measures by one weak country
will immediately complicate the task of other Member countries in
similar positions and make retaliation difficult to resist. In a multi-
country world, increased protectionism is a *minus-sum game.*"

Nevertheless in a world characterised by high energy costs, low or
stagnant growth and serious labour unemployment, trade protectionism is a game that many industrial countries will be increasingly
tempted to play. At the time of writing the perilous state of the
American Steel industry, faced by fierce import competition from
Western Europe and Japan, is causing particular concern. It remains an
open question whether this and other threatened national industries
will force President Carter's Administration into a more trade protectionist stance. The American industrial economy developed behind
tariff walls. It remains to be seen whether they will be reintroduced in
response to the trade challenges of the contemporary world.

## The Development and Role of Multinationals

During the past decade or so perhaps no subject has aroused greater
controversy and debate, from a wide variety of quarters, than the rapid
expansion and impact of multinational enterprises, investing, manufacturing and selling, in a wide range of worldwide markets. The
question of the sovereignty of control over wealth creating possibilities
bedevils relationships between national governments on the one hand,
and huge multinational organisations on the other. Taken in historical
perspective, it is of course apparent that multinationals as such are by

no means new phenomena. As we have seen from the time of the great mercantilistic trading empires of Spain, Portugal, France, Britain and Holland, which extended from the 16th to the 18th centuries, trading enterprises and companies of adventurers and merchants developed as the means of expanding the influence of a mother country, into newly acquired colonies. Thus, in the history of economic thought, the problem of multinational, or more accurately international, operations have reverberated thoughout both theoretical and practical discussions. The history of the British East India Company for many hundreds of years attracted a mixture of concern and awareness on the part of legislators, administrators and academics alike. In the early 17th century Thomas Mun found it necessary to defend the company and its export of bullion on the basis that more wealth would, in consequence, come back to England later on. The story of the great trading companies is part and parcel of the story of imperial expansionism. For a long period of time up to the Indian Mutiny of the late 1850s, the East India Company virtually ran India as a commercial enterprise, with its own armies, administration and officials all dedicated to facilitating trade and drawing wealth back to the mother country. Following the publication of his book on the *History of British India*, James Mill became a long-standing senior administrator of the company in London, while three other leading 19th century classical economists, Thomas Robert Malthus, John Stuart Mill, and William Thomas Thornton, also found lucrative employment in her service.

Likewise in Canada, the Hudson Bay Company had a long history of development starting from its 1670 Charter given by Charles II (1630–1685), and extending through to the present day. Only in recent years has the head office been moved from the original London base to Canada. Moving south, most of the original American colonies were set up by trading companies, which had an important role in the development of the British colonial mercantile system. Thus by no means can it be said that international enterprise is a new phenomenon in the world economic scene. Rather it is a very old phenomenon associated with the expansion of the internationally based commercial and industrial capitalistic system well known for the support of its progenitors, extending from Sir Walter Raleigh (1552–1618) in 16th century colonial Virginia, to Lord Clive (1724–1727) and Warren Hastings (1732–1818) in 18th century India, and Cecil Rhodes in late 19th century Southern Africa. Conversely Marx and his followers, including Hobson and Lenin, wrote powerful criticisms of the extent and impact of such enterprises on the world economy – seeing them as part and parcel of the need for capitalism to extend and monopolise wider and wider market areas. Indeed they considered that only in this way could capitalism escape from constricted markets and a falling rate of profit. Again, the British Prime Minister Benjamin Disraeli (1804–1901) early perceived, in *Tancred* that 'the East is a career' and all too frequently, as expressed in the House of Commons in 1863 – 'colonies do not cease to be colonies because they are independent'.

\*     \*     \*     \*     \*

For many contemporary economists educated in the neo-classical liberal democratic tradition, the success or otherwise of the multinationals would be seen to be part and parcel of the historical growth in the scale of business enterprise as a whole. The economies of scale and the modern industrial division of labour, in particular based on the success of highly centralised systems of research and development, might all suggest a perfectly reasonable extension of the activities of large companies as being to expand into market locations abroad. This in turn means gradually moving from the stage of purely trading to the establishment of local branches, and finally to the creation of manufacturing on an international basis. In-so-far as this type of activity has facilitated the post-war growth of world trade and the rise and broadening in living standards generally, many contemporary Western democratic economists would regard this as a beneficial development. However in line with their thinking about the problem of scale and potential abuses of market power, they would also be concerned when such enterprises showed a tendency to internalise markets unnecessarily, and to pursue what might appear to be monopolistic or quasi-monopolistic practices, to secure undue advantages and security for their own activities. Yet in general it would be seen as requiring individual host governments to make their own decisions about these types of activities and to legislate, or by other means prevent multinational enterprises from unduly exploiting local market dominance or shares. To this line of thinking there was nothing particularly unique about a multinational, other than its great size and general ability to exploit for the benefits of shareholders, workers and customers alike the opportunities of further widening the possibilities of the economies of scale. Given the assumption of a liberal society and an informed body of opinion with efficient legislative safeguards, there is no reason why the sovereign state should not deal with the multinational enterprise in light of its perception of where the 'public good' lies. Nevertheless even some well established sovereign states throughout Western Europe during the 1950s and 1960s became increasingly conscious of, and sensitive to, the impact that multinationals, particularly from the United States, were beginning to have on traditionally secure domestic markets.

Increasingly critical views about multinationals and their influence became particularly common in France, and to some extent were associated with Gaullist political and philosophical attitudes, towards national sovereignty and independence. In a very real sense these views reflect back to longstanding French policies, from mercantilistic time onwards, for strong central government. In the early 1960s a leading French intellectual, M. Servan Schreiber, published an important book called *The American Challenge* in which he presented the many problems of large American multinationals extending their influence throughout Europe. As he emphasised, the multinationals' great source of technology from a base in the United States, plus their ability to raise large Eurodollar loans against the security of a powerful parent company, gave them enormous market strength, particularly in markets associated with high technology, from computers to aircraft manufacture and such like.

Another current work, which considered similar themes in a detailed analytical way is by Dr. Y. S. Hu on *The Impact of U.S. Investment in Europe*, a case study of automotive and computer industries published in 1973. He pointed out that neither in the automobile nor in the computer industry did the United States start with a technical lead over Europe. However in cars the development of the mass consumer market and the mass production technology gave the great American companies, General Motors, Ford, Chrysler, etc., a powerful market base, which their lead in management and production engineering enabled them to transfer successfully into Europe. More recently the onset of the energy crisis and the need for small cars has caused the American owned companies to develop small cars – witness Ford's Fiesta. Again in computers the market and money provided by the American Government in the 1960s gave American based manufacturers a massive domestic market position. In turn this allowed IBM Ltd. to develop successfully and achieve a commanding position in the world market. Hu's book contains a detailed account of how Machines Bull, the technological leader on the Continent, collapsed into the arms of the General Electric Company of the United States. From a nationalistic viewpoint this is a sad tale and shows how the French Government was manipulated by a strong multinational firm. But it is no less revealing that the take-over, far from injecting new managements and technology, seems merely to have led to Machine Bull's accelerated demise. The important point associated with many such discussions is that the impact which imported investment, in this case American, has on facilitating or otherwise the introduction of new technology and management skills into the market. It cannot simply mop up local skills without having marked local costs or benefits. Thus the implicit moral of Hu's account, which is applicable widely in many other situations, is that the benefits from foreign investment and technology depend on the ability of the host country to define its true long term interests and needs. This is a critical debate, not only in the case of multinational operations in the advanced industrial countries, but perhaps even more critically in the case of their many activities in the less developing world.

Another recent book which deals with such issues in relation to the developing world is by Mr. Louis Turner on *Multinational Companies and the Third World* published in 1973. As he provocatively points out, the subject of multinational companies in Southern Africa is impossible to discuss 'without asking political and moral questions'. Even if one seeks to stick to such issues as, what has been the economic impact of multinational companies in the Third World, Turner emphasises that it is often impossible to answer without making major assumptions about what would have happened if the companies had never invested or if they had been used for only part of a project. Plainly in many such cases economists may disagree about the value of sheer growth, arguing that it might be achieved at the expense of other values, not least of which might be the social instabilities engendered by a small industrial and foreign influenced élite getting rich-quick. Turner, in his book, reflects on most of the difficult issues raised by multinational investment in the contemporary less developed world, and illustrates his themes by telling stories, filling in historical background, and discussing the role of the personalities who have influenced events.

Somewhat similar lines of debates have also been followed by a number of other popular authors, including Mr. Anthony Sampson in his fascinating book on *The Sovereign State – the Secret History of ITT*, and also more recently in his important work on *The Seven Sisters*, an account of the great oil companies and the world they made. Again in the book *Do you sincerely want to be rich?*, a Sunday Times insight team – Charles Raw, Bruce Page and Godfrey Hodgson, examined the story of Bernard Cornfeld and I.O.S.; an international swindle. At a more academic level one would have to refer to Professor John Dunning's

pioneering work on *The Multinational Enterprise* (1971), (in association with a group at Reading University), and also the work of
Michael Brooke and Lee Remers in respect to *The Strategy of Multinational Enterprise*, (1970). Follow up work is now associated with
the International Business Unit in the University of Manchester, Institute
of Science and Technology. Finally the recent book by Professor
Raymond Vernon *Storm Over the Multinationals* published in 1977
reviews many of the issues involved.

*     *     *     *     *

There are many other examples of these types of wide ranging
enquiries, not least of which is the United Nations' *Report on Multinational Corporations in World Development*, published in 1973. The
difficulty from the viewpoint of academic or officially based exposition
is that nothing in the contemporary scene presents an easy or tidy
picture. Rather one perceives an extremely confused and rapidly
changing picture of great multinational companies, operating in diverse
and many changing markets, and in widely different circumstances,
from the great cities of the Western World to the Middle East and the
less developed world as a whole. The overriding issues remain the
desirability or otherwise of political, economic and social power and, in
particular, market power on a multinational basis: often easy to
describe but difficult to analyse or judge. Plainly the growth of
industrial and commercial activity has involved companies located
initially in Britain, Western Europe, the U.S.A. and elsewhere, gradually
extending their scope and activities into other markets. In line with
neo-classical doctrine such companies frequently demonstrate the
characteristics of oligopolistic or monopolistic structure and market
behaviour. Their great size inevitably tends to internalise many markets, while in many external markets they face few major direct
competitors, though they frequently have to face competition, at least
initially, from locally based competitors for many products. However,
in general the classical free market test does not fully apply. Moreover
during the great period of post-Second World War growth in trade and
development, the activities of multinational large enterprises have
become increasingly significant throughout the world. According to a
recent United Nations' survey of multinationals, eight of the ten largest
companies now operating derive from the United States. Of these ten
predictably eight are involved in the oil and chemical industries, and the
other two, General Motors and Ford, are concerned with vehicle

manufacture. Figure 17 (overleaf) taken from *Fortune* Magazine, in 1974, indicates the contemporary position.

It is thought that the multinationals ultimately owned and directed from the United States, today account for something more than half of the world's current stock of foreign direct investment, estimated at some $1,650 billion. In fact the multinationals based on the United States together with those of Great Britain, the Federal Republic of Germany and France, probably represent over four-fifths of direct foreign investment. Such foreign direct investment also tends to be concentrated in a few firms within each home country which, to a considerable extent, is a reflection of the increasingly concentrated nature of industrial ownership and control throughout the Western world. The exception is Japan where, in addition to large corporations, a number of smaller firms also seem to have participated significantly in foreign investment. Many multinationals are much larger than individual national economies. In the early 1970s, for instance, production of each of the top ten multinationals, in terms of added value, was estimated to be in excess of £2.5 billion, greater than the individual gross national product of over 80 countries at that time. Paradoxically as the breakup of the Western European Colonial empires increased apace, and many new countries came into existence and applied for membership of the United Nations, the scale and extent of multinational operations extending over countries increased, both relatively and absolutely. Some two-fifths of all activities are now thought to be in manufacturing activities, and approximately one third in petroleum, etc. In the industrial developed economies, something like half of the multinationals' investments tends to be in manufacturing, and less than one third in mining and extraction. However in Third World countries, half of the estimated stock of foreign investment is concentrated on the mining and extractive industries, and little more than a quarter in manufacturing.

The United Nations also reports the increase of multinational investments in the developing countries' manufacturing and servicing sectors, and a decline in primary industries, particularly those associated with agriculture and the traditional plantation crops which, in the second half of the 19th century, were one of the main facets of colonial commercial development. Multinationals have also become far more active in other growing service activities, including airlines, travel, tourism, banking, insurance, consulting, and such like. In these types of changes one can see reflected, as much as anything else, the rapidly changing nature of the technical-economic systems of parent countries.

FIG. 17   THE WORLD'S FIFTY LARGEST COMPANIES, 1974

| Sales Rank | Company | Headquarters |
|---|---|---|
| 1 | Exxon | New York |
| 2 | Royal Dutch/Shell Group | London/The Hague |
| 3 | General Motors | Detroit |
| 4 | Ford Motor | Dearborn, Michigan |
| 5 | Texaco | New York |
| 6 | Mobil Oil | New York |
| 7 | British Petroleum | London |
| 8 | Standard Oil of California | San Francisco |
| 9 | National Iranian Oil | Tehran |
| 10 | Gulf Oil | Pittsburgh |
| 11 | Unilever | London |
| 12 | General Electric | Fairfield, Connecticut |
| 13 | International Business Machines | Armonk, New York |
| 14 | International Tel. & Tel. | New York |
| 15 | Chrysler | Highland Park, Michigan |
| 16 | Philips Gloeilampen-fabrieken | Eindhoven (Netherlands) |
| 17 | U.S. Steel | Pittsburgh |
| 18 | Standard Oil (Ind.) | Chicago |
| 19 | Cie Francaise des Petroles | Paris |
| 20 | Nippon Steel | Tokyo |
| 21 | August Thyssen-Hutte | Duisburg (Germany) |
| 22 | BASF | Ludwigshafen on Rhine |
| 23 | Hoechst | Frankfurt on Main |
| 24 | Shell Oil | Houston |
| 25 | Western Electric | New York |

| Sales $m | Main Industries | Assets $m | Employees |
|---|---|---|---|
| 42,061 | Oil, Chemicals | 31,332 | 133,000 |
| 33,037 | Oil, Chemicals | 30,194 | 164,000 |
| 31,549 | Cars, Trucks | 20,463 | 734,000 |
| 23,620 | Cars, Trucks | 14,173 | 464,731 |
| 23,255 | Oil | 17,176 | 76,420 |
| 18,929 | Oil | 14,074 | 73,100 |
| 18,269 | Oil, Chemicals | 15,088 | 68,000 |
| 17,191 | Oil, Chemicals | 11,633 | 39,540 |
| 16,802 | Oil | 6,935 | 50,000 |
| 16,458 | Oil, Coal | 12,503 | 52,700 |
| 13,666 | Food, Detergents | 7,116 | 357,000 |
| 13,413 | Electrical Products | 9,368 | 404,000 |
| 12,675 | Computers | 14,027 | 292,350 |
| 11,154 | Telecommunications | 10,696 | 409,000 |
| 10,971 | Cars, Trucks | 6,732 | 255,929 |
| 9,422 | Electronics | 7,717 | 412,000 |
| 9,186 | Iron & Steel | 11,304 | 187,503 |
| 9,085 | Oil | 8,915 | 47,217 |
| 8,908 | Oil | 8,266 | 27,400 |
| 8,843 | Iron & Steel | 9,456 | 97,814 |
| 8,664 | Iron & Steel | 5,212 | 150,888 |
| 8,497 | Chemicals | 6,074 | 110,989 |
| 7,821 | Chemicals | 7,795 | 178,710 |
| 7,633 | Oil | 6,128 | 32,287 |
| 7,381 | Electrical | 5,239 | 189,972 |

| Sales Rank | Company | Headquarters |
|:---:|---|---|
| 26 | ENI | Rome |
| 27 | Continental Oil | Stamford, Connecticut |
| 28 | ICI (Imperial Chemical Industries) | London |
| 29 | E.I. du Pont de Nemours | Wilmington, Delaware |
| 30 | Atlantic Richfield | Los Angeles |
| 31 | Siemens | Munich |
| 32 | Volkswagenwerk | Wolfsburg (Germany) |
| 33 | Westinghouse Electric | Pittsburgh |
| 34 | Bayer | Leverkusen (Germany) |
| 35 | Daimler-Benz | Stuttgart |
| 36 | Montedison | Milan |
| 37 | Hitachi | Tokyo |
| 38 | Toyota Motor | Toyoda-City (Japan) |
| 39 | ELF Group | Paris |
| 40 | Occidental Petroleum | Los Angeles |
| 41 | Mitsubishi Heavy Industries | Tokyo |
| 42 | Nestlé | Vevey (Switzerland) |
| 43 | Bethlehem Steel | Bethlehem, Pennsylvania |
| 44 | Renault | Boulogne Billancourt (France) |
| 45 | British Steel | London |
| 46 | Union Carbide | New York |
| 47 | Goodyear Tire & Rubber | Akron, Ohio |
| 48 | British-American Tobacco | London |
| 49 | Tenneco | Houston |
| 50 | Petrobras (Petroleo Brasileiro) | Rio de Janeiro |
|  | TOTALS | |

Source: *Fortune*

| Sales $m | Main Industries | Assets $m | Employees |
|---|---|---|---|
| 7,172 | Oil, Chemicals | 11,379 | 92,241 |
| 7,041 | Oil | 4,673 | 41,174 |
| 6,911 | Chemicals | 7,428 | 201,000 |
| 6,910 | Chemicals | 5,980 | 136,866 |
| 6,739 | Oil | 6,151 | 28,771 |
| 6,701 | Electical | 6,246 | 309,000 |
| 6,568 | Cars | 5,841 | 203,730 |
| 6,466 | Electrical, Nuclear | 4,301 | 199,243 |
| 6,300 | Chemicals | 6,800 | 134,837 |
| 6,288 | Cars | 2,607 | 154,865 |
| 6,189 | Chemicals, Synthetics | 6,864 | 153,200 |
| 6,183 | Electrical | 7,147 | 144,863 |
| 5,948 | Cars | 3,900 | 58,862 |
| 5,900 | Oil | 7,432 | 22,331 |
| 5,719 | Oil | 3,325 | 34,400 |
| 5,664 | Machinery, Ships | 8,243 | 114,100 |
| 5,603 | Food | 5,105 | 138,899 |
| 5,380 | Iron & Steel | 4,512 | 121,623 |
| 5,341 | Cars, Tractors | 2,207 | 206,000 |
| 5,340 | Iron & Steel | 6,378 | 223,000 |
| 5,320 | Chemicals | 4,882 | 109,566 |
| 5,256 | Rubber Products | 4,241 | 154,166 |
| 5,152 | Tobacco, Paper | 4,507 | 81,016 |
| 5,001 | Oil, Engineering | 6,401 | 157,019 |
| 4,089 | Oil | 4,995 | 43,783 |
| 538,592 | | 439,173 | 8,273,016 |

In short the multinational enterprise has become a force to be reckoned with, on a world wide basis, in both developed and developing countries alike.

*   *   *   *   *

In line with these developments in recent years academic and public controversy about multinationals has extended far beyond the scope of traditional economic thinking. Indeed this area provides an outstanding example of the merging of political, economic and social debates. Political considerations apart much analysis, of a multi-disciplinary nature, has focused on definitions: what in today's world can truly be described as a multinational organisation or enterprise? Plainly there are many great enterprises, both public and private, with activities which cross national boundaries and most national governments today operate information and commercial networks in other countries. There is also the traditional trade of large companies buying and selling goods and services and knowledge over wide trading areas. Many governments now also participate directly and indirectly in this type of activity, particularly through state owned industries and state trading corporations, and this is especially true of countries in the Soviet inspired COMECON bloc.

Professor Howard Perlmutter has suggested three models of 'international management', the first two of which are clearly recognisable and correspond to the phases of development which many multinationals have gone through since the end of the Second World War, while the third is a speculation about a style which may evolve, though as yet no company has fully adopted the pattern. These three styles may be summarised as the *ethnocentric*, the *polycentric* and the *geocentric* organisation, the characteristics of which are listed below. In academic terms such definitions and analysis involve several different disciplines and, to this extent, indicate the way in which simplistic economic model classifications no longer fully comprehend the nature of the large scale enterprise.

Most multinationals begin as *ethnocentric* organisations. They are characterised by having decision-making highly centralised on a home company, with frequent references by local managers back to headquarters in London, New York, Paris, etc., even for matters of tactical detail and day to day operations. This central control system often takes the form of elaborate reporting by Telex, etc., on a weekly and monthly basis. Most important overseas managers are expatriates from the parent company (which remains the principal repository of managerial and technical skills) and foreign employees are given little freedom of action. Although the ethnocentric approach means tidy organisation charts, it tends to be unstable in the longer run, because it attracts hostility wherever local nationalism becomes articulate. The call to 'indigenise local management', starting first with personnel, but finally going through to the most technically demanding posts, faces most such multinationals today. As many such companies are finding, from Hong Kong to Mexico City, Nairobi to Dakar, the 'training commitment' towards local staff becomes overwhelming. Moreover in an extreme form, as has become increasingly apparent in Latin America, expatriate managers and their families may be under strong threat of kidnap, ransom or death.

Second, the *polycentric* organisation apparently evolves as the commonsense way of getting an increasing number of management decisions taken near the markets, as increasing autonomy is encouraged, if not demanded, by more governments in the developing world. Autonomy of management is accorded to the subsidiary and the ethnocentric centrally controlled organisation is rapidly replaced by the other extreme, the polycentric company. The tight ethnocentric hold is loosened and greater consideration is given to local needs. More decision-making takes places on the spot, and subsidiaries are increasingly seen more as trade investments, and run predominantly by local nationals. Such a polycentric company takes increasing account of the existence of local nationalisms, and recognises that local situations are different. Non-executive members frequently appear on local boards, often more on the basis of their knowledge of local political situations than of technical or marketing detail. The parent company relies more on financial controls than on a formal, centralised command structure. However it tends to remain the sole repository of all research findings, and is in a position to provide, or cut off, funds for development. It remains unusual for foreigners to be promoted to positions of real responsibility within the head offices of parent companies.

Today many large multinationals can be seen as predominantly polycentric in management structure and style. However by emphasising the national differences, they may encourage national, rather than international, attitudes, and thereby divorce subsidiaries from valuable ideas and innovations in other group companies in other countries. They may also, by expensive duplication of plant and by creating competitive export situations between subsidiaries, face difficult issues

of choice between subsidiaries. Though there are a number of examples
of companies run successfully on polycentric lines, others have experienced intractable difficulties. Plainly when there is a loss of performance by the subsidiary, reasserting disused powers of central
intervention takes such time, and can involve serious disruptions. In
some cases, increasing technical complexity, and the need to co-
ordinate resources and opportunities on a worldwide basis, may require
a more integrated approach. The attempts by the major American
motor companies, General Motors, Ford and Chrysler, to develop
European wide integrated manufacturing and marketing strategies,
indicate many of the problems involved.

Third, in the idealised *geocentric* organisation of the future, neither
the home company nor the expatriate executives working in the
international subsidiaries, are seen as being inherently superior. Such a
company seeks to find the best men for the managerial positions at
headquarters and round the world, regardless of nationality. All senior
men in headquarters have international experience, even those who do
not come from the parent company can reach top positions. In the
subsidiary, the chief executive need not come from the country in which
he is working. In practice the nationalism of many governments makes
this idealised concept impossible to achieve. Moreover few managers,
either in headquarters or the subsidiaries themselves, are sufficiently
cosmopolitan to accept it as a normal pattern. Executive remuneration
problems arise, complicated by exchange controls, varying types of
effort and reward schemes in different countries, and differing taxation
practices. Nevertheless a company adopting a geocentric philosophy
would carry out research on an international basis, and it would make
its research and development findings, from its laboratories and
development workshops located round the world, freely available to all
subsidiaries. Ideally the geocentric approach aims at an inter-
nationalisation of corporate outlook, which is brought about primarily
by organisational and management development on a global scale, and
by involving the top executives of the subsidiaries and associations in
the full process of corporate and strategic planning.

Finally some of the more general issues associated with corporate
strategic planning are considered elsewhere. Clearly multinationals face
particular problems in seeking to co-ordinate strategic planning on
a global basis. Necessarily this becomes an on-going process of
reviewing all aspects of a multinational's philosophy, aims, objectives
and strategies and relating them to the total environment in which it is
operating. Few international enterprises are satisfied with the ways in

FIG. 18. THE DEVELOPMENT OF AN INTERNATIONAL MARKET

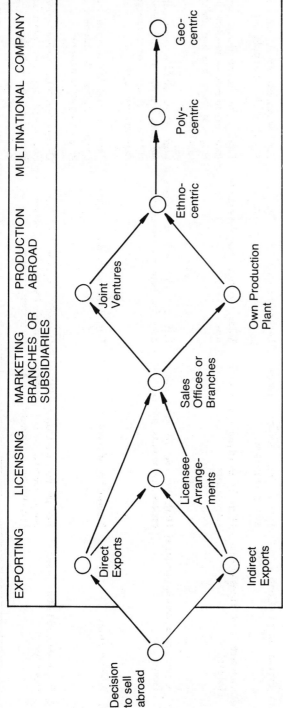

The forms of trading and the business activities listed above represent a typical pattern of evolution; from exporting domestically produced goods, through manufacturing the products partly and then wholly abroad, to a final position in which there is no capital holding, no export of goods but technology and know-how are exported on a franchise basis.

An enterprise developing its international business does not have to go through all the stages outlined; indeed its first international transaction could conceivably be the setting up of a franchise agreement involving no exports of goods at any stage. But some, or even all, of the stages could apply.

In practice the escalation in operating abroad, from exporting – via export houses, agents or marketing subsidiaries abroad – to production subsidiaries or joint ventures may develop over years, or be very rapid indeed. The possible progression is illustrated by the diagram.

FIG. 19. PERLMUTTER'S MODEL—TYPES OF HEAD OFFICE ORIENTATION TOWARDS SUBSIDIARIES IN AN INTERNATIONAL ENTERPRISE

| Social-Technical Design | Ethnocentric | Polycentric | Geocentric |
|---|---|---|---|
| (a) Work Flow | Complex in home country simple in subsidiaries | Varied and independent | Increasingly complex and interdependent |
| (b) Authority/Decision-making | High in headquarters | Relatively low in headquarters | Aim for collaboative relationship between headquarters and subsidiaries |
| (c) Evaluation and Control | Home standards applied for persons performance | Determined locally | Find standards which are universal and locally applicable |
| (d) Rewards and Punishments Incentives | High in headquarters, low in subsidiaries | Wide variation: may be high or low | Equity for international and local executives in rewards for reaching local and worldwide objectives |
| (e) Communications/Information Flows | High volume to subsidiaries: orders, commands, advice | Little to and from headquarters. Even less between subsidiaries | Both ways, and between subsidiaries. Heads of subsidiaries regarded as part of corporate management team |
| (f) Identification | Nationality of owners | Nationality of host country | Truly international company but concerned about the interests of all participating nations |
| (g) Succession and Management Development | Recruit and develop people of home country for key positions everywhere in the world | Develop people of local nationality for key positions in their own country | Develop best man everywhere in the world for key positions everywhere in the world |

Note: No enterprise will correspond in its entirety to any of these three stereotypes. Indeed the characteristics of two, or even three, of them may be found within the same company.

which they are doing this, particularly because of the difficulty in setting up a central planning system which is capable of identifying the essential world wide strategic issues which, over time, will determine the enterprise's success. The contemporary age of 'discontinuity' and 'uncertainty' presents too many intangibles to be fully comprehensible on a world basis, as well as on a time scale forward. Moreover, as has been shown, there are very real difficulties of achieving effective integration of the operations of the enterprise in the international market. One benefit which might arise from the geocentric approach is the improvement in strategic planning which occurs when the subsidiary or affiliated units participate substantially in the planning process. In this way the headquarters should have a better international feel, resulting from the inclusion in the process of senior managers who are nationals of the countries where the more significant of the enterprise's activities are located. The tug of war between the sovereign nation states and their diverse regional interests, and the multinational enterprise, will remain an overriding political, economic and social debate into the foreseeable future. The essence of power will remain! How and by what means can the future be influenced? The multinational enterprise, however defined or circumscribed, will remain a potent instrument in the wealth creating process of the future.

## The Meaning of Development and Growth

During the years since the end of the Second World War and concomitant with the break up of colonial empires, and perhaps, paradoxically, the emergence of 'one world views', the ideas of development and growth have received increased prominence in economic literature. One of the most significant of contemporary thinkers on these issues has been the Swedish 1974 Nobel Prize Winner Professor Gunnar Myrdal who published his book on *Economic Theory and Undeveloped Regions* in 1957, and is also widely known for his work on *Asian Drama*. Plainly in everyday discussion, ideas about economic development and growth are often mixed together, development being used to imply growth, and vice versa. Broadly economic growth may be described as some outward evidence of a process of economic development, and in this sense it is 'quantitatively' measureable and may be used to describe an expansion in the work force, the growth in the amount of capital employed in industry, the expansion of trade, an increase in consumption, or most commonly the growth of output per head of population, etc. In this sense growth equates to the increase of wealth in the old classical sense. Conversely economic development is often used to describe underlying 'qualitative' determinants of growth, such as changes in personal and social attitudes and institutions, which are conducive to encouraging an economy or society to seek a higher, as opposed to a lower rate of growth or indeed a stationary state, if that is what is desired.

However defined, the idea of economic growth is very much a product of the thinking of Western economic man from the 'age of enlightenment' onwards, to Adam Smith, through to Marx and Keynes and their many disciplies. Though ideological differences may still separate our understanding of the progress or otherwise of industrial and urban societies, which today make up the Western mixed economy democratic world as opposed to the Marxist inspired Socialist camp, both systems are a long way, in philosophical and practical terms, from life as lived in static primitive and/or purely agriculturally based societies. A static Tibetan or preferably Tahitian lifestyle, with little if any social or economic change for thousands of years, is almost incomprehensible to contemporary 'Western man' or Western influenced man, with his desires for excitement, innovation and ceaseless change. In this characteristic at least 'convergency' can be seen between the Western and Eastern European industrial systems. All the modern urban industrial and service based societies, western democratic and Marxist alike, have become accustomed to a continuous pace of innovation, to new methods of production, machinery, and products being introduced. Efficiency and success in the wealth generating process is given a high priority in the goals of society. However, 'divergency' may be said to apply between the two ideologies in the ways in which income distribution between social groups and the national balance between savings and investment are determined. Yet there are signs that many industrial societies, having achieved a certain rate of 'development', become tired of growth for growth's sake, and seek 'non-economic' goals, which may reflect the preferences of many workers for an easier, less discontinuous, and possibly less alienated, lifestyle. Mr. Schumacher's challenging book, *Small is Beautiful* or Mr. Mishan's *The Costs of Economic Growth*, and the need to 'preserve the environment' became catch phrases expressing a possible turning away from 'growth for growth's sake', within the main motivations of industrial economic man. Indeed one of President Carter's publicly stated reasons for adopting a neutral position, vis-a-vis Concorde's landing rights in New York, is the strength in the America of today of environmental lobbies against noise, etc. Certainly it by no means follows that growth leading to greater economic wealth necessarily implies greater happiness or satisfaction in any full sense for all of the population. There is much evidence to suggest that the reverse is often the case. Increased national wealth can allow a higher proportion of any population to change their scale of preferences, to prefer leisure to more material wealth and indeed to shift up Mr. Maslow's 'hierarchy of needs' scale.

There are a number of ways of measuring national economic growth in the quantitative sense. One difficulty is that an increase in the total real national income over a period of time may be obscured because of the changes in the value of money, due to inflation or conceivably deflation, and again cyclical swings and changes in output have to be allowed for. Another area of contention is that growth in national wealth may be accompanied by an even faster growth of new population increase, so that in real terms less is available for each person, and the average standard of living, as measured in quantitative terms, may have been reduced. A second measure of economic growth is achieved by dividing the increase in national income by the increase in population, so that the indicator becomes an increase in income per head. It is of interest that the West Indian, Professor Arthur Lewis, in his important book on *The Theory of Economic Growth* published in 1954, emphasised growth of output per head of population. His primary concern was with optimising real output, and not with questions of distribution or consumption per se, a traditional concern of many economists, from Ricardo onwards. Nevertheless very real difficulties are associated with the distribution of the new income. If, for the sake of argument, the increase in national wealth all goes to a small and relatively well-off élite social class, and the share of the expanded national income going to the remainder of the population remains the same as numbers grow, much of the population would be both relatively, and in some cases absolutely, worse off than before. This is often seen to be the case during the early stages of moving from agrarian to commercial cum industrial development, when the newly emerging middle classes, often an externally influenced military, commercial or industrial élite or an absentee rentier class, gain far more of the benefits of the new growth and affluence than the rest of the population.

If economic growth is seen as a process which genuinely raises the real wealth and standard of living of the community, taken as a whole, another indicator of the growth is income per head, supplemented by information on the distribution of income, and the degree to which national resources are being used to satisfy the preferences of society as a whole. Plainly this definition of economic growth involves substantial 'value' judgements on what is a desirable, or undesirable, change in the distribution of national income. Often a national desire for investment and economic growth to raise the standards of living is seen as a long term objective which, during the shorter run, may require living standards to be restrained to facilitate the necessary saving to accumulate industrial capital and knowledge, know-how and such like. Forced saving now, to allow for basic investment and 'pie in the sky' in the future. In order to avoid such value judgements and for simplicity's sake, many economists prefer to use the crude figure of real national income as the measure of economic growth and then, if required, make adjustments for increases in population by categories as may be required. Underlying all such discussions is the assumption that statistics are validly collected. This, particularly in the case of the less developed, and for that matter many industrial countries, is far from always true. Indeed one measure of development might be the avidity and competence with which governments seek to assess accurately new wealth being created.

## Historical Stages of Growth Theories

Having moved through debate about the problems of defining economic growth or development in 'quantitative' terms, many economic thinkers have thought of growth as part of a series of historical stages of development. In general those able to accept economics as part of an 'inductive' historical approach to knowledge have found this easier to accommodate than those committed to development of its 'deductive' scientific respectability. The founder of the classical school, Adam Smith, in his early writings, suggested that society could be considered as falling into hunting as the 'lowest and rudest state' such as 'we find among the native tribes of North America'; 'pasturage such as we find among the Tartars and Arabs or the Hottentots of the Cape of Good Hope'; 'agricultural': 'alloidal and feudal' leading finally to the emergence of the exchange economy, with the usual division between town and country. The towns cum cities of Smith's time were generally small and composed of those merchants, tradesmen and mechanics who were not bound to a particular place, but who found it in 'their economic interest to congregate together', and indeed whenever possible, given the frailty of man, 'to concoct schemes to raise prices'! However in Smith's view the increasing 'division of labour' and skill in industry and the productivity gains thereby, could be expected to increase gradually the manufactured goods which workers could afford to buy. Indeed early in *The Wealth of Nations*, Smith pointed out that as a result of the division of labour the industrial and frugal peasant enjoyed, as well as enough food for subsistence, a woollen coat, a coarse linen shirt, shoes, a kitchen grate, knives and forks and kitchen utensils, earthenware or pewter plates, and glass windows, with the result that 'his accommodation greatly exceeded that of an African king'.

In Smith's theory, however, capital accumulation allows increasing population and employment and, providing that the market for manufactured goods is sufficiently widened by this increasing division of labour, will in turn have favourable effects on labour productivity and wealth creating possibilities as a whole. If competition is sufficient, and an increase in capital will generally increase competition, the prices of manufactured goods will then fall with unit labour costs, with the result that the quantity and range of goods that workers can afford to purchase, will increase. Faster capital accumulation is associated with a faster rate of growth of employment, output and living standards. This optimistic view of growth possibilities was not of course fully accepted by Malthus, Ricardo or the younger Mill, who, in their various ways, saw diminishing, or at best a trend, to constant returns to scale, inevitably leading to the need for a 'stationary state', however defined. Marx's historical determinist views have also been referred to. The six-stage view of society, evolving through from primitive tribal communism, through systems of slavery, feudalism and thence to capitalism and on to socialism and communism, continue to have a powerful impact on the thinking and policies of much of the world. For Marxists, much of the dynamics of economic growth, and eventual decline, are continued within each stage of development, up to the final culmination in pure communism, in an advanced urban and industrial society.

Like Marx and many others of the German school, Professor Joseph Schumpeter also saw an historical pattern of development. He gave especial emphasis in his theory to the impact of large scale technology, on both the system of government and also on the decline of the strength of the family, with its emphasis on the importance of private property and capital accumulation. His works cover all branches of economics: *Capitalism, Socialism and Democracy* in 1942, and a *History of Economic Analysis* published in 1954, give some indication of his wide range of interests. In his earlier *Theory of Economic*

*Development* originally published in 1912, and *Business Cycles* published in 1939, he undertook an extensive analysis of the capitalist system and suggested the theory that 'innovations' made by entrepreneurs were a critical factor in economic development, and had an important position in the process of the trade and business cycle. In many ways his analysis, based as it is on an historical perception of development, is similar to Marx's, though his conclusions were markedly different, leading as they do to the evolution of modern capitalism towards large scale corporate organisations controlling new financing, product innovation and the development of markets. Like Marx, he also perceived the uneven pattern of boom/bust and the cyclical ups and downs of overall activity, as being a central feature of the way a modern industrial economy moves forward.

Other leading economic historical authors associated with historical development growth theories, were the Germans, Professor Werner Sombart, who emphasised the spirit of accumulation as a creative force in the evolution of modern capitalism in *The Modern Capitalism* (1916), and Professor Max Weber, who wrote about *The Protestant Ethic and the Spirit of Capitalism* in 1930. The influential British economic historian Professor R. H. Tawney, also emphasised the importance of the Protestant ethic in his book on *Religion and the Rise of Capitalism* (1938). Again Mr. Andrew Schonfield's book on *Modern Capitalism, the Changing Balance of Public and Private Power* (1965), surveyed changing institutions in the growth of major Western economies since the end of the Second World War. Similar themes have also been developed by Professor J. K. Galbraith, also of Harvard University, in his various writings about modern capitalism, notably in his books on the changing nature of capitalism, including *The Affluent Society* (1957), *The New Industrial State* (1967), and *The Age of Uncertainty* published in 1977.

\*     \*     \*     \*     \*

In considering debates about economic growth in the world at large it is of interest that during the past two centuries economic activity, in the 'advanced' countries, is thought by some economic historians to have experienced a curious half century-long rhythm – known as 'Kondratieff long waves'. It is suggested that they appear at intervals of some 25 years or so; periods of inflation, expansion and high business confidence being followed by comparable periods of price fluctuations, deflation and a general business environment of malaise and political and social tensions. As we have seen, in the case of Britain there seems to have been a period of a strong upswing in economic development and growth, which from the 1780s onwards coincided with the early years of the industrial revolution and continued to the end of the Napoleonic Wars. The next period, roughly from the Peace of Vienna in 1815, to the repeal of the Corn Laws, was a time characterised by much less certain growth, and prolonged political and social disturbance. In the rural areas – notwithstanding the degree of protection offered by the Corn Laws – the enclosure movement and the introduction of new farming machinery and methods occasioned great social distress. In the expanding industrial areas of Lancashire, and later the Midlands and in Greater London and elsewhere, large scale industrial and urban living, combined with the unprecedented inflow of population, and the general uncertainty of trade, often produced appalling social conditions, unmitigated by the fact that they were matched by huge profits for reinvestment, in Ricardo's new machines and the 'wage fund'. It was this uncertain situation that minds as diverse as Robert Owen, Friedrich Engels, Mrs. Gaskell and Charles Dickens were to write about so critically. Yet the subsequent economic upswing from perhaps the Great Exhibition of 1851, and the gold discoveries of California and Australia, to the mid-1870s, was to make it appear that many of the overwhelming problems of the previous three decades seem solvable. Thus John Stuart Mill's call for a 'stationary state' and Marx's and Engels' call for revolution, in the *Communist manifesto* of the same year, 1848, both fell on barren ground. Yet from the mid-1870s onwards the slowing off and deflation of the 'great depression' bore especially adversely on many of the less privileged – especially in the rural areas, where declining grain prices made emigration, for large parts of the population, well-nigh inevitable. There then followed, from 1896, the upswing to the Edwardian 'Indian summer', and the culmination in a world war which so many, including Hobson and Lenin, had predicted as the inevitable outcome of big power rivalry, massive overseas investment and 'exploitation' and imperialistic ambitions. It remains a subject of keen debate whether the stimulus of the 1896 South African gold discoveries was a critical stimulant in the pre-1914 boom. The post-war period saw a brief upswing and the beginning of industrial transformation away from the old staple trades; cotton textiles, heavy manufacturing, shipping and coal. The world depression from 1929 onwards was only really ameliorated by the onset of rearmament and the Second World War. The post Second World War decades – so influenced by Keynes' ideas of demand management originally presented in his *General Theory* in 1936, both at home and

FIG. 20.    KONDRATIEFF 'LONG WAVES' OF ECONOMIC GROWTH

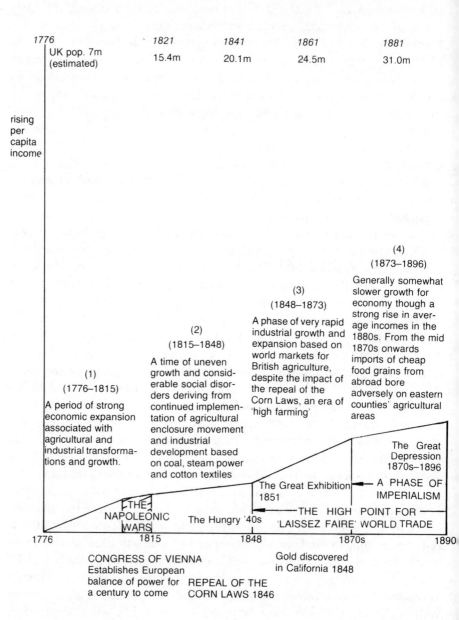

AS APPLIED TO BRITISH ECONOMY 1776–1976 (NOT TO SCALE)

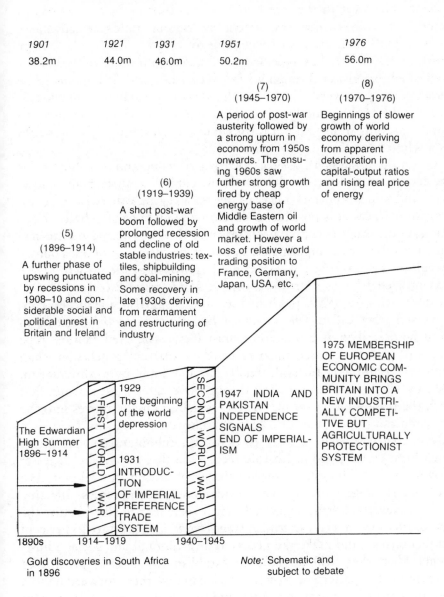

| 1901 | 1921 | 1931 | 1951 | 1976 |
|---|---|---|---|---|
| 38.2m | 44.0m | 46.0m | 50.2m | 56.0m |

**(7)**
**(1945–1970)**

A period of post-war austerity followed by a strong upturn in economy from 1950s onwards. The ensuing 1960s saw further strong growth fired by cheap energy base of Middle Eastern oil and growth of world market. However a loss of relative world trading position to France, Germany, Japan, USA, etc.

**(8)**
**(1970–1976)**

Beginnings of slower growth of world economy deriving from apparent deterioration in capital-output ratios and rising real price of energy

**(6)**
**(1919–1939)**

A short post-war boom followed by prolonged recession and decline of old stable industries: textiles, shipbuilding and coal-mining. Some recovery in late 1930s deriving from rearmament and restructuring of industry

**(5)**
**(1896–1914)**

A further phase of upswing punctuated by recessions in 1908–10 and considerable social and political unrest in Britain and Ireland

1975 MEMBERSHIP OF EUROPEAN ECONOMIC COMMUNITY BRINGS BRITAIN INTO A NEW INDUSTRIALLY COMPETITIVE BUT AGRICULTURALLY PROTECTIONIST SYSTEM

The Edwardian High Summer 1896–1914

FIRST WORLD WAR

1929 The beginning of the world depression

1931 INTRODUCTION OF IMPERIAL PREFERENCE TRADE SYSTEM

SECOND WORLD WAR

1947 INDIA AND PAKISTAN INDEPENDENCE SIGNALS END OF IMPERIALISM

| 1890s | 1914–1919 | 1940–1945 |
|---|---|---|

Gold discoveries in South Africa in 1896

*Note:* Schematic and subject to debate

abroad, brought another strong period of unprecedented economic
growth. However in the late 1960s some observers suggested that a
deterioration in capital investment to output ratios in advanced
technological industries was beginning to inhibit growth. The energy
crisis of the 1970s has now led to a further blunting of hopes for
continued expansion throughout the Western world. It remains to be
seen if strong recovery can be stimulated by Keynesian type methods –
in the light of the underlying 'supply constraints' which now seem to
apply, not only in Britain but throughout the Western industrial world
as a whole.

Given the basic neo-classical doctrines of value and distribution; of
the factors of production, land, labour, capital, management, know-
how and education, and ideas of the efficacy or otherwise of competitive markets, it is possible to develop any number of debates about
the ways the wealth creating process is most likely to occur, in historical
time-periods or by comparing the apparent performance of one country
or culture with another. A recent bold approach at the growth theme
was projected by the American economic historian Professor W. W.
Rostow, who, in 1959, published an interesting if academically controversial tract called *The Stages of Economic Growth*. Rostow, in
what he described as a non-communist manifesto, used Marxist type
stages of growth, but led them forward to different conclusions than
that of revolutionary turmoil, finally culminating in pure communism.
He saw all societies as evolving through five categories: starting first
with the traditional primitive society, which gradually moves into the
pre-conditions for 'take-off'. This is followed by the third stage of
take-off, succeeded by a drive to maturity, culminating in an age of
'high mass consumption'. Rostow recognised that during the stages of
moving from traditional society to the preconditions for take-off and
the take-off stage there will be considerable 'discontinuities' affecting
society. Nevertheless he suggested that if societies are able to raise the
rate of investment at these critical stages from 5 per cent to 10 per cent
(in real terms), and make the necessary institutional and social adjustments, then they will be able to establish, by a long process of
development, a pattern of growth which can take them forward on to a
sort of learning curve to maturity and an eventual age of high mass
consumption. In this sense all the advanced industrial systems, whatever their ideological complexion, show signs of 'convergency'.

Rostow supported this vision of development by an extensive examination of historical periods of growth, as experienced in different
societies from 18th century England moving into the Industrial Revolu-

tion, through to growth in Western Europe and the United States in the 19th and 20th centuries, and also to certain developing countries who are moving into industrial/urban living at the present time. At the stage of high mass consumption, which Rostow postulated as the ultimate any human society can hope for, he saw a wide diffusion of consumer durable goods with suburban living, and a college education for a third to half of the population. However he conceded that this stage of development may be inhibited by the onset of social welfare legislation in the pursuance of non-high mass consumption goals, by the build up of the need for national defence and aggrandisement which may inhibit expenditures on growth. Paradoxically as the individual wealth and well being may increase, the society as a whole feels what Voltaire called the 'tyranny of possessions' . . . and the need to defend what it has achieved. There is also often a lack of ability to make the right critical long term investments for the generation of power, electricity, and other crucial basic industries. Interestingly, writing in 1959, Rostow failed to give any significant weight to environmental or other resource constraints to growth, which have since featured so prominently in the 'Club of Rome' and Massachusetts Institute of Technology conservationist world growth models of the late 1960s onwards. The 'energy crisis' of the 1970s was also unforeseen in Rostow's late 1950s scenarios. Nevertheless his five stages have considerable interest to them. During the 'drive to maturity' phase which immediately precedes the stage of high mass consumption, particular characteristics are the speed of technical change and an improved efficiency in all sectors of the economy, the habit of growth becoming ingrained in the population, and the rates of growth consistently outstripping population increase, leading to rises in per-capita income. Immediately before this stage, in the take-off stage, essential requirements include a rise in the overall rate of growth in compound interest, while in the pre-condition stage there are slow changes in attitudes of organisation, the gradual mobilisation of resources, and of new productive activities in agriculture and industrial capacity. Rostow called his work a 'non-communist manifesto' because he considered it suggested a viable alternative to the socially disruptive aspects of the Marxist model, which originally derived from *The Communist Manifesto* published by Marx and Engels in 1848.

It remains to be seen whether the developing world as a whole will follow Rostovian or Marxist/Leninist industrial patterns in their developmental processes – or in fact eventually opt for self-help agrarian development programmes, as followed in much of Mao's

FIG. 21. W. W. ROSTOW'S FIVE STAGES OF ECONOMIC GROWTH (1959)

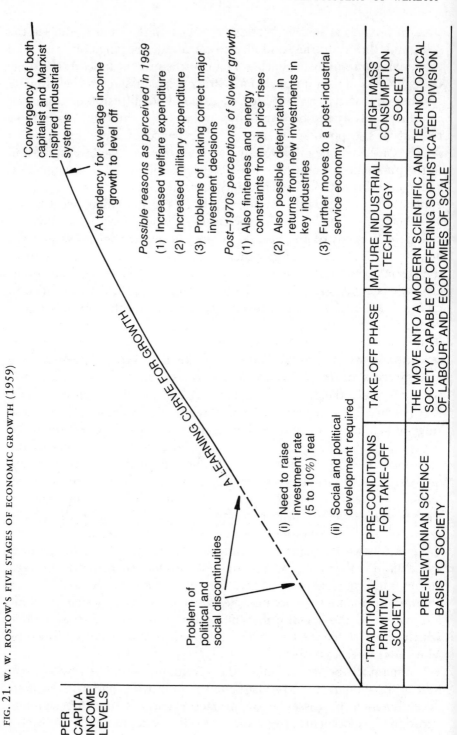

post-1949 revolutionary China. Again the Club of Rome, cum Massachusetts Institute of Technology type restraint arguments, as to the urgent need to conserve basic finite resources, are reminiscent of early classical views of diminishing returns, acting as a longer term constraint to affluence for everyone. In a number of advanced economies from the late 1960s onwards, economists have also drawn attention to a possible worsening in capital investment to output ratios experienced by basic capital intensive industries – and the implications of this for further rapid growth prospects. Certainly the impact of high energy prices imposed by the OPEC countries, from 1973 onwards, suggests the increasingly alarming scenario of a world economy divided into three Ricardian type groups; a rentier monopoly group of emerging primarily oil producing states, able to demand a pure 'scarcity rent' for their goods; an advanced urban/industrial group of countries with the know-how and ability to at least break even and in some cases earn a substantial surplus, especially those like the U.S.A. and potentially the U.S.S.R., and the combined E.E.C., endowed with both industrial and military power and substantial mineral and agrarian resources as well. Finally an intermediate group of less developed countries, devoid of both cheap energy and critical raw materials, or of specialised managerial cum technical resources, able to do little more than exist on their own limited resources and sell a small margin of raw materials, foodstuffs, etc., to unstable, or at best uncertain, world markets. The latter groups will find it difficult to escape from their current position and indeed, from time to time, will inevitably require continual and substantial financial assistance from the more industrially developed or resource-abundant world. Thus Ricardo's early 19th century England, of rentier landlords, frugal capitalists and 'subsistence' wage, industrial and agrarian workers may, in very broad terms, be translated into late 20th century national groupings. For Ricardo the way out was free trade abroad, which in England's case eventually followed the Repeal of the Corn Laws in 1846. Wherein lies the contemporary solution for the modern world remains the unanswered $64,000 question. Expanding output and wealth via trade with other planets or solar systems does not seem to offer immediate practicable possibilities!

## Neo-Keynesian Ideas about Economic Growth

It will be apparent from the foregoing that many of our ideas about growth owe little, if anything, to a totally secure statistical base, which has increasingly been regarded as critical to the development of modern economic science. Yet the problems associated with economic growth and development clearly hold a fascination for those immersed in economic statistics, and to a greater or lesser degree many of their ideas have found their way into national economic planning – as practised both in industrial cum post-industrial and would-be industrialised developing economies. To some extent this has been undertaken by Keynesian minded economists who wish to extend, if possible, the benefits of new ideas to the more fundamental problems of economic growth per se. There are many examples of this type of work: particular reference might be made to Walther Hoffman's pioneering work on the growth of industrial economies, published in 1931, which was based upon the relationship of industrial production to capital goods. In the 1930s the Australian agricultural economist, Professor Colin Clark, also examined in detail the relationship between the primary agricultural, the secondary manufacturing, mining and construction, and the tertiary service sectors. Later, Professor Simon Kuznets, the 1971 winner of the Nobel Prize in Economic Science was an important implementer of Keynesian ideas, as part of his interest in national income accounting he undertook a series of international investigations on the quantitative aspects of economic growth of nations and also a deeper historical study of statistical data, which leads on to a consideration of seeking to isolate what have been the critical variables in the long-term growth process. Attention should also be drawn to work by Professor Jay W. Forrester's *World Models* developed at the Massachusetts Institute of Technology – linking together short and longer term cycles of economic activity, in a computer based study of the U.S. economy extending over long time periods. Finally, some of the 1973 Nobel Prize winner Professor W. Leontief's ideas about input–output tables fit into similar uses. Some of his current quasi-optimistic projections on *The Future of the World Economy* are included at the end of the book.

It will be recalled that in the classical Ricardian model the major limitation on growth was imposed by the finiteness of land (and other raw materials), which in turn affected the price of food and eventually influenced the long term growth of population and supply of labour. The intellectual justification for the harshness of the Ricardian model with its ordering of society into three classes: rentier landlords safeguarding the productivity of the finite soil, of the capitalist classes looking after long term investment needs, and of the working classes toiling for a 'subsistence wage', was that only by this ordering of society and wealth distribution, could the necessary resources be mustered to

FIG. 22.   GROWTH CYCLES ACCORDING TO JAY W. FORRESTER

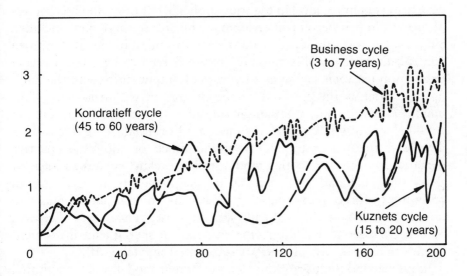

A computer-based simulation by Professor Jay W. Forrester and his M.I.T. colleagues reveals cyclical behaviour by much of the U.S. economy: labour demand in the consumer-goods sector in the three- to five-year business cycle, capital demand from the consumer-goods sector in the 15- to 20-year Kuznets cycle, and capital-equipment demand in the capital sector in the 45- to 60-year Kondratieff cycle. But Professor Forrester suspects that there is an even larger 'life cycle of economic growth' which represents a 300-year process of maturation.

The question arises as to the contemporary impact of the 'ups and downs' in the American economy on the world economy as a whole. It was once said that when 'America caught a cold Britain got the 'flu'. The growing interdependence of the modern American economy with the world economy as reflected in its requirements to import up to half of its oil supplies, and as a major market for the other industrial nations' products, means that what happens in America is of critical importance to what happens to the world at large.

finance the future. These sorts of ideas, dressed up in more humane form, were also apparent in subsequent neo-Keynesian growth models. In practice Keynes' ideas for interventionist financial demand management policies have had most immediate application in the advanced democratic industrial economies. Nevertheless several of his disciples have also sought to develop theories applicable to promote higher rates of growth in less developed economies. In Britain these have included Sir Roy Harrod and Lord Kaldor. For instance, in the well-known 'Harrod-Domar model' economic growth is seen to be a result of the interaction between saving and the capital output ratio, with the build up of capital as the essential engine of growth within society. Thus intended savings and the capital output ratio achieved sets out an equilibrium growth path, from which in a Keynesian sense it is easy to deviate if there is instability from too much or too little effective demand. In other words this model seeks to relate Keynesian ideas of short term demand management to the longer term needs of an economy to forgo via savings for critical investment, and increases in future output. As we have already seen, Rostow, in his stages of growth model, considered that lifting the *real* rate of saving cum investment from 5 to 10 per cent of GNP, was essential for 'take-off'.

In intellectual discussion the Harrod-Domar model was later shifted somewhat in a neo-classical direction by Messrs. Solow and Mead, who allowed for far more substitution amongst the factors of production rather than the fixed proportions between capital and labour, etc., as assumed in the Harrod-Domar model. Again Kaldor, in a further development of ideas about growth, gave rather more emphasis to the importance of what he called the 'technical progress' element relating to investment. In seeking long term growth, capital investment per se is simply not enough; rather advanced industrial societies need to move continually into areas of greater technical sophistication, and this in turn extends investment to include not only machinery but also consideration of investment in human capital via appropriate education, increased organisational efficiency and government policies, etc. Indeed all the advanced Western economies are locked in a sort of 'devil take the hindmost race', with each country seeking to move 'up market' into areas of high technology and greater value adding possibilities. Whether they will be able to continue to do this smoothly, if at all, in a world characterised by a rising real price of energy, and by an apparent threat of deteriorating capital investment to output ratios in key industries, is the dilemma facing much of the highly industrialised world in the last quarter of the 20th century.

FIG. 23.   A. H. MASLOW'S 'HIERARCHY OF HUMAN NEEDS'

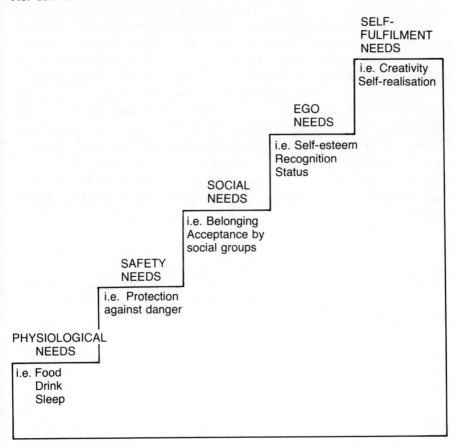

1. Maslow assumes that man is a continually wanting animal, and that these needs and wants operate in a hierarchy of urgency as shown above.

2. This means that the lowest unsatisfied need at any time overrides the other needs and motivates the behaviour of a person to satisfy that need.

3. A satisfied need is no longer a motivator.

4 The highest need is the need for self-fulfilment, that is the desire to become everything that one is capable of becoming.

A full statement and discussion of these ideas can be found in *Motivation and Personality*, A. H. Maslow (Harper & Row, 1970).

In sum, despite all the discussion there has been in recent times about economic growth, it cannot be said that a coherent ongoing 'predictive' model has yet been achieved. Economic doctrine has a long way to go before it can devise an ideal rationalisation of the processes by which all societies, at any stage of development, at any time in history, might be seen to be encouraged to develop and grow to a higher stage of material well-being, assuming always that is what they desire in the first place. Underlying all macro-growth wealth creating discussions remains the fundamental issue of human motivation. Is this normally guided by truly 'economic man' as postulated by the classical, neo-classical and Marxist economists? Alternatively do deep cultural and religious values, with different 'hierarchies of need' on the lines suggested by Mr. Maslow or others provide a more rational explanation for the way most societies will continue to grow or not to grow into the future? Only time will tell!

# Chapter 4

# DOMESTIC PROBLEMS AND POLICIES

"Qu'ils mangent de la brioche."
Let them eat cake."

Marie-Antoinette (1755–1793)

"Population, when unchecked, increases in a geometrical ratio. Subsistence only increases in an arithmetical ratio."

Thomas Robert Malthus (1766–1834)
*The Principle of Population*

"The rich man in his castle, the poor man at his gate, God made them, high or lowly and ordered their estate."

Cecil Francis Alexander (1818–1895)
*All Things Bright and Beautiful*

"It costs a lot of money to die comfortably."

Samuel Butler (1835–1902)
*A Luxurious Death*

"When every one is somebodee, Then no one's anybody."

Sir William Schwenck Gilbert (1836–1911)
*The Gondoliers*

"He (Gladstone) told them he would give them and all
other subjects of the Queen much legislation, great
prosperity, and universal peace, and he has given them
nothing but chips."

Lord Randolph Spencer Churchill (1849–1894)
Speech House of Commons, 7 March 1878

"I'll let you into a secret folks,
I'm buying land. They've stopped
making it."

Will Rogers (1879–1930)

"I see one-third of a nation ill-housed,
ill-clad, ill-nourished."

Franklin Delano Roosevelt (1882–1945)
Second Inaugural Address, 20 Jan. 1937

"How ya gonna keep 'em down on the farm,
once they have seen Paree?"

Popular song refrain by
Walter Donaldson

"Private affluence, public squalor."

John Kenneth Galbraith

## Land, Natural Resources and Rent

As has been emphasised in earlier chapters, the problems and debates
associated with the possession of and price for land, and related finite
natural resources, as reflected in rents, totally preoccupied the thinking
of many of the early classical economists. Land as a primary source of
wealth and store of value, for nations and individuals alike, dominated
the pre-industrial world. Necessarily the same issues remain among the
most politically and socially contentious debates facing society today.
The possession and use of land is critically important, both as a source
of basic materials and food production, and as a provider of essential
living and working space. It presents critical policy and public welfare
problems for Western democratic and Marxist governments alike. In
the agrarian based developing countries of Asia, Africa and Latin
America the effective utilisation of land resources is still central to
economic survival.

Professor W. G. Hoskins, in his work on *The Making of the English*

*Landscape*, published 1955, examined the evolution in the economic use of the countryside from early settlement to modern industrial times. However, most of our intellectual ideas about land as a uniquely scarce resource date from the beginnings of the industrial age. It will be recalled that the end of the 18th century and early years of the 19th century saw an unprecedented growth in Britain's population and increasing demands for food production – the more so in the light of restrictions of imports by the impact of the Napoleonic Wars and the later working of the Corn Laws and trade embargoes against cheaper foods from Europe and elsewhere. Thus, land was the *critical* factor which, beyond a certain point, no increase in price could increase supply given the ultimate finiteness of nature. In classical doctrine it was seen to fulfil two distinct functions. In the productive process its fertility and location enabled its possible use for food production. However, land also provided space for other economic activities, including the rapid expansion of new towns and cities to accommodate the growing population and expanding industrial scene. The justification of rent centred around first the importance of land as a scarce and irreplaceable resource, and as a measure of its 'scarcity value'. Second, a justifiable additional price for land which, by the expenditure of capital would be made inherently more productive, by the introduction of drainage, or new methods of husbandry, or the clearing of scrubland and woodland. Land as a natural resource in its raw state had no supply price, in that there would be no reduction in the available supply even if it earned nothing. In this sense the earning capacities of land depended entirely on the extent of the demand for its use, and its relative scarcity. As time went by and more and more hitherto common land was enclosed and brought into production, man-made capital improvements were incorporated into the soil, and it became impossible to separate the returns from these man-made improvements, from the returns to land as a scarce and finite resource. A third stage of classical thinking was that the closer land was to some specific demand for its produce or for its use, the higher its price was likely to be. A particular piece of land with high fertility and the advantages of situation, such as land suitable for market gardening near a growing town, would naturally be able to sustain a higher level of rents than land which had low fertility and was remote from commercial use.

The early classical economists were further impressed with the fact that land became a resource with 'diminishing returns'. As we have seen, they illustrated this by referring to what was known as the 'law of variable proportions', a principle that described the relationship between inputs of productive resources and the resultant output of a product. Whenever increased output requires the combined services of different factors of production, such as labour and land, and one of which is limited in supply, such as land, any attempt to overcome its relative scarcity by combining it with larger amounts of other factors will eventually slow down the rate of increase in total output. More precisely the law stated that 'as equal increases of a variable factor are added to a constant quantity of other fixed factors, in this case land, the successive increases in output will after a point decrease'. The law applied to all forms of productive organisation providing one or more of the productive factors is fixed in supply. Successive units of the variable factor were assumed to be of equal efficiency, such as further inputs of work by similar labourers, and where the state of technological knowledge remains constant. The law rested on the common observation that factors are imperfect technical substitutes for one another. Diminishing returns were and are the physical effects of continuing the substitution of the less available or fixed supplies of a factor, particularly land.

In their classical policy prescriptions, Ricardo and Malthus were mainly concerned with the application of the concept in respect to the growth in population, relative to finite agricultural land forcing up rents and food prices. The 'dismal science' prophesies of these classical thinkers was based on the view that technical progress in agriculture, such as the introduction of new crops, fertilisers, drainage, machinery and suchlike, would eventually prove insufficient to offset the effects of the law of variable proportions, and diminishing returns to further inputs of labour, etc. was bound to apply. In fact the history of British agriculture witnessed sustained periods of innovation and change, from the early clearings of woodland, draining of fen and marshland and application of improved methods of husbandry. As it turned out the real increases in agricultural productivity from the later 18th century to the present day have gone far beyond those contemplated by classical doctrines, and they do not seem to have been borne out by subsequent events. Most importantly, the British economy moved away from its dependence on its own land as a finite resource and as a basis to feed its population. Following the disaster of the Irish potato famine in the mid-1840s and the subsequent Repeal of the Corn Laws in 1846, the growth of *laissez-faire* trade with other parts of the world enabled the exchange of manufactures for imported food from more abundant land surplus countries. These, in respect to national food supplies and income, were able to compensate for the diminishing returns inherent in the domestic agricultural system. Nevertheless the possibility of diminishing returns, especially as applied to agriculture and food production, remains an important and fundamental constraint underlying the working of any economic system. The ability of any nation to feed its people from its own land resources remains a trump card in a world of scarcity.

In the history of economic thought very similar diminishing returns discussions and debates have also occurred in respect to the commercial situation of coal, and other finite mineral resources. In 1864, for instance, Professor Stanley Jevons, noted for his pioneering work on marginal utility, published a pessimistic book called *The Coal Question* in which he examined the diminishing returns apparently inherent in British coal mining, moving as it was into less and less easily workable seams. Fortunately mining technology developed rapidly, and new, deeper and more productive seams were also discovered. In recent years the basic output per man hour shift in coal mining, greatly aided by investment in mechanical methods, has continued to rise slowly. In the British coal industry current hopes lie in developing large new mechanised mines in the East Midlands at Selby to overcome rising costs elsewhere. Moreover during the 1960s, there was a massive switch into another finite source of energy, Middle Eastern crude oil, which was coming in great abundance on to the world markets at the time. At present we are seeing a further reappraisal of the costs of all finite forms of energy, following on from the 1973 oil price rises, and a renewed questioning as to the diminishing returns energy basis of society as a whole. Britain, and indeed the Western world, is reappraising long term energy needs in the light of security of supply and other critical considerations.

*     *     *     *     *

In terms of public policy the question of the justification of payment of rent, for a finite and scarce resource, to a rentier class however defined, be they 18th century landowners or 19th century coalmine owners, or 20th century oil sheikhs, had persisted throughout economic reasoning. Plainly as population has increased, and the demand for land as either a productive resource to grow food, or to extract minerals, or for housing and industrial purposes, has grown, those who have unlimited rights of property vested in land or resources are apparently able to obtain a continually increasing rent. For this reason Ricardo, in his theory, divided discussion of the return from land into two categories: returns that would be justified because of the natural *scarcity* of land; and returns which were justified because of improve-

FIG. 24. THE ROLE OF LAND AND FARMING IN THE EUROPEAN ECONOMIC COMMUNITY, 1977

| | farming profile | importance of farming in each country | | importance to EEC of each country's farming | | | size of farms | |
| --- | --- | --- | --- | --- | --- | --- | --- | --- |
| | | % of country's income farming provides | % of jobs provided by farming | % of total farmland in EEC | % of total EEC farm production | contributes more than 20% of EEC production of: | average size of farm (acres) | average number of cows in dairy herd |
| UNITED KINGDOM | Largest farms in the EEC. Not as high yielding as Denmark or Netherlands. Farms usually produce more than one type of food. Net importer of food | 2.1 | 2.6 | 20 | 11.7 | barley, potatoes, lamb/mutton | 159 | 40 |
| BELGIUM | Small farms. Emphasis on pig farming and horticulture. Net importer of food | 2.8 | 3.6 | 2 | 4.0 | nothing | 35 | 12 |
| DENMARK | High-yielding. Emphasis on pig and dairy farming. Farms all pretty much the same size. Net exporter of food | 6.0 | 9.2 | 3 | 4.3 | nothing | 56 | 16 |
| FRANCE | Big contrast between relatively large and rich grain farms of north and north-east, and relatively small and poor farms in certain other areas. Dairy sector politically powerful. Net exporter of food | 4.9 | 11.2 | 35 | 27.6 | wheat, oats, barley, maize, sugar beet, tobacco, oil seeds, fruit and veg, milk, beef and veal, flax and hemp, poultry, lamb/mutton, wine | 60 | 11 |

| Country | Description | | | | | Products | | |
|---|---|---|---|---|---|---|---|---|
| ITALY | Mixture of advanced agriculture in northern plains, and very small peasant holdings in middle and south. Net importer of food | 8.3 | 15.5 | 19 | 20.8 | wheat, maize, rice, tobacco, olive oil, fruit and veg, wine, silk, poultry | 19 | 5 |
| LUXEMBOURG | Steep wooded slopes make farming difficult. High rainfall, so unsuitable for anything but livestock. Net importer of food | 2.9 | 6.2 | less than 1 | 0.1 | nothing | 58 | 16 |
| NETHERLANDS | Small farms, with exceptionally high yields – includes reclaimed, very fertile land. Emphasis on livestock and horticulture. Net exporter of food | 4.7 | 6.5 | 2 | 7.8 | seeds | 36 | 23 |
| REPUBLIC OF IRELAND | Mainly grassland for livestock. Production time for beef slow; yields low. Farms generally worked by one person only. Net exporter of food | 15.9 | 24.1 | 5 | 2.0 | nothing | 44 | 10 |
| WEST GERMANY | Small farms, with two out of three farmers part-time. Farms usually produce more than one type of food. Net importer of food | 2.5 | 7.3 | 14 | 21.7 | rye, oats, barley, sugar beet, milk, beef and veal, pork, hops, eggs, wine, seeds | 34 | 9 |

Figures based on latest information available (mainly 1975) from EEC Commission.

ments in the *productivity* of the land. He thought in terms of improvements in land in such a way as it raised labour productivity, as opposed to improvements in land which simply enhanced the inherent productivity of the soil. He also considered land as such a finite and scarce resource, with an inherent ability to sustain high rental incomes, that he considered that rents were one of the few appropriate sources of income which could be used as a basis for taxation, in that it was taxing a resource which none could escape the consequences of its scarcity. This also became the origin of the 19th century American socialist, Henry George's (1839–1897) idea of basing all taxation on a single tax of land values. It also underpins all ideas, from Tudor times onwards, of the desirability of taking land into public ownership.

Other important ongoing theoretical discussions about the relationship between land, rents and public policy, are still associated with Johann von Thünen, the German agricultural economist and the son of a landowner. He developed a highly mathematical technique concerned with the principles to determine the best system of cultivation, especially in terms of distance from the market, and in this sense he became the forerunner of modern ideas of industrial location being based on rational analysis of alternative costs of different locations, and distances from supply and demand markets. However, his analysis also occasioned him to build up a theory of rent very similar to that propounded by Ricardo. Because of his denial of the subsistence theory of wages, and his use of marginal analysis, he played a considerable part in stimulating the later development of neo-classical economic analysis.

By the second half of the 19th century and the time that Marshall was writing, the view was that as the British population continued to grow, rents would inevitably gradually increase to exceed income again from all other material resources. The question of land ownership, use and prices has continued to persist as an important social and political issue until the present day, and is reflected in Britain in much of the debate about Town and Country Planning legislation, from the 1947 Act onwards to the Community Land Bill of 1972. A high price of land for building purposes is a reflection both of the natural scarcity of appropriate land, and the intensification of this scarcity by the requirements of planning, which limits the amount of land available, and lays down the services to be provided for housing on such land. Both requirements have naturally tended to force prices up. Land for housing today generally constitutes a higher proportion of the cost of a new house and land combined, than was the case in previous times. In urban renewal and development schemes, the question of the economic price for land being negotiated between previously fragmented small property owners and the public authorities charged with taking land over for redevelopment, or for public purposes, is often a matter of critical debate. In all western democratic countries policy is frequently torn between desire to sustain the rights of a 'property owning' democracy on the one hand – yet encourage a 'socially desirable' use of land for housing and productive purposes on the other. However Marxist-inspired states generally opt for public ownership and the elimination of 'rentier classes' as a whole. In Soviet Russia the Kulaks, a more prosperous class of peasants, who had gradually acquired land following the abolition of serfdom and the break up of great estates, suffered grievously at the hands of Communists with the forced introduction of state owned collective farms, during the 1930s.

Figure 25 gives some indication of the current worldwide relationships between land area, population nucleus and density per square kilometre which today apply. Plainly even within the European Economic Community very wide variations exist – with Ireland and France having especially abundant land resources while Belgium, Holland, Germany and the United Kingdom have high population densities. The high population density of Japan is also especially significant. Perforce countries with very high densities of people to land have generally sought a way out through the creation of advanced industrial, commercial urban based societies.

FIG. 25.   AREA, POPULATION, DENSITY PER SQ. KILOMETRE AND ESTIMATED POPULATION GROWTH—MID 1974

| | Country | Area '000 sq km | Popu-lation '000 | Density per sq km | Projected population '000 | |
|---|---|---|---|---|---|---|
| | | | | | 1980 | 1985 |
| | EUR-9 | 1 528.2 | 257 835 | 169 | 263 507 | 268 962 |
| 1 | Germany | 248.6 | 62 054 | 250 | 61 940 | 61 814 |
| 2 | France | 547.0 | 52 507 | 96 | 55 302 | 57 744 |
| 3 | Italy | 301.3 | 55 413 | 184 | 57 181 | 58 773 |
| 4 | Netherlands | 40.8 | 13 545 | 332 | 14 190 | 14 729 |
| 5 | Belgium | 30.5 | 9 772 | 320 | 9 867 | 9 933 |
| 6 | Luxembourg | 2.6 | 357 | 137 | 364 | 370 |
| 7 | United Kingdom | 244.0 | 56 056 | 230 | 56 214 | 56 878 |
| 8 | Ireland | 70.3 | 3 086 | 44 | 3 309 | 3 519 |
| 9 | Denmark | 43.1 | 5 045 | 117 | 5 140 | 5 202 |
| 10 | Greece | 132.0 | 8 962 | 68 | 9 479 | 9 740 |

FIG. 25 *continued*

| Country | Area '000 sq km | Population '000 | Density per sq km | Projected population '000 | |
|---|---|---|---|---|---|
| | | | | 1980 | 1985 |
| 11 Turkey | 814.6 | 38 270 | 47 | 45 767 | 52 010 |
| 12 Norway | 323.9 | 3 987 | 12 | 4 100 | 4 196 |
| 13 Sweden | 450.0 | 8 161 | 18 | 8 334 | 8 436 |
| 14 Switzerland | 41.3 | 6 481 | 157 | 6 636 | 6 864 |
| 15 Austria | 83.9 | 7 528 | 90 | 7 778 | 8 018 |
| 16 Portugal | 91.6 | 8 735 | 95 | 9 283 | 9 663 |
| 17 Finland | 337.0 | 4 682 | 14 | 4 570 | 4 524 |
| 18 Spain | 504.8 | 35 225 | 70 | 36 413 | 38 061 |
| 19 USSR | 22 402.0 | 252 064 | 11 | 270 634 | 286 882 |
| 20 USA | 9 363.1 | 211 909 | 23 | 229 000 | 244 000 |
| 21 Canada | 9 976.1 | 22 479 | 2 | 25 299 | 27 347 |
| 22 Japan | 370.0 | 109 671 | 296 | 115 972 | 120 798 |
| **World** | **135 897.0** | **3 890 000** | **29** | **4 401 000** | **4,858,000** |

Looking to the world at large, as population continues to expand rapidly, and the productivity of the economic system struggles to maintain pace with the demand for foodstuffs and other raw materials, the price of land and related finite natural resources is bound to remain a highly contentious issue. In world terms countries endowed with abundant amounts of land of high agricultural fertility appear to be well placed in the future balance of world power. In recent years the productivity of the American grain growing regions, arising from both their adequate endowments of suitable soils and the high efficiency of their energy-intensive privately owned farming system, has enabled the United States to have a powerful bargaining tool in world diplomacy. In turn, in the mid-1970s this has become particularly associated with the failure of the Soviet large collectivised agricultural system, the grain growing of which is generally confined to somewhat more northern climes than the United States' grain growing areas, to produce sufficient foodstuffs for the growing Soviet population. In the mid-1970s the Soviet Union became critically dependent for some margin of its grain foodstuffs to be imported from the United States. Other examples of the critical importance of land and its use, both as a source of foodstuffs and for underlying minerals and raw materials, will be familiar to all and require no further reiteration at this stage. They remain central practical and doctrinal issues, in the economic and political life of both democratic and Marxist inspired states alike.

## Population Increase and Labour Supply

During the past two hundred years economists have also been strongly aware of the problems associated with a rapid increase in population, and this was often associated with discussions about the use of finite land, and other resources. Between 1850 and the 1970s the world's population quadrupled from 1 billion to 4 billion souls. By the end of the century it may be approaching 8 billion, much of the increase being concentrated in less developed agrarian societies. Most of these countries face public policy problems which would have had immediate meaning for the classical and early Marxist economists alike. For Adam Smith the answer to the rapid increase in population and the associated enclosure movement of the agricultural improvements, was to look for suffcient economic growth and wealth creation in the new manufacturing methods to absorb and sustain the rapidly increasing workforce. As we have seen, his perception of the problems presented by population increase in relation to the working of the economic system as a whole were generally optimistic. He believed that freeing economic systems from the shackles of mercantilist restrictions would, through the beneficent working of *laissez-faire* and the benefits of the 'invisible hand' on the division of labour, generate aditional wealth. In time this would be sufficient to deal with the problem of providing work and sustenance for the increasing population and workforce. Smith also looked to the further development of colonies abroad as a way by which expansion of trade could be found, and where surplus population and capital would be able to find creative outlets.

For Malthus, however, closely associated with land by family and occupation, the world seemed a far less optimistic place. In time, following his 1798 essay on the *Principle of Population*, Malthusian ideas were to sweep away the optimistic hopes generated by the philosophers of reason, particularly Adam Smith and Godwin. They suggested that as population increased less fertile land would have to be brought into cultivation, and the increase in food production could not possibly keep pace with demand. This seemed a reasonable proposition at the time in England, and throughout Western Europe, where population had begun to increase at a previously unprecedented rate, and there was considerable distress in the countryside. In Britain this distress was compounded by the effects of the enclosure movement which were forcing many landless workers off the land, and by the failure of the new factories to expand fast enough to provide alternative employment opportunities. Later Marx was also to note the distress of a pauper landless peasantry forced off the land to provide a 'reserve army' of unemployed, available for 'exploitation' and 'immiseration' in the new industrial system.

For Malthus, famine could only be avoided if the labouring population undertook moral restraint, by which he meant marrying later and having fewer children. Given the conditions of the age, only the most optimistic conceived of this as being remotely possible, and Malthusian ideas eventually had much influence on policy makers who wished to adopt a more 'cost effective' policy towards public relief for the poor. This is an *important story* which is worthy of considerable examination, in that very similar debates and policy description are occurring in many of the developing countries of today. From Tudor times English poor relief had been administered by local Justices, in relation to the price of bread and the size of the pauper's family. In the late 18th century the system had been further liberalised by linking under the Speenhamland system some agricultural workers' wages to corn prices, which prevented the need for relief in the first place. In light of the full application of Malthusian theory, a policy of being kind in the present would seem to lead to greater hardship in the future, in the sense that it would increase the possibility through feeding and 'over indulgence' of a tendency to overpopulation. In fact the 1834 Poor Law Amendment Act was conceived by its architects as a great measure of fiscal and administrative reform, and the ideas of the leading classical economists of the day, including Professor Nassau Senior, had a hand in its framing and implementation. Their 'penny pinching' efforts were later to be the subject of vituperative attack by Marx and other anti-bourgeousie writers. It set about attempting to unify the previously somewhat chaotic Tudor local poor law system. Thus a central Poor Law Department was set up with Edwin Chadwick (1800–1890) as its first Secretary with the task of directing and advising the Boards of Guardians elected by local ratepayers to administer the Poor Laws, while in some cases parishes were combined into Unions. Unlike the previous unco-ordinated system, a distinction was made in respect to relief given between the able bodied and the sick and disabled poor, and in particular no outdoor relief to the able bodied was allowed. This meant that all those who wished to obtain relief had to enter the Workhouse, where conditions were intentionally hard. Indeed, in the Malthusian/Ricardian tradition they were intended to discourage people from having ideas that relief was in any way pleasurable, and to stimulate the feeling that everyone had an obligation to work.

Several weaknesses of the 1834 Act soon became apparent. It took no account of seasonal fluctuations in employment, which meant that many men who were willing to work were unable to do so, but increasingly resented the implication that they were 'work-shy'. Again, many of the sick, the young and the old who were without means of support, necessarily shared the shame and humiliation of harsh conditions of the Workhouse, which were by no means deserved. These soon became the target for exposure by the writings of Charles Dickens, notably in his depiction of Oliver Twist and other orphan children left to the ministrations of Mr. Bumbles, and also by other socially reformist authors. However, financially the Act seemed to be justified, and national expenditures on poor relief decreased, although other reasons may account for this, apart from the improvement in administration which the Act had brought. In particular the expansion in the 1840s of the new railway system soon provided considerable new employment and for a number of years after the introduction of the Act, agricultural harvests were good and considerable employment existed. Again the general gradual development of the manufacturing and commercial sectors of the economy generally raised living standards. In later years there were various changes in the application of the 1834 Act. In 1843 an outdoor labour test was applied which allowed relief to be paid to the able bodied if they were engaged in approved activities, and in practice relief was given even if this was not strictly complied with. Other rules were relaxed which had previously caused the separation of husbands and wives when falling under the Poor Law system. Later, in 1847, the Poor Law Board was replaced by a central government department and from this time onwards it was administered by a Minister. By the 1860s the Poor Law Unions in large towns were beginning to follow the example of London and to build hospitals for the poor. In 1888 the property qualifications required for election to the Boards of Guardians of Workhouses ended, more working class guardians were appointed, and the day to day administration of the Poor Law system began to be considered more sympathetically. Nevertheless the Poor Law system, and in particular the 1834 Amendment Act, caused great resentment and indeed was a focus for much of the political agitation associated with the Chartist movement of the time. If nothing else, the submitting of 'the People's Charter' to Parliament demonstrated that the working classes were able to mobilise public sympathy and politically became a force to be reckoned with. Yet it was to be a long road between the Charter of 1839 to the election into office of the first Labour Government under the Prime Ministership of Ramsay MacDonald in 1924. However the reformist Liberal administration, under the Prime Ministership of Herbert Asquith (1852–1928), in the years immediately before the First World War, relied substantially upon working class and Labour and Co-operative Party support.

To contemporary eyes the classical economists found it easy to move from the ideas associated with rapidly increasing population as a national problem, to the idea of the same population providing a labour supply, as a basic factor of production, employed in combination with land and capital to produce commodities or render services. They regarded much of the labour of their time as a homogenous workforce, most of whom were leaving, or being forced off the land and seeking employment in new factories. They therefore made very broad assumptions about the relationship between the supply of labour and wage levels, which in turn fed back through to the tendency for population to increase. They generally believed that there was, in Ricardo's words, a 'subsistence wage' for labour which in the England of his time was sufficient to maintain husband and wife in modest comfort, and at a level sufficient to reproduce themselves. This idea persisted in various forms. For instance in Australia Mr. Justice Higgins in the early years of the Commonwealth Court of Arbitration, following the Harvester Judgement of 1907, specified a basic wage for a family unit – sufficient for a husband and wife and two children to live in reasonable comfort. However if average wages were allowed to move above subsistence level then this would, in a Malthusian sense, encourage the population to increase. Thus increases in national wealth were seen by most of the classical thinkers as flowing through into the wage bargain, which in turn would feed through to increase levels of affluence and an eventual increase in total population. This would lead eventually to more labour on offer for hire at the average wage, which, given the state of competition, must eventually equal the marginal wage. In agriculture diminishing returns were likely to apply and lower average wages would be paid, if all else remained the same. However in manufacturing, there was at least the possibility of 'constant returns' which, as time went by, became 'increasing returns', with the increased productivity which manufacturing scale, the division of labour, and improved machinery allowed. In turn this would allow average wages to be increased.

*     *     *     *     *

In Britain one of the leading economists concerned with labour market studies has been Professor Henry Phelps-Brown at the London School of Economics. Many of his ideas were expressed in his book on

*The Growth of Industrial Relations* published in 1959. In modern economic thinking the supply of labour has increasingly been recognised as being unlike other factors. While an increase in the price of a commodity will generally induce an increase in supply, the supply of labour is influenced by a wide variety of other conditions, particularly in the shorter run. Plainly the number of any workforce available depends on the total size of the population, and the proportion of it which is customarily at work. In Britain some 48 per cent of the total population of some 56m is today regarded as being 'economically active', of whom just over one third are customarily female. Moreover of the present workforce of some 26.6m, some 1.6m are currently unemployed. The majority of those employed are today in the service industries, just over one third in manufacturing and less than 500,000 in agriculture. The structure of employment and the nature of the workforce, its skills and expectations, is thus far removed from the assumptions underlying the early classical model, which assumed a great mass of agrarian workers slowly moving into industrial and, in the case of many women, domestic service.

In practice very similar proportions apply for most advanced countries today. For instance, the O.E.D.C. statistics given in Figure 26 (which are compiled on a somewhat different basis than U.K. statistics for comparability with other countries) suggest in 1974 8.9 per cent of European civilian employment was regarded as working in agriculture, 42.6 per cent in industry and 48.5 per cent in services. Of the other countries listed Turkey with some 63.4 per cent in agriculture was by far the least industrialised – and a ready source of potential factory and service employees for Western European industry and services.

Today many people can choose, within broad limits, whether or not they will work; (a most obvious example are married women) and therefore the net effect of real higher wages on the numbers at work can be uncertain. It may, for instance, increase because more money and higher wages attract new workers, or it may diminish because some married women will tend to give up work, when the real incomes of their husbands increase. The number of hours worked depends on the relative preference of the employee for money income, as opposed to leisure. If he or she wishes to earn a higher income, they will tend to work longer hours and forego leisure. The concept of a *backward sloping supply curve* for labour when with rapid increases in real wages some workers decide that, given their present scale of preferences, they prefer to forgo part of the higher wage and take more leisure, has become a well-known feature of modern industrial society. When the

FIG. 26. CIVILIAN EMPLOYMENT BY MAIN SECTORS OF ECONOMIC ACTIVITY 1974

| | Country | Agriculture '000 | Industry '000 | Services '000 | Total '000 | Agriculture % | Industry % | Services % | Total % |
|---|---|---|---|---|---|---|---|---|---|
| | **EUR-9** | **9 085** | **43,595** | **49 590** | **102 270** | **8.9** | **42.6** | **48.5** | **100** |
| 1 | Germany | 1 882 | 12 221 | 11 586 | 25 689 | 7.3 | 47.6 | 45.1 | 100 |
| 2 | France | 2 452 | 8 301 | 10 412 | 21 165 | 12.0 | 39.2 | 49.2 | 100 |
| 3 | Italy | 3 111 | 8 256 | 7 348 | 18 715 | 16.6 | 44.1 | 39.3 | 100 |
| 4 | Netherlands (b) | 304 | 1 625 | 2 650 | 4 579 | 6.6 | 35.5 | 57.9 | 100 |
| 5 | Belgium | 140 | 1 565 | 2 096 | 3 801 | 3.7 | 41.2 | 55.1 | 100 |
| 6 | Luxembourg | 10 | 74 | 67 | 151 | 6.6 | 49.0 | 44.4 | 100 |
| 7 | United Kingdom | 705 | 10 467 | 13 596 | 24 767 | 2.8 | 42.3 | 54.9 | 100 |
| 8 | Ireland | 254 | 326 | 467 | 1 047 | 24.3 | 31.1 | 44.6 | 100 |
| 9 | Denmark | 227 | 760 | 1 368 | 2 355 | 9.6 | 32.3 | 58.1 | 100 |
| 10 | Greece | 1 134 | 852 | 1 334 | 3 320 | 34.2 | 25.7 | 40.2 | 100 |
| 11 | Turkey | 8 760 | 2 090 | 2 960 | 13 810 | 63.4 | 15.1 | 21.4 | 100 |
| 12 | Norway | 189 | 560 | 905 | 1 654 | 11.4 | 33.9 | 54.7 | 100 |
| 13 | Sweden | 276 | 1 428 | 2 175 | 3 879 | 7.1 | 36.8 | 56.1 | 100 |
| 14 | Switzerland | 220 | 1 435 | 1 442 | 3 097 | 7.1 | 46.3 | 46.6 | 100 |
| 15 | Austria | 489 | 1 219 | 1 331 | 3 039 | 16.1 | 40.1 | 43.8 | 100 |
| 16 | Portugal | 895 | 1 052 | 1 162 | 3 109 | 28.8 | 33.8 | 37.4 | 100 |
| 17 | Finland | 369 | 769 | 1 016 | 2 154 | 17.1 | 35.7 | 47.2 | 100 |
| 18 | Spain | 3 406 | 4 879 | 4 559 | 12 844 | 26.5 | 38.0 | 35.5 | 100 |
| 19 | USSR | | | | | | | | |
| 20 | USA | 3 452 | 26 745 | 54 212 | 84 409 | 4.1 | 31.7 | 64.2 | 100 |
| 21 | Canada | 571 | 2 738 | 5 450 | 8 759 | 6.5 | 31.3 | 62.2 | 100 |
| 22 | Japan | 7 030 | 19 470 | 25 830 | 52 330 | 13.4 | 37.2 | 49.4 | 100 |

EUR-9: figures 1974; other countries 1973. *Source:* O.E.C.D.

British coal mines were first nationalised in 1947, an increase in the average wage of coal miners to some £15 a week, was paralleled with a reduction in the number of hours worked. The same phenomenon is also apparent in Africa, or other less developed countries, where domestic servants have a certain requirement for a level of real wages, to pay for mission school education for their children. However, if this level of income rises from say 150 to 200 shillings per month, then the domestic servants may well opt out of full time domestic work and use more time in their traditional subsistence agricultural pursuits.

Another way in which the modern labour market is markedly different from that assumed in classical doctrine is the power of trade unions in the market place. Indeed in Britain we have become increasingly accustomed to trade union leaders becoming key elements in the success, or otherwise, of counter-inflationary powers. In recent years the application of long standing collective bargaining agreements have been disrupted by introduction of national, if somewhat intermittant wage and price control policies, Phase I and II etc. Throughout the democratic world the support of key trade unions for 'social contract' type policies is becoming central to national economic strategies. The control or influence of governments on average annual wage settlements, and the linking of these to cost of living changes, has become a central feature and debate in political life. Morover at industry level it depends greatly on political view whether one considers the power of trade unions must be strong, in order to provide a 'countervailing' power to the organised bargaining strength of employers, or whether trade union restrictions on the free working of market forces act as an undesirable brake on longer term labour mobility, and economic efficiency and growth. Plainly, immobility of both labour and enterprise capital may be aggravated by trade union restrictions, demarcation rules and regional national wage agreements which are used to prevent local and/or skilled wages differentials.

Generally, the labour market, in the western urban-industrial economies is of an extremely heterogeneous, varied and generally skilled workforce. It falls into many different professional and trade union groupings; which organise collective wage negotiations on a national basis. The issue of appropriate differentials for different skills and scarcities in the changing labour market have also become matters of acute concern and grievance. What is the fair relativity between coal miner, railwayman, fireman, civil servant, traffic controller, teacher, surgeon etc.? This is increasingly affected by the existence or otherwise of national incomes and prices policies, and ideas about a social contract, etc. All this is far removed from the early *laissez-faire* model of a largely similar propertyless workforce, moving from agriculture into small factory or manual construction work. At the factory level the way the production system works is highly dependent on the extent of capital investment in modern plant and machinery, and on the education and training of the workforce, for the effective use of this capital. Labour productivity in much of modern industry depends not only on the motivation of the workforce, but also on the levels of skill and training in that workforce, and the distribution of this skill between appropriate capital equipment and processes. For instance, one evaluation by Mr. T. M. Rybczynski of sources of 'contributions to economic growth' in Britain between 1950 and 1962, suggested that nearly one third came from technical improvements, over one fifth from additions to capital, 15 per cent from economies of scale, 13 per cent from labour (net additional man-hours), 12 per cent from education and 5 per cent from improved resource allocation. The position in a number of other leading industrial nations is shown in Fig. 27.

FIG. 27   CONTRIBUTION TO ECONOMIC GROWTH (SHARING OF THE MAIN FACTOR %)

|  | U.K. 1950–62 | U.S.A. 1948–69 | Japan 1953–71 | Germany 1950–62 | France 1950–62 |
|---|---|---|---|---|---|
| 1. Education | 12.2 | 11.0 | 4.1 | 1.7 | 6.2 |
| 2. Labour (net additional man-hours) | 13.0 | 21.5 | 16.9 | 20.1 | 3.4 |
| 3. Technological Improvement | 33.2 | 29.7 | 22.4 | 13.9 | 32.1 |
| 4. Economies of Scale | 15.1 | 10.5 | 22.0 | 25.7 | 21.3 |
| 5. Improved Resource Allocation | 5.1 | 7.5 | 10.8 | 16.1 | 20.2 |
| 6. Additions to Capital | 21.4 | 19.4 | 23.8 | 22.5 | 16.8 |
| Rate of Growth % p.a. (standardised rate) | 2.4 | 4.0 | 8.81 | 6.27 | 4.7 |

*Source:* T. M. Rybczynski.

Another important debate relates to *labour mobility*. If labour were completely mobile between areas and occupations, movement from low productivity occupations paying low wages, to high wage productive activities would be encouraged. Such a movement of labour would be reinforced by a drift of new enterprise and capital to areas where wages are relatively low. In practice the mobility of labour between occupations is limited by a variety of considerations, including lack of education, training experience and ability, and the cost and difficulties of movement. This in turn reflects the social and political structure of the country as a whole, and in particular that housing may not be available in areas where work is on offer. In Britain nearly half the population and workforce live in government subsidised council housing which is not readily available in all areas. Moreover those owning or purchasing houses on mortgages may be disinclined to move if the housing market is difficult. For these and other reasons in recent times much of British government policy has been devoted to seeking to attract to areas of high labour unemployment, new industries which can absorb the unemployed. This has been seen to be a more efficient policy than seeking to encourage very high degrees of labour mobility out of areas of traditional high unemployment, to areas where a large demand for labour exists.

Despite the application of *regional policies* of this sort, there has historically been a continuous drift of labour out of areas of relatively high unemployment, notably the central belt of Scotland, Northern Ireland, and parts of the north of England where staple industries, textiles, shipbuilding, coal mining, have long been in decline, towards areas which are offering new employment opportunities. In the inter-war years many new light industries making household, electrical and consumer goods, food processing, confectionery and suchlike, were started to the west of London and in the Midlands, and labour was attracted in from the more depressed northern parts of the country. However in the post-war years, government industrial policies have directed many new industries into areas with persistent high unemployment, particularly South Wales, Lancashire, Teesside and the Northeast coast and the central areas of Scotland, and this has been associated with the New Towns policy and investment grants to industry. Similar regional industrial development policies have been applied in many parts of the European Economic Community, though these have been more concerned with attracting manufacturing value adding activities to areas of poor agricultural conditions such as southern Italy, Sicily, south-western France and the Central Massif. On the other hand, many of the post-war factories, construction industries, catering and hotel trades and public services of France and West Germany, Switzerland, and Scandinavia, rely on drawing in from poorer Mediterranean and Middle Eastern countries a reserve work-force, which can supplement the local workforce. Throughout the European Community as a whole some 4.5m workers now come from countries other than where they presently work. As recent experience has shown, during periods of recession these 'gaste arbieter' are soon encouraged to return from whence they came. Thus the cutback in the European motor industry of 1975–76 was accompanied by massive traffic jams from Munich to Istanbul as Turkish and other Balkan workers left Germany to return to their homelands in the south. Truly a Marxian 'reserve army' of the unemployed, 1970s style!

## Savings, Capital and Know-how

In all the Western 'mixed' democratic economies, debate about the effective utilisation and productivity of labour is linked with the problem of encouraging adequate saving and investment and capital formation in productive enterprise. One effect of the Keynesian revolution in economic thought was to question the neo-classical assumption that money saved automatically flowed into real investment. In practice the rate of interest is now seen to be one of a number of variables, which may induce people to forgo liquidity or present consumption for savings, and conversely encourage or discourage businessmen from new investment in machinery and stock for expansion. In the contemporary industrial world, especially in Britain and the U.S.A., considerable amounts of financing for the future come from retained profits, and as such are not subject to an open market test. Thus in the economic system as a whole, the act of postponing or forgoing consumption (a necessary but not sufficient condition for capital formation) would today be called saving, rather than automatically supplying capital, as was thought to be the case in earlier classical doctrines.

Capital, in the broadest sense, might be defined as the stock of resources, available at a particular time, to help satisfy future wants. This definition may be applied to a nation's stock of material wealth in the form of machinery, goods, raw materials and know-how, plus its claims against, and minus debts owing to, people in other countries. It may also be regarded as an individual's private assets, which includes material objects and claims against his countrymen and government as well as claims against people in other countries. Capital has also been used to refer not only to material wealth or stock, but also to flow of savings in such terms as the supply of capital and the amount of free or floating capital, *potentially* available for productive use. As we have seen, the classical and neo-classical economists had a view of real capital being gradually developed in the expanding industrial system. Thus saving and matching accumulations of capital in new factories and processes could lead to increasing the division of labour, in the economies of scale and a gradual improvement in overall productivity. In general Ricardo however took a somewhat pessimistic view of possibilities of the return from capital in manufacturing, which he regarded as becoming constant and as unlikely, at least in his time, to fully compensate for the onset of diminishing returns in agriculture. In fact throughout the 19th century the returns from capital invested and reinvested in the new manufacturing processes improved significantly, and the increased economies of scale and the benefits of the division of labour fed through into the creation of additional wealth for society as a whole. In the second half of the 19th century such was the effectiveness of the British industrial system in producing a capital surplus that not only did the country become a major source of capital for its own purposes, but the City of London also became the centre for the export of capital throughout the world. During the second half of the 19th century the capital exports of London, going to both private industrial, mineral and transport projects and to public loan raising by the British Dominions and Colonies, became a key feature in world industrial and trade development. They also became associated with a steady and increasing flow of British and Irish emigration to the U.S.A. and to the new white Dominions. In return for the capital exports Britain received an increasing flow of dividends and other invisible earnings plus expanding trade opportunities. Many of these early investments and associations remain of great importance to the present day.

Marx, while being on record as decrying capital as 'the domination of living men by dead matter', was more than the early classical economists aware of the possibilities of the impact of new ideas and new technology on creating increasing returns to scale in the new industrial system. However in the Marxian model, the tendency for the capitalist classes to take the 'surplus value' and continually seek new investment outlets was based on the Achilles heel, of a grossly unequal distribution of income between the labouring and the capitalist classes. This meant that there would eventually be a failure of 'effective demand' for the system as a whole. To Marxists the capitalist system was predetermined to progress through a series of increasingly disastrous slumps, with periods of brief boom and an increase in the demands for raw materials and production of capital and consumer goods, being followed by disastrous depressions, arising particularly out of the inability of the system to sustain demand for its products. Marx, together with several other classical economists, including Sismondi and Malthus, took an 'under-consumption view' of the economic system, and thought that capital was likely to be locked in an increasingly desperate search for profitable investment outlets. A continuous tendency for a fall in the rate of profits would lead to increasingly desperate competition between large monopolistic manufacturers for at best static or slowly growing markets, incapable of absorbing the output of the increasingly productive factory system. Indeed both Hobson and Lenin later considered that a main imperative behind late 19th and early 20th century imperialist expansion was the need for the industrial nations to escape from collapsing profits at home.

Both the classical economists and early Marxists thought primarily of an increase in the capital stock as providing a way of gradually absorbing more labour into the factory system. As time went by there was increasing awareness that an overall increase in the total capital stock of the community at large would not only encourage *internal economies* of scale within factories, but also, by a widening of the total environment, provide *external economies of scale* within the urban and industrial system as a whole. Marshall gave particular emphasis to these possibilities, as the total capital stock of the community increased, in line with an increase in the educational standards, skills and know-how of the workforce as a whole. Today the average worker in the advanced industrial and urban countries from the U.S.A. to Western Europe, or for that matter, the industrial countries within the Soviet led COMECON group, generally enjoy a far higher standard of living than average workers in under-developed agrarian countries, largely because they work with more capital, technical knowledge and industrial managerial organising experience at their disposal. The same is true in contrasting the average incomes of workers in, say, Singapore or Hong Kong to those in nearby agrarian societies.

*     *     *     *     *

Figure 28 shows Gross Fixed Capital Formation by products in a number of countries in 1973. For the nine European Economic Community member countries on average 25.7 per cent was in dwellings, 32.2 per cent in non-residential buildings and civil engineering works, and some 44 per cent in equipment. This table indicates the broad proportions of capital formation which today applies in a cross section of contemporary industrial and urban societies.

FIG. 28.   GROSS FIXED CAPITAL FORMATION BY PRODUCTS 1973

| | Country | Dwellings % | Non residential buildings and civil engineering works % | Equipment % | Other products % | Gross fixed capital formation % |
|---|---|---|---|---|---|---|
| | **EUR-9** | **25.7** | **32.2** | **44.0** | **3.0** | **100** |
| 1 | Germany (a) | 24.4 | 34.6 | 44.0 | 1.8 | 100 |
| 2 | France (a) | 28.7 | 31.8 | 46.5 | 2.0 | 100 |
| 3 | Italy | 29.4 | 26.9 | 40.0 | 3.7 | 100 |
| 4 | Netherlands (a) | 27.4 | 33.4 | 44.2 | 1.1 | 100 |
| 5 | Belgium (a) | 22.6 | 38.9 | 38.7 | 5.1 | 100 |
| 6 | Luxembourg (a) | 21.6 | 45.8 | 35.2 | 2.7 | 100 |
| 7 | United Kingdom | 19.5 | 28.5 | 44.0 | 7.9 | 100 |
| 8 | Ireland | 23.7 | 30.2 | 39.8 | 6.3 | 100 |
| 9 | Denmark (a) | 30.2 | 34.3 | 45.9 | 0.1 | 100 |
| 10 | Greece | 32.7 | 34.6 | 32.8 | — | |
| 11 | Turkey | 19.2 | 34.8 | 46.0 | | 100 |
| 12 | Norway | 17.6 | 40.9 | 41.5 | −0.02 | 100 |
| 13 | Sweden | 24.4 | 38.6 | 37.0 | 0.02 | 100 |
| 14 | Switzerland | — | — | — | — | — |
| 15 | Austria | 56.8 | | 38.1 | — | 100 |
| 16 | Portugal | 17.3 | 39.9 | 42.8 | — | 100 |
| 17 | Finland | 25.5 | 38.1 | 36.4 | — | 100 |
| 18 | Spain | 15.4 | 34.1 | 49.7 | — | 100 |
| 19 | USSR | — | — | | | |
| 20 | USA | 23.6 | 34.7 | 41.7 | | 100 |
| 21 | Canada | 24.4 | 40.8 | 34.9 | | 100 |
| 22 | Japan | 24.0 | — | 76.0 | — | 100 |

(a) The total of the groups of products is not equal to 100, the difference being constituted by the V.A.T. deductible on purchases of fixed capital goods.

A modern industrial nation's capital stock is now widely regarded as consisting not only of durable producers' goods such as machinery and equipment and stocks of raw material, and semi-finished goods and products held by manufacturers and distributors, but also of the housing and other buildings of society as a whole. Again the individual citizen's possessions of household stocks also range from possessions with low durability, such as foodstuffs consumed in a short time, through to semi-durables such as clothing, to consumer durables such as furniture, cooking stoves, refrigerators and motor cars, some of which, in an economic sense, might be regarded as providing the possibility for society to be more productive as a whole. However in economic discussions, it is usual to exclude such household stocks from capital, partly because their purchase calls for a separate explanation than that of capital goods intended to assist with further production, and also partly because household stocks are difficult to value in themselves. Indeed one of the problems facing the private citizen living in an 'affluent' urban and industrial society is to cover the rapid depreciation in money value of consumer durable goods – the more so if they have been purchased on costly hire purchase or loan schemes.

In modern economic theory, productive capital stock is therefore generally considered as falling into two groups – fixed and working. Fixed capital includes all kinds of buildings, machinery, improvements to roads, land drainage, etc., while working capital consists of goods in process of being prepared for consumption, raw materials, semi-finished goods and finished goods in the hands of manufacturers, wholesalers and retailers. The distinction is made for two main reasons. First that income yielded by fixed capital may, for long periods, depart from current market return on replacement cost, because the capital is usually specialised and takes time to increase or decrease in amount, its supply being relatively inelastic. In the meantime, its income depends on the demand for its products and the quantity of the fixed capital in existence. Conversely, working capital can be more quickly adjusted, if its yield departs from the market return on replacement. As Marx and others clearly saw, those industries supplying fixed capital goods tend to be subject to larger fluctuations in demand because durability allows discretion in the timing of replacements, and additions to fixed capital are not usually made at a regular rate.

It is important that the development of capitalism has not so far borne out the Marxian scenario of internal contradictions in the system inevitably leading to its total destruction. This prophesy has not been supported by the expectations of increasing concentration in industry being unmitigated by a more even distribution of income, so as to make it impossible since the end of the Second World War to sustain consumer demands. As we have seen, the effect of the Keynesian contribution to contemporary democratic economic doctrine and policy has been to facilitate a more even pattern of growth in demand and, at least in the advanced industrial countries, the real standard of living of wage and salary earners has risen steadily, notwithstanding the problems of inflation. During much of the post-Second World War era, real per capita incomes in Britain are thought to have increased by some $2\frac{1}{2}$ per cent per annum, while in several West European countries some 4 per cent per annum became the usual rate of increase – until the onset of the 'energy crises' years of the mid-1970s. Moreover the social transformations and levelling processes within Western industrial society since Marx's time has tended to blur the distinction between the proletariat and the bourgeoisie, rather than aggravate them on the basis of his inevitable two class conflict model.

\*     \*     \*     \*     \*

Nevertheless during the present century there have been many continuing disputes accompanying the evolving nature of the capitalist system, with its continued reliance on the substantial private ownership of capital, and decentralised market related decision-making. One particular aspect of this has been to focus discussion on the continuing role of the large *limited liability joint stock company*, which differs markedly in its operations and functions from the one man firm or private partnerships of the early 19th century classical model. Indeed it might be considered that the introduction of limited liability companies, and the spreading of risk which they facilitated, was one of the key inventions of the Victorian age. However as company ownership has become diffused and widely held, often through investment by pension funds, insurance companies, etc., there has been a break between ownership and control over a company's affairs. Salaried directors may manage in a way which is not seen to be directly accountable to the full interest of shareholders, and there is seen to be a widening gap between ownership and control considerations. This tendency towards a bureaucratisation within the capitalist system was early analysed by Schumpeter, and others of the historical school, as part of a more general development into a new type of corporate industrial society. Similar themes have been taken up by a number of contemporary economists, notably Professor J. K. Galbraith, in his book *The New Industrial State*, published in 1967. However other neo-classical thinkers, such as Professor Hayek and Lord Robbins, have continued to emphasise the responsibility of the legal framework of companies, for the forms of industrial structure which have been allowed to develop within the capitalist system. For this anti-corporatist and institutional view the answer to the problems presented by large industrial capital grouping forming cartels or monopoly is not to nationalise them; or to seek to co-ordinate decision-making through 'Tripartite planning agreements'; and such like. Rather the solution lies in reintroducing the benefits of competitive markets, instead of considering their demise as an inevitable consequence of the development of big technology, big governments, big unions and the mass production system as a whole. Recently Professor Milton Friedman has also been expressing similar *laissez-faire* views, with great vigour and reference to current British political, social and economic tendencies.

In Britain and other Western European Democratic economies, another important debate centres on the relative balance of the large scale private, as opposed to publicly owned, sectors of the economy. The question of decision-making about future investment planning, and of appropriate research and development programmes, also comes into focus, especially by multinational companies who make decisions about these on an international basis. For instance the creation in the early 1960s of the National Economic Development Council brought together the tripartite interests of big industry, the unions, and of government. Its various committees examine in detail the aggregate supply problems of major segments of the industrial economy. This is seen as putting the supply side of the economy back into some form of creative relationship with attempts to financially demand manage the economy by the Treasury and other agencies. Thus the Keynesian revolution, which started as an interventionist philosophy to deal with the problems of unemployment in the 1930s, has become a broad demand management system which, in turn, has required a supply management response. This in turn, is the subject of a wider political debate about whether investment decisions, made on a 'co-ordinated' central basis, are likely in the long run to be more effective, in national terms, than decisions taken on a decentralised basis. Certainly 'convergency' of opinion about such issues is far from achieved, and many of the associated issues are considered later in the book.

## Profits, Rates of Return and Corporate Survival

Associated with the role of capital are debates about both its cost and its rate of return as reflected by profitability. In everyday language profit is still associated with a surplus of income over outgoings in an industrial or commercial enterprise. To the pure capitalist it is a justified reward for risk taking or uncertainty: to the true Marxist a measure of exploitation and the 'immiseration' of the working class. In fact practical businessmen in both capitalist and Marxist inspired systems are increasingly demonstrating a remarkable convergency of opinion in emphasising the importance of an *adequate rate of return*, however defined, to finance the future. In the development of classical doctrine, profit was regarded in a number of different ways. To some it was the wages paid to the individual entrepreneur for his work, and particularly for his role as a risk-taker. To others it was rent paid for his special knowledge and ability; and yet to others an interest on his capital. In fact, accounting for profit by a small businessman, such as a shopkeeper or a farmer, may include elements of all three kinds of payment. The neo-classical economists, faced with both the increasing scale and rapidly changing nature of large scale industry and markets, came to regard profit as essentially a recompense for *risk taking*. This is still an influential view, though given the vast scale and organisational extent of much of contemporary industry, it is often difficult to see it applied in full rigour or extent. It is not easy to see how risk is divided between the shareholders, who receive what is left after paying taxes, and given the application of 'dividend restraint' policies leave considerable income in the company, and the decision-makers who in theory are the risk-takers, but as directors are usually salaried servants of the enterprise. Again, in present circumstances, some risks can be foreseen and discounted, while large numbers may be grouped together and converted into a known cost by insurance. Alfred Marshall regarded profit as a reward of enterprise or the earnings of management, and in this sense profit became a special type of wage or salary paid for specially unique kind of labour service. Later the American, Professor John Bates Clark, considered the nature of profit to be justified as a reward as a result of change. He argued persuasively that in a static and perfectly competitive economy the price of commodities or services would cover their costs including management and no more. However, change would upset this equality, because the effect of increasing income would take time to spread throughout the economy. In the meantime some sectors would exceed costs as defined, giving rise to true profits, or costs would exceed prices giving rise to losses. Another American, Professor F. H. Knight, developed the theory beyond this point, and argued that change as such could not explain profit, because some changes would be anticipated and could be allowed for before they happened. Indeed if there was perfect foresight, all change could be foreseen and therefore change would not bring any profit at all. Thus for Knight the root cause and justification for profit was *uncertainty*, profit arose not from change itself but from the unpredictability of change, which made precise rational judgement of future change and profits difficult to achieve. To view a profit as a kind of risk premium is useful for a number of reasons. It suggests that in the absence of monopolistic practices the cost to society of risk bearing is likely to be large. It also indicates that profits in the sense of a risk premium is likely to be present in any kind of economic system, whether based on private enterprise or on state ownership and control. The only way in which any system can abolish 'profit' is by preventing change, so that the future can be seen without uncertainty. More recently the 1972 Nobel Prize winner Professor Kenneth J. Arrow has also been associated with developing new theories on 'risk' and 'uncertainty' in business judgement.

Recent experience in Britain, American and throughout Western Europe, has demonstrated the extreme political and social difficulties which arise when large capital and labour intensive enterprises cease to earn profits, and indeed pile up large losses. As the recent examples of Lockheed, Rolls Royce, British Leyland, Volkswagen and numerous fringe banks and property companies have shown, too much is at stake. For the best of political and social reasons Mr. Edward Heath's Conservative Government, from 1970 onwards, found it more difficult to allow 'lame ducks' to die, than many of their more 'backwoodsmen' supporters had imagined, or desired. Too much is at stake, from national employment, to exports and import replacement, and pension fund equity to allow a quick death by the market test. Yet, in the day-to-day working of the modern mixed economic system, profit is still regarded as an essential surplus, to allow enterprises to retain for investment in the future. An adequate rate of return (taking into account the true rate of inflation) is essential to allow the enterprise to finance the depreciation of its existing capital and to invest for future possibilities. The tendency for there to be an apparent fall in true profitability – and a lack therefore of adequate investment funds for further industrial development – has been widely suggested as a prime reason underlying Britain's lack of competitive strength against overseas competitors – both at home and abroad. It must however, be recognised, that average rates of return have also tended to fall in other Western economies as well, though accompanied at the same time by, until recently, a steady growth in output. Needless to say, for the committed Marxists, the apparent widespread deterioration from the late 1960's in capital to output ratios and the associated decline in profitability, is taken to presage the long predicted demise of capitalism, and its eventual replacement by a completely socialist system of ownership and control.

*    *    *    *    *

Doctrines apart, a strong practical interest is being shown in the importance of 'real profitability' to the operation of the modern industrial economy. Neo-classical and Marxist thinkers are in agreement in the need for an adequate surplus, however defined, to finance the future with, and in both systems a convergence is apparent in the wide recognition of the need for adequate 'surpluses'. Moreover, for different reasons, business in both types of economy has shown an increasing tendency to do this from retained 'profits', than from outside sources. In a study published on profitability in Britsh industry between 1960 and 1975 in *Trade and Industry*, 8 October 1976, it showed that while the level of profitability, measured in historic cost terms, has remained in a range between about 19 per cent and 13.5 per cent over the last 15 years, it has declined from about 13 per cent in 1960 to about 4 per cent in 1975, when measured realistically in light of inflation, and the depreciation of money as any sort of store of value. Faced with such a downward trend in real rates of return it is understandable that individual managers and owners might be tempted to postpone new investment in fixed assets, even if they judge that they can have or can get adequate funds, to put to productive future use. Rather they may well decide to employ the retained profits of companies to reduce debt, or to employ their funds in making financial investments where they will have high immediate rates of return. Early in 1977 the average yield on British Government short term securities was some 14 per cent, as opposed to something over 6 per cent, as reflected on a dividend yield of ordinary shares. Yet in making such a comparison it is necessary to recognise that the dividend return on Government Bonds stays the same in cash over the years, losing their real value in proportion to the rate of inflation over the period. On the other hand investment in productive assets offer a prospect of a real return, which is likely to grow as the fixed assets come fully into operation, and the cash value of many such assets may well also increase in line with inflation. Thus, in theory at least a low but certain yield in real terms, together with the prospect of capital gains, may still be preferable to a money rate of return, which is nominally higher.

The British Government has become increasingly aware of the many dangers implicit in the declining trend of industrial profitability in real terms, and its current 'industrial strategy' is based on the idea of 'regeneration' of a profitable industrial sector producing tradeable commodities in export markets. To this end the Government's Price Code was revised to take better account of companies' need for adequate profit, with modifications designed to favour investment and the adjustments for the inflated cost of depreciation. Moreover there have been tax allowances for investment in fixed capital, with further adjustments for stock appreciation which operate to reduce tax liability. The Chancellor of the Exchequer Mr. Dennis Healey has also publicly recognised the importance to industry and commerce of a stable tax environment, that is, one which does not make frequent changes in coverage and rates, which make financial forecasting so difficult. There have also been outright grants for capital investment in assisted areas under the 1972 Industry Act and in addition £205 million was allocated by the Government since 1975 to provide low interest loans for modernisation in specific industries, such as clothing, machine tools, etc. Some £120m was allocated to provide 'pump priming' loans to promote accelerated investment for counter-cyclical purposes starting before September 1976. Further allocations of £108m in 1977, 1978 and 1979 of selective industrial support from public funds were announced by the Chancellor on 15 December 1976.

During 1976 the Government also reviewed planned public expenditure in the light of economic and financial developments and announced cuts designed to ensure the resources and finances of private industry were not 'crowded out' by demand in the public sector. Again, in its monetary policy, the Government has attempted to control the growth of the money aggregate in a way which supports the Government's policy on counter-inflation and industrial expansion, while helping to maintain orderly conditions in foreign exchange markets, in particular the 1976 'December package' was designed to create conditions for which, in the longer run, it considered would be good for industrial investment.

At the present time a committee, under the chairmanship of Sir Eric Roll, is examining, under the auspices of a National Economic Development Committee, sources of finance for industrial development. In longer term the Committee on Financial Institutions, under the chairmanship of Sir Harold Wilson, is also looking at the performance of existing financial institutions to provide adequate finance for industrial development. In these various ways the hope is that the essential requirement of profit, in real terms to the economic system, will continue to be recognised. Finally one can do worse than to quote from a speech by the Prime Minister, Mr. James Callaghan, at the Labour Party Conference on 28 September 1976, in which he said:

> "Let me add one more thing that we are a little shy of saying in conference about industrial regeneration. The willingness of industry to invest in new plant and machinery requires not only that we overcome inflation but that industry is left with sufficient funds and sufficient confidence to make up the new investment. When I say they must have sufficient funds I mean that they must be able to earn a surplus which is a euphemism for saying they must make a profit. Whether you call it a surplus or a profit it is necessary whether we live in a socialist economy, a mixed economy or a capitalist economy."

Finally, as Mr. Dennis Healey, the Chancellor of the Exchequer, speaking to the Overseas Bankers' Club at Guildhall on 21 January 1977, affirmed:

> "Firms will only expand and invest if they can see scope for making profits."

Who can best decide what should be invested in for the future; the government, big business, the unions or small business is another story, which is pursued in somewhat greater detail elsewhere in the book.


## The Balance of Production to Welfare

The two parts of Figure 29 suggest both the regularities and the proportions of the use of Gross Domestic Product which today apply in some leading countries. For the European Economic Community as a whole in 1974 some 61.4 per cent was as private consumption, 15.5 per cent on government consumption and 22.8 per cent on Gross Fixed Capital Formation. Among other countries listed the very high proportion of 34.3 per cent devoted by Japan to Gross Fixed Capital Formation is especially significant as to the way that economy operates as a world-wide industrial competitor – and is considered in greater detail in Chapter 6.

In neo-classical economics, theories of value (in use or exchange) and

FIG. 29. USE OF GROSS DOMESTIC PRODUCT AT MARKET PRICES 1974

| Country | Private consumption on the economic territory | Collective consumption of general government | Gross fixed capital formation | Change in stocks | Balance of exports and imports of goods and services | Gross domestic product at market prices | Private consumption on the economic territory | Collective consumption of general government | Gross fixed capital formation | Change in stocks | Balance of exports and imports of goods and services | Gross domestic product at market prices |
|---|---|---|---|---|---|---|---|---|---|---|---|---|
| EUR-9 | 559.5 | 140.5 | 210.3 | 11.2 | −3.3 | 918.1 | 61.4 | 15.5 | 22.8 | 1.3 | −1.1 | 100 |
| 1 Germany | 177.4 | 42.4 | 69.5 | 0.3 | 15.2 | 304.9 | 58.2 | 13.9 | 22.8 | 0.1 | 5.0 | 100 |
| 2 France | 131.3 | 27.6 | 53.4 | 3.9 | −3.2 | 213.0 | 61.7 | 13.0 | 25.1 | 1.8 | −1.5 | 100 |
| 3 Italy | 80.2 | 16.8 | 28.0 | 2.2 | −7.3 | 119.8 | 66.9 | 14.0 | 23.4 | 1.8 | −6.1 | 100 |
| 4 Netherlands | 30.9 | 9.5 | 12.3 | 1.3 | 1.4 | 55.4 | 55.8 | 17.2 | 22.2 | 2.3 | 2.5 | 100 |
| 5 Belgium | 24.7 | 6.2 | 9.6 | 0.9 | 0.8 | 42.1 | 58.7 | 14.7 | 22.7 | 2.1 | 1.8 | 100 |
| 6 Luxembourg | 0.9 | 0.2 | 0.4 | 0.0 | 0.1 | 1.7 | 53.4 | 12.1 | 25.5 | 1.8 | 7.1 | 100 |
| 7 United Kingdom | 96.4 | 31.1 | 30.4 | 2.1 | −8.6 | 151.4 | 63.7 | 20.5 | 20.1 | 1.4 | −5.7 | 100 |
| 8 Ireland | 3.8 | 1.0 | 1.3 | 0.2 | −0.9 | 5.3 | 71.0 | 18.2 | 24.7 | 3.3 | −17.2 | 100 |
| 9 Denmark | 13.8 | 5.7 | 5.4 | 0.4 | −0.8 | 24.5 | 56.5 | 23.2 | 21.9 | 1.6 | −3.2 | 100 |
| 10 Greece | 10.9(c) | 2.1 | 3.3 | 0.6 | −1.5 | 15.3 | 70.9(c) | 13.6 | 21.7 | 3.7 | −9.9 | 100 |
| 11 Turkey (a) | 10.9(c) | 2.1 | 2.7 | 0.0 | −0.6 | 15.1 | 72.2(c) | 14.0 | 17.6 | 0.3 | −4.1 | 100 |
| 12 Norway | 9.6 | 3.1 | 6.0 | 0.3 | −0.3 | 18.7 | 51.4 | 16.5 | 32.1 | 1.8 | −1.8 | 100 |
| 13 Sweden | 23.5 | 10.7 | 10.0 | 0.9 | 0.1 | 45.3 | 52.0 | 23.6 | 22.0 | 2.1 | 0.3 | 100 |
| 14 Switzerland (b) | 18.1 | 3.7 | 9.3 | 0.3 | 0.8 | 32.2 | 56.1 | 11.6 | 28.8 | 0.8 | 2.6 | 100 |
| 15 Austria | 14.2 | 4.0 | 7.4 | 0.8 | −0.2 | 26.3 | 53.9 | 15.3 | 28.0 | 3.3 | −0.6 | 100 |
| 16 Portugal (b) | 6.4(c) | 1.2 | 1.8 | −0.0 | −0.5 | 8.9 | 72.3(c) | 13.5 | 20.1 | −0.1 | −5.8 | 100 |
| 17 Finland | 8.7 | 3.0 | 5.1 | 1.5 | −0.8 | 17.6 | 49.6 | 17.1 | 29.0 | 9.0 | −0.5 | 100 |
| 18 Spain (b) | 34.7 | 5.5 | 10.5 | 0.9 | 3.1 | 48.6 | 71.4 | 11.3 | 21.7 | 1.9 | −6.3 | 100 |
| 19 USSR | — | — | — | — | — | — | — | — | — | — | — | — |
| 20 USA | 703.1 | 215.2 | 195.2 | 11.2 | — | 1,118.4 | 62.9 | 19.2 | 17.5 | 1.0 | −0.6 | 100 |
| 21 Canada | 64.6 | 22.4 | 27.0 | 2.2 | 0.2 | 116.5 | 55.5 | 19.2 | 23.2 | 1.9 | 0.1 | 100 |
| 22 Japan | 190.9 | 36.6 | 124.7 | 13.7 | −1.9 | 364.0 | 52.4 | 10.1 | 34.3 | 3.8 | −0.5 | 100 |

(a) 1972.
(b) 1972.

theories of distribution together came to constitute that of price. Additionally theories of welfare relate to options or choices open in the distribution of wealth, which may or may not relate to the price mechanism. In Britain the work of Sir John Hicks, the 1972 Nobel Prize winner with Kenneth J. Arrow, is especially associated with pioneering work in both general equilibrium and welfare theories. As has been emphasised throughout, a persistent underlying debate in economic doctrines is the distinction between production and wealth distribution, in both its current income and existing capital forms. Most leading economists at one time or another, during the course of their careers, have been concerned with the relationship of production to wealth. In the late 18th and early 19th century the physiocrats and early classical economists made great play of dividing society into different classes, some of whom were regarded as being inherently more productive than others. For the physiocrats the productive classes were the tenant farmers, whereas the land owning and merchant classes were essentially non-productive, the former taking the rent for land, while the latter simply passed on wealth, which had already been created in the sowing and harvesting process. Again, Smith and the other early classical economists were aware that some people were apparently more productive, in a wealth producing sense, than others. For Smith, increased production came essentially out of the division of labour, and from those people who were pursuing their own interests, working for either a profit or for a wage, in the new industrial system. On the other hand there were many other people – landlords, judges, professors on secure salaries with lifetime tenure, servants of the Crown, the armed forces and such like – who needed to be justified by other criteria, though in an over-all classical economic sense they appeared to be largely non-productive. Similar themes also occupied most other classical economists, anxious both to encourage wealth creating activities, yet at the same time to justify a social system which allowed, nay encouraged, many to remain 'unproductive' in a strictly economic sense. Finally for Marx, society divided into two diametrically opposed economic classes – within which the productive group, the working classes, toiled for a subsistence wage, whereas the new capitalist class, having expropriated the position of the old land-owning classes, took the 'surplus value' and used it for a continuous programme of reinvestment. For him the disproportionate distribution of income between his two classes was the weakness underlying the classical system, and as such would eventually lead to its demise. The narrowly based capitalist class would be unable to sustain an adequate level of demand necessary for the highly productive industrial system, based as it was on the returns from new and increasingly productive capital investment, and from the sweated labour of the working classes.

Throughout the 19th century economists of all persuasions debated these issues, and indeed the classical economists found more and more exception to the rule, to people being rewarded purely on the basis of their supply of one of the productive factors, possibly land for rent and certainly labour for a wage, capital providing for interest, or risk taking for a profit. Within the main body of doctrine was the idea that wealth was only due to people in terms of their contribution to the productivity in the total system, and that all other distributions of income should be seen very much in the light of charity. As we have seen from the British 1834 Poor Law Amendment Act onwards, legislation was deliberately designed to discourage people from wishing to live on charity, and to emphasise to them the rightness of the 'work ethic'. In the U.S.A. this philosophy supported by the 'survival of the fittest' logic of Spencer, became reinforced as the 'Protestant ethic' of salvation, through toil. Yet as the century went by, the claims of welfare for both political and other reasons became increasingly pressing. Moreover as the wealth producing system became more effective, social reforms as advocated by Seebohm Rowntree, in his early study of industrial poverty in York, and other Quaker and Socialist inspired reformers became more possible. Underlying British society was a rapidly rising population, matched by the ability of the new industrial system to sustain increasingly high levels of average output and income, and in turn provide a greater surplus for distribution as wealth, unrelated to direct tangible contribution to the productive process – that is as potentially some form of *welfare* payment.

Looked at broadly, the history of the growth of industrial and urban living in 19th century Britain brought a gradual increase in the proportion of income devoted to things which the classical economists, guided by the precepts of Smith, Malthus and Ricardo, had regarded as at best suspect, and at worst positively harmful, to the efficient functioning and growth of the system as a whole. It will be recognised that these changes went hand in hand with vast increases in population, in Britain from over 15m in 1821 to some 38m in 1901, and in patterns of employment and income. Moreover as we have seen, these changes were concomitant with changes in thinking about political, economic and social conditions, stimulated by minds as diverse as John Stuart Mill, Marx and Spencer. In fact, throughout the 19th century all manner of working condition improvements occurred, starting with Sir

Robert Peel's 1802 Act – for the protection of pauper children – and going on through the 1833 and 1844 Factory Acts, to reforms in the mining industry under the 1842 Act, the abolition of chimney sweeps and the climbing boys under the 1864 Act, and of widespread improvements in public health. This started with the 1848 Public Health Act, which created a central Board of Health and encouraged local authorities to set up their own board and appoint sanitary inspectors. Educational conditions also changed drastically, and there were major improvements in all forms of education, from the 1870 Education Act onwards. Whereas in 1819 it was estimated that some 80 per cent of British children had been almost entirely uneducated, facilities were gradually improving throughout the 19th century. However even in 1870 onwards, half of all children were still thought to be uneducated. But Britain was beginning seriously to lag behind Germany and the U.S.A. in world trade, and investments in both new technology and new education were recognised as being essential for sustained industrial progress. Later still, the 1902 Education Act further greatly extended the public education system, and rationalised its organisation in view of changes in local government. After the First World War Fisher's Education Act of 1918 contained many radical proposals, which again extended the provision of public education. Similar reforms occurred in many other areas of education – the old Grammar Schools were affected by the Taunton Commission, whose recommendations were written into the Endowed Schools Act of 1869, while the great public schools were reformed at the same time. The Public Schools Act of 1868 generally reorganised such schools on the lines originally developed by Dr. Thomas Arnold (1795–1842) at Rugby between 1828 and 1842. Again the second half of the century saw some reform at the old English Universities of Oxford and Cambridge, and the extensive development of scientific, medical and engineering education at the new University of London and at many other civic universities as well. Most of these types of reforms, in respect of conditions of employment, public health and welfare, and education, eventually meant a gradually increasing burden to be borne on public funds, from a beneficent state. During the present century we have been conscious of a continued growth in the extent of the welfare state, which, since the end of the Second World War, has been powerfully influenced by the foundations established under the 1942 Beveridge Report on Social Security System and the 1944 Butler 'Education Act'. It will be apparent that many of the origins of ideas and reactions to the welfare state are both political and sociological. The trend of recent times has been for its services to become increasingly *comprehensive* and *universal*.

* * * * *

A remarkable feature of all the contemporary urban-industrial societies is first the scale and nature of taxes and actual social contributions, and second the high proportion which they, in welfare terms, constitute as a percentage of Gross Domestic Product. The Figures 30 and 31 indicate the proportions in the present day European Community – where in 1974 on average actual social contributions constituted nearly one third of the total. There are variations between countries with some like the U.K., Ireland and Denmark obviously bearing much of the cost of welfare expenditure on other taxations. The second table suggests that on average approximately one fifth of Gross Domestic Product in European countries today goes on social security expenditures.

The economic implications are seen increasingly as the effects of welfare expenditures, become in some way competitive with those of investment for future production. In the 17th century the pioneering English statistician and economist, Sir William Petty, drew attention to the tendency for the structure of employment to shift in the direction of services with increased economic development, a process which became known as 'Petty's Law', while economists from the physiocrats onwards have been concerned with the balance of 'productive' to non-productive elements in the economic system. In our present society, by ensuring high minimum standards of education and health, etc., the welfare state may well be regarded as assisting to increase production, and to this extent will be regarded generally as a 'good investment' in that it can pay for itself by increasing the wealth creating possibilities of the nation. However the adverse effects may be seen in a 'lack of incentives'. For instance, many might consider that high marginal taxation, especially on income, to support welfare and a wide range of other government expenditures, limits the urge to increase earnings by risk taking enterprise and work. Moreover the provision of extensive 'free' and subsidised services may blunt the urge to earn money to buy them with.

In practice there would appear to be three main limits to the provision of minimum welfare standards – the first being the need for those at work to have higher standards than those who do not, and in recent times this may have been lost sight of. The second is to avoid labour becoming totally passive and immobile; and third, to keep the

FIG. 30.   TAXES AND ACTUAL SOCIAL CONTRIBUTIONS 1974

| Country | Taxes and actual social contributions, total | Taxes linked to production and imports | Current taxes on income and wealth | Capital taxes | Actual social contributions |
|---|---|---|---|---|---|
| | Eur mio | in % of total | | | |
| **EUR-9** | **342 441** | **34.9** | **32.1** | **0.6** | **32.4** |
| 1  Germany | 116 064 | 32.4 | 33.7 | 0.2 | 33.7 |
| 2  France | 77 493 | 40.2 | 20.4 | 0.6 | 38.8 |
| 3  Italy | 37 846 | 36.4 | 20.9 | 1.0 | 41.7 |
| 4  Netherlands | 25 596 | 25.2 | 34.8 | 0.5 | 39.6 |
| 5  Belgium | 16 555 | 30.2 | 37.7 | 0.7 | 31.4 |
| 6  Luxembourg | 687 | 28.0 | 43.2 | 0.4 | 28.4 |
| 7  United Kingdom | 55 552 | 36.8 | 43.4 | 1.3 | 18.5 |
| 8  Ireland | 1 779 | 55.8 | 30.9 | 1.7 | 11.7 |
| 9  Denmark | 10 869 | 36.2 | 62.2 | 0.4 | 1.3 |

FIG. 31.   SOCIAL SECURITY EXPENDITURE AS PERCENTAGE OF GROSS DOMESTIC PRODUCT AT MARKET PRICES

| Country | 1962 | 1968 | 1969 | 1970 | 1971 | 1972 | 1973 |
|---|---|---|---|---|---|---|---|
| 1  Germany | 17.7 | 20.4 | 20.0 | 20.7 | 21.2 | 22.3 | 22.7 |
| 2  France | 16.7 | 19.1 | 19.1 | 18.9 | 19.1 | 19.4 | 19.8 |
| 3  Italy | 14.4 | 19.0 | 19.1 | 18.8 | 29.2 | 21,7 | 21.4 |
| 4  Netherlands | 14.1 | 19.7 | 20.0 | 20.8 | 21.9 | 23.2 | 24.0 |
| 5  Belgium | 15.8 | 18.1 | 18.1 | 18.5 | 18.9 | 20.3 | 20.5 |
| 6  Luxembourg | 15.2 | 18.8 | 17.5 | 16.6 | 18.4 | 18.8 | 18.1 |
| 7  United Kingdom | — | — | — | 16.3 | 16.7 | 17.1 | 17.4 |
| 8  Ireland | — | — | — | 13.2 | 13.7 | 13.7 | 15.0 |
| 9  Denmark | — | — | — | 19.9 | 21.4 | 21.6 | 23.2 |

overall costs within national means. Some classically minded economists have argued that as national income rises, it is wasteful to give
equal benefits to education, health and other public services which
should, as much as possible, be confined to people in need, the
remainder being free to pay for the state service, or apply for one if they
need it. However as the scale of state welfare and related services has
increased, the difficulty, both administratively and ideologically, of
allowing the 'wealthy' to opt out, has become more and more apparent.
In recent times, a lively debate has been developing, stimulated by
Messrs. Eltis and Bacon, of Oxford, of shifted attention on to the total
weight of public expenditure, which in terms of the gross national
product as variously measured, is thought to exceed half the total. They
argue that this represents an excessive burden on non-productive public
expenditures which leads to a high proportion of 'non-tradeable,' i.e.
often welfare, goods and services being produced, as opposed to
'tradeable' commodities, which can be readily sold on world markets.
In turn it is argued that much of the reason for Britain's poor export
performance and a loss of share in world markets in recent years, has
been a misallocation of national investment funds into public service,
housing subsidies and tax reliefs on mortgages and welfare expenditures, as opposed to critical investment projects, for re-tooling of key
industries and the revitalising of the industrial sector, which should
provide a surplus of goods for world exports. Much can be said for
these lines of thought, but in specific terms it becomes very difficult, in
many instances, to argue it through. For example, public expenditure
on roads may be seen to be a form of non-productive expenditure, in
the sense that it does not immediately provide a tradeable good or
service which can be sold abroad. On the other hand, if the roads to
major ports are inadequate this may well preclude an easy flow of
goods for export, and as such is an investment which should be
undertaken. Again a subsidised coal and steel industry, by its lower
market prices give very real assistance to private industries whom it
supplies. Many other forms of public expenditure, which are clearly
supportive to the 'productivity' of the private sector, may be regarded in
a similar light.

The key issue is when does expenditure on public services cum
welfare cease to be a type of investment in the form of better
education, better health, better facilities as a whole and become a form
of pure consumption, which does not help the nation in general to be
more efficient, or more effective in the world economic growth stakes.
The type of economic thought particularly associated with such issues is

known as *welfare economics*. This was associated with some of the writings of Professor Cannan, at the London School of Economics, who was regarded as being critical of the classical tradition in that he defined economics as being a study of 'material welfare'. It was also the product of the ideas of Professor Pigou of Cambridge who, in 1920, published *Economics of Welfare*. In this pioneering work he examined particular policies in relation to their effects on the distribution and size of the national output, and on the divergence and effects of economic activity on those who conducted it (marginal private net profit), and on society as a whole (marginal social net profit). In post-war years this distinction has been increasingly directed to national policies, transport, social, welfare, land planning and such like. In post-war years the work of the Dutch Professor Jan Tinbergen, on *cost benefit* analysis, the primary accountable and secondary generally longer term less easily quantifiable benefits, has also been used in attempts to clarify investment choices. Certainly the issue of the relative productivity of different forms of both public investments and welfare expenditures, and their impact on the longer term productive resources of the community as a whole is a fundamental debate, and one which shows no likelihood of being diminished in the future. As Petty perceived long ago, as economic development occurs, agricultural employment is replaced by manufacturing, and then the service sector grows. In Britain, for many years we have relied on part of our service sector to support key export industries, especially through provision of banking, insurance and other services. However, a point is ultimately reached when some service activities cease to be beneficial to the overall 'recreation' in Schumpeter's world of the economic system as a whole. The key task for effective social democratic planning in times of peace is to strike a sustainable balance between the claims of consumption, and particularly welfare on the one hand, and the claims of production, and especially creative industrial reinvestment on the other. Moreover in an open world trading economy such as Britain, policy must always be conscious of the need for production of tradeable goods and services for export, as for any claim on the public purse. In this sense at least the mercantilist view of the value of a trade surplus, for national sovereignty and power, just as surely as the poor, is always with us. The current debate stimulated by Messrs. Eltis and Bacon, with their call to reduce welfare and other public spending, and Mr. Wynne Godley and the 'new Cambridge school', with their proposals for domestic expansion, matched by some resort to tariff controls against cheaper overseas imports, is in a long and distinguished tradition. Long may it remain so!

# Chapter 5

# THE EVOLVING NATURE OF INDUSTRY

"Avarice, the spur of industry"

David Hume (1711–1776)
*Essay of Civil Liberty*

"Be no longer a chaos, but a world, or even worldkin. Produce! Produce! Were it but the pitifullest infinitesimal fraction of a product, produce it in God's name! 'Tis the utmost thou hast in thee: out with it, then."

Thomas Carlyle (1795–1881)
*Sartor Resartus*

"Government and co-operation are in all things the laws of life; anarchy and competition the laws of death."

John Ruskin (1819–1900)
*Unto this Last*

"When every blessed thing you hold
Is made of silver, or of gold,
You long for simple pewter.
When you have nothing else to wear
But cloth of gold and satins rare,
For cloth of gold you cease to care –
Up goes the price of shoddy."

Sir William Schwenck Gilbert (1836–1911)
*The Gondoliers*

"The public be damned!"

William Henry Vanderbilt (1821–1885)

Reply to a question whether the public should be consulted about luxury trains. A W. Cole's Letter, New York Times, 25 August 1918.

"We demand that big business give the people a square
deal; in return we must insist that when any one engaged
in big business honestly endeavors to do right he shall
himself be given a square deal."

Theodore Roosevelt (1858–1919)
*Autobiography* (1913)

The Managerial Revolution

Book title (1941)
James Burnham

"The Unacceptable Face of Capitalism"

Mr Edward Heath
*Extract from a speech in 1973*

## Competitive Structure and Behaviour

Some of the debates associated with multinational companies operating
across national boundaries has already been considered. Notwithstanding
the wide public recognition of the existence of large scale industry
operating in domestic and international markets, much theoretical discussion about business capital, its profitability or otherwise, is still associated with competitive small market patterns of industrial structure and
behaviour. Indeed, as we have seen, since Adam Smith's time much of
*laissez-faire* inspired economic thinking and policy making has been
dominated by the distinction between the idea of a perfectly competitive, as opposed to a monopolistic form of market organisation. In
the classical doctrine as developed from Ricardo onwards, perfect
competition was projected as the essential norm, with monopolistic
organisation being regarded as an undesirable aberration, which from
time to time, through the power of particular vested interests, may
persist. To this line of thought the freeing of the market of all such
monopolistic practices and restrictions was seen as a desirable goal for
economic policies. The classical cum neo-classical perfectly competitive
deal, in its pure form, suggests that a market would be most desirable if

there were many sellers of absolutely identical products in relation to their total sales, so that none could influence market price by varying the quantity they are prepared to put on the market. Buyers and sellers are assumed to have full knowledge and complete certainty as to prices and opportunities available everywhere in this, and every other market. Significant economies of scale are absent, so that no seller or buyer can expand to the stage of dominating or influencing the market unduly. Finally that there are no barriers of any kind to the movement of factors of production, or of risk taking entrepreneurs from or to the rest of the economy. Probably such a pure or perfect market has never existed, save in a primitive tribal or rural community where producers, sellers and buyers all live in close proximity and 'truck, trade and exchange' limited range of goods; tomatoes for potatoes, baskets for fishing nets, etc.

Under such idealised perfect market conditions it is assumed that competition among rival manufactures should, in the long run, ensure that every producer is operating with the most efficient lowest cost output, and is only able to earn the minimum amount of normal profit necessary to maintain the minimum number of producers in the industry. The perfectly competitive model is assumed to produce the ideal output, in the sense that the price consumers would have to pay to obtain additional supplies of a commodity produced under these conditions would, both in the short and longer run, be just sufficient to bid the necessary resources away from alternative uses. If production were everywhere organised in this ideal way the price system would thus secure an optimum distribution of economic resources, to meet consumers' preferences in the most efficient way. The model is seen to provide a norm for economic efficiency in the allocation of resources for the individual, for business and for society as a whole. Figure 32, compiled in 1970, lists no less than 156 products where one producer controlled over 50 per cent of United Kingdom supplies. The highly concentrated nature of modern industry inevitably means that a substantial part of the supply of many products will come from one or at best a few producers – though imports from the European Economic Community and increasingly Japan now elsewhere provide a potent new competitive element for much of British industry.

\*     \*     \*     \*     \*

In truth the idealised state of perfectly competitive markets was seldom, if ever, achieved. As we have seen, all the classical economists, from Malthus onwards, were aware that land tended to be a scarce and

FIG. 32.  MONOPOLISED AND OLIGOPOLISED PRODUCTS IN THE UNITED KINGDOM, 1970

A high degree of market concentration has long been a feature of modern industrial society. Some Economists have come to regard it as an inevitable result of large scale technology and the need for economies of scale in mass production and distribution. They have therefore suggested the need to control such groupings by Nationalisation, by regulatory boards through price controls or by other means. The interests of trade unions, with their members largely employed in such large organisations, have often appeared to coincide with the desires of the employers and government to promote 'stability' in market conditions and processes. However, other Economists have claimed the need to encourage the restoration of competitive conditions, in the long term interests of consumer choice, efficiency and growth.

The following list, published in *Hansard* for 6 April 1970, is of 156 products where one producer controlled over 50 per cent of United Kingdom supplies at that time.

Baker's yeast
Cotton linters
Cellulose acetate tow
Man-made fibres*
Phosphorus
Soda ash
Hydrogen peroxide
Boric acid
Oxygen
Urea
Lithopone
Phosphates
Nylon polymer
Polyethylene terepthalate
Polytetrofluoroethylene
Rubber contraceptive goods
Rayon yarn
Plate and sheet glass
Unwrought nickel†
Magnesium metal
Gas cylinders, welded, low-pressure
Heavy safes and strong-room doors†
Lawn mowers
Hosiery and knitting machinery
Motor scrapers
Non-electric carpet sweepers
Mustard
Rayon staple fibre
Salt, industrial and rock*
China clay
Phosphoric acid
Calcium carbide
Shock absorbers
Fuel injection equipment for diesel engined vehicles
Bicycles†
Speedometers
Heater devices for motor vehicles
Matches
Drop forged crankshafts
Tyre valves
Basic slag

Certain frozen foods*
Soups*
Cereal breakfast foods*
Canned peas†
Canned baked beans†
Sugar*
Margarine*
Vinegar
Whisky*
Gin
Cigarettes and tobacco*
Refined petroleum products*
Caustic soda
Chlorine
Glycerine
Dynamos, current-voltage control units, starter motors for motor vehicles
Doors locks and fittings for motor vehicles
Methanol
Polypropylene
Soap*
Synthetic detergents*
Potash
Gelatine and glue*
Polyethylene
Cellulose film*
Asbestos goods*
Safety glass*
Brass 'semis' extruded†
Nickel alloy 'semis'†
Metal containers*
Overdrives, line drive shafts
Steering gears for vehicles
Steering wheels
Timing chains
Clutches
Petrol tanks and axle casings
Caravans†
Rubber footwear*
Cinematographic equipment
Parking meters
Photographic film
Refined borax

Pyridine
Dissolved acetylene
Ammonium carbonate and bicarbonate
Nitrogenous fertilisers†
Sporting cartridges
Polymethyl methacrylate
Celluloid
Casein plastics
Wallpaper*
Metallic yarn
Iron pressure pipes and fittings
Unwrought zinc†
Gas cylinders, seamless, high-pressure
Wood screws
Precision chains
Tufted carpet machinery
Boot and shoe machinery
Weighing machinery
Diaphragm valves
Ignition coils, magnetos, distributors, ignition suppressors for motor vehicles
Windscreen wiper motors
Lamps, horns, trafficators, relay units for motor vehicles
Automatic transmissions for motor vehicles
Universal joints for transmission systems
Wire rope
Diamond dies
Oil well drilling bits
Crown corks
Needles†
Pistons and piston rings
Brake linings and clutch facings
Plasterboard
Cylinder block castings
Stencil duplicators
Punched-card machinery

Cash registers
Steel works plant
Bearings and bushes for motor vehicles†
Sewing machines, domestic and industrial
Grain milling machinery
Excavators
Road rollers
Towed scrapers
Dish washers
Packaging machinery
Tonnage oxygen plants
Rubber-working machinery
Tobacco machinery
Brushmaking machinery
Vacuum cleaners†
Electricity house service meters
Gas welding equipment
Fire and burglar alarms
Dry (primary) batteries†
Electrical instruments for motor vehicles†
Sparking plugs, compression ignition heater plugs
Electronic valves†
Cathode ray tubes†
Semi-conductors†
Carburettors for cars
Tanning and leather working machinery
Drum and disc brakes
Electric clocks
Brass band instruments
Mechanical lighters
Fuel lift pumps for vehicles
Engine valves for vehicles
Bottled gas
Oil seals for vehicles
Razors, (safety) and razor blades†
Nylon yarn
Linoleum†
Cement

Among the products missing from this list we may note paper-making machinery, cod liver oil, incandescent mantles, steel sheet, tinplate, tin and three-wheeled vehicles.

* The 1963 Census of Production published concentration ratios for these twenty products.

† The 1963 Census of Production included these twenty products in larger groups of products for which concentration ratios were published.

FIG. 33.   MONOPOLISTIC COMPETITION DIAGRAMS

In a modern economy monopolistic competition is considered to apply in many markets. By this is meant that most products such as industrial machine tools, cars, household consumer goods, prepared foodstuffs, package holidays, banking and insurance services and such like, are differentiated by brand names but that entry into the market for alternative suppliers is still possible. In these circumstances heavy expenditure on advertising and product promotional activities is a common feature. The main aim of the competitive monopolist is to preserve as much of his monopoly position as possible while at the same time the industry as a whole will tend to operate at less than optimum capacity, and non-price competition will be an important feature.

The following four diagrams illustrate the theory of monopoly and monopolistic competition as they usually appear in contemporary economic text books.

(A)   THE MARGINAL REVENUE OF A MONOPOLIST

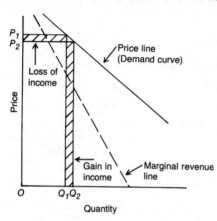

*Notes:*

1. At $P_1$ the monopolist sells $Q_1$ articles.
2. If he increases output by one unit to $Q_2$ he will receive a lower price because of the downward-sloping demand curve.
3. The whole quantity $Q_2$, will be sold at the price $P_2$, bringing in an average revenue of $P_2$ to the monopolist.
4. The marginal revenue (i.e. the increase in total revenue to the monopolist from the sale of the extra unit) is not $P_2$, but $P_2$ less the loss in income sustained because of the lower price on all the other units.

(B)   PRICE DETERMINATION IN MONOPOLY CONDITIONS

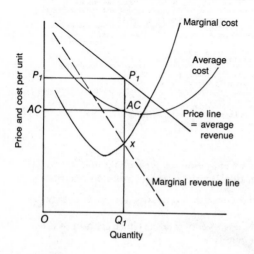

*Notes:*

1. The marginal-cost curve cuts the marginal-revenue curve at $x$, and well below the price line. Output ceases at this point with an output of $OQ_1$.
2. Price will be decided by the point where a line from $Q_1$ parallel to the price axis cuts the price line, at price $P_1P_1$.
3. The entrepreneur will earn revenue of $OQ_1P_1P_1$ at a cost (including normal profit) of $OQ_1$, AC, AC. He is therefore earning super-profits of AC, $P_1P_1$, $P_1$, AC. *But these super-profits will not be competed away, as they would in competitive conditions.*

(C) THE SHORT-RUN POSITION OF A SUPPLIER IN MONOPOLISTIC COMPETITION

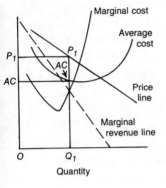

*Notes:*

1. The supplier is making super-profits with his brand equal to $AC$, $P_1$, $P_1$, $AC$.
2. New firms will be attracted into the industry, selling the same goods in a differentiated form. The new supplier or suppliers will have to aggressive in advertising and pricing policies if they are to make inroads on the market of the established brand, and to the extent that they are successful there will be a change in the conditions of demand.
3. The demand curve for the supplier of the established brand will move to the left, a decrease in demand.
4. The marginal-revenue line will also move to the left, and some of the entrepreneur's super-profits will be competed away.

(D) THE LONG-RUN POSITION OF A SUPPLIER UNDER MONOPOLISTIC COMPETITION

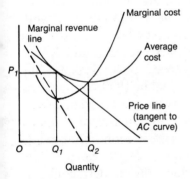

*Notes:*

1. The demand curve has moved, owing to the changed conditions of demand, so far to the left that it has become tangential to the average cost curve.
2. At this point all super-profits are competed away and the firm is making normal profits only.
3. There is excess capacity in the industry; the supplier could increase output to the optimum level of minimum average cost at $OQ_2$ and decrease unit costs by doing so, but the marginal revenue would decrease *even more*, leaving him worse off. It is therefore a feature of monopolistic competition that excess capacity exists in the industry in the long run.

finite resource, and that the owners of land inevitably have some form of monopolistic power over its use as an income earning resource and in their ability to charge rents. Labour had been often organised as guilds and combinations which, during the early years of the British industrial revolution, were gradually abandoned and prohibited by law. Later, trade unions became illegal under the Combination Acts of 1815, which were, however, repealed in 1824. Under the inspiration of Robert Owen, 1834 saw the formation of the abortive Grand National Consolidated Union. After three decades of strife, the foundation of the Trade Union Congress, in 1868, and the passing of the Trade Union Act 1871, recognised the legality of such unions, and the Criminal Law Amendment Act following the Taff Vale case in 1906 later opened up the way to peaceful picketing. Thus changes in the law, and the eventual development of large, well organised trade unions, inevitably made the real world market of labour supply far less perfect than Smith, or many of his disciples would have deemed desirable. Professional skills from accountants to doctors, airline pilots, lawyers and estate agents also tend to be somewhat limited as to entry, and organised in various restrictive arrangements.

British governments, from Tudor times onwards, and indeed throughout the mercantilistic era, found good reason to seek the regulation of trade and many interests, in the pursuance of what they saw to be the 'national interest'. Yet in the purely classical model the functions of government came to be regarded as 'non-productive' and, at best, limited to the minimal provision of domestic law and order and defence, and the provision of money as a means of exchange and, linked to gold, as a store of value. However even to such a purist as Smith, the Navigation Acts, which from 1651 to their repeal in 1849 confined the carriage of goods to and from British ports to British ships, were seen as being desirable, in that they assisted in the maintenance of Britain's naval supremacy. As we have seen, other classical economists, while generally supporting the widest extension possible of the perfectly competitive model, found exceptions to which the model should or could not be fully applied. Aspects of social welfare, the provision of posts and telegraphs, and a variety of natural public utilities, were all increasingly regarded as areas in which the state might legitimately create a monopoly, under the supervision of Parliament, and a concern with national welfare. It is therefore apparent, even in the most perfect of worlds, monopolistic arrangements may apply for good reasons.

In our present age we are well familiar with the justification that governments have seen for a wide extension of public ownership to many basic industries, from transport to energy, iron and steel, shipbuilding and such like, and to the provision of many forms of service, from welfare, health and education. In agriculture statutory marketing boards have, since the 1930s, been concerned to provide orderly marketing arrangements for many products, and indeed the whole recently applied paraphernalia of the European Common Market with careful regulation of the European Agricultural Market and the green £, and protective measures against cheaper imports from areas outside the Market, might be seen as extensions of a monopolistic 'Corn Law' type of regulation on a wide scale. Again, monopolies are often granted by government for long periods of time, patents and copyrights have been seen to be justified, because they are regarded as necessary to stimulate national research and inventiveness and such like.

Apart from the concerns and extension of the scope of big government, other monopolies naturally arise out of scarce natural resources. Scarcity of finite resources from land to salt, diamonds, gold and silver, are traditional natural monopoly situations. In the present world basic energy in the form of oil and natural gas, gives many multinational companies and increasingly sovereign states or shiekdoms concerned with their production, a natural quasi monopoly position. The current position of the O.P.E.C. group of oil producing states, and the virtual stranglehold they have established over Western Europe for up to 70 per cent of basic energy requirements, and the U.S.A. for nearly 50 per cent of its oil needs, indicates the power of a 'monopoly' position applied to a finite natural resource in high demand. The ability of the fortunate possessors to charge a long term 'pure rent' for its supply – over and above production costs – is a measure of the power which such a natural monopoly confers. It also, incidentally, allows many other *high cost* energy producers – such as Britain, Holland and Norway in the North Sea – to come into the market, with oil and natural gas supplies.

Another type of monopoly which has developed during the last hundred years of capitalist development, are processes, associated with very large units of production, which led to declining costs per unit of output. Whereas, as we have seen, Ricardo generally assumed constant returns, Marx, and later Marshall, were aware of greatly increasing returns to scale in manufacturing and commercial processes. Marx foresaw large scale monopoly capitalism developing in the middle of the 19th century. He saw the trend to bigness and a tendency for monopoly capitalists to compete with each other, for what he thought would be static or shrinking markets, and inevitably absolute declining rates of profit. In fact the Marxian nightmare did not transpire, and the markets for most capital and consumer goods, and the cash flow of total profits derived from them, have expanded enormously during the past 100 years. Nevertheless the problems of ownership and control of very large units of output has been a continuing preoccupation of government. One of the first reactions which was developed strongly in the second half of the 19th century and the first 15–20 years of this century, was the creation of public utilities for such basic local needs as water, gas, electricity, sewage, and much of public transport. As time went by the economies of scale also became far more manifest in the production of many other basic goods and services, iron and steel and especially chemicals, of which the creation of Imperial Chemical Industries Ltd. in 1926, under the leadership of Alfred Mond, the first Lord Melchett (1868–1930), as a counter to the market power of very large American and German chemical producers, was but one example. Others have included the bringing together during the inter-war and post-war period of much of the textile industries fragmented patterns of ownership and production into larger units. Plainly all such very large organisations of which today there are a considerable number present the potential abuse of monopoly of quasi-monopoly power. The creation of the European Coal and Steel Community in the 1950s was as much intended to control monopolistic competition between a few large producers in Europe in the interests of the community at large, as for any other purpose.

Other forms of industrial monopoly situations arise from time to time, when companies produce commodities which are perishable or bulky in relation to their selling price, and are therefore protected from competition in local markets by the transport costs for distant producers. Such goods as bread and beer, cement, bricks and a variety of others which are traditionally regarded as natural local monopolies, though in recent times modern transport and distribution methods have tended to break down many such local market situations. However merger and takeover activities of many such industrial groupings became a feature of the 1960s British industrial scene. A further type of monopolistic activity, which has been extensively practised by many large firms producing consumer durables, is when they seek to create a degree of differentiations between their own, and other comparable products. Such companies use extensive advertising, branding and packaging and other product differentiation devices to persuade the consumer that their products from soap flakes, to washing machines and cars, are different from others of the same kind. Many well known economists, from Marx to Schumpeter and Galbraith, have seen a particular problem associated with the very large scale companies controlling particular markets, and shaping consumer tastes to suit their production facilities. Given the growth of scale of manufacturing and the control that many companies are able to exert over hitherto small and relatively free markets, the degree of competition may be seriously reduced by such activities. One public reaction to this has been a growth of all manner of consumer representation organisations, and the publication of such magazines as *Which* to check on the actual qualities of goods produced. In our contemporary world, the power of multinationals producing, operating and marketing many such goods over worldwide markets has also presented particular problems of sovereignty and power which, have also been referred to earlier in this book.

## The Theory and Practice of Monopoly Control

In debates about monopoly it is sometimes argued that abuses have been over-emphasised by critics, who take a too partial and static view; too partial because they do not allow sufficiently for competition between the products of near monopolists, which today commonly apply in advanced Western economies, and too static because they have looked at a still of the economy, and not a moving picture, in which such monopolies are rapidly broken up by new competition in the form of new ideas, products, know-how and such like. Since the 1930s one of the leading writers about *The Economics of Imperfect Competition* has been Professor Joan Robinson, at Cambridge, while in the USA the writings of E. H. Chamberlain were also influential. Monopolistic competition is one of a number of market conditions; these range from pure competition through monopolistic competition and ologopoly, to pure monopoly. Monopolistic competition is seen when there are many sellers of products which although close substitutes for one another, are not perfect substitutes because of product differentiation supported by branding and advertising, etc. In these circumstances individual sellers have some degree of control over the price at which they sell. Where there is no collusion or substantial agreement between sellers to restrict the entry of new competitors, the degree of monopoly power conferred is considered unlikely to be significant in the long run.

As has been suggested, when looking at the subject of monopoly or imperfect competition *laissez-faire* inspired economists have often made the simplifying assumption that the producer, in the imperfectly competitive market, will only seek to produce such output as will maximise his profits. However, other critics of the competitive market model have pointed out that this does not necessarily yield the best results in terms of economic wealth. In reality most markets are always, to some degree, imperfectly competitive. Indeed for the reason stated earlier the perfectly competitive model is impossible to achieve, in any full sense, in a modern industrial system. In order to judge adequately an imperfectly competitive market it is necessary to make allowance for a degree of imperfection that is created, if only its unavoidable elements due to the need for large scale economies of scale production and consumer preferences, etc. remained. This situation might then be compared with the practical alternatives under any other system. The contrast that immediately comes to mind is a centrally planned, fully Socialist economy, where property is not privately owned and where production is not conducted in response to consumer preferences in free markets, but to orders from computer based central planners with authority to enforce their plans. This type of planning has been extensively practised in the Soviet Union and its COMECON group satellites, and also in a number of other ideologies as well. The difficulty about such comparisons is that all sorts of other considerations must be taken into account, not the least of which is the political one that a centrally planned economy does not normally allow people, as consumers, freedom of choice, or as workers, freedom of occupation. Thus a comparison on purely economic terms of efficiency is incomplete, and analysis may be forced back to more micro plant by plant comparisons of the methods actually used, and the products actually produced. In such 'scientific management' style enquiries one is seldom comparing like with like.

*     *     *     *     *

Viewed empirically, the need for monopoly control has been variously interpreted, in different countries in different ways. For instance, the United States which, as we have seen, initially developed its manufacturing industry behind extensive tariff protection against British and European competition, became highly sensitive, towards the end of the 19th century and early 20th century, to the abuses of large monopolistic Trusts. These were seen to be monopolising production of many basic materials and industries: railways, coal and oil, iron and steel, etc. Indeed most of the great founding families of American capitalism, from Andrew Carnegie (1835–1919), to Pierpont Morgan (1837–1913), the Astors and Vanderbilts, the du Ponts and the

Rockefellers, were variously regarded as having profited from such arrangements. The response to this was seen in the introduction of strong, legally based anti-Trust laws known as the Sherman Anti-Trust Act, 1890, and from that time onwards they tended to dominate American thinking about the desirability of breaking up monopolistic groupings. One of the first victims of the Sherman Anti-Trust legislation was the extensive interlocking trust of John D. Rockefellers' (1839–1937) Standard Oil Co. of New Jersey, which was forced to break itself into many separate companies. This was later followed by the Clayton and the Federal Trade Commission Acts of 1914 onwards, and many subsequent legal rulings and legislation as well.

In Britain the classical view as expressed by neo-classical doctrine and law, was strongly against monopolistic practices, though from the First World War onwards trade associations became a vehicle for Government recognised arrangements, initially to assist with war production, and later to consolidate and run down surplus industrial capacity revealed by the inter-war depression and slump for many old staple industries, from coal, to cotton textiles and shipbuilding. During the Second World War many of the same arrangements were used as a basis for wartime planning, and it was only after the war that more attention was given to the problems of monopolistic practices in the private sector. In 1948 Monopolies and Restrictive Practices Inquiry and Control Act set up a permanent body which could be requested by the Board of Trade to investigate the monopolies and restrictive practices of industry and trade. Under this Act the Board could refer a case to the Commission whenever at least one third of the output would supply the market by one firm, or a group of related firms in the U.K. or a substantial part of it, or by an association of firms whose conduct prevented or restricted competition. Some of the Commission's early reports on individual industries commented adversely on the effect on the *public interest* of collective agreements between firms which restricted competition, and in 1955 it produced a report on collective discrimination and dealt with restrictive agreements generally. As a result, a Restrictive Trade Practices Act was passed in 1956 to provide judicial machinery for dealing with these agreements, which were therefore excluded from the scope of the Commission. Later, in 1965, a new Monopolies and Mergers Act was introduced. Whereas the 1956 Act established a framework of the appraisal of monopolies situation once they had developed, the Government now had power to prevent industrial concentration which might lead to monopoly power. The Monopolies and Mergers Act was intended to tidy up the whole field of

monopoly legislation. The existing framework of the Restrictive Practices Court and the Monopolies Commission was retained, but the
criterion for a monopoly was altered to a market share of 25 per cent.
In addition, the Act contained many provisions for the protection of
consumers from abuses. To supervise the implementation of Acts the
provision of a Director-General of Fair Trading was instituted, and the
early indication is that he is beginning to have a vigorous effect on
trading practices.

In general, the philosophy underlying all British legislation from
1948 was that each case must be considered on its merit, though the
onus was on the parties concerned to an agreement to show that it is in
the public interest. The 1973 Fair Trading Act attempted to erase
defects in old Acts and practices, though its approach still rests on such
terms as an ad hoc appreciation of relationships between 'structure,
conduct and performance'. However, it can undertake a wider range of
investigations, it has new procedures for reference and new definitions
of the public interest. The problem of lack of speed, arbitratiousness of
reference, division of responsibility and conflicts of legislation, and a
failure to face up fully to difficulties of scale, efficiency and such like,
remain. A further complication is that Articles 85 and 86 of the Treaty
of Rome applying to monopoly and restrictive practices on a European
wide basis, are also beginning to apply to the United Kingdom. The
fears of many are that the more legalistic approach of the European
Community will be in conflict with the empirical approach hitherto
followed in Britain. The fact that the British Government of today
through a wide number of other means, including the existence of the
Price Commission from 1973 onwards, also affects pricing and market
practices, has yet to be fully appreciated or thought through. Certainly
the developing 'corporatism' is far removed from any easy congruence,
with the neo-classical *laissez-faire* basis for judging the public desirability of competitive market behaviour.

\*     \*     \*     \*     \*

By way of summary one can do worse than look at the conclusions of
*Recent Trends in Monopoly in Great Britain* by Mr. G. Walshe,
published for the National Institute of Economic and Social Research in
1974. This work is the second of two Occasional Papers containing the
interim results of the research project on mergers and concentration in
British industry, undertaken at the National Institute, under the direction of Professor P. E. Hart. It deals with British industries selected for
their high concentration, either with over 90 per cent of sales made by

the top five firms in 1958, or with so few firms participating that the Concentration Data in the 1963 Census of Production was restricted by the risk of disclosing information on individual firms. The project stated out with three aims; first to ascertain the relative importance of internal and external growth in promoting business monopoly and near monopoly; second to show whether monopoly or near monopoly was durable; and third to assess the constraints on the exercise of monopoly and oligopoly power.

Mr. Walshe's work refers back to the survey of 36 trades initially categorised by Messrs. Evely and Little as high concentration trades in *Concentration in British Industry*, published by Cambridge University Press in 1951. Out of the 36 trades it is revealed that in no less than 32 cases monopoly and oligopoly had proved durable. Twenty-five of the trades had experienced an increase in concentration after 1951 up to the late 1960s. In another seven cases no perceptible change had occurred, and the instances where monopoly or tight oligopoly had shown a tendency to dissolve were very few. A second and related finding was that in British industry over the period under review, mergers were often used to buttress or entrench the monopoly and oligopoly market power achieved by 1951. Indeed in only eight of the 36 trades could no evidence of merger activity since 1971 be discovered. Most of the firms which had grown internally up to 1951, that is to say without merger activity, used external growth as a means of increasing their market power after that date.

Mr. Walshe suggests five *contemporary* constraints to monopoly power. Monopolists and oligopolists may encounter significant import competition which is not controlled by themselves; or they may be operating in rapidly declining markets, and thereby find themselves unable to extract monopoly rents from customers who are deserting the product. In fact these two types of constraint were significant for four and three products respectively out of a total of 44. For three other products countervailing power could have been exercised for the benefit of consumers. For a further four products there were low, or moderately low, entry barriers which provided scope for potential competition, and so constituted a constraint on the unbridled exercise of market power. Finally, the Monopolies Commission had investigated 12 of the products and it may be reasonably assumed that their surveillance had proved some kind of check on the exercise of monopoly or near monopoly. For the remaining 22 products monopoly power was apparently still a serious matter. These products faced little import competition, market decline did not constitute a check on the

leaders' activities, there were high entry barriers encircling the producers, and there were no immediate sources of countervailing power
pitted against them. None of these products had, at the time of writing
Walshe's book, been investigated by the Monopolies Commission.
Overall, his study provides a survey of recent developments in a study
of monopolistic structure and its relationship to current policies in the
United Kingdom. However, little attention was given to the growth of
constraints on monopoly power likely to come from Britain's entry into
the European Common Market, from which it might be assumed that
greater competition will arise. Plainly the study for the next decade is
the effect of Britain's membership of the European Economic Community, on monopoly power and market practices in British industry as
a whole.

## The Changing Role of Management

The question of the appropriate role, purposes and rewards for
management, however defined, have been a subject for continuous
economic, political and social debate. Indeed the respective role of
'them and us' is central to any understanding of how any economic
system works, both in terms of meeting present needs and defining
future goals. As we have seen in the early classical model, the
management of society was seen as lying in the hands of landowners,
who looked after the irreplaceable qualities of the soil, for which they
received a scarcity rent. The new capitalist classes were concerned with
the risky creation of new enterprises, often on a small scale basis, and
within which there was a close identity of ownership with control.
Overseeing society was the traditional ruling class, generally the landed
aristocracy, who undertook the functions of state. In Adam Smith's
view much of this class were economically non-productive, yet were
justified in the sense that they maintained the stability of the system,
law and order and the defence of the realm. In the doctrine as refined by
Ricardo, the role of the capitalist class was to forgo for the present to
invest for the future, in that it was assumed that the working class,
living on 'subsistence wages' would be unable to do this adequately, if
at all. Later, Marx saw the economic organisation of society in still
starker terms, seeing the demise of the old rentier landowning class, and
their replacement by the new capitalist bourgeoisie who owned and
managed the increasing extensive means of industrial production.
Inevitably opposed to this class, and its interests, was a propertyless
urban proletariat, many of whom had but recently been forced off the

land, to provide a reserve army of unemployed available, as need arose, for wage labour in the new factory system. Thus in place of Smith's and Ricardo's three tier society, Marx saw two tiers, the new increasingly monopolistic capitalist class, in eventual outright confrontation with the ever expanding industrial workforce. Confrontation between the interests of the capitalist class, anxious to use continually a 'labour surplus value' for reinvestment, and a working class who survived on a subsistence wage, was the central means by which capitalism was to evolve, eventually through revolution into a socialist state in which the ownership of the means of production would be commonly owned. This socialist state would in turn eventually be replaced by a state of pure communism, in which the abundance of production would be so great that the functions of government would entirely wither away, and universal abundance would apply, in theory without the need for a master/servant relationship in any form. Marx also perceived the growing division which was developing within the capitalist system, between those who owned the means of production, through the on-going possession of capital inherited from one generation to another, and those who managed it on behalf of the capitalist class. In this sense the interests of many of the new managers were seen as potentially identical to those of the working class. The managers were by the nature of their roles essentially 'lackeys' of the capitalist system.

*     *     *     *     *

Many subsequent authors have speculated on similar themes: one in particular had an important impact in the United States. The somewhat eccentric American economist Thorstein Veblen developed a number of ideas about the way the new capitalist system would work, and increasingly saw power falling in the hands of technocratic engineers who would understand and control the new means of production. Veblen also wrote important works about the structure of the economic system as a whole, including *Theory of the Leisure Class*, in 1899, and *Theory of Business Enterprise*, in 1904. Both of these works contained criticism of what he described as 'conspicuous consumption' and the tendency of new investment to destroy continually the profitability of existing investment in machines and other facilities. Like Marx, Veblen saw this tendency inevitably leading on to financial failures and slumps. The power of his ideas led to him becoming the founder of *institutional* cum *evolutionary* school of economics in the United States, and which later enthusiastically embraced New Deal Keynesian demand management economics, during the Roosevelt years of the 1930s. As we have seen throughout, what all writers, from Veblen to Schumpeter, had to grapple with was that, with the on-going development of capitalism, the increase in scale of plants was entirely changing the nature of organisational structure and behaviour. The thesis became broadly, as capitalism developed, the owners of wealth in the form of the capitalist classes were gradually being replaced by a managerial class, as the dominant element in economic and political life. Ownership was becoming gradually divorced from control in the modern industrial enterprise. With the continued growth of large firms the massive concentration of capital implied the ownership of business become much more corporate in nature. This was in marked contrast to the world that Adam Smith and his immediate disciples had conceived, when the man was also his own capitalist. Of particular importance in this pattern of evolution was not only the tendency for many industrial processes to require scale for efficient least-cost operations: it was also the on-going success of the invention of the limited liability company, with its wide extension of ownership. Inevitably ownership, through wider dispersion of shares, etc., tended to be dispersed, and control in large companies inevitably fell into the hands of small groups of professional managers or directors, who owned only a small proportion of voting capital. Although nominally control of 51 per cent of votes is needed for controlling an enterprise, the wide dispersion of votes and the practice of professional management made it possible to control firms with small shareholdings.

In these circumstances the professional manager, in day to day touch with the conduct of business, and often with high technical competence of the particular requirements of that business, naturally came to occupy increasingly key positions in the industrial and commercial scene. One, later, author who had a wide impact, was the American James Burnham, whose book *The Managerial Revolution*, in 1941, described in close detail what had gradually become recognised as an important feature in the organisation of modern industrial society. He suggested that the control over the instruments of production would inevitably be augmented by state ownership, and that inevitably the managers would come to control the state, thus achieving a form of 'revolution' with the managers becoming a new ruling class. These views also had a parallel to the ideas expressed somewhat earlier by Schumpeter that the changing structure of the capitalist system inevitably meant that the leadership of the Western democratic European state would move away from traditional aristocratic ruling classes, towards a new managerial class which would emerge out of the industrial situation. Moreover the sheer scale of modern enterprise would also gradually eliminate the role of the family firm, as an important element in the functioning of system. Although Burnham was at the time regarded as presenting his views in an extreme form, there has been wide acceptance of the idea that much political control and influence has passed from the old landowning and 'nouveau riche' capitalist classes to the professional industrial manager. In their different ways Sir Harold Wilson's 'White Hot Technological Revolution' of 1964, and Mr. Heath's new Tory efficiency 'Selsdon man' of the early 1970s marked the changing world. In recent times, particularly in Britain, the situation has become further confused by other developments. One has been the vast growth of the public sector, particularly the large nationalised industries and welfare services as a dominant element in society. The second has been the extension of the power of large scale organised trade unions, into most aspects of industrial and political life. The latter support, as the British coal miners', strike of 1974 illustrated, can make or break democratic governments. Politicians are increasingly judged by the electorate for their ability to 'get on with the unions' and keep the system functioning, whatever the cost.

Today throughout Western Europe, under the stimulation of the European Communities Fifth Directive, large scale industry and commerce is also being encouraged to introduce 'worker participation' to the boardroom, however that may be defined. It will be recognised that in the member states company organisation is on a very different basis. For instance, in Germany and Holland, much of company financing has come from high gearing and bank loans, and bankers have usually had a seat on the Upper Supervisory Board, in partnership with trade union organisations. Again in France, and even more so in Italy, government financing of companies has involved a degree of participation between government representatives, and others representing shareholders, and worker interests, and similar conditions apply in Scandinavia. However in Britain, the board of the typical joint stock company has traditionally consisted mainly of representatives of equity shareholders, which today for many companies are most importantly the investment managers of life insurance and pension funds, unit and investment trusts, etc. The idea of worker participation on the board is a new departure for most public companies. At the time of writing, the publication of the Bullock Report – on *Worker Participation and the Boardroom* – whose majority recommendations is for trade union representatives on the board of all British companies with over 2,000 employees, has caused great controversy. It is too early to say in what form these proposals will eventually become law. It is certainly by no means clear that all British trade union leaders wish to be involved in upper management decision making in this way.

* * * * *

Plainly the form of managerial revolution which the capitalist system is now passing through is a further stage on from that originally envisaged by Burnham. In countries such as Britain we seem to be evolving into a form of corporatism in which the leading professional managers drawn from both the public and the private sectors of industry regularly meet, with representatives of government and of the trade unions to argue about, and hopefully to decide wisely the future directions for national policy. Thus Burnham's managerial revolution has moved beyond the stage of simply recognising a transformation in the relationship between the owners of capital, and the direction of enterprises into a stage when the upper managerial group for society as a whole is drawn from the government, from the major boardrooms of industry often as represented by the Confederation of British Industry, and from the Trade Union Congress. The meeting place in the present British industrial scene is the National Economic Development Office, which has become increasingly concerned with the 'supply side' of the national economy – broken into major industrial groupings. It thereby provides a counterpoint to the Kenyesian demand management side – as represented by the Treasury and Bank of England in shaping the aggregate level of short term financing demand.

The evolution or drift into a form of 'corporatist state' has not gone unnoticed, by critics on the social democratic Left, or the Right. Many on the Left would see it as a desirable development, which still, however, needs to be brought into a full relationship with the state's overall planning objectives and needs. Long term national investment planning – to this line of reasoning – can only be effectively directed by close agreement of objectives over the 'commanding heights of the economy' and by concensus and support of all the work force. Planning agreements involving participation from big companies, the unions and government are seen as one way to co-ordinate long term national goals. Again the National Enterprise Board also has a growing role in co-ordinating government aid to and links with problem industries, notably British Leyland. In turn these relate to the total structure of central control and influence which are further listed in Appendices II and III. Critics on the political Right would see all this as inevitably leading to a disastrous misallocation of resources and eventual economic collapse. Thus Professor Milton Friedman, a leading advocate of both the need to control money supply to curb inflation, and also a strong supporter of *laissez-faire* market principles, has proposed three ways to change the 'present path to disaster and intellectual bankruptcy of policy directing that Britain has followed in the past decade'. As cited in the Financial Times in January 1977, these embraced:

> "First, a 'drastic reform' of taxation was needed which would sharply curtail the top marginal rate. The 98 per cent top rate on investment income was not there to yield revenue but as a punitive measure.
>
> Second, reform was needed in the area of social services. Social welfare programmes were not selective. 'They tend to be inefficient and create an enormous bureaucracy to interfere with the freedom of the ordinary individual'.
>
> The ultimate objective of reform in this area should be to replace all services in mind by a straightforward negative income tax providing aid to people that need assistance in the form of money.
>
> Third, he said, the nationalised industries were a 'drain upon your budget; they promote inefficiency, and if you have a major problem with trade unions a large part of that is because so many of the trade unions are in the nationalised sector."

Plainly with a wide diversity of possible national strategies to pursue the role of the manager and decision maker in the modern 'mixed economy' is a 'far from happy one'. Yet the essential point remains. Someone somewhere, has to take responsibility for the functioning of the industrial cum economic system, both in its day-to-day operational sense and in terms of its need to 'recreate' itself continuously, for 'the future possibilities of mankind.'

Unfortunately missed from much of the intense contemporary planning debates is the historic role of the small enterprise and 'risk taking' entrepreneur in this process. It could be argued that before all else what is really necessary for a viable manufacturing and commercial future is the willingness for management to risk *innovation* and *change*. It is by no means apparent this process is always most successfully undertaken by committees working in large organisations.

## Ideas of Scientific Management

During the second half of the 19th century, and the first half of the present century, a number of practical businessmen cum academic thinkers and consultants became increasingly concerned with the need to improve the organisational and functional aspects of industry. The early management science thinkers were, in their various ways, looking at similar issues to those which concerned many academic economists, both of the classical cum neo-classical and Marxist schools. These concerns included the phenomenal growth in the scale and capital intensity of industry, the increased productivity which flow line methods of production was making possible, and the need for recruiting, training and motivating an increasingly skilled and disciplined work force, to service the new technologies. The management of flow line production in large motor plants, and later of a wide range of consumer durable goods, were rapidly changing the context within which the practical manager in any highly urban and industrial society had to operate. In particular, labour could no longer be thought of as purely homogeneous, easily substitutable one for the other. Moreover given huge overhead costs, disruption of production for even limited periods could become devastatingly destructive to profitability. These environmental changes forced considerable new thinking about the basis upon which 'scientific management' could be effectively applied. A useful compilation or readings about those developments are included in the book on *Management Thinkers* edited by A. Tillett, T. Kempner, and G. Willis and published in 1970.

It is of interest that in contrast to the story of economic doctrines the idea of scientific management was often non-ideological in content, in that the basic purpose was in seeking to establish the most efficient and practical means to produce the right goods, of the right quality, and at the right time. At its simplest form this could be conceived of, at plant level at least, without undue reference to the underlying social structure, or distribution of wealth or of incomes. Thus the interest of the great burgeoning capitalist enterprises, such as Fords, General Motors, Firestone, Westinghouse, etc., in the possibilities of scientific management, were matched by the early Marxist–Leninist inspired Soviet planners, in the application of such techniques to their own factory requirements. Lenin in particular was highly attracted by the possibilities which an understanding of accountancy and book keeping, of scientific methods and of 'electrification' as a source of basic motive power, held out for the rapid industrialisation of post 1917 Russia. A similar interest in many of the techniques of scientific management has persisted in the Soviet Union and other countries of the Soviet led COMECON group, to the present day. Among other things, they have become major purchasers of Western computers as aids – indeed essential facets of scientific management in a centrally planned economy. Thus efficiency in management, whether it came through scale of operations, from amounts of power or capital intensity employed, or methods of labour training and motivation, were of as much interest to those in a Marxist inspired system as they were to those in a capitalist system. The imperatives of big technology for efficiency of methods had similar application in both ideological systems. However, the underlying conceptual idea of man, his social needs and his motivations, is clearly often very different.

*   *   *   *   *

The pioneers of scientific management frequently demonstrated a range of versatility and eccentricity, bewildering to modern specialist managers. For example the Frenchman Frederic Le Play (1806–1882) was a man of action cum original thinker about the relationship between industrial change to social needs, and also as to the possibilities of improving the management of both industry and the world at large. During the course of a long and extremely active and varied life he moved from being a L'ecole polytechnic trained mining engineer to become a leading figure in public affairs as a Commissioner-General of Exhibitions in the second empire of Napoleon III, and thence on to function as an influential pioneer social thinker. Indeed he is regarded by many as a forefather of modern sociology, being especially known for his analysis, based on extensive case studies and field work throughout Europe, of the family as a basic unit in society. In 1856 he became the founder of La Societe d'Economie et de Science Sociale. His ideas about society and economic affairs at large later impressed many thinkers including the leading English neo-classical economist Alfred Marshall, and the pioneer industrial sociologist Elton Mayo.

Le Play for many years successfully combined the role of a professor of mining engineering in the Ecole des Mines in Paris with extensive travelling and consultancy arrangements concerned with mining and related industrial development schemes throughout Europe, North Africa and, as far East as the Donets Basin and Crimean Regions of Czarist Russia. His writings and notes reveal a wide understanding of the acute social and economic changes which the new industrial technologies were bringing to European civilisation in the middle years of the 19th century. He frequently expressed a strong scepticism for the economic wisdom of the English classical *laissez-faire* school of political economy, which reigned at that time. Yet as a basically conservative mind he recoiled from the revolutionary remaking of society implicit within Marxist ideas, which were coming to the fore in the middle years of the 19th century. As Dr. Michael Brooke aptly points out in his book on *Le Play Engineer and Social Socialist* published in 1970, his ideas were inevitably compounded of 'a sense of danger, a sense of tragedy and a sense of the future'. The sense of danger derived from the revolutions through which France had passed. The sense of tragedy from the sufferings which were all too apparent in much of industrial society, and the sense of the future from his studies which suggested social trends that he had to accept, without being able to like. He thus became increasingly regarded as an advocate of social peace at any price, and was all too aware of the fact that 'scientific progress had outpaced moral advance'.

In his work on *L'Organisation du Travail* published in 1870 Le Play defined six essential needs for the worker which still have their meaning for the successful management of the mass industrial society to the present day. As summarised by Brooke, the first was permanent contracts, both between the employer and the worker and vice versa. The second was a complete understanding between the two on wages. This was an optimistic suggestion, but was intended to prevent exploitation and maintain peace at the same time. Custom was to settle wages, rather than bargaining or the authority of the employer. The third was local diversification. Le Play noticed the problem, so often discussed since, that it was dangerous for a region to be overdependent on heavy industry. There was need to ensure that in any area a balanced industrial development took place. Heavy industry alone made the district liable to chronic unemployment, and meant a lack of any suitable employment for disabled men or for women. The fourth need was the provision of suitable means of saving. Some of this should be compulsory, in the form of obligatory insurance schemes. Le Play and members of the Societe d'Economie Sociale had deduced from their studies that the bulk of workers' savings was through compulsory saving. They lived through the rapid increase of both compulsory and voluntary schemes by savings banks, co-operative organisations, mutual benefit societies and insurance companies. But, clearly, only a limited number of people made adequate provision for their future needs voluntarily. The fifth and sixth needs embraced Le Play's view of the family – they are protection from eviction, and protection for women.

Among those whom we, in the Anglo-Saxon world, particularly associate with the introduction of the idea of the 'criteria of efficiency' in scientific management, is the pioneering work of Frederick Taylor (1856–1915), an American engineer cum conceptual management thinker. Taylor, like Ricardo and Marx before him, emphasised the importance of productivity to production. The workshop was the main unit of application for his system, and the activity measurement as the chief source for improvement. Taylor's philosophy, later developed by Henry Ford, and other large scale volume manufacturers, was to seek to limit the action used in performing a task to the most essential, and to improve the flow of work between individual workers in the workshop. He considered that men would maximise their efforts, and consquently the efficiency of the factory, if they felt they were doing the job in the best way, and were thus able to earn more. To Taylor, administration was regarded as little more than a means of introducing and controlling the new methods, but labour was at work within the framework of administration, and an improvement of work is partner to the improvement of the administration.

Another American thinker associated with the introduction of efficiency ideas into management was Frank Gilbreth (1868–1924) who was particularly concerned with the measurement of work; and later Henry Fayol (1841–1925), a Frenchman who was concerned with the principle of organisation. For Fayol the source of efficiency was proper management procedure, the unit of application was administration, and the method for its attainment the establishment of correct principles. He used as a strategy of analysis the establishment of principles for managers, which would result in organisational control. He was writing in the early 20th century, at a time when such ideas on management were uncommon. Indeed he helped to move the perspectives of 'management sciences' away from Taylor's workshop practice and a preoccupation with the worker, towards problems of industrial administration as a whole. Organisational problems were increasingly seen not merely as the result of unco-operative workmen, but also of failures in communication and co-ordination inside the enterprise as a whole.

Later still the science of 'operational research' came to be associated with search for more efficient means of production. This particularly developed during the Second World War, and was concerned with the improving of production activities of factories concerned with war munitions and also in the planning of many wartime operations, including the strategic bombing of Nazi Germany. In particular, it is based on a number of disciplines of which statistics is the most important, to convert observations to numerical values, which can then be interpreted to improve management effectiveness and performance. Similar ideas were also used in calculating likely targets in Britain for flying bombs, and in devising counter measures. In America the wartime work of Mr. Robert McNamara in these respects was later translated to rebuilding Ford's as a powerful vehicle manufacturer, then transferred to the Pentagon as Defence Secretary for the Johnson administration, and finally today finds a place in his role as President of the World Bank.

Another line of thinking for scientific management, which also had parallels in economic ideas, particularly associated with Professor Cannan in London, and Pigou at Cambridge, involved the introduction of 'welfare criteria' for judging the desirability of policy. In respect to the introduction of welfarist perspectives it is important to emphasise that for much of the 19th century in Britain, America and also in Western Europe, poverty was commonly associated with drink, idleness, sexual excess and degradation, and as such was regarded primarily as a moral problem. The wide impact of Malthusian cum Ricardian and indeed Spencerian ideas on the thinking of the successful and the affluent, suggested a particular perspective of the poor, far removed from the tolerance orginally extended by the old English Poor Laws. As we have seen in Britain, these were made more rigorous in the 1830s by the introduction of new Poor Laws, which set up a far more rigorous centrally controlled system of supervision and of outdoor relief generally. Indeed it became widely felt during the Victorian age on both sides of the Atlantic that the poor were naturally indolent and lazy, and that the new urban poor were not only less successful in material terms, but were also morally inferior to the achieving, saving and investing middle classes. If the poor were given material aid in the form of welfare payments or suchlike, Marx's 'reserve army' of the industrial unemployed was likely to continue to prefer idleness and sloth and, more importantly, to be encouraged to breed, as Malthus had suggested, in excessive numbers. In turn the increasing population would eventually push up the labour supply, and the demand for wages and sustenance far beyond the available means of subsistence, and this in turn would be at the expense of investment needs, for both new machinery and for sustaining the Ricardian wage fund.

An influential English critic of such simplistic views of the 'truths' of the classical economic dilemma became Mr. Seebohm Rowntree (1871–1954), a Quaker liberal industrialist, who began his early research into the nature of poverty within the industrial workforce of his home city, York. Arising out of this experience Rowntree developed a strong social conscience, and also a belief in the need for a democratic approach to industrial relations and the need for social improvements derived from the possibilities of scientific management generally. In his work on *The Human Factor in Business*, he observed that under any satisfactory industrial system two conditions would always be observed in the process of wealth production. First industry must pay the greatest possible regard to the general welfare of the community, and pursue no policy detrimental to it; and second, that wealth produced must be distributed in such a manner as will best serve the highest ends of the community. These notations did not prevent Rowntree in his own business life from upholding the requirements of good work and efficiency. He was, however, instrumental in broadening the perception of the goals of business to include not only the classical concepts of efficiency and profit, but also ideas of social harmony and welfare. The extension of such ideas into the scientific management debate later became extended to include ideas about 'personnel management' as well. In scientific management such welfare ideas also led to the development of improved organisational techniques. Yet as economists at large had recognised, welfare is often more difficult to identify than simple efficiency in the management of a firm. Indeed decisions about welfare cannot be made in isolation by managers, because they affect the society as a whole. The usual approach to industrial welfare became increasingly concerned with the whole man; this is his social as well as economic well-being, and this in turn involved concern with the dignity of labour and the social good that can be achieved through working in a business environment. Another welfare-based approach included attempts to diminish waste and to make the workforce more content and hence more stable, and to accept the standards set by society in order to preserve the independence of the business.

A further group of ideas associated with scientific management involved attempting to include the importance of *co-operation* between many groups engaged in the industrial process. This is particularly associated with the work of Elton Mayo (1880–1949), an Australian who became Professor of Industrial Research at the Harvard Graduate School of Business. In fact the questions that people and writers increasingly asked about human beings in organisations, were also posed by political philosophers and political economists about society as a whole. How is a productive organisation possible, when the people in the organisation have many interests which must conflict, and what are the obligations which must be filled by a person entering an organisation, and by the organisation, during the period of employment? The rejection of the simplicity of classical economic man and 'individualism' turned out to be a common theme. Rather, Mayo and his disciples put forward the idea of man as being primarily a social animal who worked not only for money, as some of the purist classical economists might have been supposed to have suggested, but also for a wide range of other considerations, including non-pecuniary social prestige and acceptance.

One of the major factors used by Mayo and others in explaining human action was to take the group as a fundamental unit of social activity. The human being is bound together not only by self interest, but also by values they hold in common. In the process of getting to know each other, people form expectations of each other's behaviour, and these mutual beliefs about the actions of others are known as circularity of response. Men value and accept the norms of their fellows as a legitimate standard, and a *normative man* often replaces a purely *economic man* which the classical economic doctrines had placed such reliance on. The co-operative line of thinking led on to a major discovery in respect of what management thought about the influence of the informal group of workers. Thus those working in organisations felt loyalty to their workmates and not to the goals of the company. Mayo's well known Hawthorne plant experiments showed the importance to employees of the friendship, and good esteem, of the colleagues in the informal group. Such ideas necessarily led to a new conception of the role of management, and the idea of the creation of common values, which everyone in the organisation could accept. Communication and the establishment of trust became more important than the authority of the leader's position, be he a heroic risk taker as so often portrayed by the individual classical entrepreneur, or a 'lackey' of the bourgeoisie, as suggested by the Marxists. In contrast for co-operation thinkers, people faced a choice between working hard, or not working hard, and whether they liked or disliked their work. All could be strongly influenced by a creative managerial style, and a new organisation of values. The result of these types of enquiries and views was to place great emphasis on workers' morale, and the creation of common responsibility.

It is apparent that many of the ideas of scientific management thinkers ran, to some extent, on parallel lines to those of economists in thinking about the problems of business. However in other ways, by their emphasis on different and more complex patterns of human motivation, and in particular on relationships within groups signified radical new lines of departure. Nevertheless the problem remains one of introducing into industrial organisations a sense of human scale, and a freedom of the sense of 'alienation', which will overcome the social disadvantages of large scale, yet will be economically viable in production costs terms, and eventual selling prices to the consumer. Recent experiments by the Volvo company in Sweden in organising car production around co-operative groups of workers, as opposed to flow line methods, represent a bold attempt to achieve this compromise in the modern industrial system.

## The Challenge of Strategic Planning and Forecasting

Any consideration of the complex decisions facing a modern large-scale organisation, be it primarily national or multinational, necessarily brings into focus the development and role of strategic planning and forecasting, as an essential element in modern business management. As has already been seen, in the neo-classical *laissez-faire* model, the assumption of large numbers of relatively small highly competitive enterprises, with a close identification between ownership and management, made the link between the past, the present and future easier to comprehend. However in the contemporary industrial scene, generally characterised by very large-scale, capital intensive and often multi-purpose multinational companies, the question of adequate decision-making and judgement, about both present needs and future directions, become more difficult. The sheer scale of modern enterprises presents many similar problems in Western democratic and Marxist inspired economies, and in this area at least considerable 'convergency' in approaches and techniques may be discerned. The total business environment has changed drastically, and in the Western mixed economy the extension of big government into the functioning of most aspects of the market, from demand management to pricing, quality standards and capital raising, etc., raises many new issues. Again in the democratic world powerful unions and social welfare criteria, affecting the functioning of the labour market has changed the context within which business decision-making is now undertaken.

Much of the stimulation for developing more sophisticated forms of business planning and forecasting has come out of the United States. This is hardly surprising in the light of the scale and extent of the present large-scale American business operating in both domestic and overseas markets. For many large companies formal strategic planning systems were first introduced during the 1950s and 1960s, on the lines of corporate planning then advocated by the management author Professor Igor Ansoff; by the Stanford Research Institute, and by various management consultants. Corporate planning also developed out of the increasingly involved relationship between the partners in what President Eisenhower called in his 1960 final address to the nation, the 'Industrial-Military Complex', particularly in association with major defence projects. Initially such planning took the form of programme budgeting and planning systems, and was particularly associated with the influence of Mr. Robert Macnamara, the Secretary for Defence in the Johnson administration and previously a 'whiz kid' cum systems expert and senior planner with the Ford Corporation. Macnamara earned his early experience with the wartime Strategic Air Command and had also attended the Harvard Business School.

Plainly all such planners whatever their organisational setting are concerned to guide decisions on a logical basis. Yet it has become increasingly apparent that many formal company planning systems, originally devised in response to particular budgetary needs, have limitations of application as a general rule. It has therefore been increasingly suggested, that it should now be possible for planners to abandon their hitherto rather limited system analysis and management scientist views of corporate planning, as a formal exercise in resource allocation. Indeed, it is proposed that rather than trying to sell, install and maintain planning procedures, the evolving role of the company planner lies increasingly in seeing his contemporary role in broad terms; by seeking to improve the quality of strategic decision, by whatever means seem to be appropriate. Thus it is increasingly recognised in many large organisations that comprehensive formal planning systems are of limited use, and may produce strong resistance from line managers, principally because they require too highly a disciplined approach, and involve substantial costs in time and money. It is also possible to recognise situations where comprehensive formalised planning is totally inappropriate. For instance, a traditional first generation entrepreneur, especially in a small business involved in rapidly changing competitive markets and heavily reliant on innovation and change, often succeeds because of his opportunism and willingness to take risks. Moreover, the day-to-day, and indeed the longer term planning of a highly volatile activity or an unpredictable environment, in even a very large business, may be better directed towards developing broad strategies and contingency plans. In these circumstances the modern big company chairman has to hold together a balanced coalition of opposing interests, often needing to avoid making policies too explicit, for fear of stimulating open conflict. Thus it is increasingly recognised that formal systems are by no means the panacea they once seemed to be. It may be a safer policy for planners to consider a wider range of alternative strategies, for which they will be able to present a number of different approaches and techniques. One might be operational planning only, with strategy being determined elsewhere. The second could be extended budgeting, extrapolating the consequences of the present policy; while a third might be ad hoc analysis of policy issues, as they are selected by management from time to time. The fourth approach might lead on to special studies, using research including attitude surveys, and future studies of likely developments. The fifth could include co-ordinated planning for key areas, if the company needs facilities or manpower in a particular special skill. A further might include the setting up of new venture groups, including a diversification task force or corporate development unit. Another would be for strategic management attempting to promote entrepreneural attitudes, by organisational and management development and such like. Alternatively it might include comprehensive strategic planning, which has followed on from a company merger or crisis situation. Finally, for very large companies contingency planning should enable the group to be better prepared to deal with the unexpected, as it affects its markets or sources of supply.

It will be apparent from the foregoing that a great deal depends on the nature of the business organisation being planned for, and this would seem to apply equally well in Western democratic or Marxist inspired industrial states. In large, mature, companies in a stable environment with little opportunity for rapid growth, timing tends to become routinised and focused around capital budgeting processes. However in organisations which are growing rapidly, and have to cope with a very dynamic environment, corporate planning does not consist only of a series of project development and marketing programmes Indeed, if the nature and extent of environmental change precludes the development of long-made plans, much greater emphasis is necessarily placed on achieving flexibility. In some business situations planners have found that after establishing a formal planning procedure, their role changes to that of a futurist or corporate guru with, as one of their principal purposes, the encouragement of line management to think and perceive, in a more unorthodox manner, and to ask less obvious questions. In such organisations it may be that top management is seeking guidance from the planner for a new corporate philosophy or mission.

In such changing circumstances it would seem that in the future the company planner's best approach would not be that of a technician with a ready-made solution, but like the doctor through a prognosis who would be able to advise senior management to ask critical questions. Such questions might include ideas about the limits of the authority in the management team: the role of the organisation as prescribed by its owners or stakeholders. Who has the power to make strategic decisions, an individual or a policy committee, or a coalition of several groups or teams? What is the prevailing management style, participative or authoritarian? Where will present policies lead to, and how do they compare with other goals? What are key strategic issues for organisations, and how do they need to develop new capabilities to deal with them? How can we change the organisation, in what direction, and by what means? Finally, and perhaps the most critical question: how in very large-scale organisations can one foster creativity and innovation and maintain it over a long period of time?

Moving beyond the large company into the contemporary business environment, the central strategy question has probably changed. It may no longer be what business are we in, but why are we in business at all? The traditional neo-classical economics answer to such a question – to make a profit, or in a more refined sense, to grow and to give an adequate return to shareholders, have in recent times all been questioned. They are being questioned both because the scale and nature of enterprises have changed, and relationships to government and the community have evolved radically. In this area particularly the move to convergency between many of the issues faced by planners everywhere in democratic and centrally planned systems of Western and Eastern Europe is remarkable. Increasingly, large companies are being required to take cognisance of many issues, of a wider social and welfare nature. These include whether a company provides satisfying jobs, or is helping solve social problems or assisting in providing employment of regional development. Thus possible conflict between business goals and social goals has become a central strategy issue, and in this sense reflects similar issues to those which have been the preoccupation of welfare-minded economists for many years. Large business enterprises, like other organisations, tend to develop their own distinctive sub-cultures, with their own value systems, which may differ markedly from the values accepted in society generally. Indeed the more effective their management selection, training and reward systems may appear, the more such *normative* values may be reinforced. However looking more broadly, a simplistic acceptance of business values from whichever source these may stem, can lead to major difficulties, when society at large begins to reject these in favour of other priorities. This has

FIG. 34.  CORPORATE PLANNING DIAGRAM

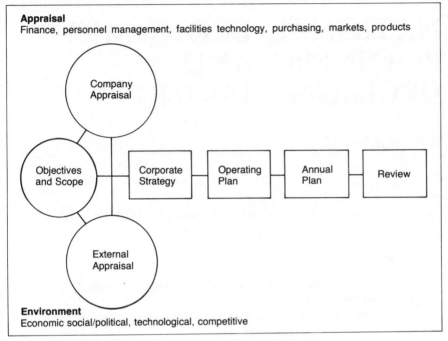

*Source:* Prof. B. Taylor

1. Specific objectives (company, division, function)
2. Environmental appraisal
3. Company appraisal
4. Assumptions and forecasts
5. Alternative strategies
6. Integrated plan
7. Action programmes
8. Budgets
9. Review

been becoming particularly apparent at a time when the power and autonomy of large management was being challenged and corporate planning is increasingly being transformed, in Professor Bernard Taylor's words 'from an internal dialogue between managers in headquarters and managers in divisions, into an open debate involving public servants, employees and self-appointed representatives of community interests'.

In sum, planning for business forecasting and decision making is increasingly being regarded as too important to leave solely to the judgement of businessmen. In this sense alone it is a world away from the assumptions of autonomous decision making, implicit within the neo-classical inspired competitive model. It reflects the move, by much of large scale industry and commerce, into a closer, more explicit relationship, with the changing values and goals of society as a whole. It also represents an essential response, on the part of big business to the changing nature of government and society today.

# Chapter 6

# NATIONAL ECONOMIC PLANNING AND DECISION MAKING

"It is much safer to obey than to govern"

Thomas Kempis (1380–1471)
*Imitatio Christi*

"*Boswell:* So, Sir, you laugh at schemes of political improvement?
*Johnson:* Why, Sir, most schemes of political improvement are very laughable things."

Samuel Johnson (1709–1784)
*Boswell's Life*

"A state without the means of some change is without the means of its conservation."

Edmund Burke (1729–1797)
*Reflections on the Revolution in France*

"All dressed up, with nowhere to go."

William Allen White (1868–1944)

*On the Progressive Party in the U.S.A. in 1916, after Theodore Roosevelt had retired from the Presidential campaign.*

"We get fat in war and thin in peace."

Will Rogers (1879–1935)

"We are the first nation to starve to death with a storehouse that's over-filled with everything we want."

Ibid

"Guns will make us powerful; butter will only make us fat."

Hermann Goering (1893–1946)
Radio Broadcast, summer of 1936

"It sure makes me feel proud to belong to a country that can afford peace and war at the same time."

*Captain on a cartoon in the* New Yorker *magazine at the time President Lyndon B. Johnson (1908—1973) stated there was no need to restrict the domestic economy because of the Vietnam war.*

## Public Ownership and Planning: Western Democratic Style

As will have become apparent from earlier chapters the present age has seen the evolution of much of the previously laissez-faire inspired capitalist countries, into the so called 'mixed economies' of today. Professor Paul A. Samuelson, one of the most widely read and respected of contemporary American economists succinctly described, in his work on *Economics*; the transformation into a more planned and regulated industrial social democratic society as follows:

"After World War I, new governments were set up all over Europe. By 1925 an impartial observer might have said that the future of the capitalistic way of life appeared serene and assured. Yet within a half dozen years, country after country succumbed to dictatorship: totalitarian fascist governments covered the map of Europe. The depression decade of the 1930s finally ended in a great world war.

At the end of World War II, the outlook had changed. The world was divided into great blocs; Soviet Russia and her satellites of Eastern Europe stood within the Iron Curtain in an uneasy alliance with mainland China, and outside was the rest of the world. But nations outside the Iron Curtain were far from homogeneous. Labor-socialist governments were ruling in Britain, in Australia and New Zealand and in all of Scandinavia. Various forms of dictatorship still lingered on in Spain, Portugal, Egypt and Latin America. France, Japan, and Italy had within them noisy and articulate left-wing political parties. The awakening nations of Asia and Africa did not view the world with laissez-faire tinted glasses.

Only the United States and a few other nations remained as islands of declared capitalism in an increasingly collectivised world. But even here, the scene was drastically changed; almost unconsciously ours had become a mixed economy with both private and public initiative and control. The clock of history, sometimes, evolves so slowly that its moving hands are never seen to move. After the New Deal, the American economy was permanently changed. We have converged with Western Europe to the mixed economy."

*    *    *    *    *

Any discussion of the contemporary role of national economic planning within a 'mixed' urban industrial society inevitably means drawing together a great many loose ends, touched on in previous chapters. At its simplest, such planning might be defined as organising the use of factors of production by central direction, instead of by the profit motive as in a purely *laissez-faire* market system. In between these two extremes are the many variations of 'mixed' social democratic style economy planning which have been followed throughout Western Europe since the end of the Second World War. As we have already seen, the early classical economists, from Adam Smith onwards, were able to assume a considerable degree of competition between large numbers of small firms. Thus the conclusion of much of classical and neo-classical economic theory, as developed through from Smith to Ricardo and on via Jevons and Marshall to 'marginal utility' analysis, was that in a freely competitive world the working of the profit motive would result in the best possible allocation of resources. However, as time went by this was inevitably challenged, by a number of different points of view. Within the Western market economies the problems of a different scale of social priorities and the need to develop a broader perspective of welfare criteria inevitably results in the development of arguments for more centralised economic planning. The increasing size of many large scale manufacturing and commercial enterprises also suggested that in many cases it was simply impractical to seek to break up such enterprises, because this would destroy the very advantages which they offered; that is a highly efficient division of labour and economies of scale inherent in flow-line production. The solution, therefore, to the problem of scale in large-scale industry, once the re-introduction of a highly competitive ethic was abandoned, was to suggest ways in which they might be made more amenable to social need, hopefully compatible at the same time with a sustained upward rate of growth.

Inevitably a wide variety of solutions arose, ranging on the one hand from syndicalist ideas, originally developed from the ideas of the French Socialist philosopher, François Fourier, in early 19th century France, that the ownership and control of industries and factories would best lie in the hands of people who worked within them; to co-operative ideas dating from Robert Owen, and later, the Rochdale pioneers of 1844, that the activities of enterprises would best be governed by groups of consumers. Finally in Britain we arrived at Socialist cum British Labour Party ideas, that large scale enterprises were best taken into public ownership. It is of interest that the nationalisation solution was followed so enthusiastically by Mr. Clement Attlee's (1883–1967) Labour Government between 1945 and 1951. One reason is that leading members of the Labour Party, and particularly Mr. Herbert Morrison, (1888–1965) had been impressed by the benefits of public ownership as indicated by the establishment, on the basis of a previous private monopoly, of the London Passenger Transport Board in 1929, with full powers to provide both bus and underground transport for the whole of the Greater London Area. The example of the London Passenger Transport Board and other public utilities was used as a basis for implementing a much wider nationalisation of key industries after the end of the Second World War. In time these came to embrace the Bank of England; coal mining, which for many years had had some elements of government interference and control; railways which again like coal mining had from the 1920s onwards been under strong government influence; ports, airways, steelmaking the hitherto local public utilities of electricity, gas, water, transport etc. and others. The many difficulties associated with the massive, increasingly bureaucratic nationalised industries in attempting to meet their original criteria of success, that is earning a profit taking one year with another, will be highly familiar to most readers. Again in many cases commercial dealings and relationships with major private companies, increasingly dependent on government patronage and supports also raise acute public accountability dilemmas. Two recent books: *The Dilemma of Accountability in Modern Government – Independence Versus Control (1969)* edited by Bruce L. R. Smith and D. C. Hague and *Political Responsibility and Industry (1973)* by Edmund Dell consider in detail the many issues arising. Two points deserve particular emphasis. One is the sheer difficulty of very large organisations, nationalised or non-nationalised, to be highly responsive to market needs, especially when saddled with public service obligations. Second, given the scale of the enterprises and the changing technology on which they are based, the difficulty of making effective long term investment judgements about the needs of the future. This is applied particularly in the case of large scale industries concerned with public transport, power generation, and suchlike. Current public debates stimulated by Mr. Tony Benn's 1976 espousal of 'open government' about the appropriate futures for different and to some extent competitive energy industries: coal, North Sea gas and oil, nuclear power and electricity generation, highlight many of the problems involved.

\*      \*      \*      \*      \*

It is important to recognise, however, that by no means all of our present interests in planning simply stem from the better organisation 'of the supply side of the economy'; indeed in most Western industrial countries, including Great Britain, the main inspiration of present day attempts at national planning stemmed from the demand side of the economy, from the Keynesian style attempts to establish better control over business cycle fluctuations and their effects on employ-ment, on business expectations, and on decision-making by consumers and businessmen alike. In Britain, for much of the post-war period many planning ideas started to come from the search for better methods of short term control over the way the mixed economy was operating. For instance it was an attempt to escape from a cycle of 'stop-go' policies which moved Winston Churchill's Conservative Government, elected in the early 1950s with a strong free market ideology of 'setting the people free' and of 'letting Conservative freedom work', to even-tually adopt economic planning as a central theme of their domestic policies a decade later. Interestingly enough, unlike the Keynesians of the inter-war years, the British authorities of the post-war years were not so much worried about their abilities to manage a depressed economy, floundering along at the bottom of an apparently unending stagnation in the trade cycle. Rather it was the problem of managing the strong up-turn that became their primary concern. It was how to prevent an 'overloaded economy', to use the late Professor Harry Johnson's telling phrase, from straining the balance of payments to a point where expansion had to be halted, in order to protect the gold and foreign exchange reserves, which were increasingly held in the form of U.S. dollars. Moreover, from the mid-1950s onwards, most attempts to manage interest rate adjustments in Britain were as much a reflection of external factors working on the economy, than anything to do with the internal domestic needs of the economy, through credit expansion or otherwise. In contrast to the pre-war years, in the post-war years the £ sterling interest rate moved from being a world interest rate, setting a standard which the rest of the industrial and trading world tended to follow, to a reflection of overseas attitudes towards sterling, and the running of the British economy at large. The British interest rate moved from being the 'price setter' to being a 'price taker', powerfully influenced by overseas reactions to conditions within the United Kingdom economy and their likely implications for the balance of payments and for holders of sterling securities, etc. From this time onward, the attitudes of Zurich Gnomes to the running of the British economy entered into the demonology of the Left, and into economic debate at large. The answer to these awkward Helvetian dilemmas was the idea that the economy, in both its public and private sectors, should be increasingly guided by longer term objectives, rather than the fluctuating circumstances of the short term market. Keynesian inspired economists talked increasingly about the need for a 'steadier rate of growth', year by year. Being steadier it was also piously hoped that the average rate for the period as a whole would also tend to be on a higher long term growth path.

As Mr. Andrew Schonfield pointed out in his book on *Modern Capitalism*, published in 1965: 'It is of great importance that only gradually were governments induced to recognise the fact that the forces making for inflation during periods of prosperity were different in kind from those responsible for deflation during a down-turn of the business cycle.' Thus, the British Government, during the late 1950s and early 1960s, persisted in maintaining that the major cause of their economic problems, including the slow growth in national product, was an excessive demand on resources, just as their troubles of the 1930s had been caused by excessively small demand. There was increasingly supposed to be a simple calculable figure for the optimum level of aggregate financial demand which would, at one and the same time, keep prices steady and maximise production. A most influential exponent of these views, which guided the British Treasury for several years, was Professor F. W. Paish, who considered that the equilibrium rate of unemployment corresponded to full utilisation of British productive capacity without inflationary pressure, was $2\frac{1}{4}\%$. A level of unemployment somewhat above this figure was sustained for a whole year — for the fourth quarter of 1962 until the third quarter of 1963. Guided by these doctrines the Government pursued a policy during the early 1960s which kept British unemployment at two to three times the level of those which applied in Germany. However the experiment did not justify itself, either by giving Britain the market advantage over Germany, or by raising the British rate of growth to a German level. A decade later, from the early 1970s onwards, a downward float of the £ sterling against the D Mark and other major currencies, was also to prove to be equally unrewarding. In fact at the present time, the employment and balance of payment debate has been shifted off into a new realm, by the fortuitous impact of North Sea oil on the fortunes of the economy as a whole.

*     *     *     *     *

During the 1960s the idea of national planning through influence over the 'commanding heights' of the economy took a somewhat different turn. In Britain, the creation of The National Economic Development Council, in 1962, and the subsequent attempts to use this, initially as a clearing house of ideas between government, the unions and employers about the future course of direction of large scale industry, was an important step. The current idea of planning agreements between government departments and particular major companies about the future course of investment and related activities, has also been seen as a further twist in the planning debate. Underlying all these various moves towards a more centralised co-ordination of planning is the belief, held by many, that capitalism in its old atomistic competition form, was simply inefficient. By this it meant that it tended to leave factors of production under-employed, or those employed were used with varying efficiency by different entrepreneurs cum managers. Again, perhaps more critically, it was often asserted that in a modern economy free competition simply did not exist, and unplanned private industries simply led to large scale secretly organised monopoly and restrictive practices, which were inevitably designed to maintain individual company profits by limiting production and/or maintaining prices. As indicated in Chapter 5, the many reports of the various Monopolies and Restrictive Practices Tribunals from 1948 onward did little to alter this view.

The relevant point about this in terms of the development of economic doctrine and practice was a gradual recognition that cost inflation required management of the production supply side of the economy: that simple Keynesian methods of aggregate demand management simply would not work on their own. Thus a whole new style of intervention by the Government was increasingly called for, if a 'full employment high growth strategy' was to be pursued with any consistency. Increasingly governments have become concerned with 'supply questions' such as looking for individual bottle-necks in particular industries, whether they be the availability of key goods and services or raw materials, the existence of appropriate capital equipment, or a lack of special types of skills threatening to hold up growth overall. The more that Britain and other Western industrial nations pursued these types of approaches, the more they took on the form of functioning like governments in under-developed countries, than the traditional behaviour of 'hands off' government of the liberal democratic type. Significantly intervention in the supply side of the economy was drastically changing the perception of the general public to the role of government, in its relationship both to industry and to society as a whole. Such interventionist ideas inevitably led to full scale involvement in labour questions and the eventual abandonment, at least temporarily, of free collective bargaining and its replacement by wage freezes, social contracts, and suchlike. At the time of writing (Autumn 1977) Mr. James Callaghan's Labour Government has become stuck on a voluntary acceptance of not more than an average pay increase of 10 per cent — as a central point in its economic strategy!

It is of interest that in the 1920s, long before he was known for his work on *The General Theory*, Keynes wrote a lecture about *The End of laissez-faire*, reflecting on the miseries of business depressions. In this lecture he said that:

> "I believe that the cure for these things is partly to be solved in the deliberate control of currency and of credit by a central institution, and partly in the collection and dissemination on a great scale of data relating to the business situation"....
>
> "These measures would involve society in exercising direct intelligence through some appropriate organ of action over many of the inner intricacies of private business, yet it would leave private initiative and enterprise unhindered."

The last sentence sums up the dilemma of most interventionist policies on the supply side during much of the post-war period. However, perhaps what Keynes did not fully envisage, was the problem of almost continuous expansionary control, once the menace of massive and persistent slumps had apparently been removed. As Schonfield, in 1965, pointed out:

> "A typical problem of modern economic planning related chiefly to the need for greater mobility of resources in order to take advantage of more rapid technological change did not figure in his (Keynes) thinking. The

law of diminishing returns provided his natural intellectual framework. There was no hint of an offsetting principle of increasing technological opportunity."

The experience of the mid-1970s onwards, and particularly the onset of the various crises emanating from a rapid real rise in the price of energy, particularly in the form of Middle Eastern crude, has drastically changed the scene again. It may well be that the problems facing Western planners in the future will as much rely on a perception of the traditional classical constraints of 'diminishing returns', and of the payment of pure rents to a new rentier class of Middle Eastern oil sheikhs and other possessors of cheap energy, as from any other cause. Thus the path of economic doctrines, from natural scarcity through to problems of finiteness and scarce resources, influencing supply and then via Keynes to a concern with demand management, will once again turn the full circle, at however, an entirely different level of overall activity.

*    *    *    *    *

Throughout much of the post-war era Britain's industrial production grew more slowly than those of her major European rivals. For instance between 1958 and 1976 the combined index for the original European Economic Community Six rose from 100 to 248, while Britain's only grew from 100 to 151. In face of this real challenge to her relative position during the late 1950s and early 1960s, there was an increased interest in the apparent success of national economic planning in France. This success was seen to lie in the rapid improvement of living standards in France, and the associated success of much of French industry in expanding markets both at home and abroad. The interesting contrast to the British experience was that the French perceived somewhat earlier the problems that were coming, and historically having had a lower record of growth than most industrially advanced countries, were determined to manage things somewhat better than they had done before. They also lived in an intellectual environment which, from mercantilism and Louis XIV onwards, naturally gave the state and central direction from Paris a much larger role in the working of the system. Moreover in contrast to the other major Western European powers, France, with her favourable relationship between land resources and population, also had a physiocratic tradition to support. However, the most important post-war French contribution in the words of Schonfield was 'that they did not rely exclusively on increasing the overall level of investment to achieve their ends'. Rather they sought to develop a strategy on a national scale for deploying this investment at points in the system which it would produce an especially high rate of return. Another apparent contrast with Britain was the willingness of the French Government to assume a supervisory position in the division of the prizes from economic growth. This contrasted to British planning in much of the 1960s which tended to be concerned with enlarging the aggregate volume of supplies, but tended to recoil from any highly specific attempt to plan demand. The French, in their Fourth Plan, insisted on the objective of achieving a more complete view of man, by which they meant not merely that the extra produce should be used to satisfy consumer demands finding expression through the market, but should also be devoted to broader purposes for which the ordinary citizen would not naturally choose, but for which he would presumably be grateful in the future. At about this time the French film producer, Monsieur Jacques Tatti, made a highly popular film concerned with the place of modern man in society, including an hilarious send-up of the various gadgetry which this implied. In their national economic planning the French tended to set their face against 'gadgetry' and tried to point towards a national ethical purpose, to impose choices about the longer term use of resources, somewhat different from that with which the market would probably produce. In this sense they were giving emphasis to a view, completely contrary to the older classical view of economics, that market prices in a modern society would often fail to measure up either to 'social costs or social benefits'.

*   *   *   *   *

Another decisive feature has been the awesome recovery of the West German economy during the past twenty years or so. A variety of reasons have been suggested to explain why it was that West Germany, from the early fifties onwards, developed such a high growth rate. Early on it was undoubtedly true that the wartime destruction of her economy and its subsequent rebuilding with the latest ideas and technology and the assistance of Marshal Aid from 1947 onwards provided an excellent take off point for re-development. Yet it was of course much more than simply a matter of adopting advanced machine using technologies. The destruction of the previous Nazi system of government and society meant that the population as a whole were receptive to starting things in a new way, and there was little commitment on the part of management or labour to procedures that had gone before. Moreover the mass movement of some twelve million people from Eastern Europe into Western Germany in the years immediately after 1945, also provided a highly skilled and amenable work force, ready to accept the disciplines of privation and the efforts of hard work, to re-establish both themselves and their country as a major industrial power. Later still this work force was greatly added to by an inflow of 'gäste arbeiter' from the Balkans, Turkey and Southern Europe generally. From the 1950s onwards a feature of the German system was its extremely favourable location with ready access to nearby growth markets across land frontiers. As the success of the increasingly integrated European Common Market became more and more apparent, from the mid-1950s onwards, re-vitalised German industry was in a good position to take advantage of new market opportunities as they presented themselves. Moreover internationally, German business, being somewhat paradoxically unfettered by tradi-tional ties and sentiments with captive markets (such as Britain had with her imperial preference system and France with her colonies) was more amenable to shaping her production capacity to market's needs, as opposed to simply regarding export markets as an outlet over and above what the domestic market was able to take. Additionally there was a marked difference of philosophical attitude. Under the early leadership of Dr. Ludwig Erhard (1897–1977), Germany enthusias-tically embraced a free market philosophy, which meant, at least in the early post-war years, an extensive reliance on the attitudes and dis-ciplines which Adam Smith and his successors would have applauded and admired.

The result of all these developments is that the German economic miracle became manifest for all to see and the growth rate and strength of her balance of payments, together with that of Japan, eventually vastly exceeded those of her former enemies, particularly Britain and also France. Indeed by the early 1970s, the position of Germany in many areas appeared to be well nigh unassailable. However since that time other problems have presented themselves. While the German balance of payments has remained strong, acute social cum anarchist type Bader Mienhoff gang tensions have developed within the fabric of society. There are signs of a turning away, on the part of many of the younger population, from the values and disciplines which provided the spur to effort and industrial production in the immediate post-war years. Moreover the 1973 onwards energy crisis hit the German economy in a particularly vulnerable way. Whereas Germany still has extensive deposits of coal in the Rhur, it is almost entirely devoid of any of its own resources of energy in the form of oil or natural gas. It is therefore highly dependent on the continuation of the present international system, and of an expansion of the European Common Market and of world trade in an orderly fashion.

Nevertheless the example of Germany as a free market philosophy economy stands in marked contrast, in economic growth stakes at least, in successful contrast to the slower performance of the British economy. Whether this is a function of the economic doctrines which have applied, or more a function of a whole set of other circumstances, is a matter for a continued great debate. It is certainly true that while the German economy has not had the same pressure towards central planning (which have become manifest in both France and Britain) Keynesian demand management techniques with a preference for a higher rate of unemployment, to a lower rate of inflation, have had an important impact on the way the economy has functioned. Again, close links between the banking system and the great industrial enterprises have meant that German industry has been more able to 'gear up' to market opportunities as they occur more rapidly than perhaps applies in the case of Britain, where industrial financing continues to rely more on retained profits and equity. In the case of Britain, London has continued as an important source of international finance, and the flow of 'invisibles' into the British economy remains a critical element. In contrast, the German economy had a comparatively small inflow of invisible income, but at the same time a banking system more directly geared to the needs of financing industry as opposed to the British pre-occupation with guarding the security of depositors and of financing and servicing the world as a whole. In short, before making sweeping judgements about the comparative performances of different economies, it is desirable to make sure one is really comparing like with like. Further information about the comparative industrial performance and economic growth of major countries is included in Appendix V.

\* \* \* \* \*

Looking more broadly over the history of planning and Western European democratic government relations with industry and with the consumer since the end of the Second World War, a number of strands can be emphasised. Writing in the mid-1960s Mr. Schonfield suggested three which still have validity a decade later.

First, there is 'indicative planning' in its purist form. It is made to work because the quality of the analysis done by the planners convinces the men wielding power, in private and public sectors alike, that the conclusions offered to them provide good advice. Second, there is an approach which relies on reinforcing governmental powers. The state controls a large part of the economy through the nationalised industries and public sector generally and the planner, by intelligent manipulation of the levers, can thus guide the remainder of the economy firmly towards objectives which the government chooses. The third approach eschews, wherever possible, direct government intervention and places its reliance instead on the 'corporatist' formula for managing the economy. In this approach, familiar to British readers, the major interest groups are brought together and encouraged to conclude a series of bargains about their future behaviour which will have the effect of moving the economy along a desired path. The French method of planning is generally a combination of the first and second approach, that is, indicative planning combined with reinforced government powers, whereas the British approach, the N.E.D.O. type of planning, tends to be a combination of some aspects of indicative planning together with a corporatist system for seeking to manage the economy. On top of this, in recent times has been added the concept of 'planning agreements' which will encourage the major companies within the economy to think collectively with the government towards overall goals. All these types of planning raise the issue as to the power of the technical expert, as a master of the whole operation. The relationship between these managerial experts and the political process has yet to be fully thought through. Certainly Parliament of the British pattern often seems incapable of maintaining effective control over the activities of this type of expertise, and indeed a call has been made from a number of different quarters for creating a subsidiary parliament, possibly a reformed House of Lords, which will take on the role of an economic Star Chamber, with specific responsibilities for supervising the work of the planning process, in both its demand and its supply aspects. In the late 1950s Sir C. P. Snow drew attention to the problem of the *two cultures*; of those trained in science being incomprehensible to those trained in the arts and vice versa. The many problems in recent years of seeking to relate rational decision making about long term capital intensive technology programmes, to the short term 'non-scientific' adversary based parliamentary processes, has rammed home the truth behind Snow's original perception, of the many complex dilemmas involved. 'Convergency' is yet to be found in this domestic resolution of the claims of overall national planning, *vis-à-vis* those of retaining individual freedom and choice.

## Planning for Industrial Society: Marxist–Leninist Style

Having discussed in outline the various forms that planning and government relations have taken in the democratically inspired Western world, with particular reference to Britain, France and West Germany, we can now consider briefly the nature of central planning in the Soviet led COMECON group of states. Since 1949 the economic policies of this important group of largely internally trading nations has been coordinated by the Council for Mutual Economic Assistance – C.M.E.A. As has been shown, the 1917 Russian cum Marxist revolution occurred in the wrong place, in the sense that contrary to the prophecy it did not occur in an advanced industrial urban society from a revolutionary overthrow of the capitalist-bourgeoise class, by a landless propertyless proletariat. Rather it occurred in Russia, towards the end of the First World War, in a country which, although it had some mainly foreign French owned manufacturing and service industries, was still primarily a backward agrarian society, characterised more by landless and landbound peasants, than an industrial proletariat. In the Marxist hierarchy of different historical stages of economic and social development, Russia in 1917 equated more to a state of feudalism slowly evolving into capitalism, rather than a state of capitalism with an industrial base, waiting to crumble into socialism on the onward march to pure communism. It is of interest that Marx himself had initially left Germany in the 1840s feeling that the state of Prussia and the other German Principalities, etc., required a revolution leading to the overthrow of feudalism and the expropriation of its assets by the new capitalist class, before they would be ready for a later revolution of capitalism being overthrown and replaced by socialism. Marx did not, apparently, foresee the rapid industrialisation of Germany which subsequently occurred from the 1860s onwards. Towards the end of his life Marx, though he learnt Russian, believed this to be even more strongly the case in Tzarist Russia. Serfdom cum slavery had been abolished only in 1862, which was even a further stage down the hierarchy of Marx's and Engels' historical stages. Thus when out of the chaos of war the revolution finally occurred, Lenin and his supporters were confronted with an acute dilemma. Was the new Russian state capable of supporting socialism in the true Marxian sense? The answer was surely 'no'! In order to run a system in which each would contribute according to his abilities and could be rewarded according to his labour need, let alone his ultimate need, a powerful industrial base was essential. Thus it was from this unpromising start, that once the early revolutionary turmoil was over, foreign influences had been expelled and foreign debts, particularly to France, had been repudiated, that the Soviet state began the long march from what was still basically a backward agrarian into a powerful, industrial urban society. Russia's current status as one of the world super powers has been based on the wealth and power creating success of this process.

In looking at the evolution of the modern Soviet industrial state it is important to appreciate the historical developments which preceded the revolution of 1917. The abolition of serfdom by Tsarist Russia represented more than a shift of the regime away from a dependency on a feudal self sufficient economic system. As with the emancipation of the negro slaves in the southern United States at the same period, the move away from serfdom marked the beginning of the possibility of applying more efficient types of capitalist development to Russia's extensive, if grossly under-utilised, land resources. From that time onwards free peasants were encouraged to buy land from the government, which had acquired the land from the feudal landlords following the break up of the great estates. However in order that the peasants have sufficient income to purchase the land, and to pay taxes as well, they needed cash income, which they could only acquire by producing foodstuffs for sale to the market. Gradually an extensive agricultural market economy began to develop, both to feed the expanding urban population and to provide grain exports to the growing population centres of Western Europe. Russian grain exports became an important feature in the latter years of the 19th century, in competition with American grains which were flowing across the Atlantic at the same time. The strength of grain export earnings eventually enabled Russia to move on to the gold standard in 1895, and she became a more reliable investment opportunity for Western European, and especially French risk capital. This flow of foreign funds was increasingly used to finance developments in both the public and the private sectors of the Tsarist economy. The programme of transformation was led by the farseeing Minister of Finance, Count Sergi Witte (1849–1915), who between 1892 and his dismissal by the Tsar in 1903, implemented many changes. These included the completion of the Trans-Siberian railway, placing the rouble onto the gold standard and supporting industrial development by protective tariffs. Thus it was that Tsarist Russia began the transformation from an agrarian system into a society based on a growing proportion of urban and industrial activities.

The possibilities of the changing situation were not lost on Lenin. For him the onset of capitalism, especially in rural Russia, meant the destroying of the elements of isolationism, and separatism, and the fragmentation of the rural economy into a number of isolated and petty producers. Some of the peasantry were increasingly drawn into the capitalist system, which he felt would eventually provide a strong revolutionary possibility. However, Lenin also perceived that the peasantry had a traditional subservient attitude to the ruling classes, and were therefore unlikely to provide a strong revolutionary potential in their own right. This conservative element was intensified by the fact that as some of the more successful peasants moved up into the landowning middle peasant Kulak class, they would be even less inclined to be enthusiastic participants in revolutionary social change. The question arose that given the basic importance of agriculture to the Russian economy as a whole, was it right for social democratic reformers to encourage neasants to seize farms or estates, which, by and large, were well managed and becoming increasingly mechanised? Lenin concluded that in the longer term a clash between the rural proletariat and the rural bourgeoisie was well nigh inevitable. Yet he certainly recognised that a substantial number of the rural classes would be resistant to revolutionary changes extending from the town.

The collapse under the stress of total war of the Tsarist regime in 1917, and the various events which followed up to the final expulsion of foreign interests in 1919, left the Russian economy in a pitiful state. Food production collapsed, famine was widespread and the industrial system, such as existed, had ceased to function. The first problem facing the Bolshevik regime with the end of the civil war in 1920 was to restore the agricultural system to the point of being able to feed the population. As Lenin saw it, the dual personality of the middle peasants, at once 'toilers by habit' and 'capitalist traders' by instinct, presented a major challenge to the introduction of a fully socialist system. Indeed in 1919 he spoke in conciliatory terms of the need to woo this vacillating peasant element into a firm alliance with the urban workers, separating them from the upper peasant Kulak class by a careful consideration of their needs. By 1920, alarmed by the rapid decline of agriculture, and growing peasant unrest, Lenin spoke of means of devising state compulsion to raise agricultural production. However, in time he realised this would prove disastrous, and ordered instead what became known as the 'tactical retreat of the new economic policy'. The *New Economic Policy* of 1921 could not be represented as it advanced towards a socialist society, except that it would in some ways strengthen the country economically and so give the Bolsheviks greater freedom of action. In fact the policy looked like a tremendous victory for the well-off peasant. The tax in kind which replaced the requisitioning programme, encouraged an expansion of the prosperous holdings, and the leasing of land and hiring of labour in the best capitalist tradition were legalised. Economic differentiation of the peasantry, which in spite of egalitarian land distribution had continued, now received further stimulus. At the same time an attempt was made to encourage the onward move to a Socialist society. This included the development of consumer and rural agricultural co-operatives and other forms of co-operation by means of which the working peasantry would be brought together towards gradual voluntary association on producer collectives. Lenin's ideas also included a variety of subsidies and privileges for co-operatives, and the involvement of all working peasants in such organisations. In fact, by 1923, the Bolshevik government seems to have moved against Lenin's advice and abolished compulsory membership of consumers' co-operatives. Yet earlier Lenin had insisted that co-operatives be voluntary, saying they were intended to bring about the general active participation of 'toilers', in order to make the population so civilised that they would understand all the advantages. The evolution of Lenin's attitude to the peasants and the perpetration of private property in the agricultural sector can be regarded as a tactical response to the changing situation. In the circumstances of the time it was essential to re-establish food production to the level of pre-war years, and by the mid-1920s this had been achieved. The later introduction of collective farms, from the 1929 *Five Year Plan* onwards, owed more to the ideas of Stalin than they did to Lenin. These eventually took the form of large scale socialist agricultural enterprises, owned by the nation as a whole and organised on the industrial model. The collective farm system and regulated agricultural markets also increasingly provided a large cash surplus, which was essential to the future 'risk' financing of the Soviet industrial economy as a whole.

The 1929 Stalinist inspired national Five Year Plan marked a distinct change of direction. It conceived of using the vast agricultural resources of Russia reformed, wherever possible, by the introduction of state collective farms and the virtual abolition of private ownership. In this process the rural bourgeoisie, the Kulaks, were gradually to be stripped of their assets, and either 'liquidated' or absorbed into truly large scale production units. From this reformed agrarian base the source of a 'surplus value' could be found, to finance the transformation of the Soviet Union into a leading urban and industrial society. On this basis

Soviet Russia would be able to establish a world role and be capable if need be to lead the onward march to a Communist world. Lenin himself had given great credence to the idea of industrialisation being reflected particularly in power generation and especially to the widespread diffusion of power by electrification, and also by the rapid and massive expansion of coalmining and steel making capacity, etc. The application of science and scientific management to achieving an industrial society was given high priority. Indeed during the 1930s such were the priorities given to the 'central core' activities that much of the remainder of the economic system tended to remain seriously inadequate for the burdens imposed on them. In particular the transport system often proved incapable of moving the quantities that were being produced and in linking the far flung agricultural and grain growing regions to the expanding industrial centres. Similar 'bottlenecks' were also common in respect to efficient movement of industrial raw materials from the depths of Siberia to industrial centres in the west. Nevertheless, great strides were made from the late 1920s onwards, the market mechanism was all but abolished, firm priorities were established from the Centre on a one to five years basis, and decisions went out for a programme of forced investment and industrialisation on a massive scale. It would be wrong to underestimate the achievements of the Soviet state in industrial terms; in fact, by dint of most heroic sacrifice on the part of the average Russian citizen an enormous industrialisation programme was pushed through with the utmost ruthlessness, albeit with considerable inefficiencies as well. By the Second World War the Soviet Union had established considerable heavy industrial and armaments capacity, and once the initial onslaught of the Nazi attack was absorbed by retreat and scorched earth tactics, was capable of mobilising immense resources. These came from centres beyond Moscow and indeed beyond the Urals, and supported a large, well mechanised and eventually powerful army. The same type of progress has been pushed on, with considerable further ruthlessness, during much of the post-war era. The result is that today the U.S.S.R. is a leading world industrial power, almost matching the U.S.A. in coal production, exceeding it in petroleum production, in iron-ore, in pig-iron, in crude steel and a number of other critical items. However the emphasis of much of the Soviet system has remained on the continuous re-investment in heavy industry and the support of a large military power, including in recent years a rapidly expanding deep sea navy. Moreover the scale of untapped natural resources, including oil in Siberia, promises the need for further continuous investment in transport and development plus defence *vis-à-vis* China. The Soviet system has proved far less capable of adjusting itself flexibly to more widely based consumer demands, or creating consumer and consumerable goods which are sellable into a competitive market based economy. There are signs throughout the eastern European economic system of a growing lack of 'worker motivation', deriving from the paucity and low quality of consumer goods available in the shops.

\*    \*    \*    \*    \*

Turning to other members of the COMECON group, with the collapse of the old capitalist system at the end of the Second World War, the Soviet presence was manifest throughout Eastern Europe. The initial task of reconstruction involved shipment of considerable amounts of basic industrial materials and machine tools, etc., from Eastern Germany, Hungary and other ex-Nazi installations into the Soviet Union. However as time went by, each of the new Socialist states were encouraged to begin to emulate the Soviet pattern of industrialisation, based on the surpluses of agriculture. Within the agricultural sector collective farms were established and private landowners eliminated, though in many areas they frequently reappeared as managers of collective farms. The surplus value from agriculture was then syphoned, via controlled markets, out of the agricultural system, and used as a basis for financing a new industrial and urban society. However each country within the emerging Soviet influenced bloc was encouraged to pursue 'socialism within one country', and trade with other members was initially minimised. Gradually the sheer inefficiency of each member country, of very differing factor endowments and skills, doing its own thing, became apparent, and willy-nilly a pattern of barter trading developed, one mutual assistance member country swopping with another, on a non-convertible currency basis, various tradeable goods.

As the 1960s progressed there was a tendency for the Soviet Union to develop increasingly as the supplier of many basic industrial materials, particularly petroleum products, and in turn be open to supplies of foodstuffs and consumer goods from the Soviet client states. A number of the COMECON member states began to establish trade links with Western countries to export some of their surpluses to the West. This started particularly with foodstuffs from Rumania, Bulgaria and Hungary but increasingly also included some manufactured goods, textiles and machinery particularly from those countries with an industrial tradition and a long history of trade with the West: Poland,

Hungary, Czechoslovakia, East Germany, Rumania. Poland also became a major exporter of coal. Moreover the whole of the Eastern bloc showed a tendency to open extensive lines of credit with Western suppliers. On the last count these totalled some $38 billion, with Western Germany as principal creditor nation.

Another interesting feature of the Marxist inspired system is that from the initial foundation in 1949 each member state has pursued its own Socialist development policies, and this has continued to the present day. Indeed early in the 1960s, the Soviet Union attempted to encourage member countries to co-operate more directly in formulating their one and five year plans. However this was strongly opposed by Rumania, and later by other member states, who felt that the integration of their planning within coherent overall Council for Mutual Assistance planning would be detrimental to their national sovereignty and ability to pursue their own economic interests. In this sense the organisation has pursued a very different pattern of development from that being attempted in the *laissez-faire* mixed market system of the European Economic Community. The Eastern Europeans have persisted, notwithstanding the expansion of trade with each other and with Western countries, a policy of planning within themselves on a largely self-help basis. Conversely the Western mixed economies have for most of the post-war era pursued an entirely different pattern of quasi-*laissez-faire* development, gradually running down industries in different parts of Western Europe in the interests of more efficient manufacturing in a few concentrated centres. The European Coal and Steel Community, which pre-dated the Treaty of Rome of 1955, saw as one of its main functions the rationalisation of these industries on a Western European wide basis. As such it was a retreat from autarchical national industrial survival policies variously pursued throughout Western and Eastern Europe during the 1930s.

More generally within the philosophy under fully 'Socialist conditions', as is applied in the Soviet Union and other client states, economic planning covers a very wide range. It constitutes a form of direct public planning with a distribution of resources in relation to the pre-planned distribution of income between public and private users, between investment and consumption and between groups of consumers; aspects of this are shown on Figures 35 and 36.

Worthy of emphasis is the sheer information problems of running such a centrally directed system. The centrally planned Eastern European economies have proved a fruitful market for Western computer hardware and know-how. However in some countries there has

FIG. 35.  A SOVIET STYLE CENTRAL PLANNING SYSTEM

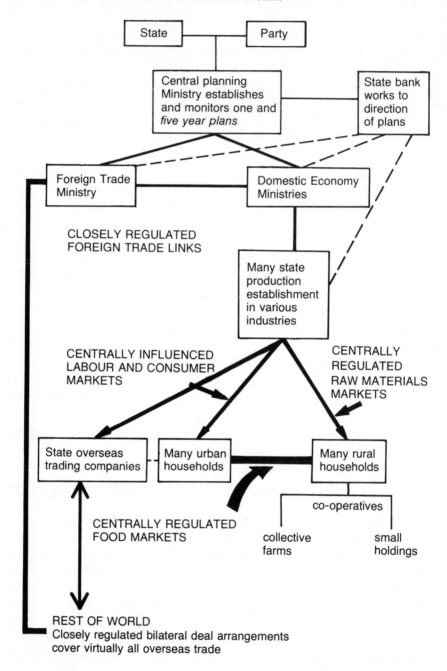

FIG. 36. SOVIET STYLE CENTRAL PLANNING INPUT–OUTPUT TABLE

| UNIT OF MEASUREMENT | PRODUCING SECTOR | Electric Power | Coal | Oil and Gas | Iron and Steel | Machinery | Chemicals | Lumber and Wood Products | Construction Materials | Textiles and Apparel | Food Processing | Agriculture | Transport | Other | Households | Government | Investment | Total Output |
|---|---|---|---|---|---|---|---|---|---|---|---|---|---|---|---|---|---|---|
| BKWH | Electric power | 15.7 | 30.6 | 51.5 | 26.9 | 1.9 | 10.7 | 412.4 | 24.7 | 21.0 | 29.9 | 27.9 | 51.0 | 29.5 | 13.7 | 36.2 | 24.4 | 16.8 |
| MT | Coal | 5.6 | 48.1 | 75.4 | 25.8 | 3.4 | 2.0 | 531.7 | 160.7 | 44.5 | .8 | 123.3 | 8.1 | 3.7 | 3.6 | 14.8 | 3.3 | 8.6 |
| 10MB | Oil and gas | 42.00 | 54.60 | 59.01 | 11.20 | 10.26 | 7.00 | 307.30 | 17.85 | .35 | 35.00 | 7.14 | 12.81 | 9.73 | 16.73 | 10.43 | 1.89 | 11.34 |
| $B | Iron and steel | .03 | .12 | .62 | .08 | .20 | 1.60 | 9.25 | .02 | .04 | .02 | 2.58 | 3.26 | .15 | .13 | .29 | .03 | .08 |
| $b | Machinery | .91 | .10 | .03 | 1.76 | 8.15 | 9.33 | 29.23 | .03 | .10 | .05 | .28 | 8.28 | .03 | .05 | .03 | .03 | .07 |
| $B | Chemicals | .43 | .42 | .58 | .60 | 1.23 | .29 | 8.07 | .01 | .03 | .06 | .10 | 1.19 | 2.21 | .18 | .05 | .61 | .08 |
| $b | Lumber and wood products | .12 | .17 | 1.16 | 2.20 | .73 | 3.01 | 12.32 | .03 | .40 | .01 | .08 | .44 | .17 | 3.12 | .18 | .14 | .36 |
| $B | Construction materials | .02 | .06 | .08 | .56 | .13 | 5.67 | 8.16 | .02 | .01 | — | .01 | .13 | .04 | .06 | 1.29 | .01 | .07 |
| $B | Textiles and apparel | — | .14 | .91 | 23.68 | .92 | .57 | 43.19 | .01 | .13 | .01 | .11 | .38 | .51 | .37 | .07 | 15.37 | .01 |
| $B | Food processing | 1.58 | — | .85 | 32.37 | 8.43 | .09 | 57.82 | .02 | — | — | .01 | .01 | .43 | .03 | .01 | .62 | 13.37 |
| $B | Agriculture | 12.44 | .02 | .21 | 18.54 | 1.49 | .01 | 53.69 | — | 59.0 | 26.8 | — | — | .01 | .03 | — | 4.47 | 16.47 |
| 10BTM | Transport | 13.9 | .3 | 2.6 | 17.2 | 12.3 | 3.4 | 230.2 | — | — | — | 24.7 | 2.9 | 4.0 | 33.9 | 17.6 | 1.8 | 9.8 |
| $B | Other | .31 | .58 | .33 | 1.55 | .58 | .10 | 8.26 | .23 | .25 | .46 | .30 | 1.04 | .81 | .43 | .43 | .33 | .53 |
| TMY | Labour | 34 200 | 6941 | 7324 | 3 696 | 13 983 | 6 302 | 94 472 | 405 | 1254 | 191 | 990 | 6915 | 754 | 3 210 | 2 037 | 3 740 | 2 530 |

BKWH = billion kilowatt-hours
MT = million tons

10MB = 10 million barrels
$B = billion dollars

10BTM = ten billion ton-miles
TMY = thousand man-years

*Source:* Soviet type economies, Robert W. Campbell Macmillan.

been an increasing tendency to experiment with the market, particularly in Hungary and Czechoslovakia since 1968. To this extent some, perhaps more optimistic observers have seen a tendency for convergency between the contemporary Eastern and Western European economic systems. Nevertheless the power of the central autocracy remains strong and seems destined to remain so. Looked at in total it cannot be said that either system, the 'mixed' economy democratic, or the centrally planned Communist, has demonstrated an overwhelming ability in the long run, to exceed the other in sheer industrial output. Undoubtedly, however, the free market mixed economy model has been proved far more amenable to the encouragement of social democratic attitudes, of the rights to own private property, and freedom of choices which have become an inherent part of the Western tradition since the ideas of John Locke, Adam Smith and Jeremy Bentham became accepted. Moreover none of the centrally planned Marxist-Lenist member states has shown any predisposition to allow 'free trade unions' or mobility of labour, which is an essential ingredient of a democratic society. 'Convergency', if it exists, is more confined to the forms of industrial and urban living, as opposed to any marked willingness of either party to embrace closely the social and political ideologies of the other. Moreover as time goes by the persistence of powerful new technocratic cadres, owing all to the way their system's ideology views them, would seem likely to keep convergency, in any full economic, political or social sense, very much at bay. Nevertheless 'liberal' tendencies will continue to manifest themselves, especially in those countries with closer associations with the West, by history, religion, traditions and trade. It remains to be seen how far these will be allowed to go, in a world beset not only by ideological divergence, but also increasingly by fundamental constraints to growth from energy and other resource difficulties.

## Planning in Developing Countries: a Mixture of Influences

If discussion about contemporary economic planning in the industrial Western democratic and the Marxist–Leninist inspired countries means drawing many threads together, debate about planning for growth in the less developed, traditionally agrarian, countries means drawing not threads, but bundles of cotton wool together. In many respects the appearance of mix-ups in both their philosophical and practical sense, are more apparent then any convergency. Earlier consideration has been given to the various philosophical and practical policy notions underlying ideas of economic growth and development. In practice in most of the so-called 'developing countries' a wide variety of complex issues arise, stemming as much from the underlying nature of traditional tribal and deeply held imported religious beliefs, as ideas of change derived from any other source. From the outset, many developing countries have only recently moved out of colonial or quasi-colonial status, linked to a metropolitan power in Western Europe, or, as in the case of the Philippines, and parts of Central and South America, with the U.S.A. In some cases such countries underwent considerable commercial and quasi-industrial development during the colonial era. This is particularly likely to be the case where there was some substantial earning capacity available from traditional primary plantation products such as tea, coffee, sugar, sisal, rubber, oil palms, etc., to large mineral resources, such as occur in Zambia and parts of West Africa. However in general terms, European based colonial government in most territories was seen simply as providing a minimum framework of internal law and order, some development of educational and medical facilities, and primarily agricultural export capacity linked to the needs of the metropolitan power – Britain, France, Beligium, Holland, Spain and Portugal. In most cases the primary export industries still remain by far the most important way in which many ex-Colonial territories earn foreign exchange. At the same time many have recently embarked upon optimistic programmes of economic cum industrial development with the creation of planning ministries and the assistance of all manner of advisers from abroad. Such development programmes were encouraged by the general expansion of world trade following the end of the Second World War, and particularly by the strong expansion of trade during the boom years of the 1960s. However, many developmental schemes, entered into boldly at that time, have now peaked out and with a slow growth of world trade in general, appear increasingly vulnerable. Moreover most developing countries have, at the same time, built up a substantial appetite for importing basic materials, notably fuel oils from the Middle East and North Africa, and also a wide range of consumer durables and capital goods from the U.S.A. Western and increasingly Eastern Europe; and most significantly from Japan and her Far Eastern satellites, Korea and Taiwan. In general, the developing countries are faced with the extremely difficult task of sustaining sufficient minimum foreign exchange earnings to finance overseas debts accumulated on both public and private account during the expansionary 1960s, and at the same time to feed the aspirations of their populations for higher living standards, which high imports of petroleum fuel, durable consumer and even foodstuffs imply.

A related issue which comes very much to the attention of anyone visiting a developing country for the first time is that, in many ways, one is seeing demonstrated problems of scarcity and runaway population growth, of which the classical economists from Malthus to Ricardo and Mill were so aware. In many countries agricultural resources are demonstrably finite and, more importantly, given the application of traditional agricultural techniques, are unproductively employed. Indeed in some countries of Africa, notably in Kenya and also in Southern Africa, the highly productive 'expatriate' farming sector, generally European, for many years fulfilled the important role of providing a cheap and secure supply of foodstuffs, to feed the rapidly expanding local population. Again, in many countries there are still the very real problems of land tenure and an absentee or indolent land owning class who, by their ownership and control of resources and their persistent failure to invest adequately the returns from agriculture back into the soil, act in a way deterimental to the long term growth needs of the society as a whole. Likewise, when one turns to population questions there frequently appears a situation which would have been entirely familiar with Malthus and his disciples. The effect of European introductions of better methods of death control through advanced drugs and medical measures have generally been to reduce greatly death rates. At the same time, by the reduction of infantile mortality, to increase greatly the numbers of population surviving beyond a few weeks of life. The effect of this is to impose an enormous 'population explosion' on the traditional social and economic framework of many countries. In many African and other developing countries over half the population is today under 16 years of age, sustained by a net population increase of over three per cent per annum! The usual effect of such population pressure in the countryside is a steady drift of people off the land, away from traditional farming and tribal areas towards rapidly expanding urban centres.

The runaway growth of cities, from Nairobi to Lagos, Rio de Janeiro to Mexico City, presents acute social problems in most less developed countries. Indeed Mr. Michael Lipton – in his recently published book *Why People Stay Poor* – a study of urban bias in world development, suggests that the most important class conflict in the poor countries of the world today is not between labour and capital or foreign and national interests. Rather it is between the 'rural classes and urban classes'. The rural sector contains most of the poverty, and most of the low-cost sources of potential advance; but in Lipton's phrase: 'The urban sector contains most of the articulateness, organisation and power'. Yet, notwithstanding the force of Lipton's argument, for a newcomer to travel in from a main airport in many developing countries, through many miles of shanty dwellings of recently arrived population, living on the fringe of an affluent or semi-affluent urban core, can still be a horrifying experience. The author of this book, with others, undertook a series of studies on urban growth problems in East Africa, as they were becoming manifest in the late 1960s. These reports were later published as a book, *Urban Challenge in East Africa*, published in 1971. All too obviously the local economic system was increasingly incapable of providing sufficient urban and industrial development to absorb population in gainful employment. To quote from my own words at that time:

"There is a natural drift to the towns as much of the countryside is unlikely to provide the basis for any easy expansion of production or productivity. The situation in the arid regions of rural Kenya and Tanzania has led some observers to point to its resemblance to the Ricardian dilemma of diminishing marginal returns from new investment in outlying land resources. There is the fact that the cities have hitherto been predominantly European and Asian settlements, with a strong administrative, commercial and mission orientation. Even cursory examination suggests that most urban employment is of a tertiary nature, ranging from law and order through banking and insurance to shop-keeping, shoe-shining and petty thievery. There is a need for continuing and increased private investment in a more diversified industrial base of employment and income generation, and for substantial public investment to keep abreast of present and future public needs. There is also a need for vigorous questioning of the role of land tenure and use, and of building standards in the contemporary scene. Thus the pressure and challenges of our present urban scene necessitates the most fundamental examination of both the goals and resources of the society at large."

More generally, writing in a special supplement of *The Economist*, in December 1969, Miss Barbara Ward suggested that:

"Urban growth in the developing world today is not so much a measure of healthy, inevitable processes of modernisation as a pathological acceleration of urban 'cell creation' which could put whole societies into a terminal crisis of social and economic disintegration."

She also emphasised another important feature:

"Urbanisation has been taken as a hallmark of successful modernisation largely because of the pattern of development suggested by nineteenth century experience. Throughout most of the developed world, cities grew in response to the new forces of industrialism. For the first time in human history, the bulk of man's work was removed from the fields and taken into the lofts and workshops of early manufacturing. As the factory system grew and railways grew in its wake, large concentrations of people and services for production and distribution proved economically irresistible. They provided ever larger economies of scale, ever wider varieties of employment and, as the whole society became more sophisticated, a far greater range of tertiary services. It was in this way that cities came to be seen as the essential and successful creators and transmission-belts of the new technological system."

Yet within the developing countries this model does not often apply, and indeed the position is frequently reversed. In many countries the proportions of population in towns is considerably higher than the percentage of men working in industry, a situation which is not simply of academic or historical interest. In Barbara Ward's words:

"They are desperate warning signals of the true nature of today's urban crisis in the developing world. Since, in contrast to the nineteenth century experience of Europe and North America, the cities exist, as it were, ahead of the industrial system, they lack the solid base of manufacturing jobs which gave cities growing a hundred years ago, for all their grime and misery, a solid base of economic life."

Miss Ward's challenging insights lead naturally on to the consideration of problems associated with savings and capital formation. In general, the less developed countries tend to have only a rudimentary or inadequate banking system which, at the outset, makes it difficult to mobilise sufficient financial resources, assuming they exist, into creative projects. However of course, the problem extends far beyond this stage. In many cases there simply is not the capacity within the traditional agrarian system to produce the necessary surplus, out of the income earning population, to finance new development projects, and resort has to be made, wherever possible, to overseas borrowing or of loan funds. Moreover it is by no means clear that within developing countries that capital necessarily flows to those projects with the greatest social priority. Rather, what may appeal to the multinational investor or local 'wheeler dealer' is a new soft drinks factory, a new hotel or casino. All tend to be somewhat precariously dependent on an uncertain flow of overseas visitors, rather than basic investment in essential roads, or irrigation schemes, or infrastructure, etc., likely to encourage sustainable long-term growth for the local economy as a whole. Truly the question of choice of key investment priorities presents a particular problem in many developing countries.

At this point the question of continuing foreign influence also presents itself with peculiar force. If a country is highly dependent on foreign aid and on foreign advisers it tends to accept, willy-nilly, the advice of these advisers as to priorities which should be established. Unfortunately advisers of a technical or other nature are frequently far from free of implicit 'value judgements' imposed by their own cultures, as to the type of priorities that should be pursued. Indeed in the experience of the author one of the main needs facing many African developing countries is to rise above the advice given by advisers, to the point of making their own choices of necessary key national priorities. As George Bernard Shaw in his *Maxims for Revolutionists* wittily puts it: 'Do not do unto others as you would they should do unto you. Their tastes may not be the same'. For instance, it is very easy for a potential aid donor country, which is skilled in drainage and irrigation schemes, to come along and suggest that an appropriate way for aid to be spent would be to embark upon the drainage of large areas of countryside, which may be low lying and water logged. The fact that there are many other large tracts of country, which could be more cheaply brought into cultivation by the use of large mechanical tractors may not appeal to representatives of a potential donor country. Their main business is giving advice on the use of the technology which they have, and for reasons best known to themselves, wish to see applied. Moreover the advisers themselves naturally develop a vested interest in justifying the contribution they and their country or company are able to give, and this frequently relates back to provision of tied-aid funds, and indeed to their own salaries, overseas allowances, motor cars, appurtenances of office, servants etc.

Another outstanding example of problems associated with development planning is concerned with schemes which, on the face of it, may offer an improved technology to a developing country and which the leaders of the country are anxious to have for prestigious, or other, reasons. For instance, a developing country might well be open to have a large number of its roads tarmaced with foreign aid and assistance from outside. If, in fact, the effect of tarmacing and improving the road system is to wipe out existing forms of employment and income for large numbers of people who are normally employed in maintaining dirt roads, the project may be of questionable value – the more so if no conceivable alternative cash employment is available. While the previous dirt roads may have been rough and dusty to travel along, they were perfectly adequate to the needs of the country's transport system at that moment in time, and also met an ongoing employment and limited cash income distribution need as well. Other examples of uncertainly justified 'prestige projects' abound: most developing countries immediately after independence have gone through a spate of building of lavish hotels and public buildings, far in excess of the ability of the country to either use or support. Another common form of developing country aspiration is the possession of a national airline, which may soon impose impossible burdens on the financial, technical and the managerial capacity available in the country concerned. Extravagant military expenditures also tend to be far in excess of any need to defend the country against external threat, or to justify law and order needs. The question of adequate choice as to the appropriate future needs of the country and the technology to be employed is critical. The need for what Mr. Schumacher typified as sensible 'intermediate technologies' to bridge the gap between the advanced and the less developed economies is paramount.

Other areas where great power rivalry frequently comes into play is in relation to educational systems and schemes of training. Many of the British Colonies immediately after independence in Africa and elsewhere began to open up links with a number of other overseas countries for their students, and this was naturally encouraged by potential host countries as a way of spreading their cultural influence. Large numbers of African students ceased to go primarily to Britain for higher education and were increasingly diverted to other countries, particularly the U.S.A. and also the Soviet Union, to Eastern Europe and to some extent India and China, for extended higher education programmes. The difficulty occurs when many of these students return from abroad. In many cases the type of prolonged higher education they have been subject to in a host country is far from appropriate to their country's real needs. There seems little value in a student being highly qualified after a decade in a succession of American universities with a Doctorate in Mathematical Economics if there is no demand for such skills in his own country, other than in teaching book-keeping to managers of agricultural co-operatives. At the time the author worked at Makerere University in Uganda, sixteen students had been sent on prolonged post-graduate degree programmes in economics to North American universities. To the best of the author's knowledge only one returned briefly to the country. The remainder were thought, no doubt to their own very real benefit as it turned out, to have found permanent posts in 'African Studies' programmes in the United States. Moreover, the particular ideological complexion of education cannot be over-looked. Many African, and no doubt other developing countries, start to suffer acute conflict between the different élites, which have been created by the experience of overseas education when they return to their country. The élites often divide into conflicting groups, between those who have had the experience of an education in North America as opposed to Great Britain, or more acutely, those who have been educated in the Soviet Union, China, India, Japan or elsewhere. The comparability of educational qualifications from different systems is a continuous on-going bone of contention, where 'paper qualifications' mean the difference between superior Western style Civil Service influence and affluence and/or a life of rural penury. The fact that the educational qualifications, no matter how prestigious and acquired at no end of expense, has little relationship to real foreseeable needs is often totally overlooked in selection processes.

This point leads on to the consideration of basic philosophical context within which development process is perceived, and how this then shapes the development programmes pursued. Most ex-British and other European colonies grew up on the tradition of a capitalist form of development, with the primary agricultural system gradually generating a surplus, or level of profitability sufficient to support a small indigenous urban commercial and professional class, and a limited amount of factory development. The immediate impact of Inde-pendence has been to encourage many African countries to seek to expand rapidly beyond this stage and to look for a way out of their basic problems by a national development plan for a rapid emulation of the Western urban-industrialisation model. In this respect the influences of Mr. Rostow's 'five stages', from primitive to high mass consumption, is often cited as the pattern to follow. Inevitably such a helter skelter rush into these types of activities, all too frequently based on ill conceived foreign loans, can lead to more problems than they solve. More acutely, those who have been educated or influenced by the Marxist/Leninist model normally see the answer lying in a much more ruthless centrally directed system of development, based on achieving as large a surplus as possible from the agricultural basis of society and using it as a source of funding for a new urban industrial base, however inappropriate that base may be to the underlying factor endowments and other resources easily available in the country. On the other hand, the Chinese Maoist model of more gradual 'bootstraps' type develop-ment, with its emphasis on rural self-help schemes and an improvement in the basic productivity of the village society, also provides an alternative way to development, which a number of countries may eventually find increasingly attractive.

In the three former British Colonies in East Africa one sees all three patterns functioning, in an extremely mixed-up way. In Kenya, where there is still a substantial European and Asian business population, the pattern of development followed since Independence in the early 1960s has been essentially on Western capitalist lines. Under the leadership of President Jomo Kenyatta, Nairobi has expanded rapidly as a commercial and trading centre, attracting a large flow of tourist revenue from abroad, and also the beginnings of significant industrialisation programmes for the assembly of trucks, vehicles and a number of other consumer durable and consumer items. On the other hand, the growth of Nairobi has probably been at the expense of 'recreative' development of agricultural resources which, if anything, since Independence have tended to run down, with the withdrawal of highly efficient European forms of agriculture.

To the south, in Tanzania, a much more sparsely inhabited and basically arid country, a different pattern of development has been followed, which owes more to the leadership of Dr. Julius Nyerere and his espousal of both principles of free will and ideas of 'togetherness for co-operation' – untainted by self-seeking or the possession of property. At the village level much is owed to the example of the Chinese self-help village system than to any other inspiration. Since the *Arusha Declaration* of 1967, Chinese inspired Ujama village co-operative development schemes have emphasised the use of the soil as the basic national resource, as the main form of Tanzanian Socialist 'self help'. Any tendency for the perpetuation or development of a rentier or capitalist class has been vigorously discouraged. At the same time, an industrial and commercial base has continued to be slowly developed, within the constraints of Socialist planning, around the capital of Dar-es-Salaam. However, much of the financing of this has required overseas loans. Moreover a Chinese financed and built railway now links the port to the land-locked copper industry of Zambia in the south. Indeed some measure of the appalling contemporary 'bureaucratic' complexities of planning within a developing economy, whatever its political or ideological complexions may be, are given by Mr. T. P. N. Mushi in the *Tanzania Management Journal* for Autumn 1976. He writes:

> "Many issues remain unresolved in connection with what approach is best suited to the Tanzanian's political social and economic environment. It is difficult to mention Industrial strategy in Tanzania without touching the

issues of ownership and control. There is still a substantial private sector in Tanzania most of which is in participation with T.D.F.L. It is not foreseeable in the near future for the government to nationalise these small production units. It is the opinion of many people that the existence of a viable private sector is a hidden asset to the industrial sector. It provides a challenge for the public sector to improve its standards to produce high quality goods. It also fills a technological gap as most of the privately owned units are small scale industries. It would involve the government in a lot of heavy overhead and administrative expenditure if these small business units were to be nationalised individually.

Another aspect which needs a mention is the role of 'rationalisation' of the parastatal sector in industrial development in Tanzania. This has been criticised and also supported by many management thinkers and economic planners. It is a current subject of controversy. Between 1971 and 1973 T.W.I.C.O., S.T.A.M.I.C.O., S.I.D.O. and C.A.T.A. have been born out of the N.D.C. family. Critics agree that it has involved the creation of new 'superstructures' (Headquarters) and hence mounting of overhead administrative expenditure which will not be matched by commensurate increase in production. This assertion is debatable at this stage as most of these organisations are still in their infancy and their impact is yet to be felt. One thing is certain, however, although most of the critics tend to overlook it, rationalisation of the industrial sector is likely to promote greater diversification and industrial specialisation. Thus in the next decade it is possible to have indigenous personnel as specialists in the mining industry, small scale industry advisers etc. It requires patience to assess the merits and demerits of promoting a large number of public corporations specialising in narrow fields."

Finally, Mr. Mushi goes on to emphasise the critical importance of the Tanzanian industrial strategy reflecting and relating to national priorities in economic development:

"Sound planning and execution backed by adequate manpower are necessary, with the Government acting as a catalyst in both an advisory and regulatory capacity. Efficient use of financial and physical resources is essential and this will enable the attainment of competitive prices on the world market. Proper reorganisation of the East African Common Market is a contributory factor to balanced industrial development in Tanzania and East Africa as a whole. The review of the Kampala Agreement is essential to remove impediments to interstate trade in industrial products. The long run solution lies in having a super-national organisation in East Africa that will have authority in licensing and industrial allocation in the three territories. To realise the benefit of the Common Market it is conceivable that a system of allocation of 'East African Industries' to each territory be adopted. This demands sacrifice of national sovereignty and closer co-operation between the partner states in defining economic priorities and avoiding duplication of industries."

In Uganda, the country which has by far the most beneficient endowments of basic agricultural resources, the removal of colonial authority and the break up of the traditional tribal system, has led to the takeover of government by an illiterate, military clique, led by President Idi Amin, representative of a small tribal group. This programme of takeover was also accompanied by the expulsion of the major commercial community of some 100,000 Asians, and a complete collapse of many of the former activities within the country of a commercial nature and in terms of the plantation system of growing sugar and other important foodstuffs. On the other hand, the natural resource base in terms of agricultural capacity in Uganda is so abundant that it is possible that the average Ugandan, working in his small farm or shamba with a limited subsistence production of bananas, mealies, root crops and cattle, has been able to survive in a somewhat better condition than the world at large might generally imagine. Nevertheless Uganda has been unable to fulfill its financial obligations to its other member partners of the East African community, and has generally lost much of its export potential in cash crops, notably coffee, cotton and sugar.

*    *    *    *    *

In the post-war world, by far the largest increase in trade has been between the industrial nations and in respect of the oil trade. Something like three quarters of all world trade occurs between the industrial O.E.C.D. member states. Nevertheless the general question still arises as to the longer term relationship of the less developed world, and of less developed countries in particular with their former colonial masters. At the moment three post-colonial world trading areas appear to be emerging and strengthening on what Professor Tibor Mende has described as 'North–South geopolitical' lines. One trading area is a tendency for North America to relate substantially to South America while, at the same time, becoming highly dependent on the supply of fuel oil from Saudi Arabia, and for certain essential strategic minerals from Southern Africa. A second area of longitudinal trading relates to the historic links which Western Europe and, to some extent, Eastern Europe have with Africa. These have certainly continued to develop and, in fact, much of Western Europe is considerably dependent on

North and West African oil for its basic energy resources. However a new scramble for Africa is on, and the increasing Soviet and Chinese influences in a number of former colonies, notably the ex-Portuguese colonies of Mozambique and Angola, can hardly augur well for future stability. It remains an open question whether the Marxist world is interested in Africa primarily for its raw materials – or as an area in which to continue Leon Trotsky's much heralded 'world revolution'. Thirdly, in the East one sees the rapid development of links between the industrial power base of Japan, with its population of some 113 million people, importing its fuels and raw materials from the Middle East, from South-East Asia and from Australia, and at the same time looking to these areas as natural market outlets. In the case of Australia, Japan has virtually replaced Britain as a key trading partner, today taking over a third in value of all Australia's exports. Coking coal, iron ores and animal fibres, particularly wool, all go to Japan. However Australia, with a relatively small but highly concentrated urban population of some 13.5 million, largely involved in a form of 'taking in each others washing' city living, and with a highly tariff protected industrial structure, can hardly provide a vast market in return. New Zealand presents an even more extreme example of a very small urban concentrated population country of some 3 million people, with a tariff protected industrial structure and reliance on agricultural exports, wool, lamb, dairy products. Another possible extension of Japan's trading interests will be with mainland China, particularly with the iron ore, coking coal and oil and timber resources of Manchuria. To this extent the Japanese have in recent years established a trading area which far exceeds the dream of a 'co-prosperity trading area', which they originally sought to achieve, by military conquest some 40 years ago.

Figure 37 overleaf indicates the gross flow of capital and technical assistance from international agencies to the third world, between 1965 and 1974, while Appendix I lists major international organisations concerned with aid. Alas there are no simple answers to the problem of development and growth *per se*. The few examples cited above suggest the complexity of issues involved, deriving from the traditional nature of society, the basic motivations of people, secular and spiritual, and the impact of the colonial cum neo-colonial inheritance. Yet for good or ill the urge to develop is abroad. It remains to be seen whether and where the doctrines of Smith, Ricardo, Mill, Marx, Lenin or Mao will prevail. Alternatively the teaching of the military academy's of Sandhurst, St. Cyr and West Point may ultimately have as much impact on

FIG. 37.   GROSS FLOW OF CAPITAL AND TECHNICAL ASSISTANCE FROM INTERNATIONAL
AGENCIES TO THIRD WORLD

| | Disbursement in million dollars | | |
| --- | --- | --- | --- |
| | 1965 | 1970 | 1974 |
| World Bank Group | 770 | 1050 | 2761 |
| I.B.R.D. | 474 | 810 | 1684 |
| I.D.A. | 277 | 163 | 910 |
| I.F.C. | 19 | 77 | 167 |
| *United Nations* | 252 | 498 | 700 |
| U.N.D.P. | 136 | 267 | NA |
| W.F.P. | 58 | 149 | NA |
| U.N.C.F. | 39 | 81 | NA |
| *Regional Banks* | 225 | 635 | 1496 |
| E.I.B. & E.D.F. | 116 | 221 | 619 |
| I.D.B. | 109 | 395 | 660 |
| As.D.B. | — | 17 | 188 |
| Af.D.B. | — | 2 | 24 |
| C.D.B. | — | — | 5 |
| Total | 1247 | 2183 | 4957 |

Source:  O.E.C.D.: *Development Corporation,* 1975 Review

the pattern of development as any thoughts deriving from Cambridge, the London School of Economics, Harvard, the Patrice Lumumba University Moscow, or the Sorbonne. Finally, one should never underestimate the deep impact which religion, both traditional and imported, may have on the thought processes and policies followed by the 'charismatic' leaders of today's developing world. The struggle for Africa and elsewhere often lies as much in the rivalry for the souls of men as for any hopes of material gain. In this sense at least it is as much reminiscent of Western Europe during and following the religious reformation of the 16th and 17th centuries, as anything else.


## Japan and China: the Special Cases

The main focus of this work is on the relationship between economic doctrines and their development and impact on world events. As we have seen thus far, the main story of the great debates underlying development of political economy cum economics as a coherent body of knowledge centred first on the experience of Britain, and later on that of the other major Western European industrial powers and of the U.S.A., during the latter half of the 18th and throughout the 19th centuries. The early classical competitive, property owning doctrines first developed against the background of Great Britain's transformation from a small population agrarian mercantile society, to a large population commercial–industrial and urban nation, trading and financing throughout the known world. In turn many of the same doctrines and practices became associated with the development of far flung colonial and imperialist systems, the largest of which became the British Empire, including India, the old white dominions and many other territories during the 19th and up to the middle of the present century. In a subtly different fashion during the past 120 years or so the highly organised but insular island kingdom of Japan has also transformed; from a backward agrarian feudal society into an industrial and trading nation of the first order. In large measure this transformation was accomplished against the background of classical Western economic doctrines, modified however by the peculiar insularity of Japanese society, and by the strong collectivist traditions and spirit of the population. The result is that Japanese industrial and urban development has always had a somewhat ruthless capitalistic face. However paradoxically it also demonstrated many of the characteristics of corporate statism which were later developed by other autocratic regimes in Western Europe and elsewhere. In the inter-war years, as in Benito Mussolini's (1883–1945) Fascist Italy and Adolf Hitler's (1889–1945) Nazi Germany of the same period, it became associated with a formidable, and expansionist minded military machine.

The alternative pattern of Marxist inspired agrarian development occurred in China, a country traditionally faced with population pressures, against demonstrably finite, if widely varied, land resources. The fact that China has consistently supported nearly a quarter of the world's known population on less than 7 per cent of the world's arable land area, is a dominant feature of her development. The 19th century had brought to China the gradual encroachment of colonial influences, especially up the long river valleys and in the great international port and industrial centre of Shanghai. The 20th century degenerated first into abortive attempts at reform under the three principles of nationalism, democracy, and livelihood by the government of Sun Yat Sen

(1866–1925). This was followed by further colonial encroachments, culminating in the aggression of Japanese imperialism in Manchuria and the Northern regions of the country, in the 1930s. Following the defeat of the Japanese by China and her Western allies in 1945, the post-war period saw the eventual overthrow of Chiang Kai Shek's (1887–1975) right wing Kuomintang government, and its replacement by a Communist regime led by Mao Tse-Tung (1893–1976) from 1949 onwards. In general, developments in the period since 1949 have followed Marxist precepts, but of a distinctive type. Much of Chinese efforts under Mao have concentrated on the transformation of the agrarian basis of society, and heavy industralisation on the Soviet model has generally tended to fall into somewhat of a second place. Thus in their different ways Japan and China illustrate a diverse response to both the doctrinal influences and practical experience of social, economic and political change, which originated against Western experience. In the case of Japan, mid-19th century capitalism evolved into what Professor Tibor Mende has described as the highly 'orchestrated' Japanese industrial urban economy of today. Conversely in China, mid-19th century Marxism developed into a philosophy supportive of the reform and development of a village self-help commune based agrarian system. It has also developed in a way strongly antipathetical to Moscow's vision of the onward development of Marxist cum Leninist philosophies.

*     *     *     *     *

Looking first in somewhat greater detail at the Japanese experience, the main pattern of her economic and social development might be summarised as follows. From the Middle Ages onwards Japan existed in virtual isolation from many of the expansionary developments of Western European mercantilism, though limited contacts with isolated groups of Portuguese, and later Dutch missionaries kept some contacts open. At this time, feudally organised Japan sustained a highly efficient agricultural system under warrior Shogun leadership capable of feeding a population of some 30 million persons, from limited but intensively used rice lands and sea resources. By the middle of the 19th century Japan's main language of contact with the outer world was Dutch. However it was to require the arrival of the American fleet in 1853, under the command of Commodore Mathew Perry (1794–1858), which became known in Japanese history as the Black Ships Fleet, to open up the country for commercial relations with the West, and the appointment of the first American Envoy, Richardson (later to die at the hands of a traditionally minded assassin) as a permanent contact between the United States and Japanese governments. Over a decade of political and social disorder and uncertainty followed, as to both the pace at which the country could be drawn into commercial relations with the Western world, and the profound impact this would have on the existing superbly organised feudal agrarian basis of society. The Meiji restoration in 1868, and the coming to the throne of a new young Emperor Mutsuhito, is widely regarded as the beginnings of modern industrial Japan. This was followed by the voluntary surrender of the Daimyo Fiefs to the Emperor, and in 1872 the introduction of compulsory education for the population as a whole. What followed was the story of an almost unbelievably rapid transformation in the nature of a traditional feudal agrarian society. In the short space of some 30 years Japan launched itself headlong into a massive economic and industrial change programme. Envoys were sent abroad to learn about what were regarded as the best ideas of Western science, education and technology for changing the basis of society. It is of interest that the founders of modern Japan were in large part lower caste retainers of the old feudal Shogun system, who had managed the previous agrarian system well. When the need arose these proved to be the men who were capable of planning and carrying out an industrial cum social revolution from scratch. In economic doctrines the ideas of both competitive capitalism at home and national economic development based on Germanic style corporatism took root, and proceeded to have a strong influence. An Army was formed, based on the Prussian model, and a modern powerful Navy was laid down, with assistance from Great Britain. At home industrialisation and urban developments continued apace, and the rapidly expanding population was increasingly drawn from the backward agrarian sectors, to work in the new urban manufacturing industries. During this period Japan also increasingly gained an equal place with that of the major Western powers, and was able to contribute to a joint Expeditionary Force for the relief of Peking during the Boxer Rebellion in 1899 on mainland China. By 1904 the Japanese industrial system and the efficiency of her Navy had reached the point of being able to meet the Russian High Seas Fleet on equal terms, and to totally defeat it in a major sea battle off the southern coastline. Later, in 1915, it made twenty one demands on China and joined the War against Germany, on the side of the Allies. In 1919 The Versailles Conference refusal to include a racial equality clause in the League of Nations Covenant was seen as a setback for

Japanese claims to equality with the main Western Powers. However the inter-war period was marked by a continued growth in population, which by 1920 was some 55 million, and a further strong nationalistic impulse to continued industrialisation, notwithstanding the severe setbacks of the great world depression of the 1930s. This time also saw the emergence of increasingly aggressive militaristic forces within the body politic. From the Manchurian incident in 1931 and the Shanghai incident of the following year and Japan's departure from the League of Nations in 1933, a period of military expansionism developed, at the expense of China. For Japanese imperialistic expansionists, increasingly dominated by 'Lebensraum' type considerations, the exploitation of the timber, iron ore and coal resources of Manchuria was seen as an essential element in the promotion of Japan's status as a major industrial and imperial power, with a co-prosperity autarchically organised trading area of her own, extending throughout mainland China and South East Asia. In 1940 America joined in attempts to limit Japan's expansionist threats, by imposing oil and other trade sanctions. The 1941 surprise attack on the American fleet at Pearl Harbour, and the subsequent rapid deployment of Japanese forces throughout South Eastern Asia and as far south as Northern Australia, posed a major threat to the Western Allies. The final surrender of Japan, following the dropping of the first atomic bombs on Hiroshima and Nagasaki in 1945, marked the end of the inter-war military aggrandisement clique.

During the immediate post-war era Japan began her restoration with American guidance and support, which to a considerable extent was influenced by the autocratic lifestyle and policies of General Douglas MacArthur (1880–1964). Her economy subsequently gained a considerable boost from the Korean War expenditures of America and other United Nations Allies. Equally important was the support which she received from the United States through the inflow of industrial know-how and investment, and the freedom of access which she increasingly enjoyed in the expanding American market. Notwithstanding these obvious advantages, the altogether phenomenal growth rate in G.N.P. of some 10 to 12 per cent per annum which Japan experienced during the post-war period, drew many commentators as to the nature and underlying circumstances of her apparent success. Writing in the mid-1960s Professor G. C. Allen, in his comprehensive book on *Japan's Economic Expansion*, listed these as follows:

1. The closing of the technical gap by the import of new technology.

2.  An exceptionally high rate of investment buttressed by a very high rate of saving, both institutional and personal.
3.  The direction of investment into uses which yielded quick returns and the absence of wasteful investment in armaments.
4.  The large reserve army of workers at the beginning of the period of growth and the successful transference of huge numbers from low-productivity to high-productivity occupations.
5.  The reconstruction of the Zaibatsu and the creation of other business groups capable of organising development.
6.  A monetary system and policy which were successful both in providing industries with the finance needed for expansion and also in cutting back credit quickly whenever the economy became 'overheated'.
7.  A taxation system which kept clear of measures likely to curb industrial investment and damage personal incentives.
8.  The effective use of official controls over foreign trade and payments.

Bolstered by these policies and circumstances, Japan's phenomenally high rate of economic growth continued unchecked, until the onset of the energy crisis in 1973–74. Indeed during the 1960s Japanese consumer and capital products began to present acute competitive threats to domestic manufacturers, from Australia, to the U.S.A., Britain and Western Europe, and in many third country markets as well. However, during this decade there were signs that the growth rate was beginning to receive checks from various difficulties, including a move away, by the younger population, from the Japanese version of the 'puritan work ethic', and toward increasing demands for a more welfare based society. Again the sheer intensity of Japan's post-war industrial development, which had concentrated something like half of its present population of some 113 million people into an intense industrial belt in the middle island of Honshu, had also created great problems of pollution, and a density of activity which was beginning to inhibit 'growth for growth's sake'. Another factor, which prior to the energy crisis was also beginning to affect Japanese society, was the impact of a demographically rapidly ageing population, and an inflationary rise in relative unit labour costs against other major industrial competitor countries. Nevertheless, writing at the end of the 1960s, Mr. Herman Kahn and his colleagues at the Hudson Institute, were able to feel sufficient confidence in Japan's onward upward development to dub it 'The Emerging Japanese Superstate' in a book of that title.

Looking to the immediate post 'energy crisis' future, a number of features are particularly significant. Notwithstanding the great success of the post-war effort, it is important to realise some of the weaknesses which are inherent in her basic position. Japan remains almost entirely dependent on imports of oil and other critical industrial raw materials, and much of her foodstuffs and similar products from abroad. The result is that she has normally found it necessary to import some ten tonnes of goods in for every one tonne of goods exported out. Of present imports some 80 per cent are of raw materials, energy and foodstuffs, whereas of exports some 80 per cent are of machinery and highly finished goods. The result of this major imbalance in trade volumes, together with the long hauls implicit in her isolated situation from major suppliers and markets, is a large invisible deficit deriving from high transport costs, insurance payments on dividends and investment incomes, licensing fees, etc. abroad. In a slowly growing and increasingly competitive world economy it has also become apparent to the Japanese that they will have to become increasingly focused on an even greater concentrated industrial cum marketing effort in the future. Much of the attention of planners is therefore now focused towards a transformation of production in the direction of 'higher value adding' products. This in turn implies a high concentration on research in many new industries, from computers, atomic energy, oceanography, on advanced methods of steel production and chemical manufacture are all seen as playing an increasing role in plans for the future. Yet all this intense research and import–export industrial system depends on the continued expansion of world trade, continued free access to world markets and an ability to sustain trade flows to and fro, over long and somewhat vulnerable sea routes. In order to maintain growth at home, a continued high level of investment, a high degree of community discipline, and a high degree of social cohesiveness will remain essential. In a social environment increasingly exposed to the influence of more permissive and perhaps anarchical social conditions in the other advanced industrial countries, it remains to be seen whether Japan will be able to maintain collective investment and work disciplines, against the claims of welfare, of calls for increased defence expenditures, of increased leisure and such like.

Turning to the specific implications of the Japanese development story for economic doctrines as a whole, it seems apparent that from the mid-19th century onwards Japan accepted much of the conventional Western wisdom of the classical economic competitive model. However given the nature of Japanese society, and in particular the strong collectivist sense of the population, the strong individualism in the original Western model has never fully applied. In contrast, much of Japanese society normally appeared to strive for subordination of the individual to attain harmony within a group, taking the position that man was inherently unequal, and each had a natural place in a hierarchy. The result is that compared to the individualistic assumptions of the Western model, the Japanese often appeared intolerant and striving for conformity, and the role of the state rather than being designed to protect and enhance individual rights, as became an inherent part of the Western democratic model, was more one of preserving a nationally directed, economically efficient and vaguely benevolent social order. As such it appears, at least historically, to owe rather more to a Bismarckian type Prussian economic and social system, with the subordination of the individual to the needs of national development, than to the rather more permissively tolerant and liberal freedoms which, in theory at least, became associated with the Anglo-Saxon classical model. Sovereignty was, in terms of the political system, traditionally seen as residing in hereditary rulers, and trickling down from the top. By Western standards citizens were politically and socially passive, and until recent times consented to the rule of the establishment. Thus as a nation the Japanese generally trusted governmental authority, and accepted the application of its powers to many facets of economic and social life. As we have recounted, these characteristics provided an unusually cohesive force during the depression years of the 1930s, and the disaster war years of the 1940s. In the immediate post-war era the same attributes were put to good use in focusing national efforts to restore the Japanese economy to a leading world position. It remains to be seen whether the disciplines of a conformist society, and the focusing of national efforts to a very high rate of investment, and to massive research and development efforts will be sufficient to sustain the upward growth of the Japanese economy into the future. In this potential growth path, trade and other relationships with mainland China which, since 1949 has increasingly followed a very different pattern of development, will become a critical element.

Whatever the future course of world events the following underlying characteristics seem likely to remain critical in the working of the Japanese political economy. The total population will remain large, if demographically ageing and densely concentrated, high disciplined and skilled. The facts of an ageing population and work force will no doubt have an important impact, both on the ways in which industries use labour, and on the pressures for increased welfare expenditures exerted by the mass of the population on the economic and political system. Again the present highly concentrated structure of Japanese industry, with a relatively small proportion of the work force employed in paternalistic 'life time' employment systems by a few huge companies, but with the great majority of the work force working in a less protected lower wage system, will no doubt become subject to increasing criticism. The support of the main industrial sectors by a reserve army of lower paid subcontract companies and labour will possibly be increasingly modified by social pressure. Again for the outside observer the growth of anarchist type groups, notably from the founding of the 'Red Army Faction' in 1970, presents unpredictable threats to continued stability. Nevertheless during the post-war era Japan has demonstrated an amazing capacity to generate a very high rate of internal savings for financing the future. It also demonstrated the value of the close 'corporatist', if to the outsider highly bureaucratic links between the government's national planning mechanism in the form of M.I.T.I., and of a centrally influenced banking system to provide a high level of financial gearing for ongoing investment, in new industries and new technologies. This system is unlikely to be substantially modified, though demands for increased domestic consumption and welfare expenditures will have some effect. Turning to natural resources, the reality of densely populated islands, with very low amounts of arable land, and large areas of relatively infertile volcanic uplands and mountainous regions, will provide a continuing constraint on both domestic food producing capacity, and also in respect to space for further extensive heavy industrialisation. Pollution and the many social and political problems of urban sprawl are also likely to be continuing problems. The resource constraints of the homeland will require her to remain highly reliant on imported supplies of basic raw materials – coking coal, iron ore, foodstuffs and such like, from such natural resource abundant countries as Australia, Brazil and elsewhere, and also on basic oil supplies from the Middle East. However the beginnings of a closer rapprochement with mainland China could offer the possibilities of drawing an increasing proportion of Japan's critical supplies of basic energy and other raw materials from nearby mainland sources. Looking at her export system it appears inevitable that the Japanese reliance on far distant increasingly 'high technology' markets will remain. Yet the pressures of population at home, and the changing social environment will no doubt lead to further decentralisation of many production capacities to other lower wage cost areas, notably in

Korea, Taiwan, Hong Kong, Singapore and elsewhere. The government's role in the 'orchestrating' of the total economic system appears likely to remain predominant. However Japan seems unlikely to move towards an influenced economic system on the British or French 'indicative' planning models. Rather it will continue to rely on the host of intangible but important links between the aims of central government for national sovereignty and promoting a high growth rate, and the needs of big private industry for a continuing high rate of profits for financing investment and research and development expenditures. External political pressures from the U.S.A. and elsewhere for Japan to reassume a larger burden of defence expenditure, and at the same time re-establish trade contacts with mainland Communist China may also influence the ways her government will react to a wide range of other problems as well.

\*     \*     \*     \*     \*

Perhaps the most cohesive study of China's present development position is that included in Professor Alexander Eckstein's book on *China's Economic Revolution*, published in 1977. The overriding reality of a vast population to be fed (reportedly some 900 million on the last count), from relatively finite amounts of good arable lands has dominated Chinese thinking in the past, conditions the present, and will continue to influence the future. It is important to recognise that in agricultural terms China is both a large and extremely diverse country, containing within itself a variety of geographic and climatic zones. In the Northern regions are extensive areas of temperate and cold wheat growing lands, while to the South the country becomes sub-tropical and rice growing. Again far in the interior are extensive zones of arid and mountainous conditions. The great geographic size of the country and the far flung population presents a series of distinct challenges, to any administrative system, whatever its ideological complexion may be. The domination in China of land and population questions means almost by definition a concern with problems with which the early Western European physiocratic and Malthusian influenced economists would be well aware of. The 19th century saw the gradual collapse of the old hierarchical Manchu system of government, especially through its inability to resist the inroads of the 'foreign barbarians'. From the time of the Opium Wars, in 1839–1842 and later in 1856–1858 onwards, China became increasingly subject to encroachments from the external seaborne forces of first Great Britain, Portugal and then France, the U.S.A., and later Japan and Russia. All in various ways established powerful trading commercial and missionary outposts within China. In particular the long river valleys and the areas around Shanghai became an important base for Western European and American colonial merchant and missionary influences. However the main foreign influences were concentrated on exploiting the great resources and market opportunities of the Chinese hinterland. The abortive Boxer uprising and its crushing by interventionist European forces, signalled a final collapse of the old regime, and the following years are marked by various reformist movements, notably the administrations led by Sun Yat Sen, which between the 1900s and 1920s attempted to modernise the old system. However, following Sun's death in 1925, anarchy broke out again, the country divided into large provinces and was pillaged and ruled by independent war lords and their vassals. In the 1930s the Japanese, as we have seen, embarked on an imperialistic phase and invaded resource rich Manchuria in North Western China, and more or less turned it into a colony, for their own exploitation purposes.

Again within the framework of China herself strong political dissensions developed, between the Kuomintang, led by Chiang Kai Shek, who generally represented the small peasant and propertied classes, and the Marxist inspired revolutionary groups, led by Mao Tse Tung. In the years 1934 to 1936 the Communists, under Mao, moved out of their besieged enclave in the middle of the country and, following the 'Long March' to the North, established a strong rebel regime in the North West. Later towards the end of the decade the Communist and Kuomintang factions came together, and formed the coalition to fight the Japanese. This situation continued, with substantial American and other allied aid, until the end of the Second World War in 1945. The post-war period saw a renewal of civil war, which led to the eventual triumph of the Communists under Mao Tse Tung in 1949.

Since that time China, under Mao's leadership and inspiration, has passed through a remarkable saga of economic, social and political developments. The main characteristics of the Chinese Communist system have been very different from those of the Soviet heavy industrialisation model, though both in their different ways became cut off from foreign influences. In the Chinese case perhaps the most important development has been the strong emphasis placed on the reform of the old fragmented agricultural system, the elimination of the previous landowning classes, and the introduction of worker agrarian communes starting first in one part of the country, and later extending to other areas as a means of mobilising agricultural food producing capabilities. The post-1949 Chinese revolution might therefore be seen as having passed through various stages. As described by Professor C. P. Fitzgerald in his book on *Mao Tse Tung and China*, published in 1976, the first stage would be regarded as a political one, by which the bourgeois state of the inter-war years, which had various allegiances with Western capitalist powers, was overthrown and the Communist party, which was seen as champion of the great unrepresented masses, came to supreme power. Next came the economic revolution by which the capitalist economy, such as existed, and the feudal land system, was first modified, and then replaced by a new Socialist form of economy of commune based land tenure. This process was generally accomplished in the years following the military victory by the Communists over the Kuomintang government in the later 1940s, and culminated first in the widespread introduction of a commune agricultural system, and second in the eventual virtual complete nationalisation of all industry and commerce in the country as a whole. However in all these revolutionary changes, as Mao himself remained strongly aware, the Chinese people in their thoughts, aspirations and tastes remained largely unaltered. There still apparently remained yet a further stage, by which the system of government needed to be changed, and the economy transformed. Thus Mao's final step was to be a 'cultural revolution' whereby these characteristics were to be remodelled, culminating in genuine Socialism. This would constitute a move away from the life and thought of their ancestors, which would be as alien as those, for example, in Western European history, from that of the pagan world, and the Christian era which followed it. Mao's final 'cultural revolution', of the period 1966–1969 which was more social and ideological than economic or political, conceived of a fundamental change in the nature of Chinese society. Within China the power of Confucian thought had established a complex structure of institutions and élitist traditions, by which the country had been ruled for over two thousand years. Thus Mao's revolution (Marxist inspired economics and politics apart) was as much directed against the old ways of thinking, as against the somewhat ramshackle governments of Emperors or Presidents who had embodied the traditional wisdoms, in his own lifetime. Yet for many thinking Chinese the conception of a genius in history remains essentially Confucian. The Sagas were and are held up as examples of the strength of the partly or wholly mystical rulers of remote antiquity, and also of the real if rather shadowy man who founded and sustained subsequent feudal regimes. Such ideas naturally led the Chinese to believe that man should be guided by the example of small élites of supreme power holders, and that as the proverb put it 'as the wind blows so the grass bends'. The masses would therefore always conform to the will and instructions of the leaders. In fact this élitist tradition of historically established hierarchies was a model that Mao came to reject utterly, as being not at all appropriate to the advancement of the Chinese people or the human race as a whole, in the second half of the 20th century. Thus much of Mao's later purposes were to overthrow such reactionary thoughts, and to place emphasis on the importance of creating a new society, based not on the example of ancient beliefs, or on the values and interests of long established élites, but rather on the collective wisdom of the masses of the people at large. Whether this populist conception can or will provide a viable ongoing model for the conduct of Chinese economic, political and social affairs into the future, remains to be seen.

In terms of sheer economic performance clearly much has been achieved, since the triumph of the Communist regime over those of the Kuomintang and their allies in 1949. Yet 1960 marked a particular period of crisis, for it was at this juncture that the Soviets, for reasons best known to themselves, withdrew technical and economic support, and dealt a heavy blow to plans for industrial development, which were under way at that time. At the same time the Yellow River almost ran dry, and a vast region remained without rain for over two years. Under previous feudal systems this disaster situation would probably have meant a major famine, the migration of millions of starving people, and the death by starvation of many millions more. It is to the credit of Mao Tse Tung's China that during the succeeding two years none of these things happened, and there was certainly no political disorders. There was, however, severe food rationing, and some malnutrition and great hardship in many rural areas. The newly introduced commune agricultural system, ineffective and clumsy as it appeared in many cases, did rest on the principle of promoting effective co-operation at grass roots level. As such the commune 'self-help' schemes probably saved the lives of many millions of people, because food resources were for the first time effectively centrally controlled, rationing was made possible and water conservancy works which had been carried out in the previous years functioned reasonably well.

In the period since that time many other developments have occurred. The reorganised commune system is reported to have become a reasonably viable method of organising and motivating a mass rural society. Moreover the stimulus given to Chinese technology and invention by the withdrawal of Russian assistance in the early 1960s, which was intended to cripple such development, has apparently had the effect of promoting a rather more rapid industrial advance, based on a wider diffusion of basic technical skills amongst the population at large, rather than on a direct reliance on foreign aid or technology. Standing on 'two legs', as Mao expressed it in 1964, enabled Chinese scientists, only four years after the Russian experts had departed, to explode their first nuclear device, without Russian or other assistance from abroad.

Finally it is important to recognise that conflicts still continue within the framework of the present political and economic system, and will influence future policies. There remains the strong historic tradition of élites and hierarchies within Chinese culture. Many similar ideas will be found within the Soviet model of a Marxist industrial state, where there is a firm belief in the importance of hierarchies, and of strict discipline and obedience to the lines laid down by the central organs of the controlling party and state. Indeed such methods had often underlain the developments of the Chinese Communist party during its many years of secret revolutionary activities, and may well appear to be essential to its continued success and survival. On the other hand, Mao himself was always much more unorthodox, and expressed strong belief in the creative forces of mass opinion, distrusting hierarchies and often encouraging criticism of the official line and of the higher party organs and its leaders. The élitists groups would still appear to believe that the economy and its development, in both its agricultural and industrial aspects, are the major priority, and that Maoist style ideological and social transformation is a second objective, only to be achieved in such a way as not to disrupt centrally planned economic programmes. It remains to be seen in post-Mao Tse Tung China which of these two lines of thinking will eventually predominate. Certainly any emphasising of Soviet style industrial development for China as a whole would appear likely to lead to some reversion to traditional Confucian systems of hierarchy and discipline, which are critical to the planning of a centrally controlled system. As has been shown elsewhere, the Soviet system of collective farms did facilitate the gathering of a financial 'surplus value' out of agriculture which enabled Russia to industrialise at a rapid rate, without much direct assistance from foreign money or technology. On the other hand the continual Chinese problem facing the new administration of Hua Kuo-Feng of needing to feed a vast population, on limited land resources, could also provide a counterpoint to such opinions. Moreover the Maoist agrarian system, based on 'rural self-help' and communal development schemes, free of foreign influences and dependant on various intermediate technologies, are likely to continue to have strong attractions for many other recently independent developing countries elsewhere in the world.

* * * * *

In sum the recent experience of the ancient civilisations of Japan and China suggest the possibility of diverse responses to political and economic doctrines, originally developed against Western European philosophical and cultural traditions. For Japan the classical capitalistic doctrines, modified by strong collectivistic and nationalistic impulses, have underpinned the evolution of contemporary industrial and urban society. Conversely in China of recent times Marxism, as applied to a large mass agrarian society, with a lower rate of industrialisation than has been contemplated in the Soviet model, has been regarded as the way ahead. It remains to be seen how in future these two powerful cultures, the insular but trade dependant island kingdom of Japan and the landbound masses of mainland China, will relate both to each other and be taken as a model or otherwise for the future advancement and progress of mankind as a whole.

Chapter 7

# SUMMARY AND CONCLUSIONS

"There are two things which I am confident I can do very well: one is an introduction to any literary work, stating what it is to contain, and how it should be executed in the most perfect manner; the other is a conclusion, shewing from various causes why the execution has not been equal to what the author promised to himself and to the public."

Samuel Johnson (1709–1784)
*Boswell's Life*

"You can never plan the future by the past."

Edmund Burke (1729–1797)
Letter to a Member of the National Assembly

"Rise! for the day is passing
And you be dreaming on:
The others have buckled their armour,
And forth to the fight are gone;
A place in the ranks awaits you,
Each man has some part to play;
The Past and the Future are nothing,
In the face of the stern Today."

Adelaide Ann Proctor (1825–1864)
*Legends and Lyrics. A Lost Chord*

"The Shape of Things to Come."

Herbert George Wells (1866–1946)
Title of book

"You ain't heard nothin' yet, folks."

Al Jolson (1886–1950)

*Remark in the first talking film, 'The Jazz Singer', July 1927*

"Remember folks today is the tomorrow you worried
about yesterday."

Mr. Terry Wogan
B.B.C. Morning Chat Show
18 November 1977

"Graduating student in Economics:
    'Unfortunately, sir, I don't see how it all hangs
together'.
His Tutor:
    'A lot of us feel like that; goodbye and good luck'."

Anon

## Resumé of Main Ideas and Controversies

By way of conclusion it may be useful for readers to survey briefly the
main characteristics of political economy, its development and impact
on world events as they have been considered in the preceding chapters.
As we have seen most of the great controversies about the validity or
otherwise of economic doctrines developed in response to changing
economic, social and political circumstances. Sometimes these changes
become apparent only over long periods of time, and were barely
discernible to the man in the field or in the street. However in other
cases, they were associated with great trade crises, upsets and social and
political revolutions, and stimulated in turn sharp or violent responses
and shifts in conventional values and doctrines. In such circumstances
uncertainty as to the relevance of past experience, for present and future
needs became manifest, and existing knowledge and opinion was
strongly questioned. Yet whatever the timescales involved most of the
debates focused on problems of the scarcity of real resources; the
propensity of man to consume beyond his immediate sustenance, at the
expense of futurity; and of the fairness or otherwise of income and
wealth distribution. These historic debates, as to the ends and means of
society as a whole, persist in ever changing circumstances, to the present
day.

Political economy cum economics as we now understand it, grew
mainly out of the Western European experience. Broadly speaking,
what occurred involved the gradual transformation of society through
from a small agrarian based feudal economy, on to merchant capitalism
at home and abroad, and thence to the great surge of changes in

economic and social life, associated with the growth in population and the 'agricultural and industrial revolutions' of late 18th and early 19th century England. Later we recalled the onset of large scale Western European and American industrial capitalism; the spread of world markets; the age of late 19th early 20th century colonial and imperialistic expansion and the move through World War, depression and slumps to a Second World War. In the Western industrialised world this was followed by a period of rapidly expanding annual compound growth in both output and trade. However, generally, trade has expanded more rapidly than output. These tendencies were only to receive serious check following on from the so called 'energy crises' of the 1970s. Meantime during the present century, economic, social and political convulsions in Eastern Europe, and especially Russia, brought the creation of the largely self-sustaining modern Marxist inspired Soviet industrial state. It also saw the subsequent creation, in Mao's post-1949 China, of a more agrarian based, but Marxist inspired society. In the West the growth of big welfare, big technology, big government and high energy dependency, notably on Middle Eastern oil, have in their turn become part of the urban and industrial world of today. Rightly or wrongly the road to a high mass consumption urban industrial society, be it capitalist or Marxist inspired, is one which many newly independent nations have increasingly sought to follow in the years after the Second World War. More recently, the need to sustain or recreate food-producing capacities and to 'redevelop' the agrarian sector has achieved renewed prominence. How to keep them 'down on the farm once they have seen Paree' has become an urgent challenge for most developing countries, faced with runaway population growth, sluggish food production, and urban sprawl.

\*     \*     \*     \*     \*

Looking back over the uncertain an uneven sequence of ideas and events described in this work the initial points of departure were the notions of *Scholasticism*, which thrived in 9th to 15th century Europe. These embraced a description of the ideas of those medieval schoolmen and monks who, during the Dark Ages and early medieval period, kept classical knowledge alive. The story embraced the early economic doctrines of St. Thomas Aquinas, who was seen as a most important thinker; in his opposition to 'usury'; while his concept of a 'just price' persists to the present day. The decline of the influence of Scholasticism in economic affairs might be seen in the later separation of the activities of the new nation states from those of the Universal Catholic Church; and also to the eventual acceptance by the Church of the working of the laws of supply and demand in commercial life.

*Mercantilism*, or the 'mercantile system', is generally regarded as the economic philosophy and practices of the new nation states, which emerged out of the religious and social changes of the Western European Reformation and Renaissance. The economic background was the agricultural and commercial developments of the 16th to 18th centuries. These included the move from feudal subsistence or small trading economies towards a greater reliance on the market and on merchant capitalism overseas. The 'Age of discoveries' and in particular the finding of gold and silver in the Americas, hastened the development of a Western Europe economic system based on money and prices. Agricultural improvements and an extension of the commercial use of land brought a decline in Church authority, and led to the development of private capitalism within the increasingly secular nation states. Mercantilism, which varied somewhat between the various European states generally, emphasised the power of the all-seeing centrally controlled kingdom. In English political theory it found its ultimate justification in Thomas Hobbes' *Leviathan* which supported the concept of the divine right of kings. A leading 17th century English mercantilist author was the Levant merchant Thomas Mun, who published important works on England's overseas trade and supported the case for the export of bullion, to finance further trade and wealth at home. In the domestic economy the state's control of wages and interest, the regulation of trades by guilds and other means, and the use of protective industrial development policies, were all considered a necessary part of government policies. A kingdom's wealth was seen in the possession of bullion and expressed through the possession of powerful armies and navies, which were often mercenary in character. Abroad, protection of trading interests abounded, and commercial links were generally confined to those regions with whom it would appear that trade would yield an export surplus. Trade was especially encouraged between mother countries and colonies, and as such the English Navigation Acts were designed to encourage the growth of shipping and the maintenance of naval power. In England and in her West Indian and North American Colonial Empire as a whole this became known as the Mercantile System, and was eventually strongly criticised by Adam Smith in his *An Enquiry into the Nature and the Causes of the Wealth of Nations,* published in 1776. For Smith the mercantile system had degenerated into a contrivance to support the interests of the 'producers' against those of the 'consumers'. Nevertheless he recognised the importance of the Navigation Acts to assisting in maintaining naval supremacy, which, between the 17th and 19th centuries, played such a large part in British strategic thinking.

Criticism of mercantilistic attitudes towards the origins and promotion of national wealth was early on associated with the *Physiocrats* of mid-18th century France. Their name derived from physiocracy, meaning the rule of nature or of natural law. The philosophy was associated with a group of intellectuals who gathered around the Court of the French King Louis XV and generally tried to save the *ancien regime* from itself. They were much influenced by the writings of a somewhat obscure Irish banker cum economist, Richard Cantillon, who had been murdered in 1734. It was considered that the basis of national wealth derived primarily from the soil, and not from a surplus on overseas trade and the possession of bullion which was the mercantilists' main doctrine. The physiocrats' leader became the Court Physician, François Quesnay, whose 'tableau economique' was a type of early input output table. This suggested that agriculture alone yielded a product net, being a 'free gift of nature' worth more than the expenses of production. For the physiocrats the truly productive class were the tenant farmers who worked the soil, as opposed to the oft absentee land owning classes who owned the soil and took the rents, or the trading merchant classes who simply bought and sold goods to the market. In general, physiocratic theories anticipated Adam Smith, by advocating *laissez-faire*, calling for the removal of obstacles to freer trade between producers and consumers. They also persist to the present day, in any society anxious to sustain and support its agricultural food producing capacities.

The *Classical economists* were philosophers and men of affairs, mainly English and Scots, who, in the latter half of the 18th century and the first half of the 19th century, formulated the principles of the new science of political economy. The founding father of the school was Adam Smith who, influenced by the writings of John Locke, David Hume, Robert Jacques Turgot and others, published his work on *The Wealth of Nations* which, both coincided with the American Declaration of Independence, which was also influenced by the ideas of John Locke about the role of private property, and also somewhat anticipated many of the economic, social and industrial changes to come. Smith expressed clearly for the first time the possibilities of complete freedom of economic activity, and opposed interventionist all-seeing government policies as were advocated by the mercantilistic doctrines of the day. The classical economists thus came to regard themselves as being reformers, seeking to abolish the defects of the restrictive mercantile institutions and habits of thought which had lingered on from the 17th and 18th centuries. Adam Smith had emphasised the values of economic and political freedom working together; that the individual could be relied upon continually to strive to better his own economic position and would best know how to spend his time and money in producing wealth, for both himself and the nation as a whole. As such a 'harmony of interests' existed within society, and if man could be encouraged to follow his self interests he would be led by an 'invisible hand' to benefit the rest of community. Again the new small manufacturers in pursuit of profit would provide the goods desired by the rest of society, in the right quantities, at the right prices and at the right time. The factors of production – labour working for the wage, capital for the rate of interest, and land being provided for the payment of rent, seeking the largest possible returns, would be used in productive activities where they were most needed. A fruitful 'division of labour' would therefore apply.

Later classical economists and other thinkers of like mind developed and refined Smith's original premises, against the basis of the experience of the new steam powered, economies of scale 'industrial capitalist, system' which was developing all around them. In particular they became imbued with a theory of human behaviour developed by the utilitarian philosopher Jeremy Bentham, and included in his 'calculus of pleasure and pain'; in an economic sense pleasure coming from consumption, which had however to be moderated – in the interests of saving and investment, for future needs. Again Thomas Robert Malthus, in his *Essay on the Principle of Population* published in 1798, discussed the possibility of rapid population increase out-running the available means of subsistence while, somewhat conversely, the Frenchman Jean Baptiste Say, propounded his law of markets which suggested that supply would automatically create its own demand and an equilibrium of employment would eventually apply. David Ricardo also developed other important ideas; in particular a theory of rent which suggested that in time, given the rise of population, and the demands for foodstuffs, landlords would benefit disproportionately at the expense of the labouring and manufacturing classes. Ricardo also became widely known for his theory of 'comparative advantages' as applied to international trade, which became part and parcel of classical doctrines. He further developed classical thinking by seeking to isolate economic activities in abstract theory, and then to devise conclusions which could be compared with activities in the real world. This so called 'deductive' approach, as opposed to the more descriptive approaches of Smith and Malthus, set the pattern for economic investigations for many years. Later, following on from Ricardo, much of the energies of the classical school became focused on the implications of his 'Labour Theory of Value'. This maintained that the value of a commodity varied with a quantity of labour used in its production. It became widely criticised but was not replaced until the 'full cost theory' of John Stuart Mill that the value of a commodity depended on the amounts of all factors used to produce it. Mill in turn carried on a long debate with a number of other classical economists, including Nassau Senior and John Elliot Cairnes, about the nature and methods of political economy. In general Mill took a liberal 'descriptive' stance, whereas Nassau Senior was anxious to emphasise the 'deductive' scientific aspects. They were thereby opening up a debate which has persisted to the present day.

In the practical worlds of business and politics the great debates shifted towards issues of the application of *laissez-faire* or protectionism in the pursuit of greater national wealth. In England the influential *Manchester school* consisted of a group who were active in promoting classical Ricardian ideas of free trade abroad, and of resisting encroachments on *laissez-faire*, in economic and social affairs at home. They were most active during the period between the 1820s and the 1850s and were particularly associated with the propaganda of the Anti-Corn Law League, which was attempting to encourage the repeal of the Corn Laws, which had been first introduced in 1815 at the end of the Napoleonic Wars and were eventually repeated in 1846, following the disaster of the Irish potato famine. Their leaders came to include the agitators and publicists John Bright and Richard Cobden. Most of their economic ideas came from Ricardo's theory of comparative advantages which suggested the need to repeal the Corn Laws, so as to allow cheap food grains to be imported; to break the power of the agricultural interests; to reduce food prices and wage costs and thereby encourage the exports of manufactures, particularly cotton goods, to the world on a free trade basis. In other ways they tended to promote the liberal economic philosophy and were often opposed to factory legislation emphasising the importance of free will, choice and individualism, bounded only by legal contract within the conduct of economic affairs.

On the other hand, as we have seen *protectionism*, in one form or another, had been an integral part of older mercantilistic traditions.

During the second half of the 18th and early 19th century, the triumph of the English classical school of political economy, and in particular Ricardo's 'Theory of comparative advantages' came to dominate public thinking. In England, and to an increasing extent in other industrial countries, *laissez-faire*, on a world-wide basis, was regarded as the model to be followed, in promoting trade and wealth creation as a whole. However as the 19th century went by, it became increasingly apparent to many countries that they might best develop, at least in the initial phases, with assistance from protective tariffs for 'infant industries' and such like. In the United States tariff policy became an influential part of national policy, behind which a *laissez-faire* industrial economy, based on imported risk capital and immigrant labour, was encouraged to develop rapidly. The tariffs of the Zollverein also played an important part in the industrial development of the industry of Greater Germany under Prussian leadership, and France and other European countries also increasingly re-adopted such mercantilistic style policies during the second half of the 19th century. Moreover protectionism continues in many forms to the present time.

In the 1930s most of the industrial world resorted to trade protectionism in answer to the dilemmas created by the slump in world trade, and this became known as *autarchy*. After the Second World War the Western inspired world economies as a whole adopted freer trading patterns, under the stimulation of the General Agreement on Tariffs and Trade and other institutions. Again the European Economic Community might be seen as anti-protectionist in the sense of its encouraging a freer and enormously greater flow of trade in industrial goods between member states. On the other hand it continues to pursue a protectionist agricultural policy against imports of food stuffs from countries outside the Community, and in this sense might be seen to be strongly influenced by longstanding physiocratic notions of the need to foster agrarian interests. Finally the COMECON group of Soviet led states have generally adopted highly protectionist and regulated trade policies, both with each other and the rest of the world.

Another important set of doctrinal debates revolved around the place of gold in the monetary system and the functioning of the banking system at large. The 19th century English *Banking school* were a group of economists and men of affairs, led in particular by Thomas Tooke, who took the view that the volume of currency was not determined solely by the quantity of gold and paper notes in existence, but included bank deposits and bills of exchange. They therefore considered that the individual banks should be free to decide how many notes to issue, subject to the control that they would be convertible into gold on demand. They believed that the number of notes in circulation should be regulated by competition between banks, and should vary according to the state of trade and the needs of the general public.

The opposition *Currency school* was supported by a number of different people, including Robert Torrens. They developed their ideas during the 1820s, in a time of violent business fluctuations, with short periods of prosperity being interrupted by financial crises and business failures. Many of the problems of the period were associated with the fall off of activity and the changes of society which were occurring following the end of the Napoleonic Wars. It was felt that these problems were aggravated by the mismanagement of currency by the banking system in its note issuing activities. Members of the currency school increasingly felt that the main duty of the banker, and in particular the Bank of England, was to maintain a sufficient reserve of bullion to safeguard the stability of public credit. It was argued that the total volume of metallic currency varied with in flows and out flows from abroad, and if credit were to remain stable a mixed currency should work in the same way. The volume of paper notes being kept in strict proportion to the amount of gold in the banking system, and the opinions of the currency school and 'principle', had a large influence on the Bank Charter Act of 1844, and this in turn subsequently shaped the relationship between the Bank of England and the joint stock banks, through the regulation of the bank rate and open market operations. It became the model which was followed by many other central banks in relation to the operating of monetary systems as a whole, which, in one guise or another, have persisted to the present day.

*Marxism*, which developed in violent opposition to classical free market doctrines, embraced a wide spectrum of social, economic and political perspectives. It derived initially from the writings of Karl Marx who, together with Friedrich Engels, published in 1848 *The Communist Manifesto*. In this work – which in part reflected the lists of grievances of the English Chartists of the 1830s, there was also the crucial idea of a historically deterministic scenario of economic development – with human society evolving via revolutionary turmoil and change, through a number of predetermined stages. These followed a Paradise Lost scenario; from primitive communism, through to slavery, feudalism and capitalism and thence hopefully on to socialism and finally to pure communism, in a fully urbanised industrial world. In these final paradise regained circumstances wealth would be all abundant; distribution problems and private property would disappear, and the state would wither away. The abolition of master-servant relationships and the dictatorship of the proletariat would ensure justice for all men – in which each could, according to the theory at least, be truly rewarded according to his total needs. As we have seen, Marx himself went on in his work *das Kapital*, the first volume of which was published in 1867, to develop Ricardo's 'labour theory of value,' and to point to the problems of the trade cycle; of the tendency for advanced capitalism to run into slumps, for a failure of consumer demands due to a mal-distribution of income, for investment losses and declining profits, and much else besides. The irony was that when the great Communist revolution actually did occur it was in the Russia of 1917, a state, in Marx's own view, barely out of slavery and feudalism – and the task of major industrialisation therefore fell onto 'Socialist' shoulders. Lenin himself seemed to have had a somewhat over-optimistic faith in the powers of 'scientific management' to solve production investment and distribution problems, at a stroke. Influenced by the works of Hobson he also saw it as an eventual task for triumphant Marxism to speed the world revolution against capitalism and imperialistic exploitation, wherever it might be regarded as having occurred. It was left to the more ruthless later regime of Joseph Stalin to collectivise Russian agriculture and massively industrialise at home – and to face up to the need to defeat Nazi Germany at war, and to the later possibilities of promoting Marxist inspired revolutions abroad. Ironically the most successful of those, in Mao's post 1949 China, has shown a dis-inclination to follow Moscow's example in all aspects of Communist central planning for creating an industrial society cum 'Paradise Regained.' The reality of nearly a quarter of mankind to feed – on some 7 per cent of the world arable land has, of necessity, forced Chinese communism to have a physiocratic face. The Maoist example of village 'self help' and sufficiency also has strong and growing attractions for many newly independent agrarian based societies.

From the 1870s onwards *Neo-classical* ideas developed against the basis of classical doctrines, but came from work by a number of different men, located in different parts of Europe. In particular they became associated with the 'subjective' theory of value which derived from ideas of Carl Menger in Austria, Leon Walras in Switzerland, and William Stanley Jevons in England. Working independently, each developed a theory that the value of commodity depended on the utility of a final marginal unit. This theory of 'marginal utility', which most importantly was capable of mathematical development, was further developed by a number of Austrian economists. In Britain however,

Jevon's ideas met with opposition from some classical economists and were not fully accepted till the publication by Alfred Marshall in 1890 of *The Principles of Economics*. In this work Marshall brought together what, at the time, was regarded as having been two competitive streams of thought, combining them together into a precise theory of value and distribution, with costs of production explaining the forces of supply, and utility their demand. Marshall's system of analysis had considerable influence on the later development of economic doctrines in Britain, Western Europe, the U.S.A. and elsewhere in the Western *laissez-faire* influenced world. In the course of time much of Anglo-Saxon neo-classical thinking took on a strong awareness of welfare questions. While late 19th century and early 20th century England became a world of rapidly expanding national income, in part fired by the benefits of new markets and the returns from new investments combined with a flow of surplus population abroad, the plight of many of the labouring classes remained poor. Thus minds as diverse as Sidgwick and Marshall, at Cambridge, and later Cannan and Pigou, became much concerned with distribution of income and wealth questions, which in their various ways, eventually led forward to Lord Beveridge's and other's ideas for the modern post 1945 welfare state. Like the younger Mill before them they were all looking for a peaceful liberal Fabian Society type evolution of society, as opposed to the revolutionary turmoil propounded as inevitable by the Marxists.

In terms of practical policies much of neo-classical doctrine was initially interpreted in favour of sustaining and encouraging more competition as opposed to less; and of the philosophy of good government being less government. In reality the growth, during the last quarter of the 19th century and throughout the 20th century, of both technical scale and concentrations of ownership and control in industrial systems; the potential power of trade unions in labour markets; the great extension of the powers of big government in industrial ownership, welfare expenditures, armaments, and imperial commitments, etc., made new doctrines necessary. Increasingly neo-classical authors, on both sides of the Atlantic, came to look upon the perfectly competitive model as but one of a number of possible stages, through to state regulated monopoly. In terms of public policy, guidance was increasingly sought as to how to effectively control and judge combinations of capital or labour, in light of new criteria of what constituted the 'public interest'. In America, from the 1890 Sherman Anti-Trust Acts onwards, policy tended towards defined legal regulation and prohibition of monopolistic practices. However in Britain a more empirical 'case by case' approach eventually applied. Throughout Western Europe practice and doctrines varied more widely. At a later period J. K. Galbraith's conception of 'countervailing powers' applying between the forces of big government, big industry and big unions also moved the possible constraint and control of such large scale economic and political forces, into the realm of accepted doctrines.

Another significant departure from the English classical way of thinking occurred in the German speaking world, where discontent with the 'deductive' approach, as advocated by Nassau Senior and others, produced a strong *inductive historical school* of thinking. In particular it provoked a great debate between Carl Menger at the University of Vienna who supported the 'deductive approach' and the historian Gustav Schmoller, who supported an inductive historical approach to economic knowledge. The historical approach continued as a strong line of development, through from Werner Sombart in Germany to R. H. Tawney and others in Britain. To some extent their ideas, from Joseph Schumpeter onwards, became involved in modern ideas of understanding and promoting economic growth. More significant, from the viewpoint of much of formal economics, the Austrian school were a group of economists mainly located in Vienna which included Carl Menger, Friedrich von Wieser and Eugen von Bohm-Bawerk. Their work paralleled similar work elsewhere. The Austrians came to be regarded as forming a separate school, particularly because their methods were so strongly opposed to the prevailing inductive historical approach followed in Germany at the same period. Apart from this the 'Austrians' main contribution to economic thinking lay in the development of both the 'subjective' theory of value, and also by the application of 'mathematical methods' to economic analysis, which had an increasingly profound impact on the perception by economists of the scope and methods of economic science during the following years.

*Keynesian economics* developed out of the writings of John Maynard Keynes in England of the 1930s. In this he was writing against many of the basic beliefs of what had become the Anglo-Saxon neo-classical school, and in particular the idea which has derived from Say's early 19th century law that 'supply would create an equivalent demand'. Keynes increasingly had come to the view that it was possible for highly advanced industrial economy to persist with high levels of unemployment for long periods of time; and that considerable government intervention particularly on the demand side of economy was necessary to get activity moving again. However in general attitude and opinions Keynes was a Liberal, and wished to facilitate the continued existence of the benefits of efficiency and choice in maintaining a *laissez-faire* system on the supply side of the economy. Much of post-war macro economic debates have centred around the effectiveness or otherwise of 'demand management' as an ongoing policy. A substantial neo-Keynesian community has developed to assist with the various disputes, both practical and doctrinal involved in this process. Much of the 'Keynesian revolution' has become associated with statistical and mathematical techniques in forecasting the performance of economies as a whole. Keynesian style policies have come to include trying to reconcile on the one hand high rates of national economic growth, with full employment and price stability, within an environment of reasonable balance of payments stability. Neo-Keynesians have in turn become involved in prolonged debates with people popularly dubbed as 'monetarists', notably represented by Milton Friedman, who are concerned with the affect of Keynesian employment and demand management policies on inflation, and of the traditional role of money as a store of value. Finally, the supply side of the economy, from labour availability and skills, to investment targets, managerial resources, raw material sources and energy supplies, etc., have also been drawn into the debate. 'Indicative' planning of the French model has, in Britain at least, also been seen as an important corollary to demand management, in many facets of economic cum political activity. The extension of National Economic Development Office sector working parties; the proposal for planning agreements between major companies and government; the importance of prices and incomes policies generally, are all part of the move towards planning the supply side. When taken together with the great size of the public sector, from nationalised industries to welfare programmes, many have thought that, for good or ill, the move to a so called 'corporate state' is already an accomplished fact.

In the U.S.A. a distinct school of *Institutional cum evolutionary* economists has also developed at least in part opposition to neo-classical 'mathematical views' about the nature of the economic disciplines. They took their early inspiration from Thorstein Veblen with his ideas of the emerging roles of the 'engineers' in the developing industrial system, and a strong dissatisfaction with a society based all to obviously on the 'capitalistic ethic' and on the mores of 'conspicuous consumption'. In turn they were also strongly imbued with a historical-institutional approach to economic development, which owed more than a little to the German school, and to the writings of such powerful intellects as Joseph Schumpeter who, in the 1930s emigrated to the

U.S.A. Subsequently, in the late 1930s and in the period after the Second World War, influenced by the ideas of Wesley Mitchell and others, they embraced the goals of the 'Keynesian revolution', and became strongly instrumental in fostering its application to the highly and intentionally diffuse American Federal and State Government 'free enterprise' economy. John Kenneth Galbraith, with his many institutional and welfare concerns, lies within this school of thought, and policy pro-posals and actions.

A further ongoing stream of economic thinking and policies relates to questions of *growth and development* – especially as has applied in the newly independent 'third world'. In early times economists, from Malthus to Marx and, in the 1930s Joseph Schumpeter, J. M. Keynes and Alvin Hansen, had all been concerned with problems of the trade cycle, and of stagnation in the growth of activity within mature industrial economies. For Keynes and others this was especially associ-ated with unemployment of all real resources as characterised in Britain and elsewhere during much of the interwar period. The great postwar upsurge in free world trade generally outran the production of manu-factured and other goods, but was especially associated with trade growing between the Western industrial economies. The Korean War boom gave many primary producing countries a brief postwar lift in activity, but later their general rate of growth in trade and output tended to lag behind those of the industrial powers. The principal exceptions to the rule proved to be the oil producing states of Latin America and later West Africa and the Middle East.

The *third world*, and increasing numbers of international agencies concerned with development and trade and financing policies, soon became involved in the great debates about the best paths to greater prosperity and growth. Most initially followed a neo-colonialist capitalist path deriving from their former status. A country does not automatically become 'free' just because it ceases to be a colony, however defined. Industrialisation was to be fostered by the import of capital and a continued growth in total markets for their goods, both at home and abroad. On the other hand, the Soviet Marxist scenario of industrialisation initially through social revolution, and thence by finance primarily from an agricultural surplus, and with technical aid from Mother Russia, also attracted some. In most developing countries the Malthusian spectre of runaway population increase and the need for a secure agricultural base reasserted the claim of that critical sector for assistance and support. W. W. Rostow's work on *The Stages of Economic Growth*, published in 1959, represented a bold attempt to

FIG. 38.  A BROAD INDICATION OF HOW AVERAGE INCOMES GREW IN SOME LEADING
INDUSTRIAL COUNTRIES, 1870–1970

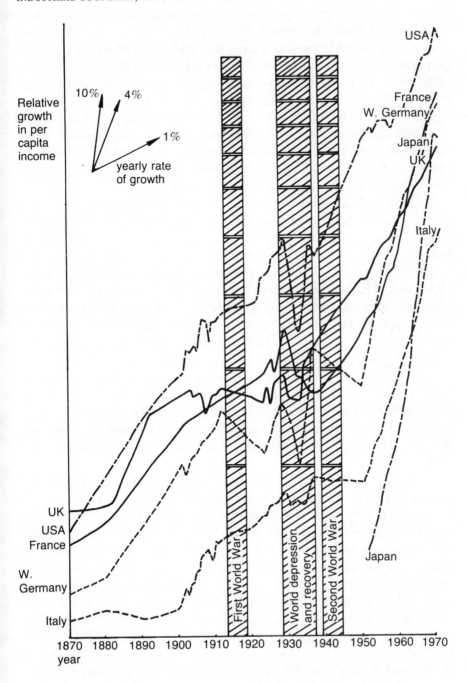

reconcile some of the issues involved. Since that time most developing nations have become highly conscious of their dependency on a vulnerable agricultural sector – and the attentions of both Robert McNamara's World Bank and the example of Mao's China has been drawn into the debate – and into the implementations of practical programmes for raising the productivity of the farming sectors. At the same time other attention has switched, in the mathematically based work of Wassily Leontief and others, towards the need for keeping world agricultural and primary product markets open, of stabilising returns to such producers and of fostering the wider dispersion of 'value adding' manufacturing activites throughout the world. Overall is a strong perception of the role of economists in guiding and assisting in the management of the future course of events.

On looking back over the history of economic doctrines and their relationships to real events one recurring theme is the ongoing nature and causes of growth, as a way out of the dilemmas of scarcity, poverty and degradation for much of mankind. In early times *the ups and downs* of economic activity were seen as reflecting underlying natural conditions of climate, aridity and cropping: of Pharoah's seven fat years being followed by seven lean years requiring abstinence in the former to provide for survival in the latter. In the 19th century, W. S. Jevons sought to relate sunspots to weather conditions and harvests and thence to food prices, wage demands and cyclical fluctuation in economic activity. Conversely, Marx regarded the trade cycle, and the persistence of long-term slumps as an integral part of the maldistribution of income and wealth between the wage-earning classes and the capitalists. A lack of demand by the former, and a decline in investment opportunities and profitability for the latter underlay long-term secular stagnation and decline.

In recent times the application of computer studies by Jay W. Forrester at the Massachusetts Institute of Technology have been to suggest that superimposed upon the familiar short- and long-term cycles of expansions and contractions built into the Western economic system, and thence to world trade at large, is a further underlying pattern of inexorable long-term change. Forrester's studies of the American economic system suggest that three distinct cycles are involved in economic fluctuations: the familiar short-term (3 to 7 years) cycle; the longer-term Kuznets (20 to 25 years) cycle and the Kondratieff (45 to 60 years) cycle of economic and political change. Preliminary results suggest that the short-term business cycle arises in the consumer goods sectors of the economy, through tardy feedback between production, inventory, and consumption. Cycles of over- and under-investment in capital goods are involved in the Kuznets and Kondratieff waves. The Forrester line of analysis and reasoning about the post-Second World War economy suggests the following logic. In the capital goods sector a large expansion to overcome accumulated shortages from the depression and war year followed World War II. By 1960, when capital plant was once more adequate, 'tremendous forces' remained – in labour unions, banks and capital sector industries themselves – to sustain capital accumulation. Finally the momentum faltered, and a decade later, as capital plant became more and more excessive, there is probably so much capital that no new investment will be needed until the 1990s.

Professor Forrester explains 'stagflation' as follows: in order to encourage growth and reduce unemployment, the government increases the money supply and providing other incentives to new investment; but if capital plant is already too large, such increases and incentives lead not to plant expansion, but to the inflation which they were designed to combat. Over all these cyclical motions is what Professor Forrester calls the 'life cycle of economic growth' – the 300-year pattern of national development and maturity in which growth first sweeps upward in an ever-steepening curve, then follows a straight line, and finally slows and ceases as demand begins to balance available resources.

In this sense, U.S. economic growth and development is now giving way to 'some sort of equilibrium' as the nation encounters limits to its resources and environment. Thus, for Forrester, America is entering a period of transition, and may have as little as 20 to 30 years in which to solve the problems it brings. Under these conditions, 'it is counter-productive for government to promote growth in per capita output; the real problem is 'how large a stable population we can support, and at what standard of living' – a hard set of trade-offs for which in this nation there is little precedent'.

Finally throughout this discussion we have followed a broad political economy approach to the questions of *scarcity, wealth and welfare.* As we have seen, this was the usual name for a study of economics until recent times. However with the onset during the last 30 to 40 years of more precise mathematical techniques to the nature of economic phenomena, the idea of trying to make it once again a more precise, scientifically provable 'science of man' became fashionable, and for some period held great sway. The majority of Nobel Prize Winners in economics from 1969 onwards, listed later in this chapter, have been noted for quantitative analysis. Yet a characteristic of contemporary economies is one of rapidly shifting dilemmas, open to continuing thought, development and debate. In all such discussions it is imposs-ible to ignore the underlying historical, institutional and political basis of society. The relevance of economists' assumptions about these changing dimensions have a decisive impact on the effectiveness, or otherwise, of theoretical approaches to the issues of wealth and welfare, in what appears to many to be an increasingly finite and scarce world.


## Contemporary Doctrines: Positive, Normative or Deterministic

In the introduction to this extended work attention was drawn to three perspectives of the economist: as a scientist, a prophet, or as a systems engineer of the 'future possibilities open to mankind'. As will have become apparent in reality the contemporary economist, in the everyday practise of his skills, is often hopelessly entangled between these three roles, lurching from debates about what appear to be scientifically established proofs, to future prophesying, and to an advocacy of social and political interventions and engineering, of all sorts and complexions. The problem of establishing realistic assump-tions, to bridge the gap between theory and reality, continues to bedevil economic analysis. The long 19th century methodological debates between the classical 'deductive' line of reason and the historical and institutional schools of thought, continue to reappear. In truth the sheer complexity and rapidly evolving nature of the contemporary world, in both the industrial and less industrial societies, involves problems and choices undreamed of by early classical or Marxist thinkers. Again the apparent onset of what Mr. Daniel Bell described as *The Coming of the Post Industrial Society* in his book published in 1974 presents new dilemmas, choices and debates for mankind in the high 'mass con-sumption' societies. Throughout it is important to recognise the con-tinuing central ambiguity which revolves around the study of the science of man, in pursuit of material wealth and welfare, in a finite and rapidly changing world. Economic 'truths' continue to come and go; the dismal science of scarcity and subsistence propounded by Malthus and Ricardo appears to have been scotched in one place, to emerge renewed and triumphant in another. The onset of the 1970's 'energy crises' (see Appendix IV) have restored to the comprehension of Western man the facts of 'diminishing returns' and the payments of 'economic rent' for scarce and finite resources, which the classical thinkers considered to be a self-evident common-sense fact of nature. An apparent worsening in capital investment to output ratios affecting many advanced technologies and declining profit margins may also appear to be a reaffirmation of the truths of limits to growth. Ideas about the need for a 'stationary state' in industrial societies, first perceived by the younger Mill in 1848, have re-emerged with renewed force in the 1970s, and have found global expression through the publications of the 'Club of Rome' and many other conservationist groups. However a more equal distribution of income, the survival and extension of private property and the growth of large scale industrial capitalism in many Western democratic societies, seems to have refuted many of Marx's prophesies as to the inevitability of economic collapse, and social revolution on a large scale. Yet many of the underlying social problems of industrial urban society which he pointed to, notably the potentially dehumanising and alienating effects of factory existence, are still live issues today. To some extent much of Western Europe has opted out of this by importing 'gäste arbeiter' to undertake more of the unpleasant and repetitive tasks which still need to be undertaken. Achieving an acceptable harmonious balance between human values on the one hand, and the economic benefits of large scale on the other – be it industrial, commercial or urban living – has yet to be done. Moreover Marx's prophesies of an inevitable revolution towards a Socialist, and eventually Communist, world continues to inspire much of mankind, as the logical path, nay goal, for social, economic and political forces. The 1930s Western Keynesian model of demand management, on a domestic and a world scale, has still to prove its staying power, as an ongoing system for the majority of mankind. The relationship of demand management to supply possibilities and constraints, as they appear in a Western industrial society, also present planning challenges with renewed force. Indeed the possibilities of 'divergence' or 'convergence' between peoples, nations and rival systems still flit to and fro like moths before a lamp – with no clear indication whether they will come to rest, or be consumed by the flame.

* * * * *

In these circumstances it is hardly surprising that, in both a theoretical and practical sense a great debate continues to rage, in both the democratic West and in the Marxist–Leninist world as to the nature of contemporary economic doctrine, its philosophical roots and practices. In the West many continue to debate the distinction between economics as a 'scientific subject', as opposed to economics concerned with 'welfare or value' criteria. As indicated, in the opening passages Professor Lionel Robbins in his important work an essay on *The Nature and Significance of Economic Science*, published in 1935 defined modern economics as a science that studies human behaviour as a relation 'between ends and scarce means which have alternative uses'. Earlier, Marshall, in the neo-classical tradition, had considered that economics examined 'that part of individual and social action which is most closely connected with attainment and with the use of the material requisites of well-being', which suggested a somewhat 'welfarist' view of the subject. Sidgwick had been concerned with social questions while Cannan had also defined economics as the study of 'material welfare'. Yet a third approach, which has been extensively referred to, derives from the 19th century Marxist view that economics can only be seen as part of a historical determinist model, with the system inevitably progressing through stages of development leading to a Socialist cum Communist form of society. To this perspective all economic, social and political actions need to be judged in relation to this pre-determined revolutionary arrived at goal.

The 'positive' *scarcity* definition of economics, as most strongly expressed by Robbins in the 1930s, suggested a subject which is an aspect of all activity focusing on questions relating to scarcity and choice. This definition separated economic considerations out from technical, historical, political, sociological or other aspects. Thus the economic problem is how best to achieve a particular goal with given resources, the choice of the best combination of differently priced resources to produce goods, or of allocating resources between different alternatives. It is a concept which continues to attract those who wish to see the further development of the 'scientifically provable' aspects of economic science. It has less appeal to those who are committed to the idea of a political economy concerned with defining both the means and the desirable ends for society as a whole. In America in particular, the important 'institutional' cum 'evolutionary' view of economics sees the subject as being in a close partnership with the other social sciences.

A concern with contemporary economic doctrines leads naturally forward to the *welfare* approach, and as to how, within a modern society, this might be maximised. Necessarily this involves comparison between the economic welfare of individuals, in considering the economic desirability of policies which would bring gain to some people but economic loss to others, both in the short and longer term. Economists guided by Bentham's principle, that policy should be judged by 'the greatest happiness for the greatest number', might see little difficulty in deciding where the welfare of most people lies. Never-theless welfare analysis is regarded as normative in that it requires the use of standards relating to *what ought to be*, as opposed to Robbins' more rigorous positive standards which requires only analysis of *what is*. At some point during welfare economic analysis, ethical or value judgements must be introduced. It may, therefore, be argued by some that such approaches lie properly outside the scope of pure economics. In practice, whilst the scarcity type of definition would seem to confine economics to scientific propositions of a positive nature, the distinction between positive as opposed to normative or value judgements is not particularly easy to make.

As we have seen, the economists in Britain particularly associated with the development of the neo-classical 'welfare' view of economics were in the 19th century Marshall and Sidgwick at Cambridge, and later Cannan in London and Pigou, also at Cambridge. The latter examined particular policies in relation to their effects on the distribution and size of national output and on their divergence in the effects of economic activity on those who conduct it, the 'marginal private net product', and on society as a whole, the 'marginal social net product'. The idea of a possible divergence between private interest and total social interest, which the early classical economists assumed to be synonymous, was most important. Pigou's distinction has subsequently been widely applied in social democratic national policies in respect of the social welfare, and in planning for many public facilities. In this sense contemporary economics ceases to be a science simply concerned with allocation problems between different factors of production to one concerned with the pursuance of socially defined goals, through the possible use of alternative means.

Finally, the Marxist view of economics being part of a historically deterministic model has been emphasised throughout, as a set of ideas which continue to influence powerfully much of mankind. Yet within the 'Socialist camp' a great debate continues to rage as to the roads to be followed, through socialism towards pure communism and the withering away of the state. Moving beyond a reliance on surpluses from agriculture and rigorous adherence to central planning direc-tives for heavy industrialisation programmes today, in a number of COMECON member states, notably Hungary, Poland and Rumania, and also Yugoslavia, there appears to be an increased willingness to use the criteria of fulfilling market demands, and the test of a 'company surplus', however defined, as one of the steps along the road. Moreover the contrast between the Marxist–Leninist model of planned industrialisation to lift society out of agrarian base, as opposed to the Chinese model of emphasising rural improvement through village self-help, continues to divide the application of Marxist principles in much of the developing world. What Marx himself would have made of all this sound and fury remains one of the great unanswerable speculations, open to economists and political philosophers alike.

## Convergency and Future Shocks and Prospects

Throughout this book the oft pivotal role of the British experience from Adam Smith through to Karl Marx and John Maynard Keynes in the development of economic doctrines and practices has been explored. Whilst the relative standing of Britain in the world economy has changed markedly – her share of world trade is today less than that of the U.S.A., West Germany, Japan and France – nevertheless she remains a key element in the functioning of the world economy. The fact that Britain developed a highly industrialised and urban trade-dependent economy before other nations means that her experience has historically often been in advance of tendencies which will eventually apply elsewhere. Recently, The Henley Centre for Forecasting in a wide ranging report on *Britain in the 1980s* outlined the following 'certainties' for the immediate future. It was suggested that the lion would not change his habit; in other words that:

(a) The pace of development and social and economic change will be much the same for most of the next decade.

(b) The birth rate will continue to decline and will continue to run below the deathrate. This means that the total population will stop growing and by the end of the decade may begin a gradual decline. In turn the smaller number of children will gradually affect both the required pattern and scale of education. Moreover the older part of the population will become relatively more important, posing problems in terms of social security requirements and demands for health services.

(c) North Sea oil and gas will eliminate the country's chronic payments problem and provide the nation with a chance to improve its rate of plough-back in investment, as well as its rate of output growth and standard of living in the 1980s.

(d) As a market Britain will continue to expand more slowly than the rest of the world.

(e) A dramatic change in technology and the application of new technology at a faster rate can be ruled out within this time-scale.

(f) Labour attitudes will continue to change and although trades unions will still concentrate on the question of pay, workers will be increasingly concerned with, working conditions and working hours, and control of their firms and participation in decision taking.

(g) The need to get more production from less working time will increase. Not only will firms have a powerful incentive to economise in the use of labour because of soaring labour costs, but shorter hours and fewer shifts will require extra investment in advanced plant and machinery.

(h) Inflation will only moderate gradually. Slackening inflation in the rest of the world and British policies in operation in 1974 and 1975 will ensure a lowering of price inflation. Businesses, however, will still be confronted with the need to adjust management policies so as to 'live' with historically high rates of inflation.

(i) The class division in Britain will continue but will be a little less pronounced by 1985. The main factor making for change in class consciousness has been the broadening of the educational system. This tendency will continue.

(j) The pressures making for regional autonomy, such as 'home rule for Scotland' will increase, and there will be growing dissatisfaction with the powers and bureaucratic systems of the central government. Dissatisfaction with large-scale organisations, including the multi-national corporation, giant firms and nationalised industries, will also strengthen. This is not to say that Britain will drift into anarchy and become ungovernable, but the tendency towards 'bigness' of organisations will be arrested.

Somewhat similar trends and tendencies are also – given circumstances – increasingly apparent in other leading industrial nations as well. However Britain's 'trump card' for the immediate future is the possible strength of North Sea oil and gas reserves in an energy-scarce world.

\*     \*     \*     \*     \*

As has been emphasised throughout, the problems of the contemporary world present many debates which would be entirely familiar to earlier economic thinkers of classical, neo-classical and Marxist persuasion – but other questions which in terms of their scale, complexity and timescales, do not fit easily, if at all, into simply analytical frameworks. It may be argued that the basic concepts of economics are comparatively simple statements of refined commonsense. The recent impact of mathematical and statistical techniques has had a profound impact on the knowledge base available for judgement. Yet as we have seen, the application of theoretical concepts

FIG. 39.  SOME DILEMMAS FACING THE WORLD ECONOMY IN 1977

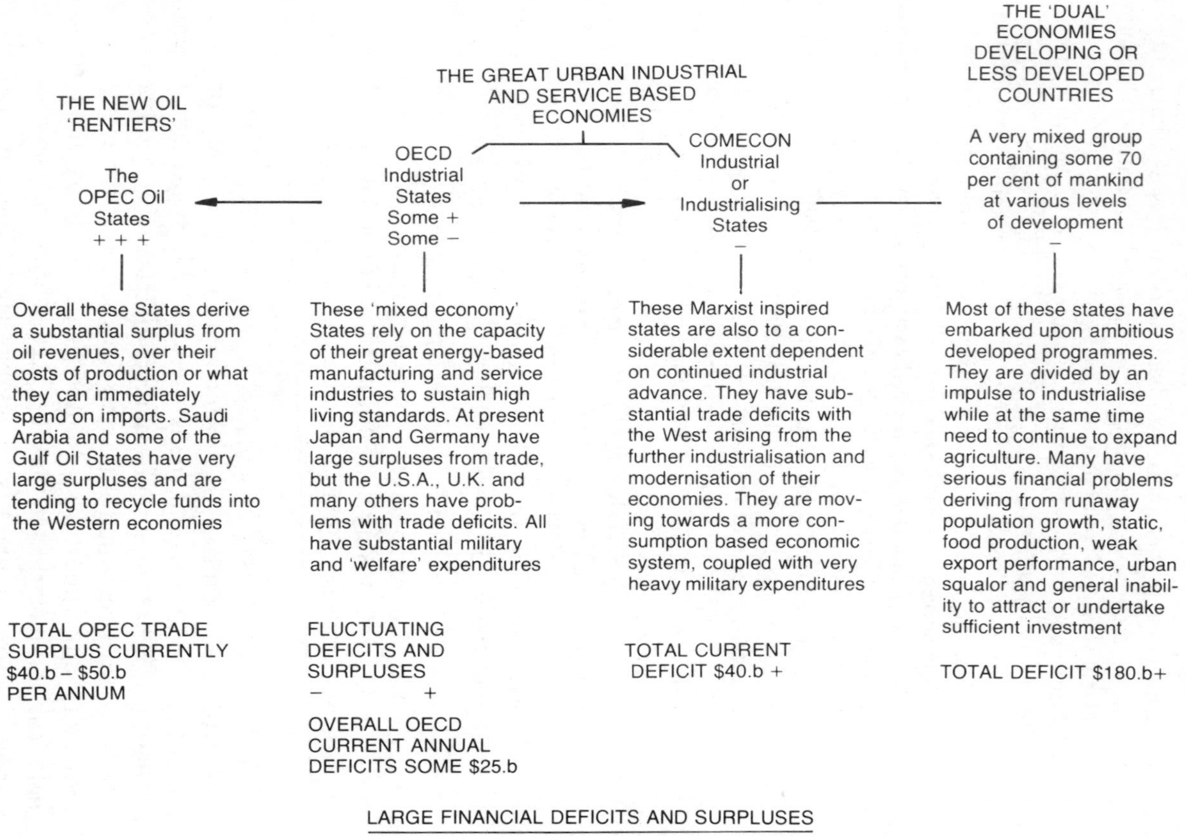

**THE 'DUAL' ECONOMIES DEVELOPING OR LESS DEVELOPED COUNTRIES**

A very mixed group containing some 70 per cent of mankind at various levels of development

Most of these states have embarked upon ambitious developed programmes. They are divided by an impulse to industrialise while at the same time need to continue to expand agriculture. Many have serious financial problems deriving from runaway population growth, static, food production, weak export performance, urban squalor and general inability to attract or undertake sufficient investment

TOTAL DEFICIT $180.b+

**THE GREAT URBAN INDUSTRIAL AND SERVICE BASED ECONOMIES**

OECD Industrial States Some + Some –

COMECON Industrial or Industrialising States –

These 'mixed economy' States rely on the capacity of their great energy-based manufacturing and service industries to sustain high living standards. At present Japan and Germany have large surpluses from trade, but the U.S.A., U.K. and many others have problems with trade deficits. All have substantial military and 'welfare' expenditures

These Marxist inspired states are also to a considerable extent dependent on continued industrial advance. They have substantial trade deficits with the West arising from the further industrialisation and modernisation of their economies. They are moving towards a more consumption based economic system, coupled with very heavy military expenditures

TOTAL CURRENT DEFICIT $40.b +

FLUCTUATING DEFICITS AND SURPLUSES
–                      +

OVERALL OECD CURRENT ANNUAL DEFICITS SOME $25.b

**THE NEW OIL 'RENTIERS'**

The OPEC Oil States + + +

Overall these States derive a substantial surplus from oil revenues, over their costs of production or what they can immediately spend on imports. Saudi Arabia and some of the Gulf Oil States have very large surpluses and are tending to recycle funds into the Western economies

TOTAL OPEC TRADE SURPLUS CURRENTLY $40.b – $50.b PER ANNUM

LARGE FINANCIAL DEFICITS AND SURPLUSES

to the contemporary world, with all the 'shades of grey' and assumptions underlying them, is still immensely difficult. Some illustration of this can be seen by looking at the nature of the present day international business and political world. Earlier in the work attention was drawn to David Ricardo's early 19th century perception of a society dividing into three main categories: landlords – who took a rent for a scarce and finite resource; capitalists – who owned and organised the means of production, and had the responsibility of investing for the future and paying wages (often in advance of work completed) to the workforce; the working classes – who toiled for a wage, which was generally at a 'subsistence' level. This assumed an infinitely elastic supply of workers at the average wage which, given the state of competition in the labour market, would equal the marginal wage. Ricardo's answer to the dilemmas of population growth and the limits of finite resources was to suggest that free trade – importing cheap foodstuffs and raw materials from abroad, and exchanging them, on the basis of the principle of comparative costs, for manufactured exports – would break the power of landlords to charge an ever-increasing rent. Indeed to a degree, this is what eventually happened, following the repeal of the Corn Laws in England, in the second half of the 19th century. However, it was a change which eventually involved a structural transformation of society – away from low income agrarian based national self-sufficiency to urban based industrial and commercial living. Britain became committed to continued international prosperity and growth for her own prosperity, and ultimate survival.

Figure 39 indicates a similar perception to the world at large, which might suggest itself today. With broad assumptions it might be considered that the present world possessors of finite resources – oil and certain key minerals and basic foodgrains – have the ability to charge a 'rent of scarcity' to the rest of the world economy. Generally the oil producing states are concentrated in the sheikhdoms of the Middle East – though it should be emphasised that certain of the trading and industrial states – the U.S.A., the Soviet Union, and increasingly Great Britain, also have substantial oil and other finite energy resources. A second category are those major urban commercial and industrial states, mainly the O.E.C.D. member countries, notably West Germany and Japan, and also certain of the more highly industrialised COMECON member states who might be equated to a middle category. They are, by the ongoing possession and creation of skilled value adding services technology and know-how, potentially able to earn a surplus for themselves. Assuming, perhaps *heroically*, that world output and trade continues to grow steadily, these types of urban and industrial societies should be able to sustain most of their populations at reasonably high living standards. However, any prolonged recession immediately reveals the 'cut-throat' nature of competition which can occur, with the densely populated island industrial economy of Japan appearing particularly vulnerable to rises in world energy raw material and food prices and any *restriction* in the growth of her world markets. Finally, a third category of states are the many less developed countries, which do not have easily available either finite resources of energy or other scarce minerals, or easy means of acquiring high technology or manufacturing techniques. In fact, some seventy per cent of mankind live in this third category of societies and a substantial body of their people, given the 'dual nature' of many such economies, are not even part of the wage earning sectors. Indeed it might be suggested that something like half of mankind is not involved significantly in the money based system at all. The question arises whether it is possible for an increasing proportion of people from this group to be drawn into industrial and commercial activities, or whether it is better, on the basis of the example provided by Communist China, Tanzania and some other countries of Africa, to encourage increased attention to maintaining the viability of 'subsistence' food producing sectors of the economy. Certainly the current tendency of the World Bank and its policies is increasingly to suggest the need to assist the less developed countries, less by providing finance for large basic projects infrastructure and suchlike, and more by directing such aid as is available to the subsistence agricultural sectors. International agencies are also advocating the need to stabilise and 'index link' commodity prices and at the same time to open up the markets of the advanced industrial economies for the products of other manufactured goods, coming increasingly from the less developed countries.

All of these issues present a series of ongoing juggling acts for mankind. At one level there appears to be a very strong technological imperative to *convergency*, both between the democratic Western industrial cum post industrial states and the Marxist centrally planned states, and also to some degree within the industrial and commercial sectors of the less developed countries. In this process the great multinational enterprise operating throughout many countries often acts as an integrating or convergency pressure. Yet it is unwise to push the convergency analogy too far: there are distinct differences of ideology, political perspective and historical tradition between the Western democratic and Marxist inspired states, which will not easily crumble away, notwithstanding the tendency for convergency in technical systems, methods of working and modes of urban living, etc. The U.S.S.R. derives many of its traditions of government and the ordering of society from highly autocratic Tsarist regimes, going back many hundreds of years. It would be fanciful to suggest that the present heirs of the system, even if they wanted to, could drastically change Russian attitudes away from a highly centralised autocratic mode of society. Within the Eastern European industrial states closer contacts with the West and traditional ideas of free will and independence are much stronger, and a tendency to convergency with patterns of behaviour in the Western social democratic economies is more apparent. No doubt they will become increasingly apparent, insofar as the Soviets are prepared to allow the process to go. In the less developed world, the difficulties of choosing which to follow are always apparent; in fact at the moment a mix-up of models is apparent. The example of the ex-colonial master may be in the heady period immediately after independence, first rejected and then rediscovered, or brought back in another form. At the same time the multinational organisation – whatever else it may do – remains a most potent force for communicating modern ideas from the capitalist industrial to the less industrialised world. Alternatively other less developed countries will feel the strong influence of Marxist ideas of various types – from post-Stalinist industrialisation programmes to Mao inspired village communes and self-help schemes.

*     *     *     *     *

Turning to look at the future and some of the challenges and shocks that it will bring, the most comprehensive and optimistic statement is a new United Nations study by Professor Wassily Leontief, *The Future of the World Economy*, published in 1977. The findings of this study, which are statistically based, are of fundamental importance to the shaping of policies throughout the world. The following summary, taken from Leontief's report, provides a fitting contemporary conclusion to this review of the development of economic doctrines and their impact on contemporary events. His principal findings have been briefly summarised as follows:

> "Target rates of growth of gross product in the developing regions, set by the International Development Strategy for the Second United Nations Development Decade, are not sufficient to start closing the income gap between the developing and the developed countries. Higher

growth rates in developing countries in the 1980s and 1990s, coupled with slightly lower rates in the developed countries (as compared to their long-term trends), would reduce, at least by half, the average income gap by 2,000.

The principal limits to sustained economic growth and accelerated development are political, social and institutional in character rather than physical. No insurmountable physical barriers exist within the twentieth century to the accelerated development of the developing regions.

The most pressing problem of feeding the rapidly increasing population of the developing regions can be solved by bringing under cultivation large areas of currently unexploited arable land and by doubling and trebling land productivity. Both tasks are technically feasible but are contingent on drastic measures of public policy favourable to such development and on social and institutional changes in the developing countries.

The problem of the supply of mineral resources for accelerated development is not a problem of absolute scarcity in the present century but, at worst, a problem of exploiting less productive and more costly deposits of minerals and of intensive exploration of new deposits, especially in the regions which are not currently known to be richly endowed with vast mineral resources, so as to reduce the unevenness in the distribution of such reserves between the various regions of the world.

With current commercially available abatement technology, pollution is not an unmanageable problem. It is technically possible to keep net emissions of pollution in the developed regions at their current levels. Full application of relatively strict abatement standards would be less of a general problem in most of the developing regions in this century and would be largely limited to abatement activites in certain industrial areas and to urban solid-waste disposal. However, even if relatively strict abatement standards were gradually applied in the developing regions, the overall economic cost of pollution abatement is not estimated to exceed 1.5–2 per cent gross product – that is, it does not present an insurmountable barrier for economic development of these regions.

Accelerated development in developing regions is possible only under the condition that from 30 to 35 per cent, and in some cases up to 40 per cent, of their gross product is used for capital investment. A steady increase in the investment ratio to these levels may necessitate drastic measures of economic policy in the field of taxation and credit, increasing the role of public investment and the public sector in production and the infrastructure. Measures leading to a more equitable income distribution are needed to increase the effectiveness of such policies. Significant social and institutional changes would have to accompany these policies.

Investment resources coming from abroad would be important but are secondary as compared to the internal sources.

Accelerated development points to the necessity of a faster growth, on the average, of heavy industry, as compared to the overall rates of expansion for the manufacturing industry. This is certainly true on the broad regional, if not on a small country, basis, increasing the possibilities of industrial co-operation between the developing countries. In many regions, however, light industry would remain a leading manufacturing sector for a long time, providing, among other things, a basis for a significant increase in the exports of manufactured products from the developing countries.

Accelerated development would lead to a continuous significant increase in the share of of the developing regions in world gross product and industrial production, as compared to the relative stagnation of these shares in recent decades. Because of the high income elasticity of the demand for imports this would certainly entail a significant increase in the share of these regions in world imports to support internal development. However, the increase in their share of world exports is expected to be slower, owing to severe supply constraints in the developing regions and the relatively slower pace at which the competitive strength of their manufacturing industries would be built up. For those reasons accelerated development poses the danger of large potential trade and payments deficits in most of the developing regions.

There are two ways out of the balance-of-payments dilemma. One is to reduce the rates of development in accordance with the balance-of-payments constraint. Another way is to close the potential payments gap by introducing changes into the economic relations between developing and developed countries, as perceived by the Declaration on the Establishment of the New International Economic Order – namely, by stabilising commodity markets, stimulating exports of manufactures from the developing countries, increasing financial transfers and so on.

A relatively stable increase in the prices of minerals and agricultural goods exported by the developing countries, as compared to prices of manufactured goods, is one way of increasing the export earnings of these countries and closing their potential payments defict. Higher mineral and agricultural prices are also called for, owing to technological requirements and the relative scarcity of natural resources, which makes them relatively more costly as time goes by. However, because of the uneven way in which mineral resources are currently distributed between various developing regions, these price changes would be of advantage to some regions, while placing an additional economic and financial burden on the others. Special schemes, providing for financial compensation to the net importing developing regions would be a possible way to reduce these imbalances.

For developing regions which are not large net exporters of minerals or agricultural goods, the main ways to reduce the potential trade imbalance is significantly to decrease their import dependence on manufactured products in the course of industrialisation, while at the same time increasing their share of world exports of some manufactured products, particularly those emanating from light industry. Building up the competitive strength of such products in the world market is an important prerequisite, combined with the reduction of tariffs and other barriers imposed on the exports of the developing regions to the developed regions. An increase in the flow of aid to the developing regions; measures to create a more favourable climate for and a better mix of capital investment flows to these regions; a reduction in the financial burden arising from foreign investment in these regions, are important but are secondary measures as compared to the necessary changes in the commodity markets and trade in manufactured products."

Finally, to ensure accelerated development, Leontief considers two general conditions are necessary: 'First, *far-reaching internal changes of a social, political and institutional character in the developing countries*; and second, significant changes in the *world economic order*. Accelerated development leading to a substantial reduction of the income gap between the developing and the developed countries can only be achieved through a combination of both these conditions. Clearly, each of them taken separately is insufficient, but when developed hand in hand, they will be able to produce the desired outcome.'

The pursuit of these many and often conflicting goals, relating as they do to hopes for material wealth and welfare on a world basis, are likely to dominate thinking and debate about economic doctrines, into the foreseeable future.

## Nobel Prize winners in Economic Science 1969–1977

The Nobel Foundation was established in 1900 to award prizes to eminent men in the fields of Physics, Chemistry, Medicine, Literature and Peace, and the award of prizes started in 1903. The need for recognising eminent men in the field of economic science was recognised by the Swedish Academy in 1969 and to date these have been as follows:

1969 – The late Ragnar Frisch (Norway) (deceased in 1973) and Jan Tinbergen (Netherlands). Both worked on the theory and applied aspects of economic development and policy. The Swedish Academy stated that they had been concerned 'with the extension of knowledge for its own sake and also in its applied aspects for the benefit of mankind'. Both were particularly associated with the development of mathematical and statistical techniques relating to economic problems.

1970 – Paul A. Samuelson (U.S.A.). A leading mathematically based economist. The Academy stated about his work on the development of new theories and for finding new applications for old theories – he has done 'more than any other economist to raise the level of scientific analysis in the field of economic theory'.

1971 – Simon Kuznets (U.S.A.). The Academy felt that quantitative precision in economic entities is a vital factor and that he had 'illuminated the facts and explained through analysis the economic growth from the middle of the last Century'. He is one of the most important of contemporary economic thinkers about the concept of national income.

1972 – Sir John Hicks (U.K.) and Kenneth J. Arrow (U.S.A.). Both economists were recognised for their 'pioneering contributions in general equilibrium theory and welfare theory'. Hicks laid the theoretical groundwork for the renewal of equilibrium theory, while Arrow followed up the theoretical models in a practical way and developed new theories on 'risk' and 'uncertainty' in business judgements.

1973 – Wassily Leontief (U.S.A.). He developed the system of input–output analysis in the 1930s. By the introduction of his simpler table, which listed on one side the sellers of goods and services, and on the other side buyers of goods and services, the detailed inter-industry analysis for an economy as a whole became more feasible. In recent times Leontief has become associated with developing models for *The Future of the World Economy* (1977) using the same techniques.

1974 – Gunnar Myrdal (Sweden) and Friedrich von Hayek (Austria). These two men were awarded the prize for their work on the theory of money and economic fluctuations and for their detailed analysis of the interdependence of economic, social and institutional phenomena. Myrdal had been concerned with macro studies including 'An American Dilemma' and 'Asian Drama'. However Hayek is better known for investigation and analysis of pure theories, and his espousal of classical ideas of free markets. Both Myrdal and Hayek were less mathematically based than previous recipients.

1975 – Leonid Kantorovich (U.S.S.R.) and Tjalling Koopmans (U.S.A.) shared the prize for their varied contributions to resource analysis. Both had 'renewed, generalised and developed methods for the analysis of classical problems of economics with regard to the optimum allocation of scarce resources to alternating ends within different economic systems'.

1976 – Milton Friedman (U.S.A.). For his contribution to the fields of consumption analysis, monetary history and theory and for his demonstration of the complexity of stabilisation policy. Friedman has long been known for his view that monetary policies, through the control of money supply are the most effective means of controlling inflation, while maintaining employment in the longer term within acceptable limits.

1977 – J. E. Meade (U.K.) and Bertil Ohlin (Sweden). Both were awarded the prize for their contribution over many years to international economic theory and policies.

# Chapter 8

# CHRONOLOGY OF EVENTS 1750–1977

"What's past is prologue."

William Shakespeare (1569–1616)
*The Tempest*

"People will not look forward to posterity who never look backward to their ancestors."

Edmund Burke (1729–1797)

"Wait and see."

Herbert Henry Asquith, Lord Oxford
(1852–1928)

"Every drop of the Thames is liquid history."

Attributed to John Burns (1858–1943)

"The inevitability of gradualness."

Sidney Webb (1859–1947)

"History is bunk."

Henry Ford (1863–1947)

"Now it is on the whole more convenient to keep history and theology apart."

Herbert George Wells (1866–1946)
*A Short History of the World*

"Time you old gypsy man,
Will you not stay?
Put up your caravan
Just for one day."

Anon.

## 1750

An age characterised by rivalry between major European powers – notably Great Britain and France – throughout the known world. Much of the iron trade was involved in the manufacture of cannons

**1756** Start of Seven Years' War

**1757** Robert Clive's (1725–1774) victory at Plassey leaves Britain supreme in India

**1759** General James Wolfe's (1727–1759) victory at Quebec leaves Britain supreme in Canada

## 1750

From 1750 onwards a new 'industrial revolution' based on a flow of new inventions, and the use of steam power, began to transform British society. It was associated with an enclosure movement in agriculture, a marked decline in infant mortality and a rapid increase in population. This led to the drift of people into small urban workshops and later factory employment. The key industries in the transformation process *became* wool and cotton textiles, coal, iron and later steel. The means of communication and transport were also improved, including roads and the beginnings of canals, in turn the same scientific and industrial developments were to gradually be introduced to other countries throughout western Europe and in the U.S.A. during the 19th century

## 1750

Politics was dominated by the interests of the great Whig land-owning families, who emphasised John Lockes' (1632–1704) ideas of individual liberty and property ownership at home, and rivalry with the absolutist regime of Louis XIV (1710–1774) of France abroad

George II (1683–1760) was the second of the Hanovarian succession. Like his father George I (1660–1727) before him he increasingly left the administration of Government to Ministers in Cabinet

## 1750

The influence of 'mercantilistic' ideas was still strong, in both domestic and overseas trade. Internally throughout Europe government and trade guild regulations controlled most commercial processes. Internationally the nation states, notably France and England, were locked in long standing trade rivalries and wars. The general belief was that trade was finite, had to be fought for and also that bullion was an important measure and store of national wealth.

New 'physiocratic' ideas were developed in France which suggested that all wealth derived from the soil and that agriculture alone yielded a 'produit net'. Denis Diderot (1713–1784) published the *Encyclopédie et Dictionnaire Raisonné des Sciences, des Arts et des Métiers*

**1758** François Quesnay (1694–1774) the leading physiocrat; published his *Tableau économique*

## WORLD POLITICS, WAR AND EXPANSION

### 1760

Britain's extensive colonial trade, regulated by the Navigation Acts, (1651–1849) provided a basis of wealth for industrial development at home

**1768**   Captain James Cook (1728–1779) commenced his great voyages of exploration to the Pacific, Antarctica and Australasia

## INDUSTRY, SCIENCE AND TECHNOLOGY

### 1760

Henry Cort (1740–1800), pioneer iron manufacturer, appointed as naval agent

**1764**   Invention of 'Spinning Jenny' by James Hargreaves (1720–1778)

**1764**   Early experiments on steam engines by James Watt (1736–1819)

**1768**   Development of water frame furthered development of 'Spinning Jenny'

**1769**   Steam engine development by Watt and Matthew Boulton (1728–1809)

| BRITISH POLITICS AND LEGISLATION | THE ECONOMISTS AND THEIR MAIN PUBLICATIONS |
|---|---|

## 1760

George III (1738–1820) succeeds as King of Great Britain and Ireland and Elector of Hanover

**1765** Sir William Blackstone (1723–1780) published *Commentaries on the Laws of England* which have had a wide influence on British society to the present day

## 1760

**1762** Jean Jacques Rousseau (1712–1778) published his *Contrat Social*

**1766** Anne-Robert-Jacques Turgot (1727–1781) published *Réflexions sur la formation et la distribution des richesses* – included discussion on 'division and productivity of labour' and competition

**1767** Sir James Stewart (1712–1780) published *Principles of Political Economy* – included ideas of finance and a theory on population which anticipated Malthus

| WORLD POLITICS, WAR AND EXPANSION | INDUSTRY, SCIENCE AND TECHNOLOGY |
|---|---|

**1770**

**1773** First Governor General of India created – Warren Hastings (1732–1818)

**1774** Death of Louis XV (1710–1774) in France

**1774** Turgot advocates a plan to restore economic stability in France

**1775** Commencement of American War of Independence

**1776** Declaration of Independence in Philadelphia, with strong influence of Benjamin Franklin's (1706–1790) ideas

**1777** Battle of Saratoga

**1778** France becomes directly involved in American War of Independence

**1778** Death of Voltaire (1694–1778) in France. His *Candide* and later satirical writings prepared the way for later French Revolution against *ancien regime*

**1779** Death of Captain Cook in Hawaii

**1770**

**1772** James Brindley's (1716–1772) Bridgwater canal introduced the canal age to Britain

**1779** Samuel Crompton (1753–1827) invented the 'Spinning Mule', which further transformed textile processes

## 1770

Growing conflicts between Tory Government of George III, supported by Lords North and Bute and Whig members about limits of power and colonial policies

**1774** John Wilkes (1725–1797), agitator and reformer, elected Lord Mayor of London and later took seat in House of Commons

**1775** A continuous preoccupation by leading political figures of what to do about the rebellion in the 13 North American colonies. The battle cry of the colonists, influenced by the political philosophies of John Locke (1632–1704) and Thomas Paine (1737–1809), being 'No taxation without representation'. The main purpose of the tax was to pay for the army of British troops, maintained in the North American colonies to fight the Indians and the French

**1778** Death of William Pitt, Earl of Chatham (1708–1778). He died in House of Lords opposing a new tax introduced in America by the Government of George III

## 1770

The beginnings of the classical *laissez-faire* school in opposition to mercantilistic ideas of central government control of trade and commerce

**1776** Adam Smith (1723–1790) publication of *An Enquiry into the Nature and Causes of the Wealth of Nations* – an attack on mercantilism and an advocacy of *laissez-faire* principles, which 'persuaded his own generation and governed the next'

**1776** Jeremy Bentham (1748–1832) published *Fragments on Government*

**1776** Edward Gibbon (1737–1794) published first volume of *Decline and Fall of Roman Empire* – a study of an earlier economic system based on conquest and slavery

## WORLD POLITICS, WAR AND EXPANSION

### 1780

Admiral Rodney's (1718–1792) victory over Spanish Fleet at Cape Finisterre

**1781** Defeat of British at Yorktown

**1782** Rodney's destruction of French Fleet off Dominica

**1783** Treaty of Versailles by which American colonists were granted independence

**1788** Magistrates in several provinces of France refused to sanction taxes unless the States General was summoned – (first time since 1614)

**1788** New South Wales colonised, as a penal settlement

**1789** Start of the French Revolution, following storming of Bastille and a history of acute economic and social grievances

## INDUSTRY, SCIENCE AND TECHNOLOGY

### 1780

Richard Arkwright (1732–1792) patents the 'Spinning Mule' which enabled steam power to be applied to spinning

**1780** Beginnings of major developments in iron industry, including smelting with coke and puddling and rolling

**1783** Montgolfier brothers, Joseph (1740–1810) and Jacques (1745–1799), fly first hot air balloon

## BRITISH POLITICS AND LEGISLATION

## THE ECONOMISTS AND THEIR MAIN PUBLICATIONS

**1780**

A period of recovery following turmoil of the previous decade. The Prince of Wales (1762–1830) (Prinny to his friends) emerges as a brilliant man of fashion and to some extent as a leader of opposition to his father's policies

**1787** Creation of Government funded debt known as 'Consolidated Stock' or Consuls

**1780**

**1787**  Bentham: *Defence of Usury*

## WORLD POLITICS, WAR AND EXPANSION

## INDUSTRY, SCIENCE AND TECHNOLOGY

**1790**

**1791** Louis XVI (1754–1793) and family arrested in France

**1792** War between revolutionary France and Prussia and Austria

**1793** Execution of Louis XVI of France and beginning of reign of terror

**1793** Commencement of Revolutionary and Napoleonic Wars which dominated European life to 1815

**1794** Earl Howe (1726–1799) defeats French Fleet, on the Glorious First of June

**1794** Executions of the revolutionaries Danton (1759–1794) and Robespierre (1758–1794) in France

**1795** Napoleon Bonaparte (1769–1821) defeats French counter revolutionaries

**1796** Death of Catherine the Great in Russia (1729–1796)

**1797** John Jervis (first Earl St. Vincent) destroys French Fleet off St. Vincent

**1798** Irish rebellion

**1798** Horatio Nelson (1758–1805) destroys French Fleet at Battle of the Nile

**1790**

**1796** Dr. Edward Jenner (1749–1823) introduces vaccination against smallpox

| BRITISH POLITICS AND LEGISLATION | THE ECONOMISTS AND THEIR MAIN PUBLICATIONS |
|---|---|

## BRITISH POLITICS AND LEGISLATION

**1790**

Edmund Burke (1729–1797) published *Reflections on the Revolution in France*

**1795** Speenhamland system attempts reform of poor law system, by relating labourers' wages to price of corn

**1799** First Income Tax introduced by William Pitt the Younger (1759–1806) as a wartime measure. Repealed in 1816

## THE ECONOMISTS AND THEIR MAIN PUBLICATIONS

**1790**

**1793** William Godwin (1756–1836) published *Enquiry Concerning the Principles of Political Justice and its Influence on General Virtue and Happiness*

**1798** Publication by Thomas Malthus (1766–1834) of *Essay on The Principle of Population as it Affects the Future Improvement of Society*

## WORLD POLITICS, WAR AND EXPANSION

## INDUSTRY, SCIENCE AND TECHNOLOGY

### 1800

Napoleon Bonaparte assumes complete control in France

**1801**  Battle of Copenhagen routs French and Danish Fleets

**1801**  Thomas Jefferson (1743–1826) becomes President of U.S.A. and encourages Western expansion

**1804**  Napoleon  proclaimed Emperor of the French

**1805**  Mehemet Ali (1769–1841) became Viceroy of Égypt

**1805**  British triumphant under Viscount Horatio Nelson at Battle of Trafalgar

**1805**  Defeat of Austria and Russia by Napoleon at Austerlitz

**1806**  Defeat of Prussia by Napoleon at Jena

**1806**  Formation of Napoleon's Continental Alliance against Great Britain

### 1800

Much of industrial activity was devoted to demands of war economy in Britain and throughout Western Europe; iron goods went to cannons, boots to armies, textiles to military uniforms. Later the techniques acquired for war-time purposes were also to find an application in peace-time markets

| BRITISH POLITICS AND LEGISLATION | THE ECONOMISTS AND THEIR MAIN PUBLICATIONS |
|---|---|

## BRITISH POLITICS AND LEGISLATION

**1800**

William Wilberforce's (1759–1833) Bill abolishes slave trade in British Empire

**1801**   Act of Union with Ireland. Irish M.P.s to Westminster

**1802**   Factories Act reduced some child employment

## THE ECONOMISTS AND THEIR MAIN PUBLICATIONS

**1800**

For the next few decades much economic writing reflected a persistent concern with 'population and land questions'. How to feed and employ a rapidly growing population became a critical debate

**1803**   Second Edition of Malthus' *Essay on Population*

**1806**   Malthus appointed a Professor of Political Economy at Haileybury College – a training school for the East India Company

## 1810

**1811**  Simon Bolivar (1783–1830) began revolt against Spanish Government in Venezuela

**1812**  Napoleon invaded Russia

**1813**  Napoleon defeated at Battle of Leipzig

**1814**  Napoleon abdicated and was exiled to Elba

**1814**  Establishment of Cape Colony

**1815**  Napoleon returned to France for '100 days'

**1815**  British and Allied Victory over Napoleon at Waterloo

**1815**  Napoleon exiled to St. Helena

**1815**  Restoration in France with Louis XVIII (1755–1824)

**1815**  Congress of Vienna establishes European political system for next 100 years

**1817**  Bernardo O'Higgins (1778–1842) defeats the Spanish in Chile

**1817**  President James Monroe (1758–1831) of U.S.A. declares Monroe doctrine concerning the Americas

**1818**  Jean Baptiste Bernadotte (1763–1845) became King of Sweden

**1819**  Stamford Raffles (1781–1826) founded Singapore

## 1810

**1813**  2,400 power looms in cotton textile industry compared to some 250,000 hand looms

**1815**  'Enclosure movement' in Agriculture largely complete. Only downland and moorland left free

**1815**  Invention of miner's safety lamp by Humphry Davy (1778–1829)

## 1810

**1811–13** Widespread political unrest in depressed agricultural areas. Luddites in East Midlands and Yorkshire smash machines

**1815** Peace in Europe was followed by beginnings of an economic slump in Britain and great social distress

**1815** Corn laws introduced strengthening home agriculture by preventing cheap food grain imports

**1815–17** Further political unrest in Eastern counties

**1816** Spar Fields riots

**1817** Suspension of Habeas Corpus

**1819** The Peterloo 'Massacre'

**1819** Gag Acts increased power of magistrates

## 1810

David Ricardo: *The High Price of Bullion*

**1814** Robert Owen (1771–1858) set up model factory in Manchester. Later moved to New Lanark in Scotland, and New Harmony in Indiana, U.S.A.

**1814** Jean-Baptiste Say (1767–1832) sent by French Government to study economic conditions in Britain. Published as *De l'Angleterre et des Anglais*

**1815** Robert Torrens (1780–1864) published essay *On External Corn Trade*

**1815** Malthus: *An Enquiry into the Nature and Progress of Rent*

**1815** Ricardo: *Essay on the Influence of a Low Price of Corn on the Profits of Stock*

**1816** Ricardo: *Proposals for an Economical and Secure Currency*

**1817** Malthus: *The Poor Law*

**1817** Ricardo: *The Principles of Political Economy and Taxation*

**1819** Jean Sismondi (1773–1842) published: *Nouveaux Principes d'économie politique* – suggested 'overproduction' and 'crisis' were inevitable

## WORLD POLITICS, WAR AND EXPANSION

### 1820

The decade was marked by relative stability in Europe, but revolutions supported by Britain throughout South America threw off the final vestiges of Spanish and Portuguese colonial rule

**1821** Brazil becomes independent

**1822** Dom Pedro I (1798–1834) becomes Emperor of Brazil

**1824** Charles X (1757–1836) becomes King of France and institutes reactionary policies

**1829** Greece achieves independence following prolonged revolutionary war

## INDUSTRY, SCIENCE AND TECHNOLOGY

### 1820

A decade marked by the application of *laissez-faire* doctrines and by continuous attempts to adjust society to new industry and technology

**1825** Stockton to Darlington railway

**1827** John Loudon McAdam (1756–1836) made Surveyor General of Roads and his ideas for improved roads extended widely

**1829** Robert Stephenson (1803–1859) demonstrated 'The Rocket' and introduced railway age

| BRITISH POLITICS AND LEGISLATION | THE ECONOMISTS AND THEIR MAIN PUBLICATIONS |
|---|---|

## 1820

In Britain between 1820 and 1850 the 'Manchester school' were active in promoting *laissez-faire* ideas and advocating the Anti-Corn Law League. Their leaders came to include John Bright (1811–1889) and Richard Cobden (1809–1865), inspired by Ricardian ideas

**1820** Cato Street conspiracy

**1821** Census of population 15.5 million

**1821** Government regulations regarding wool and linen industries removed

**1822** Political unrest in East Anglia

**1822** George Canning (1770–1827) becomes Foreign Secretary and supports independence movements abroad

**1825** 20 per cent reduction in tariffs, and navigation laws amended

**1826** Joint Stock Company banks permitted, but limited liability did not apply until 1858

**1829** Catholic emancipation

**1829** Foundation of Metropolitan Police by Sir Robert Peel (1788–1850)

**1829** Daniel O'Connell (1775–1847) takes seat in Parliament and begins Irish Home Rule Movement

## 1820

**1821** James Mill (1773–1836) published: *Elements of Political Economy*

**1821** Torrens: Essay on: *The Production of Wealth*

**1823** Thomas Joblin: *Outlines of a System of Political Economy*

**1823** Bentham: *Principles and Morals of Legislation* – the test of the 'greatest happiness of the greatest number'

**1825** John Ramsay McCulloch (1789–1864) published: *Principles of Political Economy*

**1825** Bentham: *Manual of Political Economy*

**1826** Johann Heinrich von Thünen (1783–1850): *Der Isolierte Staat in Beziehung auf Landswirtschaft und Nationalokonomie* – a publication on land use and location theories

**1826** Henry Drummond: *Elementary Propositions on the Currency*

**1827** Malthus: *Definitions of Political Economy*

**1827** Freidrich List, a German economist (1789–1846) published: *Outlines of American Political Economy*

| WORLD POLITICS, WAR AND EXPANSION | INDUSTRY, SCIENCE AND TECHNOLOGY |
|---|---|

**1830**

Charles X overthrown in French Revolution of July

**1833** Prussia, together with four other leading German states, withdrew tariffs against each other and established a customs union – 'the Zollverein'

**1830**

Second phase of 'industrial revolution' with widening of markets and improved transport facilities, etc., especially associated with the development of the railway system

**1830** Liverpool to Manchester railway line constructed by Robert Stephenson

**1830** 50 per cent of British exports cotton yarns and goods. 20 per cent other textiles, 11 per cent iron and steel manufactures

**1831** Invention of the dynamo by Michael Faraday (1791–1867)

**1835–37** 'Little railway mania'

**1837** Beginning of major improvements in agriculture production

**1838** Foundation of Royal Agricultural Society

**1838** Transatlantic steamship by Isambard Kingdom Brunel (1806–1859)

**1839** Fox Talbot (1800–1877) developed photography

## BRITISH POLITICS AND LEGISLATION

**1830**

John Doherty's (1797?–1854) National Association for protection of labour

**1830** Political unrest throughout Eastern and Southern counties

**1831** Truck Act – prevented payment of wages in kind

**1832** The great Parliamentary Reform Bill

**1833** Abolition of slavery in the British Empire

**1833** Factory Act sought to reform practices in textile industry

**1834** The Tolpuddle Martyrs

**1834** The poor Law Amendment Act – sought to reform administration of Poor Law Outdoor Relief, etc.

**1834** Robert Owen (1771–1858) formed abortive Grand National Consolidated Trade Union

**1837** Queen Victoria(1819–1901) accedes to the throne

**1839** The Chartist Movement presents first petition to Parliament of desired reforms: including universal manhood suffrage, equal election districts, vote by ballot, annual Parliaments, abolition of property qualification for M.P.s, payment for M.P.s. The Chartist Petition was rejected following riots and the movement declined in the 1840s, though its ideas lived on in subsequent reforms

**1830**

The writing of leading economists reflected a growing desire to establish a deductive 'scientific basis' for political economy

**1832** Thomas Ward introduces the 'currency principle' vis-a-vis the 'banking school'. The beginning of a long debate about relationship of bullion reserves to note issue by the Bank of England

**1836** Professor Nassau Senior (1790–1864) published: *An Outline of the Science of Political Economy* – regarded economics as a purely deductive science

**1837** Torrens: *Letters to Lord Melbourne* – a leading statement of the 'currency principle' which led to the Bank Charter Act 1844

**1838** Antoine-Augustin Cournot (1801–1877) published, *Recherches sur les principes mathématiques de la théorie des richesses* – the founder of modern mathematical economics

## WORLD POLITICS, WAR AND EXPANSION

### 1840

**1848** Overthrow of King Louis Philippe (1773–1848) in France

**1848** Revolutionary turmoil throughout Europe had profound effect on development of political, social and economic ideas

**1848** Gold discovered in California, leads to rapid westward expansion of U.S.A.

**1849** Plebiscite for presidency of France elects Louis Napoleon III (1808–1873) as President

## INDUSTRY, SCIENCE AND TECHNOLOGY

### 1840

The continued expansion of the railway system gave great boost to the development of the British and other economies

**1842** Super phosphate patented

**1842** Peruvian guano fertiliser imports begin

**1843** Invention of clay drainpipe

**1843** Foundation of Rothampstead experimental agricultural station

**1843** Samuel Morse's (1791–1872) code accepted by U.S. Government

**1844** Brunel's Iron Screwdriver steamship

**1845–47** Gigantic 'railway mania' creates vast railway system

**1845–49** U.K. wheat imports average 49,400 cwt.

**1846** Royal College of Agriculture, Cirencester, founded – helped to popularise science in context of agriculture

**1846** Government grants to improve agricultural drainage

**1847** Dr. James Simpson (1811–1870) pioneers chloroform

## BRITISH POLITICS AND LEGISLATION

### 1840

Introduction of Rowland Hill's (1795–1879) penny post

**1841** Census of population 20.2 million

**1842** Mines Act restricted use of women and children underground

**1842** Second Chartist petition to Parliament

**1842** Income Tax re-introduced, but reduced duties on many imports

**1843** Poor Law – outdoor labour test reform

**1843–44** Political unrest in East Midlands and Eastern counties

**1844** The Rochdale Pioneers established commercial aspects of the co-operative movement

**1844** Factory Act extended education for children

**1844** Bank Charter Act, based on views of 'currency school' about relationship of bullion to note issue

**1845** Irish potato famine and mass starvation and exodus abroad

**1846** Sir Robert Peel's (1788–1850) repeal of the Corn Laws, allowing import of cheap food grains from abroad – but British grain growing agriculture remained highly prosperous to the 1870s

**1847** Poor Law replaced by Government department

**1847** 10 Hours Act restricted hours of work by women and young persons

**1847** Gold standard suspended as an emergency measure

*Continued in next column*

## THE ECONOMISTS AND THEIR MAIN PUBLICATIONS

### 1840

**1841** List: *The National System of Political Economy* (emphasised importance of nation state in economic development)

**1843** William Roscher (1817–1894): *Outline of Political Economy According to the Historical Method* – the beginning of a great debate between the deductive and historical schools

**1843** John Stuart Mill (1806–1873) published: *System of Logic*

**1844** Mill: *Essays on some Important Questions in Political Economy* (originally written in 1829)

**1845** Friedrich Engels (1820–1894) published: *Conditions of the Working Classes in England*

**1847** Karl Marx (1818–1883) published first contribution to economics as *La misère de la philosophie*

**1848** Mill: *Principles of Political Economy including ideas on* 'The Stationary State'

**1848** Marx and Friedrich Engels published: *The Communist Manifesto*, including ideas of inevitable evolution from primitive society, to slavery, feudalism, capitalism, and later to socialism and pure communism

---

*British Politics and Legislation cont.*

**1848** Third Chartist petition to Parliament

**1848** Public Health Act created Central Board of Health

**1849** Repeal of Navigation Acts

# WORLD POLITICS, WAR AND EXPANSION

## 1850

Gold discovered in Australia

**1850** World population 1 billion

**1851** Louis Napoleon (1808–1873) seized power in France

**1852** Napoleon III established the Second Empire in France following his coup d'état

**1853** Commodore Matthew Perry (1794–1858) opened Japan to East–West trade

**1854** The two-year Crimean War starts

**1854** Ferdinand de Lesseps (1805–1894) obtains concession from Said Pasha to construct Suez Canal

**1857** The Anglo-French War against China is ended by the Treaty of Tientsin, which confers economic rights on foreigners

**1857** Indian Mutiny begins

**1858** Count Cavour (1810–1861) plots with Napoleon III to drive the Austrians out of Italy

**1859** Work on Suez Canal commences

# INDUSTRY, SCIENCE AND TECHNOLOGY

## 1850

200,000 coal miners produce 49 million tons of coal

**1850** Prohibition on the export of machinery and textile exports lifted

**1850** 40 per cent British exports cotton yarn and goods, 22 per cent other textiles, 13 per cent iron and steel manufactures

**1850** 224,000 power looms in cotton textile industry compared to 50,000 hand looms

**1850** The beginning of an era of 'High Farming'

**1851** The Great Exhibition in London demonstrated Britain's industrial leadership at that time – truly a workshop of the world

**1851** Sir Joseph Paxton's (1801–1865) Crystal Palace – the first major prefabricated cast iron structure

**1856** Henry Bessemer (1813–1898) invented his converter to make pig iron into steel

**1857** Louis Pasteur (1822–1895) began his pioneering study of fermentation

**1858** Rudolf Virchow (1821–1902) published his work on cellular pathology

**1859** Charles Darwin (1809–1882) completed the *Origin of Species*

## 1850

The high point of *laissez-faire* philosophy and policies

**1850** Abolition of system of colonial preferences

**1850** Mines Act – inspectors' powers extended

**1850** Ten Hours Act

**1851** Amalgamated Society of Engineers formed

**1857** Penal Servitude Act – abolished transportation to Australia

**1857** Gold standard again suspended as an emergency measure

## 1850

The following two decades were to be characterised by strong economic upswing for the British economy and the apparent triumph of the classical *laissez-faire* over the Marxist inspired historical deterministic model of political economy

**1850** Herbert Spencer (1820–1903): *Social Statics*

**1854** Professor Wilhelm Roscher published: *System der Volkswirtschaft* – historical interpretation of classical economics

**1856** Thomas Tooke (1774–1858) published: *History of Prices and State of Circulation During the Years 1793–1826* – an opponent of tariffs and supporter of 'banking school'

**1857** Professor J. E. Cairnes (1823–1875): *Character and Logical Method of Political Economy* – part of a controversy with Mill and Senior over scope and method of economics

**1857** Marx: *Critique of Political Economy* – contained essence of ideals later included in 3 vols of *Das Kapital*

**1859** J. S. Mill: publishes *On Liberty*

## WORLD POLITICS, WAR AND EXPANSION

### 1860

Russia establishes the Far Eastern city of Vladivostok

**1860** The Kingdom of Italy is established

**1861** Napoleon III begins his six-year campaign to conquer Mexico

**1861** Beginning of Civil War in U.S.A.

**1862** U.S.A. First trans-continental railway sanctioned

**1862** The first French annexations in Cochin China took place

**1862** 'Serfdom' abolished in Russia

**1862** Prince Otto von Bismarck (1815–1898) becomes Minister-President in Germany

**1862** U.S.A. Homestead Acts encouraged Westward migration

**1862** Bismarck becomes Minister-President of Prussia

**1863** Battle of Gettysburg

**1863** Abolition of slavery in U.S.A.

**1863** Insurrections in Poland inspired Socialists throughout Europe

**1864** Prussia declared war on Denmark over Schleswig-Holstein

**1864** A British trading company completes the first Persian telegraph

**1864** *The International* formed, at a meeting of European workers held in London

**1865** End of Civil War in U.S.A.

*Continued in next column*

## INDUSTRY, SCIENCE AND TECHNOLOGY

### 1860

A further decade of strong upswing for the British economy, based on rising population at home and expanding markets abroad

**1861** Ernest Solvay patents a soda-making process which drastically reduces the cost of manufacturing textiles, glass and soap

**1862** The beginning of a period of rising real wages until mid 1870s

**1864** Karl Siemens (1823–1883) and Martin introduced the open-hearth process for making steel

**1865** Joseph Lister (1827–1912) introduced antiseptic surgery

**1866** Dynamite is patented by Alfred Nobel (1833–1896)

**1866** The first transatlantic cable is laid

**1867** Werner von Siemens (1816–1892) introduces his dynamo for generating electricity

---

*World Politics, War and Expansion cont.*

**1866** The Seven Weeks' War is fought at the Battle of Königgrätz between Prussia and Austria

**1867** Dominion of Canada formed

**1869** The Social Democratic Working Men's Party is founded in Germany

**1869** The Suez Canal is opened, cutting the distance between Europe and the East

| BRITISH POLITICS AND LEGISLATION | THE ECONOMISTS AND THEIR MAIN PUBLICATIONS |
|---|---|

## BRITISH POLITICS AND LEGISLATION

**1860**

**1861** Census of population 24.5 million

**1866** Gold standard again suspended as an emergency measure

**1867** Parliamentary Reform Act

**1868** Formation of Trade Union Congress

**1868** Benjamin Disraeli's (1804–1881) first Ministry

**1868** William Ewart Gladstone (1809–1898) forms first Ministry

## THE ECONOMISTS AND THEIR MAIN PUBLICATIONS

**1860**

Walter Bagshot (1826–1877) became Editor of *The Economist*

**1864** Professor W. S. Jevons (1835–1882) published: *The Coal Question* – a study of diminishing returns in the exploitation of a finite natural resource

**1867** Marx completes Volume I of *Das Kapital* (includes important sections on commodities and money, money into capital, surplus value, wage labour and accumulation)

**1869** Bagshot: *Universal Money*

**1869** William Thomas Thornton (1813–1880) published: *On Labour* – criticised concept of the 'wages fund'

## WORLD POLITICS, WAR AND EXPANSION

### 1870

The Franco-Prussian War began

**1870** Germany annexed Alsace-Lorraine, including iron ore from France

**1870** Rome joined Italian union

**1871** Henry Morten Stanley (1841–1904) finds Livingstone in Africa

**1871** The Paris Commune seeks to set up a revolutionary government in Paris

**1871** The German Empire is established. France forms its Third Republic

**1872** Last meeting of The Socialist International, held at The Hague

**1873** The Three Emperors' League is formed by Austria, Russia and Germany

**1875** Great Britain purchases controlling shares in the Suez Canal

**1875** Gotha Congress of German Socialists

**1876** Alfonso XII (1857–1885) ascends the Spanish throne

**1877** The Russo-Turkish War begins

**1878** The Congress of Berlin reviews terms imposed by Russia on Turkey at end of Russo/Turkish wars

**1878** The International Congo Association is formed by King Leopold II (1835–1909) of Belgium, with Henry Morton Stanley and private financiers

*Continued in next column*

## INDUSTRY, SCIENCE AND TECHNOLOGY

### 1870

Growing awareness of power of overseas competition, especially Germany, France and the U.S.A. Also a growing tendency for unemployment to increase and for profitability to fall

**1870** 36 per cent British exports cotton yarn and goods, 19 per cent other textiles, 17 per cent iron and steel manufactures

**1871** Dmitri Mendeleev (1834–1907) discovers gallium to add to his Periodic Table of the Elements

**1871** Charles Darwin (1809–1882) publishes his controversial *Descent of Man*

**1873** James Clerk Maxwell's (1831–1879) study on electricity and magnetism appears

**1873** Imports of grain from North America and Russia had increasingly severe impact on agricultural prosperity

**1876** Nikolaus Otto (1832–1891) develops the four-stroke internal combustion engine

**1876** Alexander Graham Bell (1847–1922) invented the telephone

**1878** Real wage increases restricted by recession in trade

**1878** Louis Pasteur (1822–1895) lectures on his germ theory at the Academy of Medicine in Paris

**1878** Gilchrist-Thomas process of steel making

*World Politics, War and Expansion cont.*

**1879** The Dual Alliance is formed between Germany and Austria-Hungary

## BRITISH POLITICS AND LEGISLATION

### 1870

Increasing government involvement with problems of industry

**1870** Foster's Education Act allowed elementary education for girls as well as boys

**1870** Married Women's Property Act enabled women to retain earnings

**1871** Trade Union Act recognised legality of trade unions

**1871** Criminal Law Amendment Act recognised right to strike

**1873** The onset of slower growth and the Great Depression which bore especially harshly on agricultural regions and which lasted to 1896

**1874** Disraeli's second Ministry

**1875** Right to picket peacefully recognised

**1876** Sandon's Act established school attendance committees

**1879** Economic Boycott – named after a Captain Charles Boycott, with whom the Irish refused to deal in land tenure disturbances

### 1870

From the 1870s onwards neoclassical 'marginal analysis' became an important part of theory, developed both in Britain and by the 'Austrian school' in Vienna and elsewhere

**1871** W. S. Jevons *Theory of Political Economy* – this included the concept of marginal utility

**1871** Carl Menger (1840–1921) published: *Grundsätze der Volkswirtschaftslehre* – included a theory of marginal utility

**1873** Bagshot: *Lombard Street*

**1876** Bagshot: *Postulates of English Political Economy*

**1879** Professor Alfred Marshall (1842–1924) published: *Economics of Industry*

**1879** Also: *The Pure Theory of Foreign Trade*

**1879** Henry George (1839–1897) published: *Progress and Poverty*

## WORLD POLITICS, WAR AND EXPANSION

**1880**

Commencement of First Boer War

**1881** The Emperor Alexander II (1818–1881) assassinated by 'The People's Will', a Russian terrorist society, and Alexander III (1845–1894) ascended the throne and sought to crush 'Liberalism'

**1881** The French occupied Tunis

**1882** Italy joined Germany and Austro-Hungary to form the Triple Alliance

**1882** The British occupied Egypt

**1883** Bismarck established social welfare measures in Germany

**1884** Trade unions were legalised in France

**1884** Germany established colonies in East Africa

**1885** Bismarck called the Berlin Conference on the future of Africa

**1885** Death of General Gordon in the Sudan

**1886** Burma is annexed by the British

**1888** German Emperor Wilhelm I (1797–1888) died and was succeeded by Wilhelm II (1859–1949)

## INDUSTRY, SCIENCE AND TECHNOLOGY

**1880s**

The Great Depression (from 1873–1896) influenced the prosperity of many traditional trades

**1880** 500,000 coal miners produced 147 million tons of coal

**1882** Robert Koch (1843–1910) isolates the bacillus of tuberculosis

**1884** Charles Parsons (1854–1931) developed a steam turbine

**1885** Beginning of recovery of growth in real wages

**1885** U.K. wheat imports 280,600 cwt.

**1885** Hiram Maxim (1840–1916) invented the machine gun

**1885** Gottlieb Daimler (1839–1900) produced first car

**1886** Aluminium is made by an electrolytic process for the first time

**1887** Building of Eiffel Tower in Paris for Great Exhibition marked beginning for France of 'La Belle Epoque'

**1888** John Dunlop (1840–1921) produced his pneumatic tyre

**1889** Friese-Greene developed cinema photography

### 1880

Mondella's Education Act endorsed compulsory attendance at school

**1881** Census of population 31 million

**1882** Married Women's Property Act enabled women to own property separately from their husbands

**1884–85** Further Parliamentary Reform Act

**1886** Royal Commission depressed state of trade and industry – expressed concern about 'diminution of profitability' and 'declining employment' for labouring classes

**1888** Matchgirls' strike organised by Annie Bessant (1846–1933)

**1889** Dockworkers' strike led by Ben Tillett (1860–1943)

---

*The Economists and Their Main Publications cont.*

**1889** John A. Hobson (1858–1940) published *Psychology of Industry* with A. E. Mummery

### 1880

A continuing debate, especially in Germany and Austria, between those following Gustav Schmoller (1838–1917), who emphasised the 'historical method' as opposed to those led by Carl Menger (1840–1921) who emphasised the 'deductive approach'

**1881** Professor Francis Y. Edgeworth (1845–1926) published: *Mathematical Physics* – a pioneer work on statistics and mathematics in theory

**1883** Professor Henry Sidgwick (1838–1900) published: *Principles of Political Economy* – indicates a strong interest in social problems

**1884** Spencer: *The Man versus the State*

**1884** Professor E. von Bohm-Bawerk (1851–1914) published: *Capital and Interest*

**1884** Jevons: *Investigations in Currency and Finance*

**1884** Professor Thorold Rogers (1823–1890) published: *Six Centuries in Work and Wages*

**1885** Marx: Second volume of *Das Kapital* published posthumously by Engels – includes important section on circulation

**1885** John Bates Clark (1847–1938): *The Philosophy of Wealth*

**1888** Rogers: *Economic Interpretation of History*

**1889** Bohm-Bawerk: *Private Theory of Capital* relates marginal utility more closely to theory of interest

*Continued in previous column*

## WORLD POLITICS WAR AND EXPANSION

### 1890

U.S.A. Sherman Anti-Trust Act declared trusts illegal

1890 Bismarck is dismissed, assuring Hohenzollern authority

1890 Felix Méline, French cabinet head, introduces a customs tariff in France

1894 The Dreyfus case began in France

1895 New gold developments in South Africa and Australia stimulate economic activity throughout the industrial world

1896 The Italians were defeated in Ethiopa

1899 The Boer War started in South Africa between English and Afrikaners

1899 The Boxer Rebellion occurred in China, and was put down by the European powers, Japan and the United States

1899 The first Hague Peace Conference was held

## INDUSTRY, SCIENCE AND TECHNOLOGY

### 1890

Increased awareness of problems presented by scale of industry, of monopolistic tendencies, and of large trade unions for *laissez-faire* doctrines and policy

1890 Growing awareness of increased competition from U.S.A. and Germany for manufactured goods

1890 An all-steel bridge is completed over the Firth of Forth

1895 Wilhelm Rontgen (1845–1923) discovered X-rays

1895 F. W. Lanchester (1868–1946) introduced first British car

1895 Guglielmo Marconi (1874–1937) invented the wireless

1897 Charles Parsons (1854–1931) produced first steam turbine ship

1897 Rudolf Diesel (1858–1913) patented the diesel engine

1898 Radium is discovered by the Curies, Pierre (1859–1906) Marie (1867–1934)

## 1890

**1894** Sir William Harcourt's (1827–1904) Estate Duty – marked beginning of 'progressive principle' in British tax system

**1896** The beginning of recovery from the Great Depression – (1873–96)

## 1890

Marshall: *The Principles of Economics* – this work marked a reconciliation between ideas deeply imbued with earlier classical approaches and those, introduced to Britain by Jevons, which embraced the 'marginal utility' approach to economic knowledge

**1893** Professor Edwin Cannan (1861–1935) published: *A Theory of the Production and History of Distribution*

**1894** Marx: Third volume of *Das Kapital* published posthumously (including important sections on profit, credit and rent)

**1894** Sir Robert Palgrave (1827–1919) edited: *Dictionary of Political Economy*

**1897** Edgeworth: *Theory of Monopoly*

**1898** Professor Léon Walras (1834–1910) published: *Etudes d'Economie Politique Appliquée* – analysed conditions of general equilibrium

**1899** Professor Thorstein Veblen (1857–1929): *The Theory of The Leisure Class*

**1899** J. B. Clark: *The Distribution of Wealth*

## 1900

Italy's King Humbert I (1844–1900) assassinated and succeeded by Victor Emmanuel III (1869–1947)

**1901** Queen Victoria died and King Edward VII (1841–1910) ascended the throne

**1901** Commonwealth of Australia formed

**1903** The Russian Socialist groups, Bolshevik and Menshevik, split over doctrine

**1904** The Trans-Siberian Railway completed by the Russians

**1904** The *Anglo-French Entente* created

**1904** The Russo-Japanese War began

**1905** Revolution broke out in Russia, but suppressed by Tsarist regime

**1907** The Triple Entente is created between Britain, France and Russia

**1907** Dominion status for New Zealand

**1908** The Young Turks' Revolt sought to rejuvenate the Ottoman Empire

**1908** The Congo Free State became the Belgian Congo

## 1900

Period marked by continued rapid expansion of the U.S.A. and German industrial capacity

**1900** British real wages estimated to be 84 per cent above those of 1850

**1900** Max Planck (1858–1947) presented his quantum theory

**1900** Sigmund Freud's (1856–1939) ideas of psychology and personality have a wide impact

**1901** The first message is sent over Marconi's transatlantic wireless telegraph

**1903** The Wright brothers, Wilbur (1867–1912), Orville (1871–1948), made their first aeroplane flight

**1903** Curies shared Nobel Prize for Physics

**1905** Albert Einstein (1879–1955) presented his theory of relativity

**1907** Henri Bergson (1859–1941) published: *Creative Evolution*

**1909** Louis Bleriot (1872–1936) made the first aeroplane flight across the English Channel

*British Politics and Legislation cont.*

**1909** David Lloyd George's (1863–1945) First Social Security Budget

**1909** Osborne judgement sought to deprive unions of Parliamentary representation by making political levy illegal

**1909** Road Fund created, financed by taxes on motorists

## BRITISH POLITICS AND LEGISLATION

### 1900

Growing awareness of social and political problems associated with unequal income distribution. Nevertheless a period of economic growth – the 'Edwardian Indian' Summer!

**1901** Census of population 38.2 million

**1901** Taff Vale judgements threatened to make strike weapon useless

**1902** Prime Minister A. J. Balfour (1848–1930), Conservative and Unionist Government elected

**1902** Balfour's Education Act extended educational system

**1903** Foundation of Women's Social and Political Union by Mrs. Emmeline Pankhurst (1858–1928). This led to militant suffragette movement

**1903** Joseph Chamberlain (1836–1914) started campaign for 'Imperial Tariff Preferences'

**1905** Prime Minister Sir Henry Campbell-Bannerman (1836–1908), Liberal Government elected

**1906** Trade Disputes Act under which unionists could strike and union would not be liable for damage

**1906** Beginnings of major new Dreadnought ship building programme to counter new German High Seas Fleet

**1908** Prime Minister H. H. Asquith (1852–1928), a Liberal Government with Labour support

*Continued in previous column*

## THE ECONOMISTS AND THEIR MAIN PUBLICATIONS

### 1900

**1901** Professor Knut Wicksell (1851–1926) published: *Lectures in Political Economy*

**1902** Professor Werner Sombart (1863–1941) published: *Der Moderne Kapitalismus* – an important work in the German historical school

**1904** Veblen: *Theory of Business Enterprise*

**1904** Marx: Tripartite Fourth volume of *Das Kapital* published posthumously between 1904–1910 (including full treatment of Theories of Surplus Value)

**1904** Cannan: *The Wealth of Nations*

**1904** Edgeworth: *Theory of Distribution*

**1906** Professor Irving Fisher (1867–1947): *Nature of Capital and Income*

**1906** Vilfriedo Pareto (1843–1923) published: *Manuale di Economica Politica* – included concept of indifference curve

**1907** Fisher: *Rate of Interest*

**1907** J. B. Clark: *Essentials of Economic Theory*

**1909** William Henry Beveridge (1879–1963) published: *Unemployment – a Problem of Industry*

**1909** Hobson: *The Industrial System*

| WORLD POLITICS, WAR AND EXPANSION | INDUSTRY, SCIENCE AND TECHNOLOGY |
|---|---|

## WORLD POLITICS, WAR AND EXPANSION

**1910**

The Union of South Africa formed

**1910** Portugal's monarchy overthrown

**1911** U.S.A. Supreme Court ordered dissolution of Standard Oil Co. of New Jersey

**1911** Sun Yat-Sen (1866–1925) becomes President of China following collapse of Manchu Empire

**1911** Italy started its conquest of Tripoli

**1911** The Agadir Crisis took place in Morocco

**1912** Amundsen and Scott to South Pole

**1912** The Balkan wars began

**1914** Outbreak of First World War

**1914** Panama Canal opened

**1914** U.S.A. Clayton and Federal Trade Commission Acts sought further control of monopoly and restrictive practices

**1917** Russian revolution and Lenin returns to Russia

**1917** U.S.A. enters war on side of allies

**1918** Armistice with defeat of Germany

**1919** Versailles Peace Conference and Treaty – included heavy reparations for Germany, creation of Czechoslovakia and new frontiers in eastern Europe

**1919** International Labour Organisation founded (I.L.O.)

## INDUSTRY, SCIENCE AND TECHNOLOGY

**1910**

Lord Bertrand Russell (1872–1970) and Alfred North Whitehead (1861–1947) published: *Principia Mathematica*

**1911** Ernest Rutherford (1871–1937) creates a nuclear model of the atom

**1911–13** A major boom affects investment at home and overseas

**1915 onwards** Massive mobilisation of science and technology to support war effort
Rapid development of aircraft

**1915** Gas attacks introduce chemical warfare

**1916** First use of tanks at the Battle of the Somme

**1916** Battle of Jutland

**1917** Introduction of first Ford tractors into Britain

**1919** First transatlantic flight by Alcock and Brown

*British Politics and Legislation cont.*

**1918** Fisher's Education Act

**1919** Cunliffe Committee, with support of Professor A. C. Pigou, supports return to gold standard

**1919** Preferential rates on Commonwealth imports

**1919** Addison Housing Act

## BRITISH POLITICS AND LEGISLATION

### 1910

At this time public expenditure of all types constituted less than one-fifth of national income

**1911** Census of population 42 million

**1912** Miners minimum wage bill (inoperative)

**1913** Trade Union Act made political levy legal, but individuals could opt out

**1914** As part of wartime measures Britain leaves gold standard until 1925

**1915** Prime Minister H. H. Asquith's coalition Government

**1915** McKenna – duties on imports

**1915** Rent restrictions introduced as part of wartime measure

**1916** Prime Minister David Lloyd George coalition Government

**1916** Dublin Easter Rebellion

**1918** Votes for women

*Continued in previous column*

---

*The Economists and Their Publications cont.*

**1916** Lenin: *Imperialism, The Highest Stage of Capitalism*

**1918** Professor Gustav Cassel (1866–1945) published: *Theory of Social Economy*

**1919** Keynes: *Economic Consequences of the Peace*

**1919** Sir Ralph Hawtrey (1879–1963) published: *Currency and Credit*

## THE ECONOMISTS AND THEIR MAIN PUBLICATIONS

### 1910

Questions of the relationship between the large scale industrial and financial systems and human welfare increasingly predominate

**1911** Fisher: *Purchasing Power of Money*

**1912** Professor A. C. Pigou (1877–1959) published: *Wealth and Welfare*

**1912** John Maynard Keynes (1883–1946) became Editor of *The Economic Journal*

**1912** Professor Joseph Alois Schumpeter (1883–1950) published: *Theory of Economic Development*

**1913** Professor Wesley Clair Mitchell (1847–1948) published: *Business Cycles*

**1914** Philip Henry Wickstead (1844–1927) published: *The Scope and Method of Political Economy in the Light of the Marginal Principle*

**1914** Cannan: *Wealth*

**1914** Hobson: *Work and Wealth*

**1914** Friedrich von Wieser (1851–1926) published: *Theorie de Gesellschaftlichen Wirtschaft* – contained idea of 'opportunity costs'

**1915** Professor Dennis Robinson (1890–1963) published: *A Study of Industrial Fluctuations*

**1916** Cassel suggests idea of 'purchasing power parity' underlining international exchange rates

*Continued in previous column*

## WORLD POLITICS, WAR AND EXPANSION

### 1920

Post-war boom decade, but unevenly distributed. Expansion strongest in the U.S.A. until near end of decade

**1920** Kemal Ataturk (1881–1938) set about modernisation of Turkey

**1921** Vladimir Ilyich Lenin's (1870–1924): *New Economic Plan* sets about reconstruction of Russian economy – on Marxist/Leninist lines

**1922** Mussolini (1883–1945) founded Fascist 'corporate' state in Italy

**1928** President Herbert Hoover (1874–1964) gives optimistic inaugural address about 'State of the Union'

**1929** Wall Street crash precipitates world slump

**1929** Joseph Stalin's (1879–1953) *First Five Year Plan* – sets about massive industrialisation of Soviet Union, and widespread introduction of collective farms

## INDUSTRY, SCIENCE AND TECHNOLOGY

### 1920

Widespread extension of ideas and technologies developed for war purposes extended to peace

**1920** Electrification, motor transport, aeroplanes and consumer goods became more widely used

**1921** Creating of four railway companies in place of pre-war 130 railway companies

**1924** 12 major stock banks compared to 38 pre-war banks

**1924** U.K. coal production over 260 million tons, of which 75 million exported

**1926** Invention of television by John Logie Baird (1888–1946)

**1926** Creation of Imperial Chemical Industries Limited as an answer to U.S. and German competition

**1928** Invention of penicillin by Dr. Alexander Fleming (1881–1955)

## BRITISH POLITICS AND LEGISLATION

### 1920

Short post-war boom followed by problems of trade recession

**1921** Census of population 44 million

**1921** Key industry duties under Safeguarding of Industries Act

**1921** Irish partition

**1922** Prime Minister A. Bonar Law's (1858–1923) Conservative Government

**1923** Prime Minister Stanley Baldwin's (1867–1947) Conservative Government

**1924** First Labour Government led by Ramsey MacDonald (1866–1937)

**1924** Prime Minister Stanley Baldwin's Conservative Government

**1925** Britain returns to gold standard, at an 'over-valued' exchange rate (£4.2409 per fine oz.)

**1926** General Strike, following reduction of miners' wages to encourage coal exports

**1928** Agriculture Credits Act (also 1932) – to provide long-term finance to agriculture in England and Wales

**1928** Lloyd George campaigns for budget deficit to finance public works and relieve unemployment

**1929** Major impact of world depression on British life

**1929** Treasury memorandum rejects budget deficit proposals

**1929** Prime Minister Ramsay MacDonald's Labour Government

## THE ECONOMISTS AND THEIR MAIN PUBLICATIONS

### 1920

The impact of mathematical and statistical methods becomes more apparent

**1920** Dr. George Gallup and others in U.S.A. pioneered market research

**1920** Pigou: *Economics of Welfare*

**1921** Keynes: *A Treatise on Probability*

**1921** Joseph Charles Stamp (1880–1941) published: *Principles of Taxation in Light of Modern Development*

**1922** Hobson: *The Economics of Under-employment*

**1923** Marshall: *Money, Credit and Commerce*

**1923** Professor John Maurice Clark (1884–1963) published: *Economics of Overhead Costs*

**1926** Robertson: *Banking Policy and the Price Level*

**1926** Keynes: *The Economic Consequences of Mr. Churchill*

**1927** Mitchell: *Business Cycles, the Problem and its Setting*

**1927** Hawtrey: *The Gold Standard in Theory and Practice*

**1927** Professor Frank W. Taussig (1859–1940) published: *International Trade*

**1929** Cannan: *Review of Economic Theory* – defined economics as a study of 'material welfare'

## WORLD POLITICS, WAR AND EXPANSION

### 1930s

A decade of economic crises and war

**1930** Bank for International Settlements formed in Basle – to secure co-operation among central banks and organise reparations from Germany under Young plan

**1933** U.S.A. 'New deal programme' of unemployment relief and for recovery of business and agriculture introduced by President Roosevelt

**1933** World Economic Conference held in London

**1933** Adolf Hitler (1889–1945) comes to power in Germany

**1933** 'Lebensraum' becomes a policy of Nazi Germany

**1933** Persecution of Jews also a national policy in Germany

**1935** Germany reoccupies the Saarland

**1936** Germany reoccupies the Rhineland

**1936** Spanish Civil War begins

**1937** Japanese invasion of China

**1938** German Anschluss with Austria

**1938** Munich crisis – and dismemberment of Czechoslovakia

**1939** Francisco Franco (1892–1975) becomes Spanish Head of State

**1939** Nazi Germany invades Poland followed by outbreak of Second World War

## INDUSTRY, SCIENCE AND TECHNOLOGY

### 1930

Notwithstanding the Depression, widespread extension of new light industries in West London and Midlands. However there were problems of stagnation and decline in traditional staple industries – coal mining, textiles, ship building, etc. and a drift of population to Midlands and South-East. Similar tendencies were also apparent in other leading industrial countries. In Europe the effect of the depression was to encourage the major industrial countries to adopt highly 'autarchical' economic and trade policies, aimed at protecting, as best they could, national industrial and labour interests.

In Nazi Germany massive unemployment (6m) began to be mopped up by building and reconstruction works, notably the Autobahn, and later by massive secret rearmament, which increasingly unbalanced government finance.

**1934** U.K. coal production approximately 210 million tons, of which 60 million tons were exported

**1939** German military planning based on idea of Blitzkreig – rapid co-ordinated movement of fast-moving armoured forces, aircraft, etc. Widespread use of radio communications

## BRITISH POLITICS AND LEGISLATION

### 1930

Round-table conference in London on future of India

1930 Bank rate between 3 per cent and 5 per cent

1930 Mosley memorandum on economic reforms

1931 Britain goes off gold standard and effectively depreciated sterling

1931 Census of population 46 million

1931 Ottawa agreements lead to Imperial preference trade system in the British Empire

1931 Prime Minister Ramsay MacDonald's national Government

1931 National Government to deal with 'economic blizzard' – three million unemployed

1933 World trade begins to recover, somewhat in Britain's favour

1934 First Special Areas (development and improvement) Act

1935 Recovery in British overseas trade continues

1935 Prime Minister Stanley Baldwin's national Government

1935 Bank rate 2 per cent

1937 Prime Minister Neville Chamberlain's (1869–1940) national Government

1937 Rearmament programme commences

1939 Widespread rationing and rent controls introduced

## THE ECONOMISTS AND THEIR MAIN PUBLICATIONS

### 1930

During this period Professor Alvin Hansen and many other 'stagnation theorists' examined the problems of mature economies running out of investment opportunities

1930 Fisher: *Theory of Interest*

1930 Keynes: *Treatise on Money*

1931 Professor Eli F. Heckscher (1879–1952) published: *Mercantilism*

1933 Professor Bertil Ohlin published: *Inter-Regional and International Trade*

1933 Joan Robinson: *The Economics of Imperfect Competition*

1934 Professor Ludwig von Mises published: *Theory of Money and Credit*

1935 Professor Lional Robbins: *An Essay on the Nature and Significance of Economic Science*

**The Keynesian macro 'demand management' revolution begins**

1936 Keynes: *General Theory of Employment, Interest and Money*

1936 J. M. Clark: *Essays in Preface to Social Economics*

1936 Von Mises: *Socialism*

1937 Hawtrey: *The Art of Central Banking*—also *Capital and Employment*

1938 Eric Roll: *A History of Economic Thought*

1939 Schumpeter: *Business Cycles*

## WORLD POLITICS, WAR AND EXPANSION

### 1940

Dunkirk and Battle of Britain

**1940** Creation of Vichy Government in France

**1941** Destruction of much of Italian Fleet, by air attack on Taranto harbour

**1941** Pearl Harbour attacked by Japanese. America enters the war

**1941** Lend-Lease agreement between U.S.A. and the Allies

**1941** Germany invaded Russia

**1942** Beginning of co-operation between U.S.A., Canada and U.K. over atomic energy

**1942** Anglo-French forces landed in North Africa

**1943** Collapse of Mussolini regime in Italy

**1944** Bretton Woods Agreement plans future free world economy

**1944** General Charles de Gaulle (1890–1970) becomes provisional head and President of Republic of France

**1945** First atomic bomb dropped on Hiroshima

**1945** End of Second World War

**1945** Wide recognition of existence of 'dollar shortage' for Western Europe

**1945** Formation of Economic and Social Council of United Nations

**1945** Food and Agricultural Organisation founded (F.A.O.)

**1945** World Bank founded (I.B.R.D.)

*Continued in next column*
376

## INDUSTRY, SCIENCE AND TECHNOLOGY

### 1940

Widespread impact of war on 'scientific and industrial research'. Air defence of Britain based on radar and decoding of enemy signals, co-ordinating fighter aircraft interception of bombers. Operational research techniques developed from wartime operations

**1941** Whittle invented first jet aircraft

**1944** Widespread use of science and technology in invasion of Europe by Allies

**1944** U.K. coal production approximately 175 million tons

**1944** Appearance of German VI and V2 rockets

**1945** Application of wartime developments to peacetime uses (e.g. jet engines, radar, electronics)

---

*World Politics, War and Expansion cont.*

**1945** International Monetary Fund founded (I.M.F.)

**1947** General Agreement on Tariffs and Trade (G.A.T.T.)

**1947** The Marshall Plan

**1947** Formation of Organisation for European Economic Co-operation (O.E.E.C.)

**1947 onwards** Increasing Russian domination of Eastern Europe and beginning of the 'Iron Curtain'

**1947** Fourth Republic inaugurated in France

**1948** Benelux Customs Union formed

**1948** Creation of Israel

## BRITISH POLITICS AND LEGISLATION

## THE ECONOMISTS AND THEIR MAIN PUBLICATIONS

### 1940

Bank rate still at 2 per cent and unemployment persists despite wartime expansion

1940 Massive expansion of the state's powers to meet needs of 'total war'

1940 Prime Minister Winston Spencer Churchill's (1874–1965) National Government

1941 Post-war Credits introduced as a means of wartime financing

1944 Government White Paper on full employment policies

1944 Introduction of Pay-As-You-Earn income tax

1945 Prime Minister Winston Spencer Churchill's Wartime Coalition Government followed by Clement Attlee (1883–1967) Labour Government

1945 Finance Corporation for Industry founded

1945 Industrial and Commercial Finance Corporation for smaller firms

1946 Bank of England nationalised

1946 Creation of Capital Issues Committees as a non-statutory body to control new issues in public interest

1946 Beginning of nationalisation of key industries – coal, railways, public utilities, etc., and major expansion of public sector

1947 Indian and Pakistan independence

*Continued in next column*

### 1940

Questions of how to run a Keynesian 'demand management' welfare state: 'mixed economy' increasingly predominate in economic writing

1940 Robertson: *Essays in Monetary Theory*

1941 James Burnham: *Managerial Revolution*

1942 Beveridge: *Social Insurance and Allied Services*

1942 Schumpeter: *Capitalism, Socialism and Democracy*

1944 Beveridge: *Full Employment and a Free Society*

1944 Professor F. A. Hayek: *The Road to Serfdom*

1946 Mitchell: *Measuring Business Cycles*

1948 Beveridge: *Voluntary Action*

*British Politics and Legislation cont.*

1947 Introduction of National Health Scheme

1948 Monopolies and Restrictive Practices Enquiry and Control Act

1949 First post-war devaluation of the £ sterling falls from $4 to $2.80

## WORLD POLITICS, WAR AND EXPANSION

### 1950

World recovery begins to get under way

**1950** European Payments Union formed to encourage multi-national trade amongst member countries

**1950–53** Korean war influences world economy by setting off boom in commodity prices

**1952** Formation of European Coal and Steel Community to create a 'common market' in coal, iron ore, scrap and steel

**1953** Death of Joseph Stalin

**1953** Revolution in Egypt overthrows monarchy

**1954** Agreement of Association between E.C.S.C. and United Kingdom

**1956** Fidel Castro lands in Cuba

**1956** Suez crisis

**1956** Hungarian uprising against Communist regime

**1957** Treaty of Rome established European Common Market and other facets of the community, initially with Belgium, France, Germany, Italy, Luxembourg and The Netherlands

**1958** Major European countries including Britain make their currencies convertible

**1958** General de Gaulle takes power in France and abandons 'Algeria français' policies

**1958** Fifth Republic created in France

**1959** Fidel Castro overthrows Batista regime in Cuba

## INDUSTRY, SCIENCE AND TECHNOLOGY

### 1950

Continued increased application of science and technology to everyday life. Development of radio and TV, frozen and pre-packed convenience foods, wide extension of consumer durable goods of all types.

A gradual shift away from a coal-based to an imported 'oil based' industrial system

**1954** U.K. coal production approximately 230 million tons, of which approximately 15 million exported. A workforce of 700,000 men

**1958** Widespread interest in 'Indicative planning' for industry, as undertaken in France

**1959** Increased awareness of multi-national influences on progress of industry, science and technology

## BRITISH POLITICS AND LEGISLATION

## THE ECONOMISTS AND THEIR MAIN PUBLICATIONS

### 1950

Bank rate still 2 per cent – but beginnings of move to more flexible rates

**1950** Approximately 4.2 million road vehicles in Britain

**1951** Prime Minister Sir Winston Spencer Churchill's Conservative Government

**1951** Census of population 50.2m

**1951** A move away from wartime and post-war rationing. Restoration of 'free market processes' under slogans of 'setting the people free' and 'Conservative Freedom Works'

**1955** Prime Minister Sir Anthony Eden's (1897–1977) Conservative Government

**1956** Restrictive Trade Practices Act

**1957** Ghana – first African colony to achieve independence

**1957** Prime Minister Harold Macmillan's Conservative Government

**1957–59** Radcliffe Committee on working of monetary system

---

*The Economists and Their Main Publications cont.*

**1958** Professor W. W. Rostow published: *Stages of Economic Growth* – a non-Communist manifesto

**1959** Professor Henry Phelps Brown: *The Growth of Industrial Relations*

**1959** Andrew Shonfield: *British Economic Policy Since the War*

### 1950

Throughout the decade widespread interest by neo-Keynesian economists in problem of economic development, notably in recently independent less developed countries. At the same time throughout Western Europe reconstruction and balance of payments problems persist, as main issues for concern

**1950** Hawtrey: *The Balance of Payments and Standards of Living*

**1951** Professor James Meade: first volume: *Theory of International Economic Policy*

**1951** Harrod: *The Life of John Maynard Keynes*

**1952** Robbins: *The Theory of Economic Policy in English Classical Political Economy*

**1954** Schumpeter: *History of Economic Analysis* published posthumously

**1954** Robertson: *Britain in the World Economy*

**1955** Professor Arthur Lewis: *The Theory of Economic Growth*

**1955** Hawtrey: *Cross Purposes in Wage Policy*

**1955** Professor Barbara Wootton: *The Social Foundations of Wages Policy*

**1957** Professor Gunnar Myrdal: *Economic Theory and Underdeveloped Regions*

**1957** Professor Colin Clark: *The Conditions of Economic Progress*

**1957** Robertson: a leading contributor to reports of Council on Prices, Productivity and Incomes

*Continued in previous column*

## WORLD POLITICS, WAR AND EXPANSION

### 1960

Economic expansion for major industrial nations continues at unprecedented rate, but British growth increasingly lags behind that of other major European industrial countries

**1960** European Free Trade Association – reduced tariffs between 'Outer Seven Countries' – (European trade considered to be at 'sixes and sevens')

**1962** Cuban missile crisis

**1962** Beginning of Kennedy round of tariff negotiations, made possible by U.S.A. Trade Expansion Act

**1963** Assassination of President John F. Kennedy (1917–1963)

**1963 onwards** Increased U.S.A. involvement in Vietnam gradually drains America's overall economic strength by weakening the $

**1965** President de Gaulle elected for second term in France

**1967** Kennedy round of tariff negotiations completed

**1967** Six-day war between Israel and Egypt

**1968** Student riots in France

## INDUSTRY, SCIENCE AND TECHNOLOGY

### 1960

Britain's share of world manufactured exports 16.3 per cent

**1961** Russian manned space flight

**1964** U.K. coal production less than 200 million tons, with minute exports. A workforce of approximately 480,000 men

**1964** U.K. total oil imports 59.4 million tons, with Kuwait, Iraq, Libya and Venezuela principal suppliers

**1969** Club of Rome publications about need to conserve finite raw materials receive wide publicity

**1969** U.S.A. man on the moon

## BRITISH POLITICS AND LEGISLATION

### 1960

Macmillan's 'Wind of Change' speech in Africa signifies Britain's withdrawal from Empire and beginning of attempts to join European Economic Community

**1960** Bank rate between 4 per cent and 6 per cent

**1961** Census of population 52.7 million

**1961** South Africa leaves Commonwealth

**1962** National Economic Development Council formed

**1962** National Incomes Commission formed – from this time onwards growing concern with role of 'wages and incomes policies' are part of national economic planning

**1963** Prime Minister Sir Alec Douglas Home's Conservative Government

**1964** Labour Government elected under Prime Minister Harold Wilson on a 'technological revolution' promise

**1964** Balance of payment current a/c −£355m

**1965** Monopolies and Mergers Act

**1965** Rhodesia declares U.D.I.

**1965** Consumer price inflation 5 per cent p.a.

**1967** Severe balance of payments crisis leads to £ devalued to $2.40

**1967** New houses and flats completed 425,800 – postwar record

**1969** Balance of payments current a/c −£462m

## THE ECONOMISTS AND THEIR MAIN PUBLICATIONS

### 1960

Throughout the decade there was to be an increased awareness in economic writings of the problems associated with 'sustained high growth rates' in the advanced industrial societies. In the Western democratic countries there was a growing disillusionment of 'fine tuning' by Keynesian demand management economics and a recognition of the need to deal with 'supply constraints', such as energy and raw materials, adequate investment, labour supply, etc. There was also increased concern with the power and influence of multinationals. Towards the end of the decade, the tendency of the industrial countries to become highly dependent on Middle Eastern oil for basic energy also received growing attention. The idea of a 'convergency' between problems facing the 'social democratic' and the Marxist industrial societies were widely discussed

**1960** Professor Karl Popper: *The Poverty of Historicism*

**1962** Professor J. Vaizey: *The Economics of Education*

**1965** Andrew Schonfield: *Modern Capitalism*

**1967** J. K. Galbraith: *The New Industrial State*

**1969** Nobel Prize for Economic Sciences instituted

**1969** Club of Rome publications put forward 'conservationist low growth' arguments

## WORLD POLITICS, WAR AND EXPANSION

**1970s** World population approaches 4 billion

The onset of a decade of inflation and international currency crises. Also an international awareness of the recovery of West Germany and Japan as major industrial powers

**1970** Death of António Salazar (1889–1970) in Portugal

**1971** U.S.A. abandons gold and $ relationship

**1971** Helsinki Conference signals hopes for détente

**1972** £ floated against other currencies

**1972** President Nixon and Mr Brezhnev sign treaties on arms limitations, etc.

**1973** 'Floating exchange rates' widely applied

**1973** Yom Kippur War precipitating world oil price rise. O.P.E.C. emerges as major world cartel

**1973** Ideas of a 'New World Economic Order' gain attention

**1974** Revolutions in Portugal, later in Mozambique and Angola

**1974** Growing awareness of impact on international economy of oil price rises

**1974** Major world recession gains momentum

**1975** Increased Russian, Cuban and Chinese Marxist incursions in Africa

**1975** Death of General Franco in Spain paves way for reforms

**1976** Death of Mao-Tse-Tung (1896–1976) in China

## INDUSTRY, SCIENCE AND TECHNOLOGY

**1970s**

A decade marked by a strong renewed awareness of finiteness of natural resources. An increased scientific cum technical preoccupation with pollution, energy saving, etc.

**1970** Britain's share of world manufactured exports 10.6 per cent

**1974** U.K. working population 25.6 million, of whom less than 2 per cent in agriculture and just over 34 per cent in manufacturing

**1974** U.K. coal production 100 million tons, with a workforce of approximately 240,000 men

**1974** U.K. oil imports 111.8 million tons, of which nearly one-third from Saudi Arabia

**1975** Growing public awareness of importance of North Sea oil to future of British economy – approximately two-thirds of all energy comes from oil

**1975** U.K. – over 14 million passenger cars and 2 million commercial vehicles

**1975** Britain's share of world manufactured exports 9 per cent

**1976** First British North Sea oil pumped ashore

**1977** North Sea oil begins to assist strongly Britain's balance of payments

## BRITISH POLITICS AND LEGISLATION

### 1970

Britain's visible trade moved into surplus

**1970** Bank rate between 7 per cent and 8 per cent

**1970** Conservative Government under Prime Minister Edward Heath elected and seeks to restore a 'freer market economy' and membership of European Economic Community

**1971** Census of population 55.5 million

**1971** Industrial Relations Act

**1972** Abandonment by Conservative Government of 'lame ducks' policy

**1972–73** Widespread industrial unrest and three-day week

**1973** Britain joins E.E.C.

**1973** Fair Trading Act

**1974** Labour Government under Prime Minister Harold Wilson returned

**1974** The 'social contract' relates wages and incomes policy to Government economic policies

**1974** Impact of world recession strongly felt

**1974** Balance of payments current a/c −£3,668 million

**1975** Bank of England minimum lending rate between $9\frac{3}{4}$ per cent and 12 per cent

**1975** Britain confirms membership of European Economic Community following national referendum

*Continued in next column*

## THE ECONOMISTS AND THEIR MAIN PUBLICATIONS

### 1970

**1971** Professor Jay W. Forrester: *World Dynamics*

**1972** Dennis L. Meadows: *The Limits to Growth*

**1973** Science Policy Research Unit, Sussex University: *Thinking about the Future*. A critique of limits to growth

**1976** Professor J. K. Galbraith publishes *The Age of Uncertainty* – and produces first TV drama on history of economic thought

**1977** Professor W. Leontief publishes *The Future of the World Economy*

---

*British Politics and Legislation cont.*

**1975** Consumer price inflation approximately $22\frac{1}{2}$ per cent p.a.

**1975** Prime Minister James Callaghan's Labour Government

**1976** Industrial participation and worker directors becomes political issue

**1976** Unemployment persists at around 1.5 million

**1976** Budget proposals linked to continuation of wage restraint

**1976** Bank of England minimum lending rate over 15 per cent

**1977** Attempt by Labour Government to maintain 10 per cent voluntary wage restraint policy

**1977** Bank of England minimum lending rate falls to 5 per cent

# SHORT READING LIST

Raymond Aron. *Eighteen Lectures on Industrial Society,* Weidenfeld and Nicolson.

R. B. Bottomore and Maximilien Rubel. *Karl Marx – Selected writings in Sociology and Social Philosophy*, Penguin Books.

S. C. Burchall. *Age of Progress*, Time Life.

Robert W. Campbell. *Soviet-type Economics*, Macmillan.

Economist Intelligence Unit. *Key Issues in Applied Economics 1947–1997*, Longman.

John Kenneth Galbraith. *The Age of Uncertainty*, BBC/Andre Deutsch.

Roy Harrod. *The Life of John Maynard Keynes*, Macmillan.

F. A. Hayek. *The Road to Serfdom*, Routledge & Kegan Paul.

E. J. Hobsbawn. *Industry and Empire*, Pelican.

Michael Kaser and Janusz G. Zielinski. *Planning in East Europe*, Bodley Head.

John Maynard Keynes. *The General Theory of Employment, Interest and Money*, Macmillan.

Milo Keynes. *Essays on John Maynard Keynes*, Cambridge University Press.

W. Arthur Lewis. *The Theory of Economic Growth*, George Allen & Unwin.

Michael Lipton. *Why People Stay Poor*, Temple Smith.

David McLellan. *Karl Marx – His Life and Thought*, Paladin.

Gerald M. Meier. *Leading Issues in Development Economics*, Oxford University Press.

Gerald M. Meier and Robert E. Baldwin. *Economic Development: Theory, History, Policy*, Wiley International.

B. P. Menon. *Global Dialogue, The New International Order*, Pergamon.

R. E. H. Mellor. *C.O.M.E.C.O.N.: Challenge to the West*, Van Nostrand Reinhold.

Gunnar Myrdal. *Asian Drama. An Enquiry into the Poverty of Nations*, Pelican.

Boris Nicolaievsky and Otto Maenchen-Helfen. *Karl Marx – Man and Fighter*, Penguin.

Eric Roll. *A History of Economic Thought*, Faber and Faber.

W. W. Rostow. *The Stages of Economic Growth*, Cambridge University Press.

Arthur Seldon and F. G. Pennance. *Dictionary of Economics*, Everymans.

Joseph A. Schumpeter. *Capitalism, Socialism and Democracy*, Unwin University Books.

Science Policy Research Unit, Sussex University. *Thinking about the Future*, Chatto and Windus.

Schapiro and Reddaway. *Lenin, The Man, The Theorist, The Leader*, Pall Mall Press.

Andrew Shonfield. *Modern Capitalism*, The Changing Balance of Public and Private Power, Oxford University Press.

Andrew S. Skinner and Thomas Wilson. *Essays on Adam Smith*, Oxford University Press.

Michael Stewart. *Keynes and After*, Penguin.

Anthony Tillett, Thomas Kempner and Gordon Wills. *Management Thinkers*, Pelican.

# APPENDIX I Abbreviations of Major International Organisations

| Acronym | World Wide Organisations | Year Established |
|---|---|---|
| I.L.O. | International Labour Organisation | 1919 |
| I.M.F. | International Monetary Fund | 1945 |
| F.A.O. | Food and Agriculture Organisation | 1946 |
| I.B.R.D. | International Bank of Reconstruction and Development | 1946 |
| U.N.E.S.C.O. | U.N. Educational, Scientific and Cultural Organisation | 1946 |
| U.N.E.C.O.S.O.C. | United Nations Economic and Social Council including: | 1946 |
| E.C.E. | Economic Commission for Europe | |
| E.C.L.A. | Economic Commission for Latin America | |
| E.C.W.A. | Economic Commission for Western Asia | |
| E.C.A.P. | Economic Commission for Asia and the Pacific | |
| W.H.O. | World Health Organisation | 1948 |
| U.N.E.P.T.A. | U.N. Expanded Program of Technical Assistance | 1949 |
| I.F.C. | International Finance Corporation | 1956 |
| U.N.S.P. | U.N. Special Fund | 1958 |
| I.D.A. | International Development Association | 1960 |
| W.F.P. | World Food Programme (U.N. & F.A.O.) | 1962 |
| U.N.D.P. | U.N. Development Fund (U.N.E.P.T.A. & U.N.S.P.) | 1964 |
| U.N.I.D.O. | U.N. Industrial Development Organisation | 1965 |
| U.N.F.P.A. | U.N. Fund for Population Activities | 1967 |
| U.N.E.P. | U.N. Environment Program | 1973 |
| I.F.A.D. | International Fund for Agricultural Development | 1976 |

### Regional Banking Organisations

| | | |
|---|---|---|
| I.D.B. | Inter-American Development Bank | 1958 |
| C.A.B.E.I. | Central American Bank for Econnomic Integration | 1961 |
| Af.D.B. | African Development Bank | 1964 |
| As.D.B. | Asian Development Bank | 1966 |
| C.D.B. | Carribean Development Bank | 1969 |
| A.D.C. | Andean Development Corporation | 1970 |
| E.I.B. & E.D.F. | European Investment Bank and Development Fund | 1970 |

### Major International Agencies concerned with Trade

| | | |
|---|---|---|
| U.P.U. | Universal Postal Union | 1875 |
| I.T.U. | International Telecommunications Union | 1932 |
| G.A.T.T. | General Agreement on Tariffs and Trade | 1947 |
| I.C.A.O. | International Civil Aviation Organisation | 1947 |
| I.T.C. | International Tin Council | 1956 |
| I.M.C.O. | Inter-Government Marine Consultative Organisation | 1959 |
| O.P.E.C. | Organisation of the Petroleum Exporting Countries | 1960 |
| C.C.F. | Compensatory Financing Facility | 1963 |
| U.N.C.T.A.D. | U.N. Conference of Trade and Development | 1964 |
| I.T.C. | International Trade Center | 1964 |
| E.E.C. | Stabex Scheme: Lome Convention | 1975 |

### Major Pan-National Groupings

| | | |
|---|---|---|
| C.M.E.A./or C.O.M.E.C.O.N. | Council for Mutual Economic Assistance | 1949 |
| E.C.S.C. | European Coal and Steel Community | 1952 |
| EURATOM | European Atomic Energy Community | 1958 |
| E.E.C. | European Economic Community | 1958 |
| E.F.T.A. | European Free Trade Association | 1960 |
| O.E.C.D. | Organisation for Economic Co-operation and Development (a successor to the O.E.E.C.) | 1961 |
| O.E.E.C. | Organisation for European Economic Co-operation | 1947–1960 |

# APPENDIX II  The Evolution of the 'Mixed Economy' – the British Example

Attention has been given to the development of the so-called 'mixed economy' in all the advanced capitalist economies. Today all such countries rely on a blend of Keynsian style financial demand management techniques with various regulatory devices associated with external finance, trade balances, etc., and on the supply side through the operations of big government, concerned with defence and welfare programmes; with the direct ownership and control of key industries; and by means of a host of other methods of persuasion, support and direct controls. The following information gives some indication of the position in Britain in the mid 1970s.

\*　\*　\*　\*　\*

## The Public Sector in Britain in the 1970s

|  | Expenditure 1971–1972 | No. of Employees | Percentage of labour force |
|---|---|---|---|
| Central Government | £10 000m | nearly 2m | 7.6% |
| Local Government | £5 486m | nearly 2.5m | 10% |
| Public Corporations (about 35) in 1973 | £8 000m | over 2m | 7.7% |
| About 45% GNP 45% of the nation's capital assets and annual fixed investment | £23 486 | 6.3m | 25% |

R.S.A. *Journal,* July 1974, pp 481–492. Revised October 1975

\*　\*　\*　\*　\*

## Government and Industry Relationships in Britain Today

GOVERNMENT DEPARTMENTS

*Department of Industry*

General industrial policy and regional policy.

Sponsor to most private industry plus iron and steel, the Post Office and Aerospace.

Regional Offices serving Departments of Energy, Trade and Prices and Consumer Protection. Regional Industrial Directors, seconded from industry, work as from heads with an official.

The National Enterprise Board – 1975 onwards.

*Department of Trade*

Overseas trade policy, tariffs, EEC, export promotion, export finance.

Internal commerce regulation, companies, patents.

Sponsors shipping, insurance, civil aviation, tourism, newspapers, films.

*Department of Prices and Consumer Protection*

Office of Fair Trading, consumer protection, credit, standards, weights and measures, Price Commission, monopolies, mergers, restrictive trade practices.

*Department of Energy*

Energy policies.

Nationalised energy industries: Coal, Gas, Electricity, Atomic Energy Authority.

Sponsors: Oil and petrol industries, nuclear industries.

*Department of Employment*

Manpower policies.

Industrial relations – conciliation and arbitration (now under A.C.A.S.).

Conditions of employment: safety, health (now under an Agency).

Race relations, women, unemployment, pay and tax.

Incomes policy – statistics – research.

Responsible for Manpower Services Commission.

*Manpower Services Commission.* (An example of a modern 'Agency')

Ex-civil servant chairman plus nine members (three T.U.C., three C.B.I., two local authority, one educator).

   *Employment Services Agency*
      Job Centres: Employment Offices.
      Professional and Executive Register.
      Occupational Guidance.
      Employment Services for the disabled.

   *Training Services Agency*
      Co-ordinating and funding I.T.B.s.
      Filling gaps left by I.T.B. system.
      Training opportunities scheme G.T.C.s.
      Specialist training services.

*Department of the Environment*

General environmental policies – clean air, water, sewage, anti-noise functions; research into roads, building, hydraulics, water pollution, fire protection, etc.

Transport policy and industries: railways, roads, ports, etc.

Planning and local government – land use and regional planning and countryside; minerals, new towns and local government.

Housing and construction – housing programme, construction industries, Property Services Agency.

*Other departments*

Much concerned with industry include the Treasury, the Department of Education and Science and the Ministry of Defence.

## QUASI-GOVERNMENT BODIES

1. *National Economic Development Council* (N.E.D.C. or Neddy)

Membership: Prime Minister and two ministers
              Six Employers' representatives
              Six trade unionists
              Two chairmen of nationalised industries
              Two independents
              The Director-General

Meets once a month, chaired by Prime Minister, Chancellor or senior minister.

*Role:* removal of obstacles to Britain's growth. Since November 1975 it has been given an important role in government planning.

2. *Economic Development Committees* (EDCs or Little Neddies)

Membership: Government, management, unions and a chairman from another industry.

22 committees – different industries (or activities like management education and movement of exports)

*Role:* to improve the performance of their industry: review of performance and industrial prospects. They cooperated in compiling the Medium Term Review of Industrial Prospects to 1977, completed in 1973 and being followed up.

3. *The National Economic Development Office* (N.E.D.O.)

(a)   Economic Division
      Statistics, assessments, etc., for N.E.D.O.
      Statistical support for E.D.C.'s
(b)   Industrial Division
      Services for E.D.C.'s
      Industrial base for N.E.D.C.
(c)   Administrative Division

4. *Regional Economic Planning Councils*

Membership: from local government, industry and commerce, trade unions, universities and social services

Role: to assist in the formation of regional plans, implementation and integrating with national plans.

The Regional Council is paralled by a Regional Economic Planning Board, made up of civil servants, designed to co-ordinate departmental policies and plans in the region. The chairman of this board provides the secretariat for the Council.

5. There are hundreds of regulatory, administrative and advisory bodies, mostly linked with a particular department or industry.

\*    \*    \*    \*    \*

## INSTITUTIONS ON THE INDUSTRIAL SIDE

(Apart from Trade Union Congress and its affiliated unions which have links with government at all levels)

1. *The Confederation of British Industry*

(C.B.I.) represents some 12,000 companies (including subsidiaries) and public corporations and over 200 trade associations and employers' associations. It services its members with information and advice and is the spokesman for the management element of U.K. industry and commerce, especially to government and the E.E.C. Its main strength is in the central committees, though it has a regional organisation.

2. *The Association of British Chambers of Commerce* (A.B.C.C.)

The national association of some 91 chambers of commerce (50,000 members). Some chambers are powerful and effective – the central body rather less so. Their role is to serve their members by providing export and other services, organising trade missions, maintaining overseas contacts and making representations to local and central government.

3. *Trade Associations and Employers' Organisations* (T.A.s and E.O.s)

Employers' Organisations are mainly concerned with the negotiation with trade unions of pay and conditions of work.

Trade Associations look after the collective technical, economic and commercial interests of their members.

Both Employers' Organisations and Trade Associations maintain close links with government and nationalised industries and provide their members with statistical and other services. A few of them carry out both functions.

There are some 2,500 E.O./T.A.s of which about 100 are well known and effective. Most are small, poorly financed, uncooperative and ineffective. There is some reorganisation going on.


# Some Industrial Organisations in the European Economic Community

(a) Trade union link-up at the top is hindered by political and religious differences – C.E.S.L. (free T.U.s), C.M.T. (Christian T.U.s), C.G.T. (French Communist T.U.), C.G.I.L. (Italian Communist T.U.). Development of international trade unionism more likely on industry sector lines.

(b) Top industrial and commercial organisations recognised by having representatives on the E.E.C. Economic and Social Committee:

Union des Industries de la Communanté Européenne (U.N.I.C.E.) covers industry (including food processing). Membership: national federations like the C.B.I.

C.O.C.C.E.E. – the commercial and distributive world

C.E.A. – insurance

U.A.C.E.E. – handicrafts, self-employed, small businesses

C.O.P.A. – farmers and growers

C.E.E.P. – nationalised industries

The trade union federations mentioned above.

(c) F.E.B.I. – industrial sector federations of which O.R.G.A.L.I.M.E. (Organisation de Liaison des Industries Metalliques Européennes) is one. B.E.A.M.A. (British Electrical and Allied Manufacturers' Association) is a member. Many of these federations have a wider membership than the E.E.C. countries.

(d)  Product group associations, e.g. C.O.M.E.L. (Committé de Coordination des Constructeurs de Machines Tournantes Electrique du Marché Commun) of which oe.M.A. the Rotating Electrical Machines Association) is a member. It is also a member of B.E.A.M.A.

(e)  Very important is the Permanent Conference of E.E.C. Chambers of Commerce which has official links with Chambers outside the E.E.C.

*Source:* Henley Paper on Government and Industry, Paul Cherrington 1976.

# APPENDIX III  A Statement about the National Enterprise Board 1975*

The National Enterprise Board, established under the Industry Act 1975, is a public corporation whose principal objectives are to assist the economy of the U.K. to promote industrial efficiency and international competitiveness, and to provide productive employment.

The N.E.B.s activities will fall under the following main headings:

(a) *Finance for industrial investment*

The N.E.B. will be a new source of finance for industrial investment, to supplement existing sources of finance in the public and private sectors. The finance will normally take the form of equity capital but, where appropriate, medium-term or long-term loans may be provided at competitive (though not subsidised) rates of interest. The emphasis will be on financing the expansion and modernisation of productive facilities in manufacturing industry.

(b) *Finance for industrial restructuring*

The N.E.B. will be able to provide finance or advisory services to promote the reorganisation of sectors of industry where this seems likely to promote industrial efficiency and profitability.

(c) *Industrial holding company role*

The N.E.B. will act as a holding company for a number of shareholdings previously held directly by the Government, for example, those in British Leyland Ltd. and Rolls-Royce (1971) Ltd. Its job will be to ensure that the companies concerned are soundly managed and that a proper return is secured on behalf of the taxpayer. The portfolio will be added to from time to time as a consequence of the N.E.B.s role as a provider of new equity finance and through purchase of existing shares in companies, under the arrangements normally applicable in the private sector; in addition the N.E.B. has power under the Act to set up new enterprises or to participate in joint ventures with the private sector.

(d) *Assistance to companies in short-term difficulties*

The Secretary of State has powers under the Act to direct the N.E.B. to provide selective financial assistance to companies which are basically sound but in short-term financial or managerial difficulties. The assistance is subject to the 1972, and the N.E.B. will be reimbursed for any activity under this heading out of funds made available under that Act. This assistance will be separately accounted for by the N.E.B. and will normally only occur where the Government consider there is some special advantage, for instance managerial, in involving the N.E.B. in an activity which would otherwise be the direct responsibility of the government.

* The material in this Appendix was written prior to the N.E.B. becoming operational. and no longer represents current N.E.B. policy.

### N.E.B.'s investment policy

The N.E.B. is expected to exercise a commercial judgment and to look for an adequate return on its investments. At the same time, as an important instrument of Government industrial policy, it is expected to take a wider view of the benefits and opportunities that accrue from particular investments.

### Helping the assisted areas

This applies especially to the N.E.B.s role in stimulating investment and employment in the assisted areas, where it will work closely with Government Departments and the new Development Agencies which have been set up in Scotland and Wales. In addition to its London headquarters, the N.E.B. will shortly be establishing offices in Liverpool and Newcastle.

### How the Board is financed

The N.E.B.s funds will be partly in the form of loans from the National Loans Fund (on which it will pay interest at the normal rate for such loans) and partly in the form of 'public dividend capital' provided by the Secretary of State for Industry with the approval of the Treasury. The Government will set financial objectives for the N.E.B. and will decide each year, after discussion with the N.E.B. what rate of dividend would be appropriate on public dividend capital, having regard to the N.E.B.s future investment plans.

### Government's guidelines for N.E.B.

In addition, the Government is publishing certain guidelines, within which the N.E.B. is required to work. Among other things, these set out criteria for investment appraisal; they make it clear that the N.E.B. enjoys no special privileges over those of companies in the private sector (e.g. on matters like fair trading policy or the City Takeover Code); they impose obligations on the N.E.B. to consult the Government on certain matters not specified in the Act; and generally they set the framework of policy within which the N.E.B. is intended to operate.

Source: National Enterprise Board, 21st November 1975, 12–18 Grosvenor Gardens, London, SW1W 0DW.

# APPENDIX IV Energy Supplies and the Future of Industrial Society

Throughout the book attention has been drawn to the close relationship between energy usage and technology and economic growth as a whole. In recent years energy consumption and the increase in gross domestic production has been closely related, with an average energy coefficient of 1.04. Throughout the 19th century and the early years of the 20th century coal was king. However since the Second World War all the great industrial nations have become increasingly dependent on oil for up to 80 per cent of their total energy needs. The Middle East and Saudi Arabia in particular are by far the largest actual and potential source of supplies for the western economies. Since the O.P.E.C. 'energy crisis' of 1973 onwards a major rethinking of longer term energy supply and usage has been under way. The following tables, derived from an article by Dr. Norman White of the Henley Centre for Forecasting, indicates the 'critical' role of energy availability and costs in future world growth prospects.

TABLE (I)ANNUAL PERCENTAGE INCREASE IN WORLD ENERGY DEMAND 1959–1969

|  | Annual increase (%) |
| --- | --- |
| Gross domestic production (total output) | 4.8 |
| Energy consumption | 5.0 |
| Energy consumption ÷ GDP (Energy coefficient) | 1.94 |

TABLE(II) CHANGING PATTERN OF WORLD COMMERCIAL ENERGY DEMAND [EXCLUDING THE USSR, EASTERN EUROPE, AND CHINA]

|  | Solid fuels (%) | Oil fuels (%) | Natural gas (%) | Hydro-electricity (%) | Nuclear electricity (%) |
| --- | --- | --- | --- | --- | --- |
| 1920 | 86 | 9 | 2 | 3 | — |
| 1930 | 75 | 17 | 5 | 3 | — |
| 1940 | 69 | 21 | 6 | 4 | — |
| 1945 | 60 | 25 | 10 | 5 | — |
| 1950 | 52 | 32 | 10 | 6 | — |
| 1960 | 36 | 41 | 16 | 7 | (0.03) |
| 1970 | 23 | 52 | 18 | 6 | 1 |
| 1974 | 19 | 54 | 18 | 7 | 2 |

Notes: 1. Oil fuels include ocean bunkers, aviation fuels, and refinery use and loss, but exclude nonenergy products
2. Nuclear and hydro-electricity are on an input basis

Data source: Shell International Petroleum Co. Ltd.

TABLE (III) ESTIMATED RECOVERABLE RESERVES BY TYPE OF FUEL AND BY REGION EXPRESSED AS ENERGY CONTENT IN MILLIONS OF TERAJOULES

| | Solid fossil fuels | Crude oil | Natural gas | Oil shale and tar sands | Uranium (non breeder) | Total without breeder | Uraniums and thorium (with breeder) |
|---|---|---|---|---|---|---|---|
| Africa | 400 | 550 | 200 | 100 | 200 | 1 450 | 12 550 |
| Middle East | 30 | 2 170 | 360 | — | — | 2 560 | — |
| Asia | 2 720 | 180 | 90 | 900 | 3 | 3 890 | 200 |
| Europe | 2 600 | >50 | >150 | >100 | 50 | 3 000 | 9 750 |
| USSR | 3 500 | 350 | 600 | 150 | $x$ | $x+4\ 600$ | 3 400 |
| USA | 5 200 | 250 | 300 | 6 350 | 300 | 12 400 | 19 750 |
| Canada | 150 | 50 | 100 | 3 250 | 150 | 3 700 | 13 750 |
| South America | 50 | 350 | 50 | <50 | 10 | 500 | 3 750 |
| Australia | 500 | 10 | <50 | — | 100 | 600 | 6 250 |
| World | 15 100 | 3 950 | 1 950 | 10 900 | 800 | 32 750 | 66 100 |

Note: Use of uranium in breeder reactors would increase its usable energy content about 60-fold, which with thorium would treble total usable world reserves.
Data source: World Energy Conference.

TABLE (IV) ENERGY RESOURCES OF SELECTED INDUSTRIALISED COUNTRIES. (DATA TYPICAL OF PERIOD 1970–1974)

| | Dependence on imported energy (%) | Petroleum requirements imported (%) | Indigenous reserves of fossil fuels |
|---|---|---|---|
| USA | 3 (excluding Canadian imports) | 30 | Oil and gas—large<br>Coal and shale—potential surpluses |
| Canada | — | — | Coal, oil and gas—medium<br>Tar sands—Major potential surpluses |
| UK | 46 | 99.9 | Coal—large<br>Oil and gas—large by 1980s |
| France | 68 | 97.2 | Coal—large<br>Oil—very small |
| Netherlands | 63 | 54 | Gas—surpluses |
| Germany | 67 | 94.1 | Coal—large<br>Oil—very small |
| Italy | 88 | 98.3 | Oil and gas—very small |
| Norway | 51 | 99 | Oil and gas—major surpluses by 1980s |
| Japan | 75 | 99.6 | Coal—very small |

Notes: 1. In contrast to other contries the amount of petroleum imported into USA is expected increase over the next decade.
2. Continuing imports from O.P.E.C. to Canada are expected after completion of the extension of the East/West pipeline to Ontario and Quebec.

TABLE (V)  PETROLEUM PRODUCTION AND RESERVES (%)

|  | 1974 production | Recoverable reserves |
|---|---|---|
| O.P.E.C. | | |
| Middle East | 34.0 | 62.3 |
| Africa | 11.6 | 10.1 |
| S.E. Asia | 3.3 | 2.6 |
| S. America | 9.6 | 4.6 |
| *Others* | | |
| North America | 23.6 | 8.5 |
| Communist | 17.2 | 9.6 |
| Western Europe | 0.7 | 2.4 |

TABLE (VI) LEAD TIMES/TECHNOLOGY FOR NEW SOURCES OF ENERGY SUPPLIES

|  | Technology available | Time scale* (years) | Comment |
|---|---|---|---|
| *Renewable energy resources* | | | |
| Hydro | yes | over 5 | Restricted locations |
| Tidal | yes | over 5 | Limited opportunities |
| Solar | some | probably 10–20 | Practical size/location |
| *Conventional crude oil* | | | |
| Secondary recovery | yes | 2–5 | Needs skilled manpower |
| Offshore (shallow) | yes | 5–8 | |
| Offshore (deep) | some | within 10 | |
| Arctic | yes | 5 | |
| *Synthetic crude oil* | | | |
| Tar sands | some | shallow depth 5–7 | |
| Shale | some | over 7 | Large water requirements |
| Coal | some | 5+ | |
| *Conventional coal* | | | |
| Surface | yes | 5 | Environmental problems |
| Underground (land) | yes | 10 | Social considerations |
| Underground (offshore) | some | within 20 | |
| *Nuclear* | | | |
| Thermal | yes | 10 | Safety/environment considerations |
| Fusion | ? | 25+ | |

* For new operations to come into operation or for technology to be proven

TABLE (VII) RELATIVE INVESTMENT COSTS OF
VARIOUS FOSSIL FUEL SOURCES

|  | Index |
|---|---|
| *Conventional crude oil* | |
| On land (Middle East) | 1 |
| Offshore (North Sea) | 12–20 |
| *Synthetic crude oils* | |
| Tar sands | 25+ |
| Shale | 30+ |
| Coal (gas) | 30+ |
| Coal (hydrocarbons) | 35+ |
| *Conventional coal* | |
| Surface (US) | 3½ |
| Underground (deep mined) | 6 |

*Source:* Petroleum Economics Ltd.

TABLE (VIII) COSTS OF ALTERNATIVE FOSSIL
FUELS, EQUIVALENT BARREL OF OIL AT PERSIAN
GULF PORT

|  | U.S.$ |
|---|---|
| *Conventional crude oil* | |
| Middle East | 0.25–1.00 |
| North Sea | 4.00–7.00 |
| *Synthetic crude oil* | |
| Tar sands | 5.00–10.50 |
| Shale | 5.50–10.50 |
| *Conventional coal* | |
| European | 7.50–10.50 |
| USA | 5.50–8.50 |

TABLE (IX) POSTED PRICES FOR REFERENCE CRUDE OIL, 1976–1991

|  | Increase (%) | Possible band | Most probable band ($ per barrel) |
|---|---|---|---|
| 1976 | — | 100 | 12·50 |
| 1977 | 6–7 | 106–107 | 13·25–13·38 |
| 1978 | 5–6½ | 111·3–114·0 | 13·91–14·25 |
| 1979 | 6–8 | 118·0–123·1 | 14·75–15·39 |
| 1980 | 5–7 | 123·9–131·7 | 15·49–16·46 |
| 1981 | 4–6 | 128·8–139·6 | 16·10–17·45 |
| 1981–1986 | 3–7 p.a. | | |
| 1986 | | 149·4–195·8 | 20·00–23·13 |
| 1986–1991 | 0–5 p.a. | | |
| 1991 | | 149·4–249·9 | 21·88–28·13 |

*Source:* The Henley Centre for Forecasting

TABLE (X) UK INDUSTRIAL ENERGY PRICES 1975–1985

| | Coal (£ per ton) | Gas (pence per therm) | Fuel Oil (£ per ton) | Electricity (pence per kWh) |
|---|---|---|---|---|
| 1975 | 19.50 | 4.95 | 41.05 | 1.250 |
| 1976 | 22.70 | 7.00 | 47.40 | 1.468 |
| 1977 | 24.90 | 8.50 | 52.85 | 1.600 |
| 1978 | 27.70 | 9.50 | 57.60 | 1.774 |
| 1979 | 30.20 | 10.40 | 62.80 | 1.932 |
| 1980 | 32.50 | 11.30 | 67.50 | 2.000 |
| 1980–85 average annual increase (%) | 5.5 | 6.5 | 5 | 4.8 |

Notes:  1. Estimated from the average pithead prices paid for average industrial grades of coal and using average transport costs
2. The average cost per therm may not adequately reflect marginal gas prices for consumers renegotiating contracts or those on special tariffs
3. Estimated delivered price for fuel oil to medium/large customers including rebates and taxes
4. Average cost per kilowatt hour invoiced to large industrial customers

Source: The Henley Centre for Forecasting

# APPENDIX V  The Industrial World of Today

Throughout this work the long-standing relationship between industrial development and economic growth has been emphasised. As shown in Appendix IV in the contemporary world this is especially linked to the continuation of adequate energy supplies, and also to the ongoing effectiveness of research and development leading to new product innovation, improved labour productivity and higher value added possibilities as a whole. The U.S.A. emerged from the Second World War as the undisputed industrial leader and began by Marshall aid and an extensive programme of overseas investment, especially in Western Europe and Japan, to encourage the re-creation of capacity.

The following tables show that during the 1950s and 1960s the industrial growth of the original six EEC member countries was a particular feature. The economic success of the original six underlaid the desire of Britain and other countries to join the rapidly growing market. In the 1970s the relative improvement of the Western German and the Japanese economies has continued, with the important implications for the balance of power in the world as a whole.

The contribution of the Soviet led COMECON nations to world industrial production is also significant, as is the growing industrial activity in a number of other parts of the world, notably in the Indian sub-continent and South East Asia. The potential competitive strength of all these expanding industrial economies on world markets for a wide range of consumer and capital goods underlies current fears of trade wars and a reversion to protectionist policies.

TABLE (I) OECD INDUSTRIAL PRODUCTION (EXCLUDING CONSTRUCTION) SEASONALLY ADJUSTED 1971–1977

| | Belgium | Luxem-bourg | France | F.R. of Germany | Ireland | Italy | Nether-lands | United Kingdom | EEC | Canada | United States | Japan | OECD |
|---|---|---|---|---|---|---|---|---|---|---|---|---|---|
| Weights in total | 1.3 | 0.1 | 7.1 | 12.5 | 0.2 | 4.5 | 1.5 | 6.3 | 33.5 | 3.5 | 43.2 | 11.6 | |
| 1971 | 103 | 98.7 | 104 | 101.8 | 105 | 99.9 | 106 | 99.8 | 102 | 105.6 | 102.0 | 102.3 | 101 |
| 1972 | 109 | 102.8 | 112 | 105.7 | 109 | 104.4 | 111 | 102.1 | 106 | 113.0 | 111.0 | 110.2 | 108 |
| 1973 | 116 | 115.1 | 120 | 112.9 | 120 | 114.5 | 119 | 110.5 | 115 | 123.5 | 120.4 | 127.4 | 119 |
| 1974 | 120 | 119.1 | 123 | 111.3 | 122 | 119.0 | 125 | 108.5 | 115 | 127.4 | 119.9 | 123.5 | 119 |
| 1975 | 109 | 93.0 | 114 | 105.0 | 114 | 108.5 | 119 | 103.1 | 108 | 121.3 | 109.3 | 110.4 | 109 |
| 1976 | 118 | 98.8 | 124 | 112.7 | 125 | 121.1 | 126 | 104.3 | 115 | 127.4 | 120.4 | 125.4 | 119 |
| 1977 | | | | | | | | 105.7 | | | 127.2 | | |

Indices 1970 = 100.

TABLE (II) OECD UNEMPLOYMENT SEASONALLY ADJUSTED (IN THOUSANDS)

| | Belgium | Denmark | France | F.R. of Germany | Ireland | Italy | Nether-lands | United Kingdom | Canada | United States | Japan |
|---|---|---|---|---|---|---|---|---|---|---|---|
| 1970 | 71 | 24 | 262 | 148 | 42 | 616 | 46 | 602 | 495 | 4 089 | 593 |
| 1971 | 71 | 30 | 337 | 185 | 42 | 613 | 62 | 776 | 552 | 4 993 | 639 |
| 1972 | 87 | 30 | 380 | 246 | 48 | 696 | 108 | 885 | 562 | 4 840 | 730 |
| 1973 | 92 | 21 | 394 | 274 | 44 | 669 | 110 | 611 | 520 | 4 305 | 670 |
| 1974 | 105 | 50 | 498 | 583 | 48 | 560 | 135 | 600 | 521 | 5 076 | 740 |
| 1975 | 177 | 124 | 840 | 1 074 | 75 | 654 | 195 | 929 | 697 | 7 830 | 1 000 |
| 1976 | 229 | 126 | 933 | 1 060 | 84 | 732 | 211 | 1 269 | 736 | 7 288 | 1 080 |
| 1977 | 265 | 149 | 1 079 | 1 030 | | | 204 | 1 379 | 862 | 6 843 | 1 104 |

TABLE (III) THE EUROPEAN ECONOMIC COMMUNITY 1948–1975. SOME PRINCIPAL GROWTH RATES – % PER ANNUM

| **Income, finance and trade** | 1948–58 | 1958–72 | 1972–75 | **Production** | 1948–58 | 1958–72 | 1972–75 |
|---|---|---|---|---|---|---|---|
| *National income*[1] | | | | *Industrial production* | | | |
| EEC (Six) | 10.9 | 9.6 | 19.9[12] | EEC (Six) | 9.0 | 6.0 | −0.3 |
| EEC (Nine) | 9.8 | 9.3 | 11.9[12] | EEC (Nine) | 6.9 | 5.4 | −0.3[10] |
| United States | 5.2 | 7.1 | 8.1 | United States | 3.2 | 5.0 | −0.5 |
| *Standard of living*[3] | | | | *Electricity* | | | |
| EEC (Six) | 4.6[4] | 4.3 | 1.1[12] | EEC (Six) | 8.9 | 7.6 | 3.0 |
| EEC (Nine) | 3.5[4] | 3.8 | 1.0[12] | EEC (Nine) | 8.8 | 7.3 | 1.6 |
| United States | 1.5 | 2.9 | −0.1 | United States | 8.0 | 6.9 | 2.6 |
| *Cost of living* | | | | *Coal*[9] | | | |
| EEC (Six) | 3.6 | 3.7 | 10.3 | EEC (Six) | 3.1 | −2.8 | −4.8 |
| EEC (Nine) | 4.0 | 3.9 | 12.3 | EEC (Nine) | 1.8 | −3.4 | −2.1 |
| United States | 1.9 | 2.7 | 8.8 | United States | −4.1 | 2.4 | 2.9 |
| *Wages* | | | | *Steel* | | | |
| EEC (Six) | 8.6[3] | 8.4 | 15.1 | EEC (Six) | 9.7 | 4.9 | −2.5 |
| EEC (Nine) | 7.6[3] | 8.0 | 16.2 | EEC (Nine) | 7.5 | 4.2 | −3.4 |
| United States | 4.7 | 4.3 | 8.1 | United States | −0.4 | 3.3 | −4.3 |
| *Share prices* | | | | *Cement* | | | |
| EEC (Six) | n.a. | 5.8 | −2.8 | EEC (Six) | 10.6 | 6.1 | −3.1 |
| EEC (Nine) | n.a. | 7.6 | −11.8 | EEC (Nine) | 8.5 | 5.6 | −3.0 |
| United States | 11.9 | 6.7 | −7.5 | United States | 4.5 | 2.3 | −8.0[12] |
| *Money stock*[11] | | | | *Sulphuric acid* | | | |
| EEC (Six)[3] | 10.1 | 11.0 | 10.6 | EEC (Six) | 7.4 | 4.4 | −3.9 |
| EEC (Nine)[3] | 7.6 | 10.3 | 10.7 | EEC (Nine) | 6.5 | 4.1 | −3.7 |
| United States | 2.6 | 4.3 | 5.0 | United States | 3.4 | 4.9 | −2.9 |

*International liquidity*[7,8]

| | | | |
|---|---|---|---|
| EEC (Six) | 16.9 | 10.3 | 8.1 |
| EEC (Nine) | 12.0 | 9.4 | 7.2 |
| United States | -1.3 | -3.8 | 6.5 |

*Imports*[7]

| | | | |
|---|---|---|---|
| EEC (Six) | 8.2 | 12.4 | 24.9 |
| EEC (Nine) | 5.9 | 11.0 | 24.8 |
| United States | 6.4 | 10.5 | 20.7 |

*Exports*[7]

| | | | |
|---|---|---|---|
| EEC (Six) | 13.3 | 12.9 | 24.7 |
| EEC (Nine) | 9.2 | 11.5 | 24.3 |
| United States | 3.5 | 7.6 | 29.3 |

*Man-made fibres*

| | | | |
|---|---|---|---|
| EEC (Six) | 8.7 | 8.6 | -5.5 |
| EEC (Nine) | 8.0 | 8.7 | -5.1 |
| United States | 2.5 | 11.2 | -0.5 |

*Passenger motor vehicles*

| | | | |
|---|---|---|---|
| EEC (Six) | 31.0 | 8.7 | -4.6 |
| EEC (Nine) | 21.8 | 7.6 | -6.1 |
| United States | 0.9 | 5.3 | -8.7 |

*New dwellings completed*

| | | | |
|---|---|---|---|
| EEC (Six) | 16.7[2] | 2.5 | -8.1 |
| EEC (Nine) | 9.7[2] | 2.4 | -7.4 |
| United States[6] | 4.0 | 3.9 | -21.1 |

[1] Growth in terms of £ sterling at average 1975 exchange rates. [2] Excluding West Germany. [3] Excluding Luxemburg. [4] 1950–58. [5] Growth in real domestic product per head of population. [6] Dwellings started. [7] Growth in terms of US dollars. [8] Growth in total reserves of gold, foreign exchange. SDRs and the reserve position with the IMF. [9] Including coal equivalent of lignite. [10] Excluding Denmark and Ireland. [11] Growth in terms of £ sterling at end 1975 exchange rates. [12] Partly estimated.
Source: Economist Diary 1978.

THE MYSTERY OF WEALTH

TABLE (IV) OECD EARNINGS/WAGES PER HEAD IN MANUFACTURING

| | Belgium | Denmark | France | F.R. of Germany | Ireland | Italy | Netherlands | Great Britain | Canada | United States | Japan |
|---|---|---|---|---|---|---|---|---|---|---|---|
| 1971 | 111 | 115 | 110 | 113 | 116 | 112 | 112 | 111 | 109 | 106 | 114 |
| 1972 | 126 | 129 | 121 | 123 | 133 | 124 | 126 | 126 | 118 | 113 | 132 |
| 1973 | 147 | 153 | 138 | 135 | 159 | 156 | 143 | 142 | 128 | 121 | 163 |
| 1974 | 178 | 186 | 161 | 151 | 191 | 191 | 169 | 166 | 145 | 131 | 205 |
| 1975 | 210 | 222 | 194 | 165 | 246 | 241 | 192 | 209 | 168 | 143 | 229 |
| 1976 | 235 | 248 | 210 | 174 | 288 | 292 | 208 | 244 | 191 | 154 | 258 |

Indices 1970 = 100.

TABLE (V) OECD CONSUMER PRICES – ALL GOODS AND SERVICES

| | Belgium | Luxembourg | Denmark | France | F.R. of Germany | Ireland | Italy | Netherlands | United Kingdom | EEC | Canada | United States | Japan | OECD |
|---|---|---|---|---|---|---|---|---|---|---|---|---|---|---|
| 1971 | 104.3 | 104.7 | 106 | 105.3 | 105.3 | 108.9 | 104.8 | 107.5 | 109.4 | 106 | 102.9 | 104.3 | 106.1 | 105 |
| 1972 | 110.0 | 110.1 | 113 | 111.7 | 111.1 | 118.4 | 110.8 | 115.9 | 117.2 | 113 | 107.8 | 107.7 | 110.9 | 110 |
| 1973 | 117.7 | 116.8 | 123 | 119.9 | 118.8 | 131.8 | 122.4 | 125.2 | 128.0 | 122 | 116.0 | 114.4 | 123.9 | 119 |
| 1974 | 132.6 | 128.0 | 142 | 136.3 | 127.1 | 154.2 | 146.2 | 137.3 | 148.4 | 138 | 128.6 | 127.0 | 154.2 | 134 |
| 1975 | 149.6 | 141.7 | 156 | 152.2 | 134.7 | 186.4 | 171.3 | 151.3 | 184.4 | 157 | 142.5 | 138.6 | 172.4 | 150 |
| 1976 | 163.2 | 155.6 | 170 | 166.8 | 140.8 | 219.9 | 199.6 | 164.6 | 214.9 | 175 | 153.2 | 146.6 | 188.4 | 163 |
| 1977 | 174.8 | 166.0 | 189 | 182.7 | 146.3 | 249.9 | | 175.6 | 249.0 | 195 | 165.5 | 156.1 | 203.6 | 177 |

Indices 1970 = 100.

TABLE (VI) WORLD TRADE
Quarter or quarterly averages,
seasonally adjusted

US $ thousand million

|  | Exports (fob) from | | | Imports (cif) into | | |
|---|---|---|---|---|---|---|
|  | World | OECD | Rest of world | World | OECD | Rest of world |
| 1970 | 69.69 | 55.01 | 14.68 | 56.41 | 56.41 | 16.05 |
| 1971 | 78.15 | 61.51 | 16.64 | 81.12 | 62.68 | 18.44 |
| 1972 | 92.91 | 72.70 | 20.21 | 94.65 | 74.50 | 20.15 |
| 1973 | 131.88 | 99.72 | 32.16 | 132.38 | 102.71 | 29.67 |
| 1974 | 193.66 | 133.23 | 60.43 | 194.37 | 145.77 | 48.69 |
| 1975 | 199.19 | 141.81 | 57.38 | 202.24 | 146.42 | 55.82 |
| 1976 | 225.86 | 157.02 | 68.84 | 228.93 | 168.23 | 60.70 |

TABLE (VII) INDUSTRIAL COUNTRIES' TRADE
Quarters or quarterly averages,
seasonally adjusted

$ thousand million

|  | Exports (fob) to | | | Imports (cif) from | | |
|---|---|---|---|---|---|---|
|  | World | OECD | Rest of world | World | OECD | Rest of world |
| 1970 | 55.01 | 41.03 | 13.98 | 56.41 | 42.50 | 13.91 |
| 1971 | 61.51 | 45.89 | 15.62 | 62.68 | 47.29 | 15.39 |
| 1972 | 72.70 | 55.02 | 17.68 | 74.50 | 56.43 | 18.07 |
| 1973 | 99.72 | 74.57 | 25.15 | 102.71 | 76.24 | 20.47 |
| 1974 | 133.23 | 95.16 | 38.07 | 145.77 | 97.74 | 48.03 |
| 1975 | 141.81 | 96.07 | 45.74 | 146.42 | 99.82 | 46.60 |
| 1976 | 157.02 | 109.67 | 47.35 | 168.23 | 112.55 | 55.68 |

TABLE (VIII) EXPORTS (FOB) SPECIAL TRADE, SEASONALLY ADJUSTED – US $ MILLION

|  | Belgium/Luxembourg | Denmark | France | F.R. of Germany | Ireland | Italy | Netherlands | United Kingdom | EEC | Canada | United States | Japan | OECD |
|---|---|---|---|---|---|---|---|---|---|---|---|---|---|
| 1970 | 11 592 | 3 288 | 17 940 | 34 188 | 1 032 | 13 188 | 11 772 | 19 382 | 112 356 | 16 134 | 43 224 | 19 320 | 220 045 |
| 1971 | 12 081 | 3 609 | 20 592 | 39 009 | 1 308 | 15 177 | 13 953 | 22 365 | 128 084 | 17 676 | 44 211 | 23 994 | 246 037 |
| 1972 | 15 995 | 4 330 | 25 739 | 46 208 | 1 610 | 18 535 | 15 392 | 24 415 | 153 152 | 20 184 | 49 676 | 28 591 | 290 784 |
| 1973 | 22 416 | 6 120 | 35 952 | 67 440 | 2 124 | 22 236 | 23 952 | 30 662 | 210 684 | 25 200 | 71 316 | 36 936 | 398 880 |
| 1974 | 28 260 | 7 716 | 45 900 | 89 160 | 2 628 | 30 288 | 32 436 | 38 827 | 275 100 | 32 784 | 98 508 | 55 536 | 532 932 |
| 1975 | 28 812 | 8 712 | 52 212 | 90 024 | 3 216 | 34 824 | 34 440 | 44 270 | 295 992 | 32 304 | 107 652 | 55 752 | 567 804 |
| 1976 | 32 844 | 9 108 | 55 812 | 102 036 | 3 312 | 36 924 | 38 748 | 46 542 | 325 044 | 38 628 | 114 996 | 67 272 | 630 504 |
| 1977 |  |  |  |  |  |  |  | 57 526 |  |  |  |  |  |

TABLE (IX) OECD IMPORTS (CIF) SPECIAL TRADE, SEASONALLY ADJUSTED – US $ MILLION

| | Belgium/Luxembourg | Denmark | France | F.R. of Germany | Ireland | Italy | Netherlands | United Kingdom | EEC | Canada | United States | Japan | OECD |
|---|---|---|---|---|---|---|---|---|---|---|---|---|---|
| 1970 | 11 352 | 4 380 | 19 116 | 29 808 | 1 572 | 14 940 | 13 392 | 21 696 | 116 280 | 13 308 | 39 960 | 18 876 | 225 649 |
| 1971 | 12 390 | 4 476 | 21 261 | 34 356 | 1 838 | 16 026 | 15 159 | 23 918 | 129 403 | 15 460 | 45 633 | 19 716 | 250 717 |
| 1972 | 14 879 | 4 988 | 26 696 | 39 759 | 2 113 | 19 252 | 17 127 | 27 877 | 152 643 | 18 924 | 55 819 | 23 463 | 297 984 |
| 1973 | 21 936 | 7 704 | 37 380 | 54 492 | 2 784 | 27 816 | 24 360 | 38 877 | 215 232 | 23 304 | 69 120 | 38 316 | 410 820 |
| 1974 | 29 700 | 9 852 | 52 824 | 68 976 | 3 816 | 40 968 | 33 204 | 54 344 | 293 568 | 32 292 | 100 968 | 62 112 | 583 020 |
| 1975 | 30 708 | 10 332 | 54 240 | 74 208 | 3 804 | 38 364 | 35 148 | 53 618 | 300 048 | 33 960 | 96 936 | 57 864 | 587 376 |
| 1976 | 33 352 | 12 336 | 64 392 | 87 780 | 4 200 | 43 368 | 39 348 | 56 269 | 343 428 | 37 956 | 121 788 | 64 776 | 672 906 |
| 1977 | | | | | | | | 63 740 | | | | | |

TABLE (X) OECD BALANCE OF PAYMENTS ON CURRENT ACCOUNT – US $ MILLION (UNADJUSTED)

| | Belgium/Luxembourg | Denmark | France | F.R. of Germany | Ireland | Italy | Netherlands | United Kingdom | EEC | Canada | United States | Japan |
|---|---|---|---|---|---|---|---|---|---|---|---|---|
| 1970 | 713 | −544 | 297 | 848 | −183 | 902 | −522 | 1 759 | 3 270 | 1 077 | 2 383 | 1 970 |
| 1971 | 846 | −423 | 530 | 874 | −183 | 2 041 | −159 | 2 575 | 6 101 | 422 | −1 328 | 5 797 |
| 1972 | 1 142 | −63 | 297 | 748 | −125 | 2 266 | 1 290 | 289 | 5 844 | −388 | −5 824 | 6 624 |
| 1973 | 1 153 | −464 | −691 | 4 372 | −224 | −2 510 | 2 342 | −2 346 | 1 632 | 107 | 6 892 | −136 |
| 1974 | 911 | −981 | −5 942 | 9 722 | −679 | −8 039 | 2 061 | −8 443 | −11 390 | −1 540 | 1 168 | −4 693 |
| 1975 | 705 | −492 | −3 | 3 896 | −66 | −530 | 1 658 | −3 740 | 1 428 | −4 719 | 17 738 | −682 |
| 1976 | −299 | −1 906 | −6 033 | 3 396 | −271 | −2 856 | 2 385 | −2 172 | −7 756 | −4 230 | 3 507 | 3 680 |

Source: Trade and Industry Journal and OECR Statistics.

TABLE (XI) INTERNATIONAL COMPARISONS OF PRODUCTION AND PRICES IN 1976

| | Coal[1] (million tonnes) | Crude oil (million tonnes) | Crude steel million tonnes) | Electricity (thousand million kWh) | Merchant ships completed (thousand grt) | Index of industrial production (1970 = 100) | Consumer price index (1970 = 100) |
|---|---|---|---|---|---|---|---|
| Belgium-Luxembourg | 7.2 | – | 16.7 | 48.9 | 211[3] | 119[3] | 163[3] |
| Denmark | – | 0.1[14] | 0.7 | 19.2 | 1,034 | 113[8,13] | 170 |
| France | 24.8 | 1.1 | 23.2 | 191.2 | 1 673 | 123 | 167 |
| Germany, West | 131.4 | 5.5 | 42.4 | 333.7 | 1 874 | 112 | 141 |
| Ireland | 0.1 | – | 0.1[14] | 7.5[2,6] | 29 | 126 | 220 |
| Italy | 0.4 | 1.1 | 23.4 | 160.0 | 715 | 122 | 200 |
| Netherlands | – | 1.4 | 5.2 | 58.1 | 634 | 124 | 165 |
| United Kingdom | 123.8 | 11.5 | 22.3 | 279.0 | 1 460 | 102[7] | 215[10] |
| EEC[15] | 287.7 | 20.7 | 134.1 | 1 098.6 | 7 630 | 115 | 180 |
| Austria | 1.6 | 1.9 | 4.8 | 34.7 | – | 125 | 153 |
| Iceland | – | – | – | 2.4[2] | 1 | 140[12] | 399 |
| Norway | 0.5 | 13.7 | 0.9 | 82.3 | 758 | 135 | 163 |
| Portugal | 0.2 | – | 0.4 | 9.1 | 230 | 132[12] | 244 |
| Sweden | – | – | 5.2 | 84.3 | 2 515 | 113 | 162 |
| Switzerland | – | – | 0.6[14] | 34.8[11] | – | 97 | 147 |
| EFTA[15] | 2.3 | 15.6 | 12.0 | 248.0 | 3 504 | na | na |
| Poland | 191.1 | 0.5[13] | 15.6 | 104.1 | 565 | 188 | 113[13] |
| Soviet Union | 564.8[13] | 520.0 | 145.0 | 1 111.0 | 616[16] | 150 | 100[13] |
| Spain | 12.4 | 2.0 | 10.9 | 90.9 | 1 320 | 152 | 208 |
| Argentina | 0.5[13] | 20.8[13] | 2.4 | 24.5[2,13] | 39 | 127[13] | 6 539 |
| Australia | 85.4 | 20.5 | 7.8 | 80.3 | 46 | 112[9] | 185 |
| Canada | 22.4 | 64.0[11] | 13.1 | 293.4 | 244 | 127 | 153 |
| India | 102.2 | 8.6 | 9.3 | 88.1[2] | 46 | 119[13] | 161 |
| Japan | 18.4 | 0.6 | 107.4 | 475.8 | 15 868 | 125 | 188 |
| Nigeria | 0.3[13] | 102.4 | – | 3.2[13] | – | 166[8,13] | 186[13] |
| South Africa | 75.7 | – | 7.1 | 80.3 | 16 | 123[8] | 174 |
| United States | 613.6 | 401.6 | 116.3 | 2 117.6 | 815 | 120 | 147 |
| Total world[4] | 2 260 | 2 767 | 652 | 6 713 | 33 880 | 134 | 178[5] |

[1] Including coal equivalent of lignite. [2] Public utilities only. [3] Excluding Luxembourg. [4] Excluding China, North Korea and Vietnam. [5] Also excluding Soviet area. [6] Year ending March 31st. [7] Including construction. [8] Manufacturing only. [9] Year ending June 30th. [10] Retail prices index. [11] Year ending September 30th. [12] Fish only. [13] 1975. [14] 1974. [15] Including, where figures not available, estimates for 1976. [16] Incomplete information.
Source: Economist Diary 1978.

# INDEX